X-FACTOR

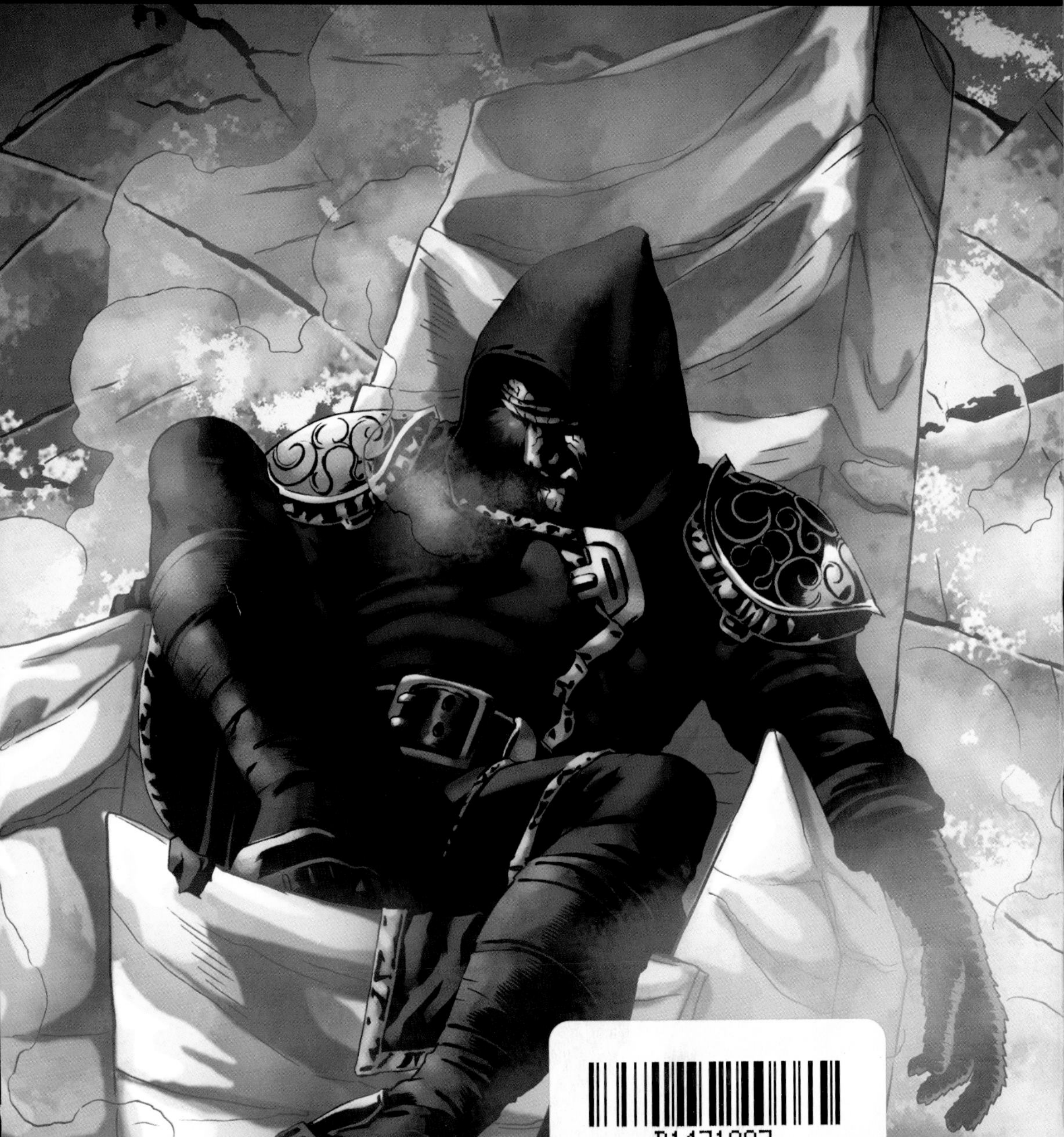

HEART OF ICE

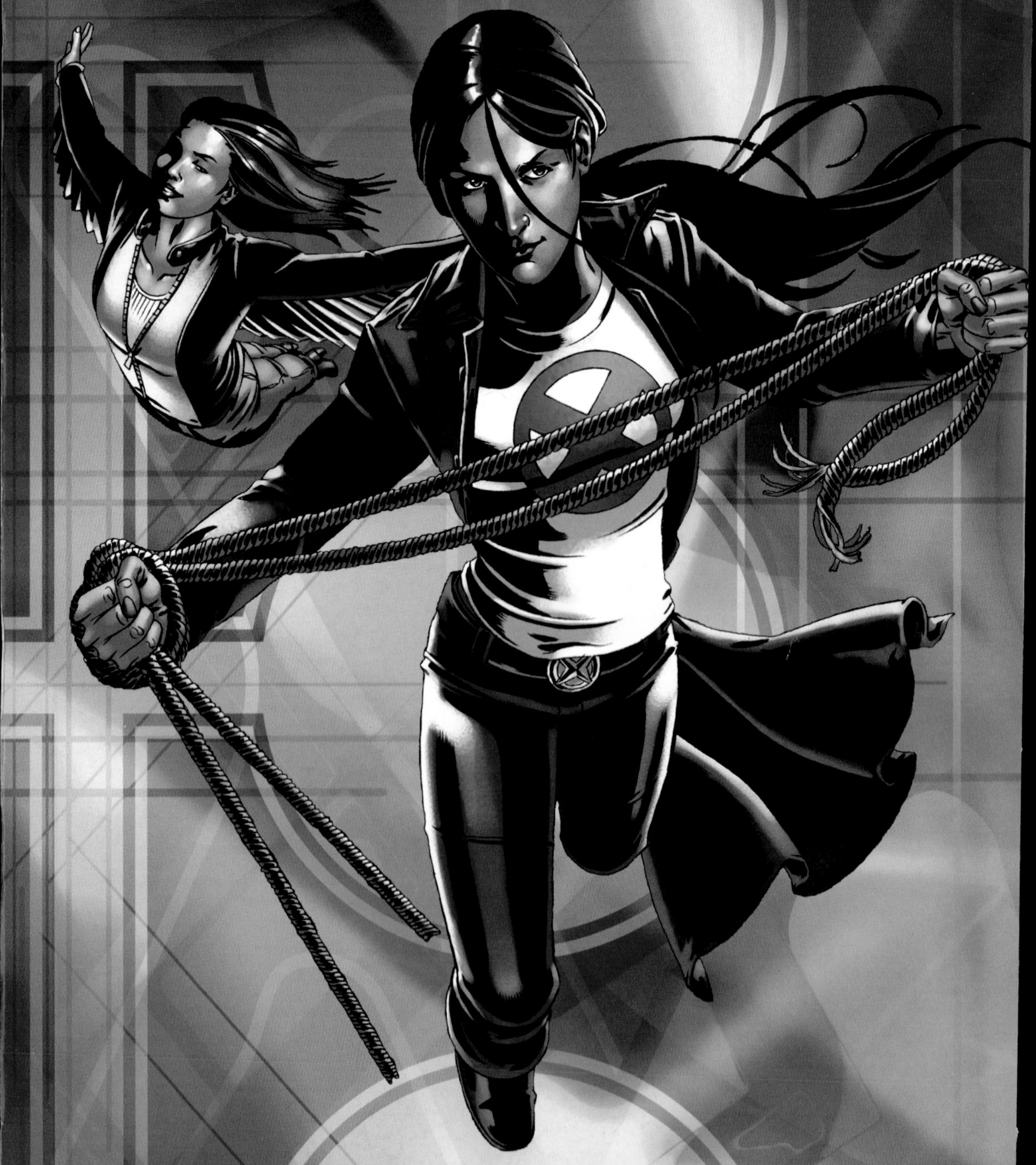

X-FACTOR

HEART OF ICE

Writer: **PETER DAVID**
Art (Issues #18-20):
Penciler: **KHOI PHAM**
Inker: **SANDU FLOREA**
Art (Issues #19-23): **PABLO RAIMONDI**
Art Assists (Issue #24): **VALENTINE DE LANDRO & DREW HENNESSY**
Colors: **BRIAN REBER (ISSUES #18, 21-24)**
& CHRIS SOTOMAYOR (ISSUES #19-20)
Letters: **VIRTUAL CALLIGRAPHY'S CORY PETIT**
Cover Art: **PABLO RAIMONDI WITH ANDREA DIVITO (ISSUE #19) & KHOI PHAM (ISSUE #20)**
Assistant Editors: **WILL PANZO & SEAN RYAN**
Editors: **ANDY SCHMIDT & NICK LOWE**

Collection Editor: **JENNIFER GRÜNWALD**
Assistant Editors: **CORY LEVINE & JOHN DENNING**
Editor, Special Projects: **MARK D. BEAZLEY**
Senior Editor, Special Projects: **JEFF YOUNGQUIST**
Senior Vice President of Sales: **DAVID GABRIEL**
Production: **JERRON QUALITY COLOR & JERRY KALINOWSKI**
Vice President of Creative: **TOM MARVELLI**

Editor in Chief: **JOE QUESADA**
Publisher: **DAN BUCKLEY**

PREVIOUSLY

Jamie Madrox, desperately dealing with the dire death of a Detroit detective dupe, discovers that Mutant Town is under serious siege by squadrons of awesomely armed army avatars. Why, you worriedly wonder? It is explained that an excess of ex-mutants called the X-Cell have expressed exasperation with the government, completely convinced that the catastrophic mutant power outage was a perfidious, unpardonable presidential plot.

To that end, they have waged war on warious...sorry, various...tempting targets and thus are themselves treated and targeted as terrorists, and have sought seeming sanctuary in Mutant Town, their quixotic quest leading them quickly to Quicksilver. Rahne and Rictor wrongly rescued an X-Cell ranger, and thus were angrily arrested by the aforementioned army. Val Cooper has ordered a muddled Madrox to make haste in extracting the X-Cell before matters escalate exponentially.

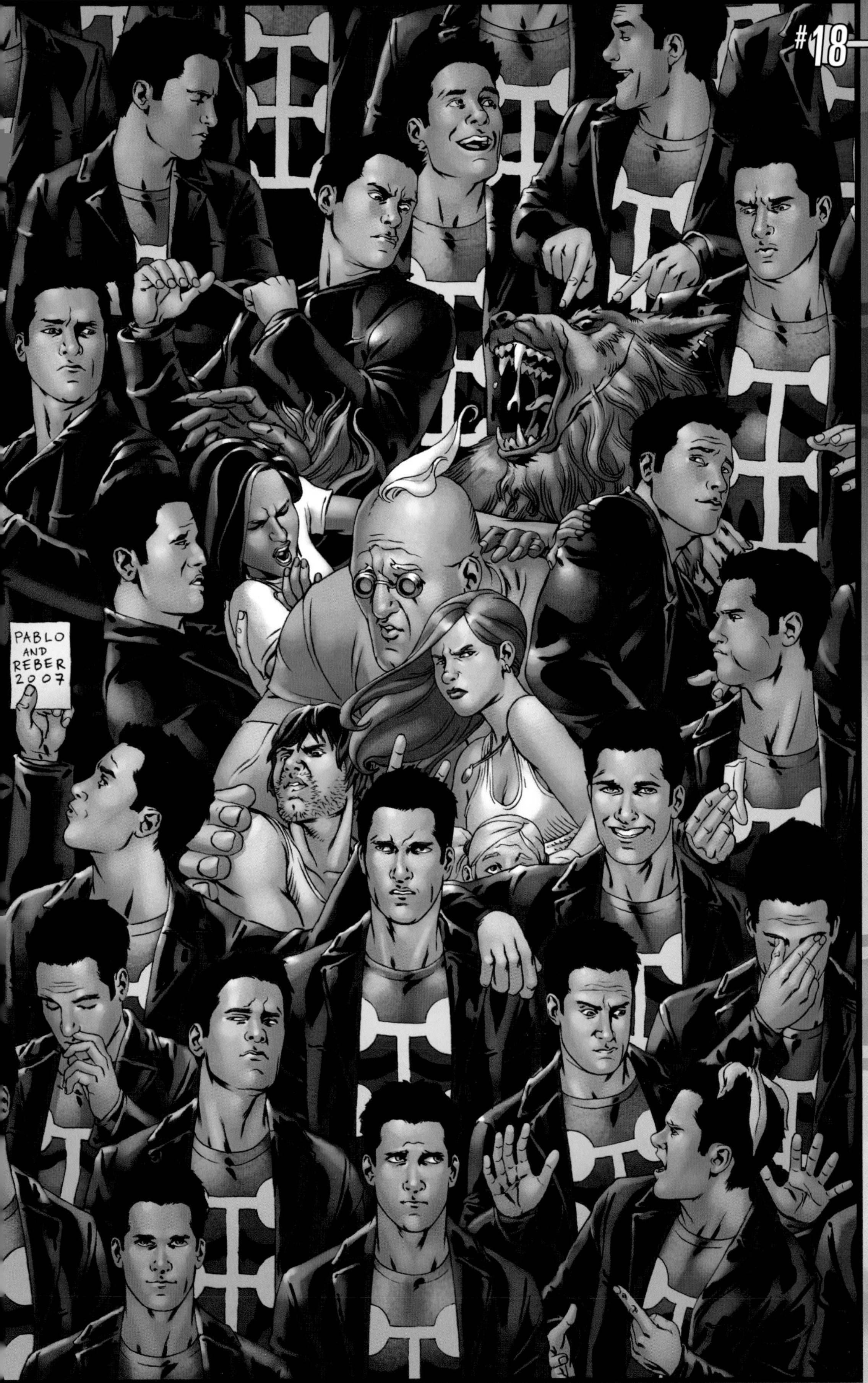
#18
PABLO AND REBER 2007

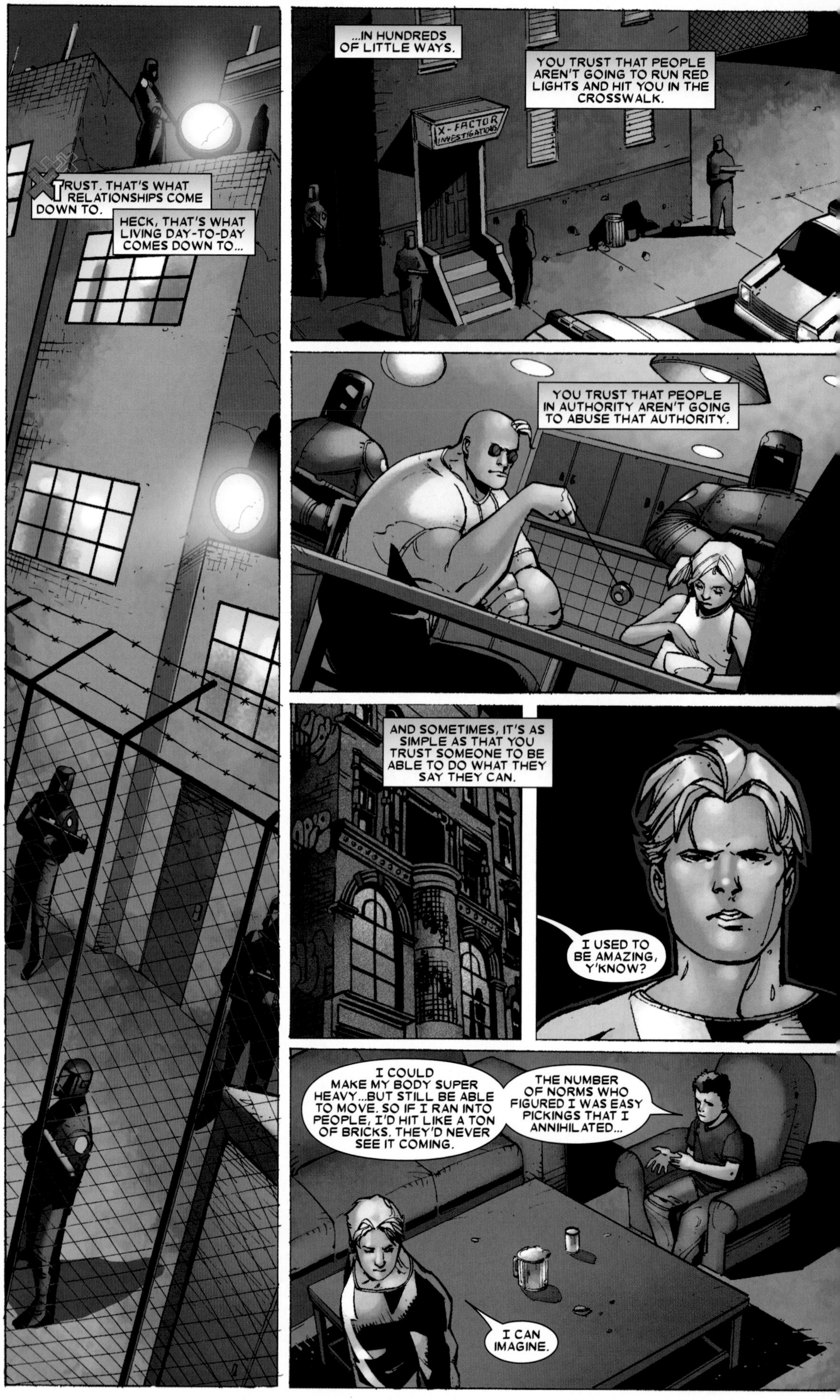

TRUST. THAT'S WHAT RELATIONSHIPS COME DOWN TO.
HECK, THAT'S WHAT LIVING DAY-TO-DAY COMES DOWN TO...
...IN HUNDREDS OF LITTLE WAYS.
YOU TRUST THAT PEOPLE AREN'T GOING TO RUN RED LIGHTS AND HIT YOU IN THE CROSSWALK.
X-FACTOR INVESTIGATIONS
YOU TRUST THAT PEOPLE IN AUTHORITY AREN'T GOING TO ABUSE THAT AUTHORITY.
AND SOMETIMES, IT'S AS SIMPLE AS THAT YOU TRUST SOMEONE TO BE ABLE TO DO WHAT THEY SAY THEY CAN.
I USED TO BE AMAZING, Y'KNOW?
I COULD MAKE MY BODY SUPER HEAVY...BUT STILL BE ABLE TO MOVE. SO IF I RAN INTO PEOPLE, I'D HIT LIKE A TON OF BRICKS. THEY'D NEVER SEE IT COMING.
THE NUMBER OF NORMS WHO FIGURED I WAS EASY PICKINGS THAT I ANNIHILATED...
I CAN IMAGINE.

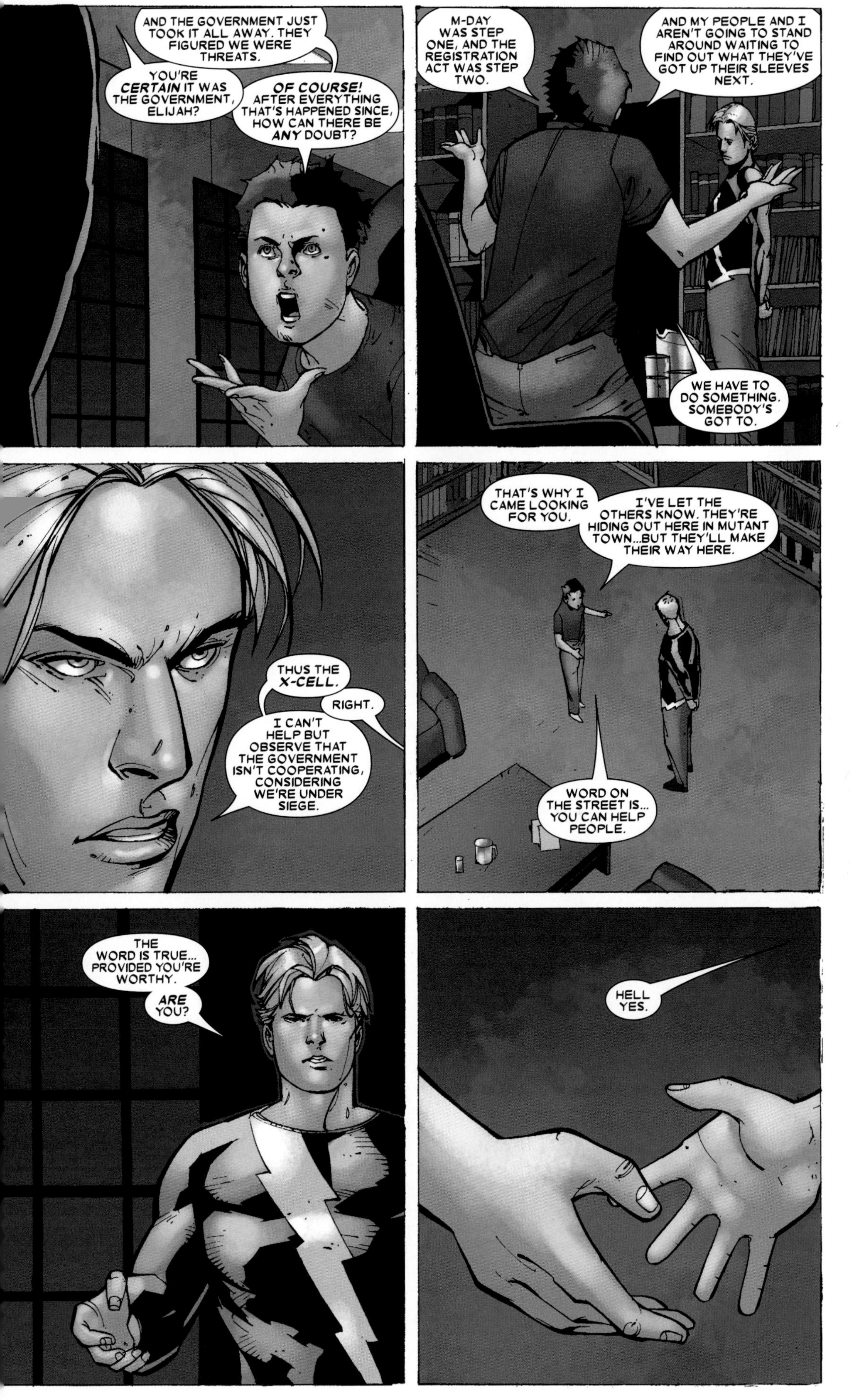
AND THE GOVERNMENT JUST TOOK IT ALL AWAY. THEY FIGURED WE WERE THREATS.
YOU'RE *CERTAIN* IT WAS THE GOVERNMENT, ELIJAH?
OF COURSE! AFTER EVERYTHING THAT'S HAPPENED SINCE, HOW CAN THERE BE *ANY* DOUBT?
M-DAY WAS STEP ONE, AND THE REGISTRATION ACT WAS STEP TWO.
AND MY PEOPLE AND I AREN'T GOING TO STAND AROUND WAITING TO FIND OUT WHAT THEY'VE GOT UP THEIR SLEEVES NEXT.
WE HAVE TO DO SOMETHING. SOMEBODY'S GOT TO.
THUS THE *X-CELL.*
RIGHT.
I CAN'T HELP BUT OBSERVE THAT THE GOVERNMENT ISN'T COOPERATING, CONSIDERING WE'RE UNDER SIEGE.
THAT'S WHY I CAME LOOKING FOR YOU.
I'VE LET THE OTHERS KNOW. THEY'RE HIDING OUT HERE IN MUTANT TOWN...BUT THEY'LL MAKE THEIR WAY HERE.
WORD ON THE STREET IS... YOU CAN HELP PEOPLE.
THE WORD IS TRUE... PROVIDED YOU'RE WORTHY.
ARE YOU?
HELL YES.

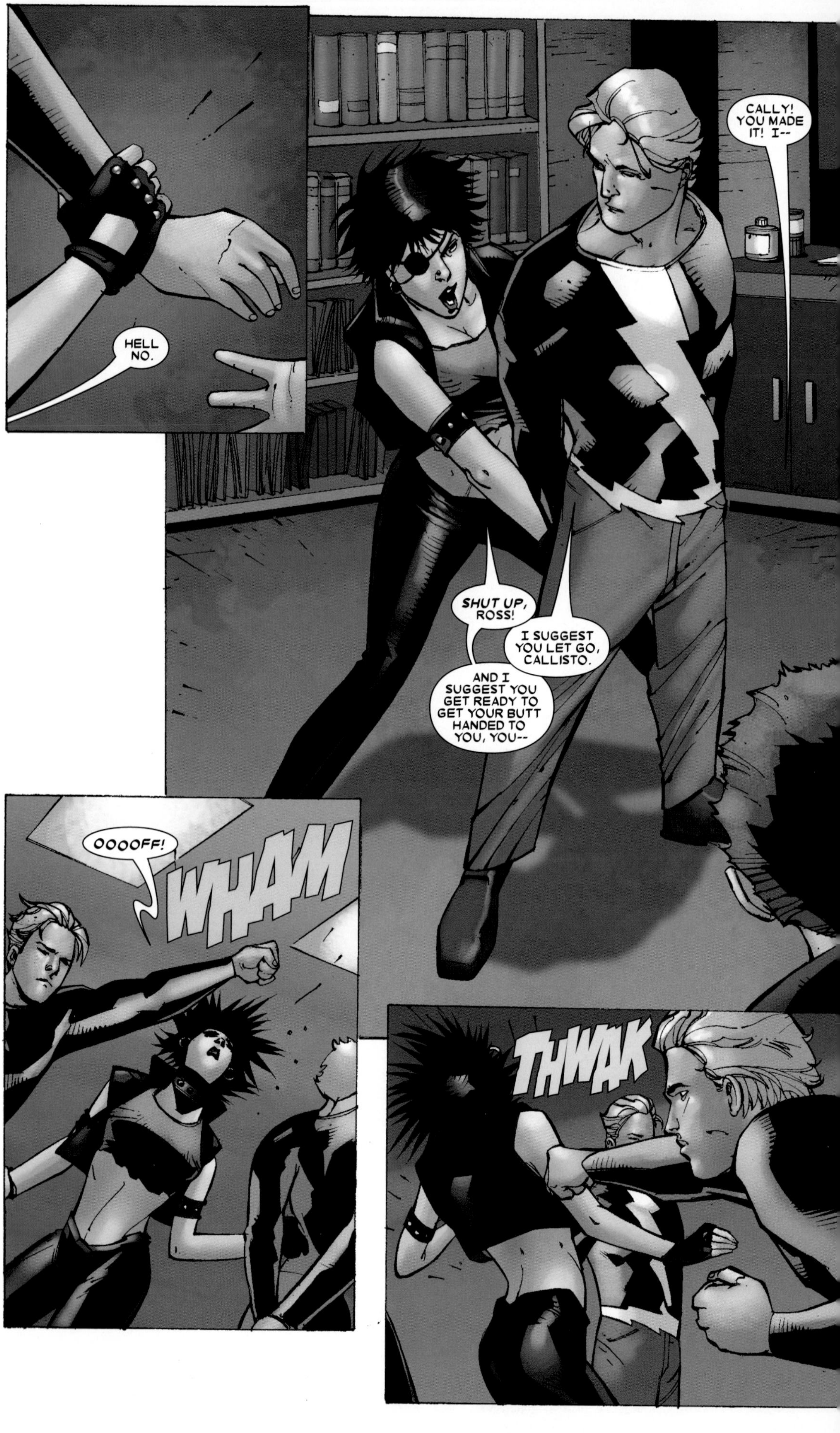
HELL NO.
CALLY! YOU MADE IT! I--
SHUT UP, ROSS!
I SUGGEST YOU LET GO, CALLISTO.
AND I SUGGEST YOU GET READY TO GET YOUR BUTT HANDED TO YOU, YOU--
OOOOFF!
WHAM
THWAK

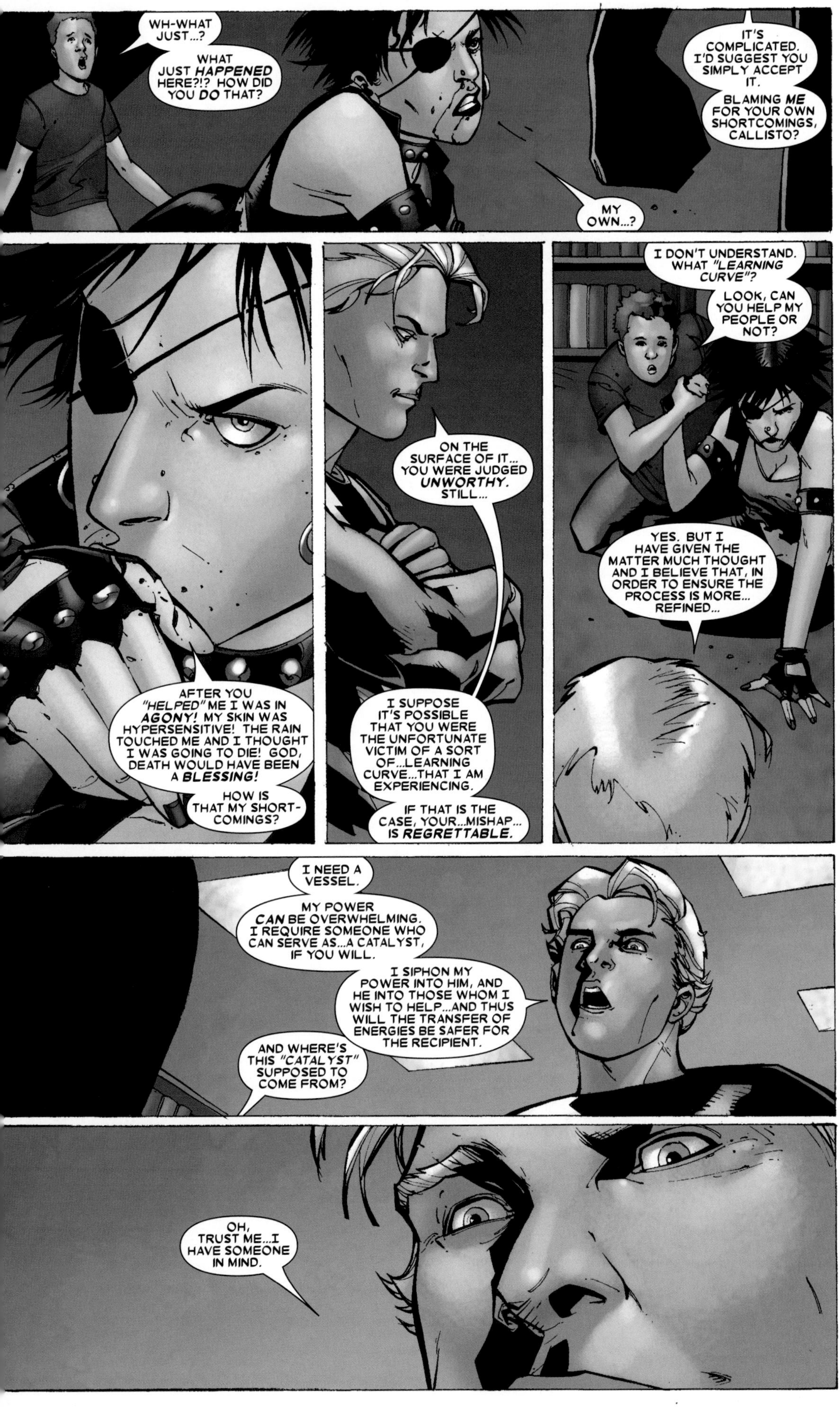

WH-WHAT JUST...?
WHAT JUST HAPPENED HERE?!? HOW DID YOU DO THAT?
IT'S COMPLICATED. I'D SUGGEST YOU SIMPLY ACCEPT IT.
BLAMING ME FOR YOUR OWN SHORTCOMINGS, CALLISTO?
MY OWN...?
AFTER YOU "HELPED" ME I WAS IN AGONY! MY SKIN WAS HYPERSENSITIVE! THE RAIN TOUCHED ME AND I THOUGHT I WAS GOING TO DIE! GOD, DEATH WOULD HAVE BEEN A BLESSING!
HOW IS THAT MY SHORT-COMINGS?
ON THE SURFACE OF IT... YOU WERE JUDGED UNWORTHY. STILL...
I SUPPOSE IT'S POSSIBLE THAT YOU WERE THE UNFORTUNATE VICTIM OF A SORT OF...LEARNING CURVE...THAT I AM EXPERIENCING.
IF THAT IS THE CASE, YOUR...MISHAP... IS REGRETTABLE.
I DON'T UNDERSTAND. WHAT "LEARNING CURVE"?
LOOK, CAN YOU HELP MY PEOPLE OR NOT?
YES. BUT I HAVE GIVEN THE MATTER MUCH THOUGHT AND I BELIEVE THAT, IN ORDER TO ENSURE THE PROCESS IS MORE... REFINED...
I NEED A VESSEL.
MY POWER CAN BE OVERWHELMING. I REQUIRE SOMEONE WHO CAN SERVE AS...A CATALYST, IF YOU WILL.
I SIPHON MY POWER INTO HIM, AND HE INTO THOSE WHOM I WISH TO HELP...AND THUS WILL THE TRANSFER OF ENERGIES BE SAFER FOR THE RECIPIENT.
AND WHERE'S THIS "CATALYST" SUPPOSED TO COME FROM?
OH, TRUST ME...I HAVE SOMEONE IN MIND.

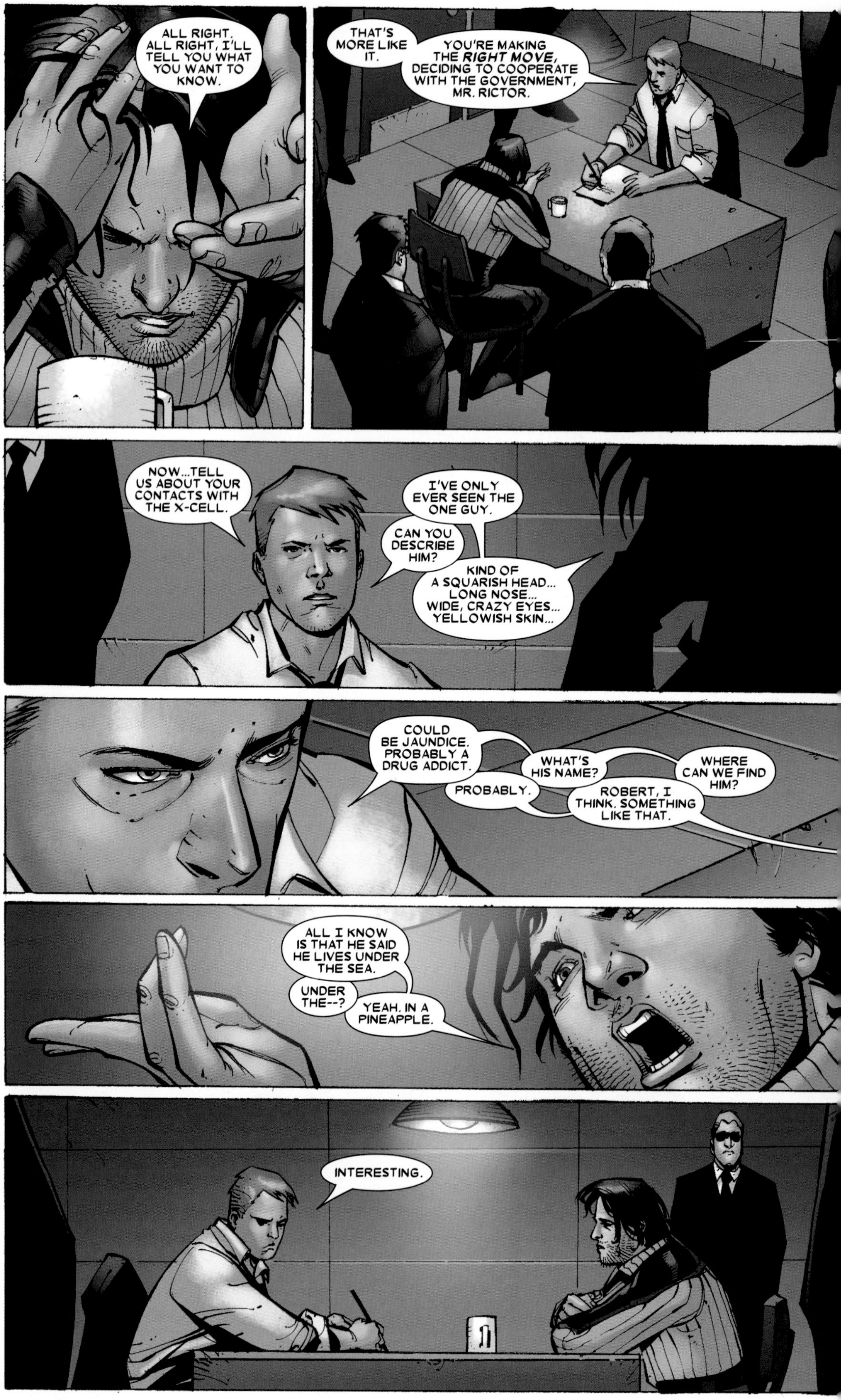
ALL RIGHT. ALL RIGHT, I'LL TELL YOU WHAT YOU WANT TO KNOW.
THAT'S MORE LIKE IT.
YOU'RE MAKING THE *RIGHT MOVE*, DECIDING TO COOPERATE WITH THE GOVERNMENT, MR. RICTOR.
NOW...TELL US ABOUT YOUR CONTACTS WITH THE X-CELL.
I'VE ONLY EVER SEEN THE ONE GUY.
CAN YOU DESCRIBE HIM?
KIND OF A SQUARISH HEAD... LONG NOSE... WIDE, CRAZY EYES... YELLOWISH SKIN...
COULD BE JAUNDICE. PROBABLY A DRUG ADDICT.
PROBABLY.
WHAT'S HIS NAME?
ROBERT, I THINK. SOMETHING LIKE THAT.
WHERE CAN WE FIND HIM?
ALL I KNOW IS THAT HE SAID HE LIVES UNDER THE SEA.
UNDER THE--?
YEAH. IN A PINEAPPLE.
INTERESTING.

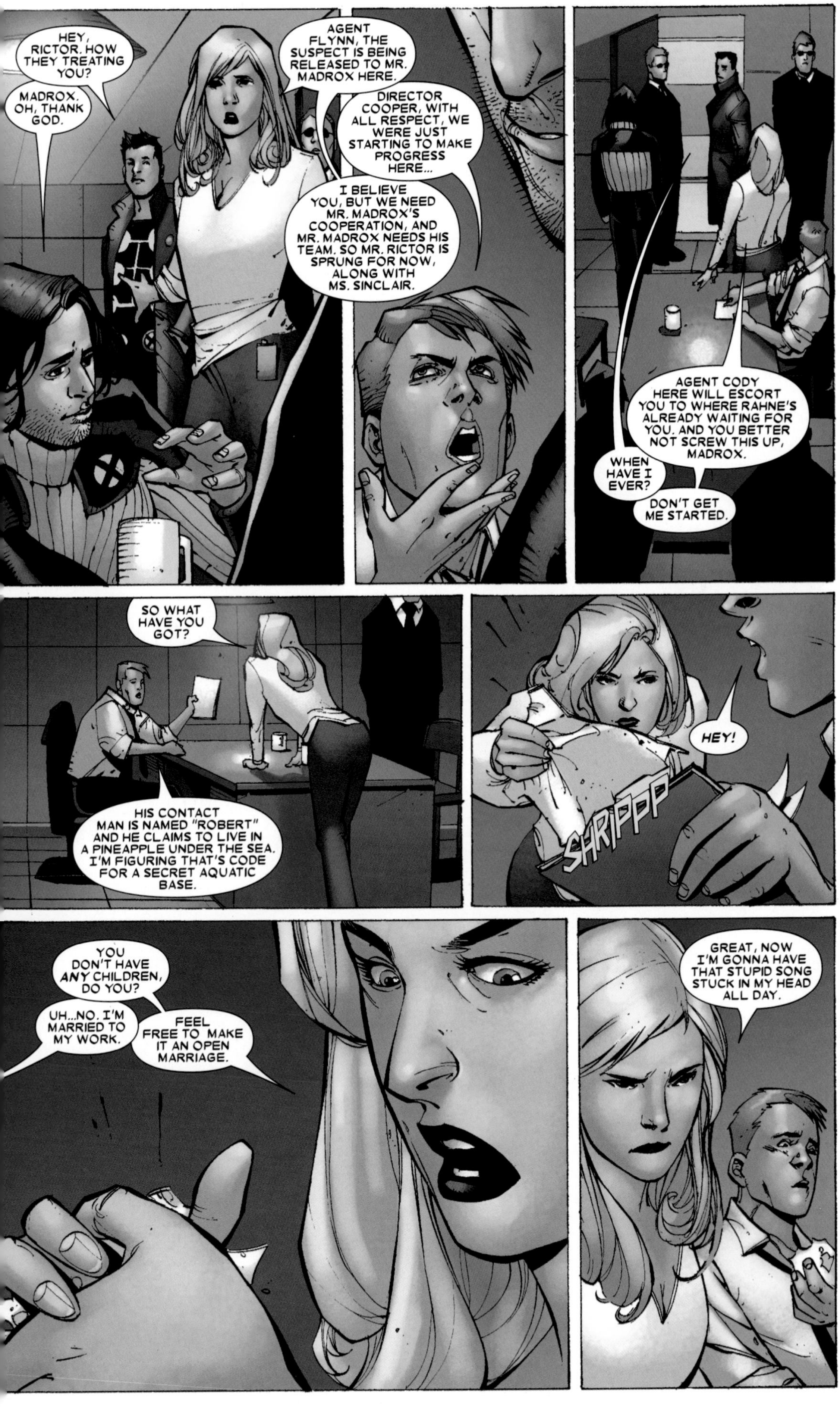

HEY, RICTOR. HOW THEY TREATING YOU?
MADROX. OH, THANK GOD.
AGENT FLYNN, THE SUSPECT IS BEING RELEASED TO MR. MADROX HERE.
DIRECTOR COOPER, WITH ALL RESPECT, WE WERE JUST STARTING TO MAKE PROGRESS HERE...
I BELIEVE YOU, BUT WE NEED MR. MADROX'S COOPERATION, AND MR. MADROX NEEDS HIS TEAM. SO MR. RICTOR IS SPRUNG FOR NOW, ALONG WITH MS. SINCLAIR.
AGENT CODY HERE WILL ESCORT YOU TO WHERE RAHNE'S ALREADY WAITING FOR YOU. AND YOU BETTER NOT SCREW THIS UP, MADROX.
WHEN HAVE I EVER?
DON'T GET ME STARTED.
SO WHAT HAVE YOU GOT?
HIS CONTACT MAN IS NAMED "ROBERT" AND HE CLAIMS TO LIVE IN A PINEAPPLE UNDER THE SEA. I'M FIGURING THAT'S CODE FOR A SECRET AQUATIC BASE.
SHRIPPP
HEY!
YOU DON'T HAVE ANY CHILDREN, DO YOU?
UH...NO. I'M MARRIED TO MY WORK.
FEEL FREE TO MAKE IT AN OPEN MARRIAGE.
GREAT, NOW I'M GONNA HAVE THAT STUPID SONG STUCK IN MY HEAD ALL DAY.

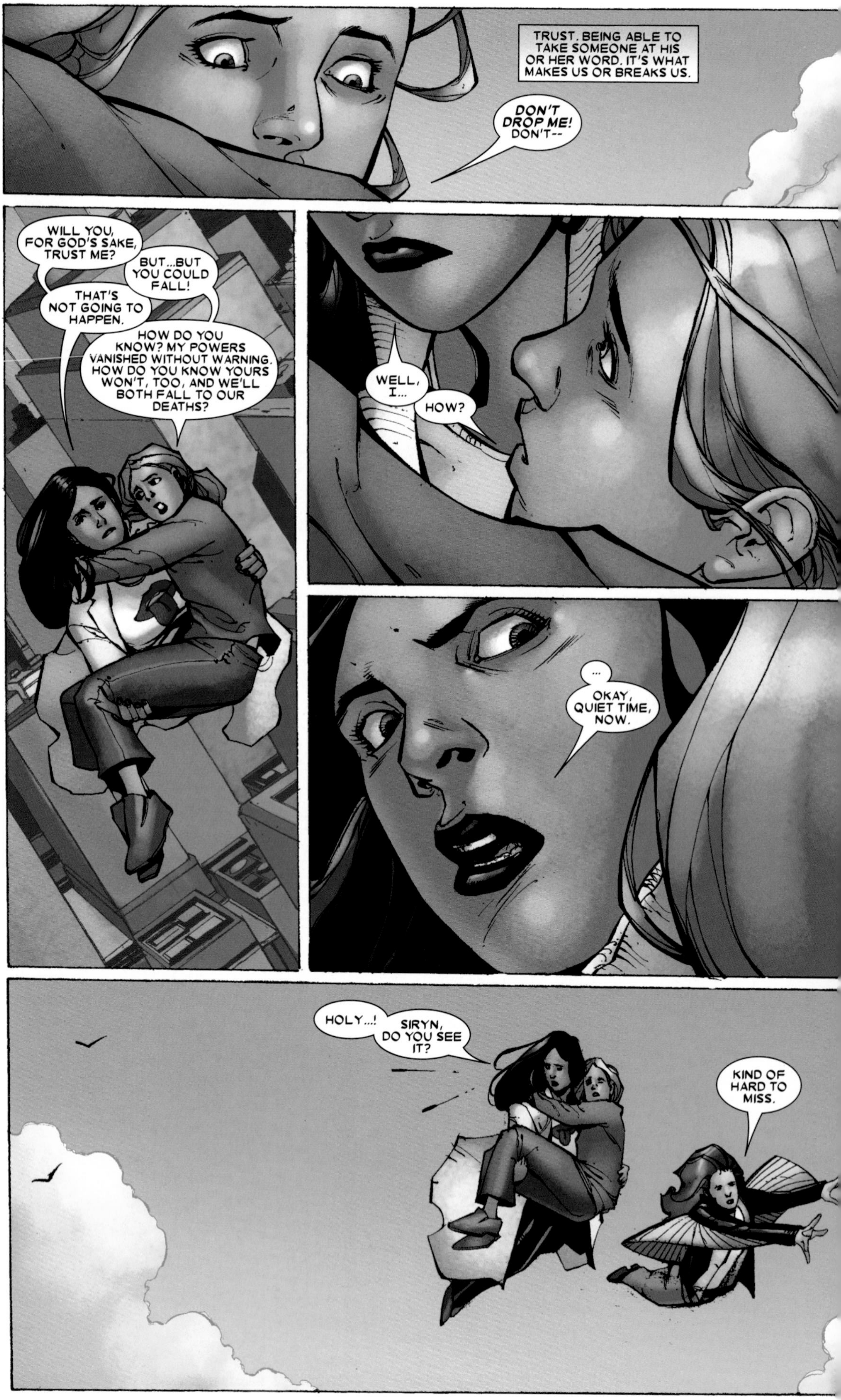
TRUST. BEING ABLE TO TAKE SOMEONE AT HIS OR HER WORD. IT'S WHAT MAKES US OR BREAKS US.
DON'T DROP ME! DON'T--
WILL YOU, FOR GOD'S SAKE, TRUST ME?
BUT...BUT YOU COULD FALL!
THAT'S NOT GOING TO HAPPEN.
HOW DO YOU KNOW? MY POWERS VANISHED WITHOUT WARNING. HOW DO YOU KNOW YOURS WON'T, TOO, AND WE'LL BOTH FALL TO OUR DEATHS?
WELL, I...
HOW?
...
OKAY, QUIET TIME, NOW.
HOLY...!
SIRYN, DO YOU SEE IT?
KIND OF HARD TO MISS.

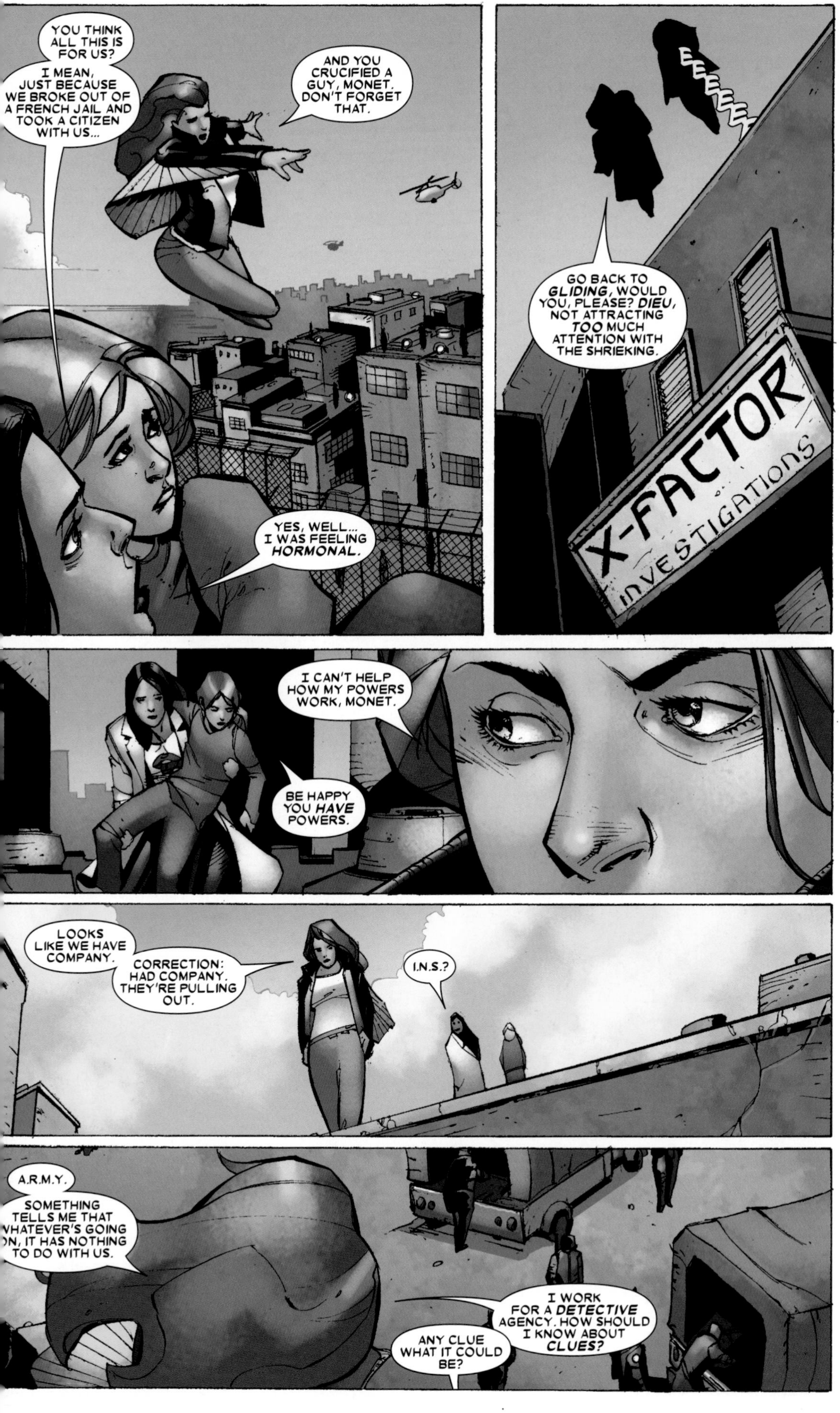

YOU THINK ALL THIS IS FOR US?
I MEAN, JUST BECAUSE WE BROKE OUT OF A FRENCH JAIL AND TOOK A CITIZEN WITH US...
AND YOU CRUCIFIED A GUY, MONET. DON'T FORGET THAT.
YES, WELL... I WAS FEELING HORMONAL.
EEEEEE
GO BACK TO GLIDING, WOULD YOU, PLEASE? DIEU, NOT ATTRACTING TOO MUCH ATTENTION WITH THE SHRIEKING.
X-FACTOR INVESTIGATIONS
I CAN'T HELP HOW MY POWERS WORK, MONET.
BE HAPPY YOU HAVE POWERS.
LOOKS LIKE WE HAVE COMPANY.
CORRECTION: HAD COMPANY. THEY'RE PULLING OUT.
I.N.S.?
A.R.M.Y.
SOMETHING TELLS ME THAT WHATEVER'S GOING ON, IT HAS NOTHING TO DO WITH US.
ANY CLUE WHAT IT COULD BE?
I WORK FOR A DETECTIVE AGENCY. HOW SHOULD I KNOW ABOUT CLUES?

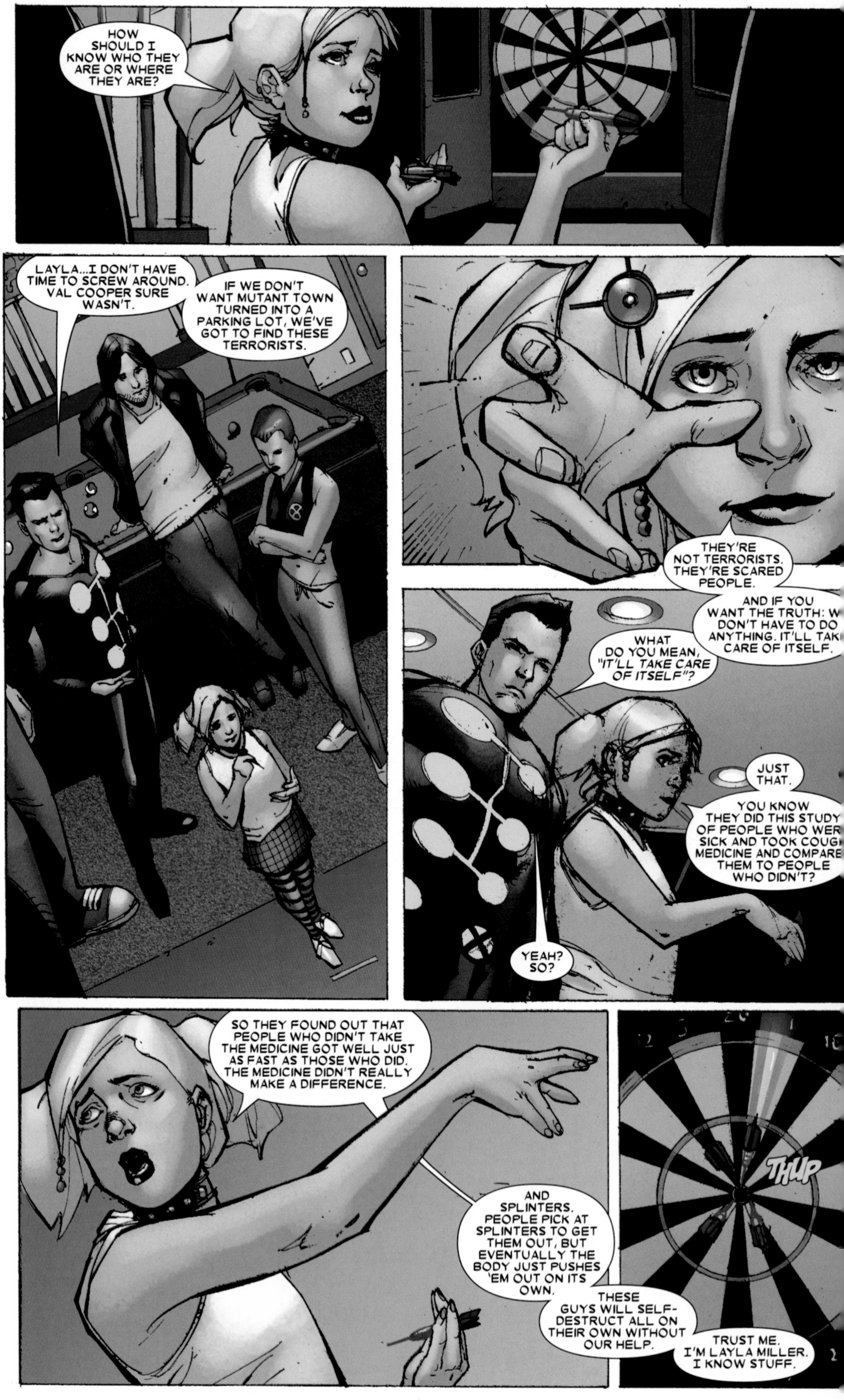

HOW SHOULD I KNOW WHO THEY ARE OR WHERE THEY ARE?
LAYLA...I DON'T HAVE TIME TO SCREW AROUND. VAL COOPER SURE WASN'T.
IF WE DON'T WANT MUTANT TOWN TURNED INTO A PARKING LOT, WE'VE GOT TO FIND THESE TERRORISTS.
THEY'RE NOT TERRORISTS. THEY'RE SCARED PEOPLE.
AND IF YOU WANT THE TRUTH: W DON'T HAVE TO DO ANYTHING. IT'LL TAK CARE OF ITSELF.
WHAT DO YOU MEAN, *"IT'LL TAKE CARE OF ITSELF"*?
JUST THAT.
YOU KNOW THEY DID THIS STUDY OF PEOPLE WHO WER SICK AND TOOK COUG MEDICINE AND COMPARE THEM TO PEOPLE WHO DIDN'T?
YEAH? SO?
SO THEY FOUND OUT THAT PEOPLE WHO DIDN'T TAKE THE MEDICINE GOT WELL JUST AS FAST AS THOSE WHO DID. THE MEDICINE DIDN'T REALLY MAKE A DIFFERENCE.
AND SPLINTERS. PEOPLE PICK AT SPLINTERS TO GET THEM OUT, BUT EVENTUALLY THE BODY JUST PUSHES 'EM OUT ON ITS OWN.
THESE GUYS WILL SELF-DESTRUCT ALL ON THEIR OWN WITHOUT OUR HELP.
THUP
TRUST ME. I'M LAYLA MILLER. I KNOW STUFF.

HI. WE'RE BACK. WE BROUGHT A FRENCH REFUGEE EX-MUTANT WITH US.

BONJOUR.

BIP

WHAT?

LAYLA, THIS IS NICOLE. SHE'S GOING TO ROOM WITH YOU IF THAT'S OKAY.

WHAT?

SHE NEEDED OUR HELP.

WHAT?

SHE *DIDN'T* SEE THIS COMING! OH, MAN, THIS IS *BEAUTIFUL!*

AYE, BRILLIANT. COULD WE GET BACK TO THE MAIN *TOPIC,* PLEASE?

RAHNE'S RIGHT.

YUP. RAHNE'S RIGHT AS RAIN.

SHUT UP, GUIDO.

LOOK, IF LAYLA'S NOT GOING TO HELP US, THEN WE GO DOOR-TO-DOOR IF WE HAVE TO...

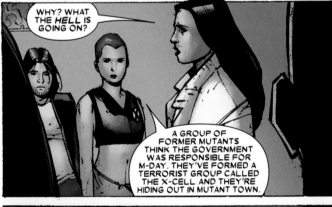

WHY? WHAT THE *HELL* IS GOING ON?

A GROUP OF FORMER MUTANTS THINK THE GOVERNMENT WAS RESPONSIBLE FOR M-DAY. THEY'VE FORMED A TERRORIST GROUP CALLED THE X-CELL AND THEY'RE HIDING OUT IN MUTANT TOWN.

AND WE'RE SUPPOSED TO TURN THEM *OVER?*

RIGHT.

BUGGER THAT!

MONET--!

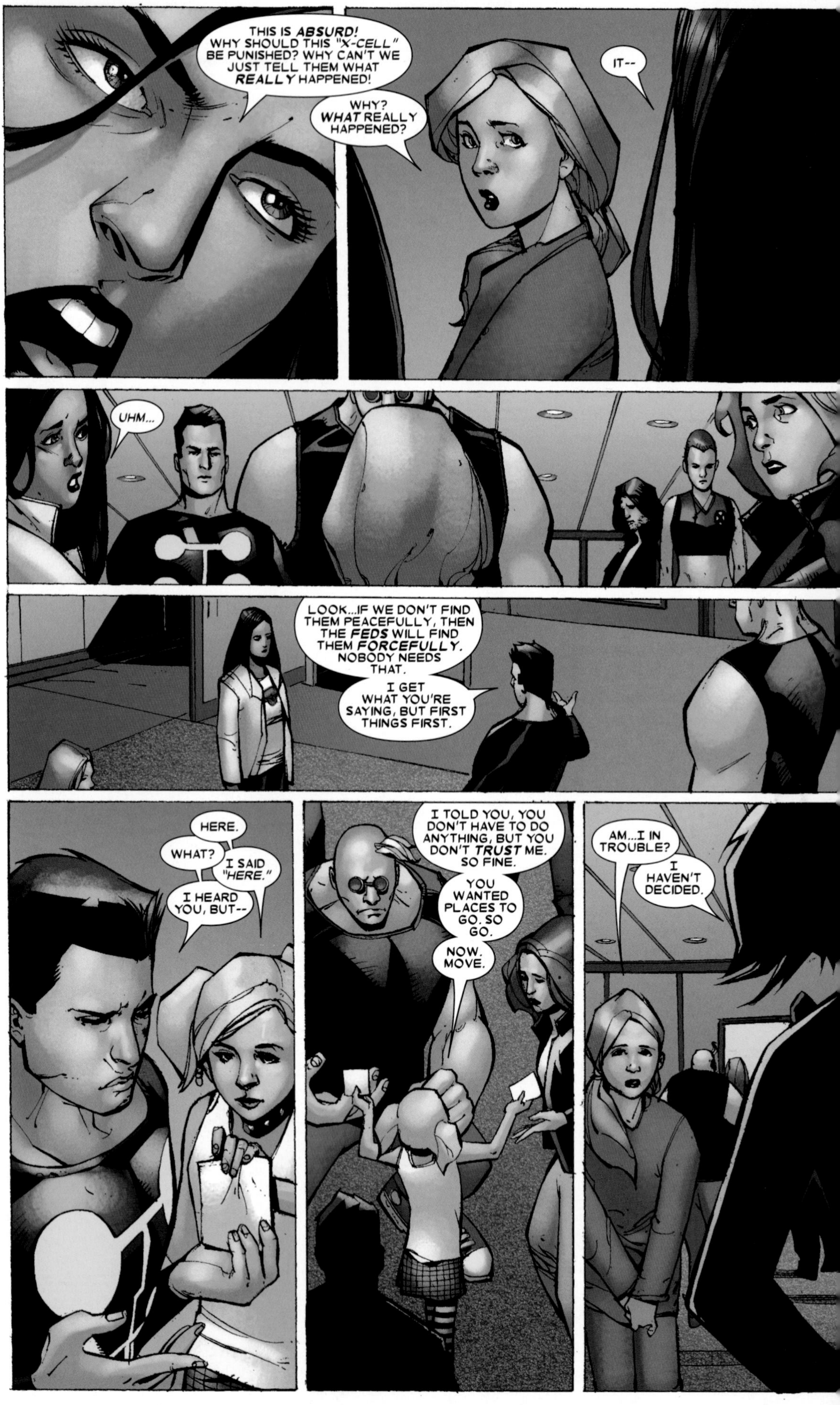

THIS IS ABSURD! WHY SHOULD THIS "X-CELL" BE PUNISHED? WHY CAN'T WE JUST TELL THEM WHAT REALLY HAPPENED!
WHY? WHAT REALLY HAPPENED?
IT--
UHM...
LOOK...IF WE DON'T FIND THEM PEACEFULLY, THEN THE FEDS WILL FIND THEM FORCEFULLY. NOBODY NEEDS THAT.
I GET WHAT YOU'RE SAYING, BUT FIRST THINGS FIRST.
HERE.
WHAT?
I SAID "HERE."
I HEARD YOU, BUT--
I TOLD YOU, YOU DON'T HAVE TO DO ANYTHING, BUT YOU DON'T TRUST ME. SO FINE.
YOU WANTED PLACES TO GO. SO GO.
NOW. MOVE.
AM...I IN TROUBLE?
I HAVEN'T DECIDED.

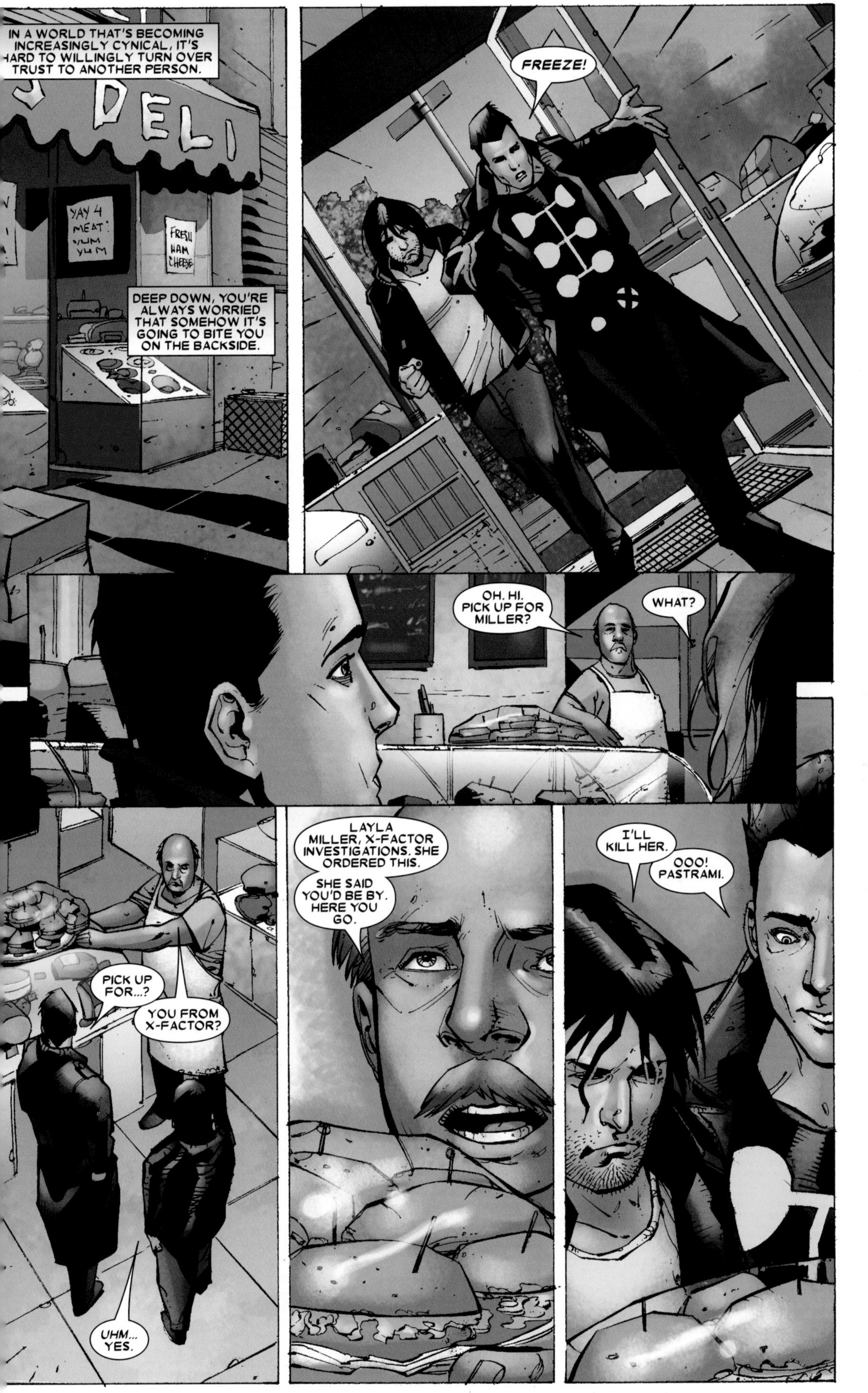

IN A WORLD THAT'S BECOMING INCREASINGLY CYNICAL, IT'S HARD TO WILLINGLY TURN OVER TRUST TO ANOTHER PERSON.
DELI
YAY 4 MEAT YUM YUM
FRESH HAM CHEESE
DEEP DOWN, YOU'RE ALWAYS WORRIED THAT SOMEHOW IT'S GOING TO BITE YOU ON THE BACKSIDE.
FREEZE!
OH. HI. PICK UP FOR MILLER?
WHAT?
PICK UP FOR...?
YOU FROM X-FACTOR?
UHM... YES.
LAYLA MILLER, X-FACTOR INVESTIGATIONS. SHE ORDERED THIS.
SHE SAID YOU'D BE BY. HERE YOU GO.
I'LL KILL HER.
OOO! PASTRAMI.

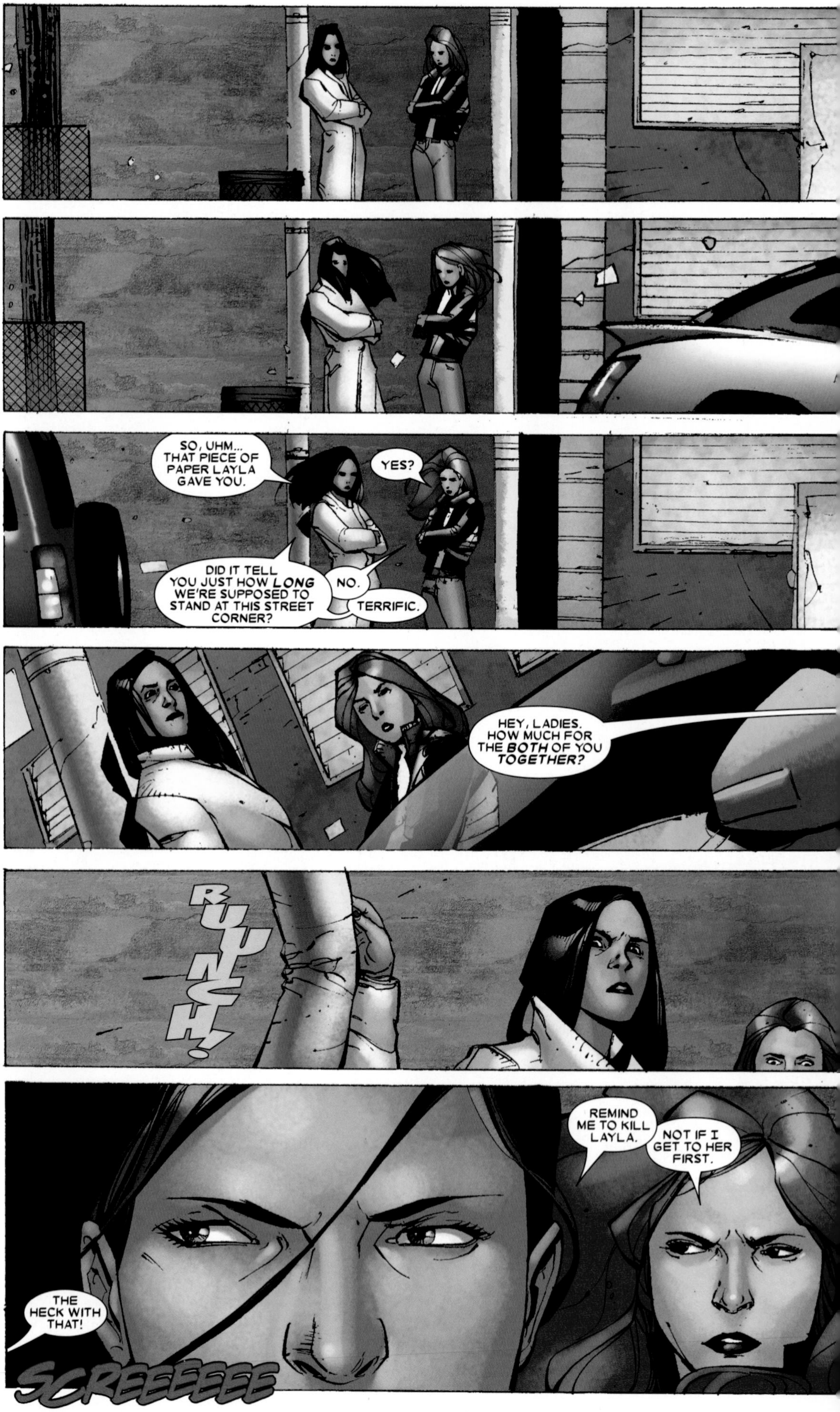

SO, UHM... THAT PIECE OF PAPER LAYLA GAVE YOU.
YES?
DID IT TELL YOU JUST HOW LONG WE'RE SUPPOSED TO STAND AT THIS STREET CORNER?
NO.
TERRIFIC.
HEY, LADIES. HOW MUCH FOR THE BOTH OF YOU TOGETHER?
RUUNCH!
REMIND ME TO KILL LAYLA.
NOT IF I GET TO HER FIRST.
THE HECK WITH THAT!
SCREEEEEEE

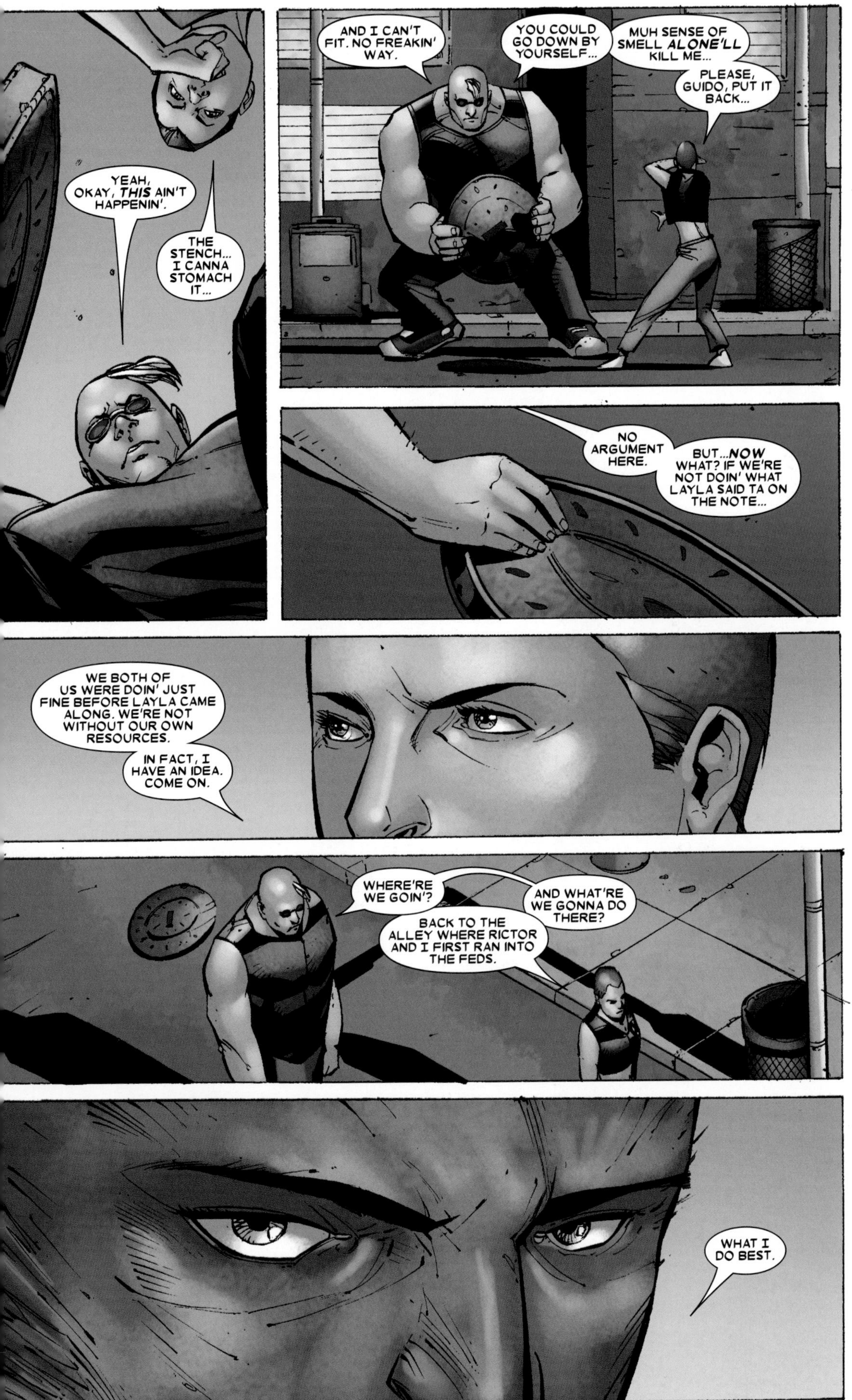
YEAH, OKAY, THIS AIN'T HAPPENIN'.
THE STENCH... I CANNA STOMACH IT...
AND I CAN'T FIT. NO FREAKIN' WAY.
YOU COULD GO DOWN BY YOURSELF...
MUH SENSE OF SMELL ALONE'LL KILL ME...
PLEASE, GUIDO, PUT IT BACK...
NO ARGUMENT HERE.
BUT...NOW WHAT? IF WE'RE NOT DOIN' WHAT LAYLA SAID TA ON THE NOTE...
WE BOTH OF US WERE DOIN' JUST FINE BEFORE LAYLA CAME ALONG. WE'RE NOT WITHOUT OUR OWN RESOURCES.
IN FACT, I HAVE AN IDEA. COME ON.
WHERE'RE WE GOIN'?
AND WHAT'RE WE GONNA DO THERE?
BACK TO THE ALLEY WHERE RICTOR AND I FIRST RAN INTO THE FEDS.
WHAT I DO BEST.

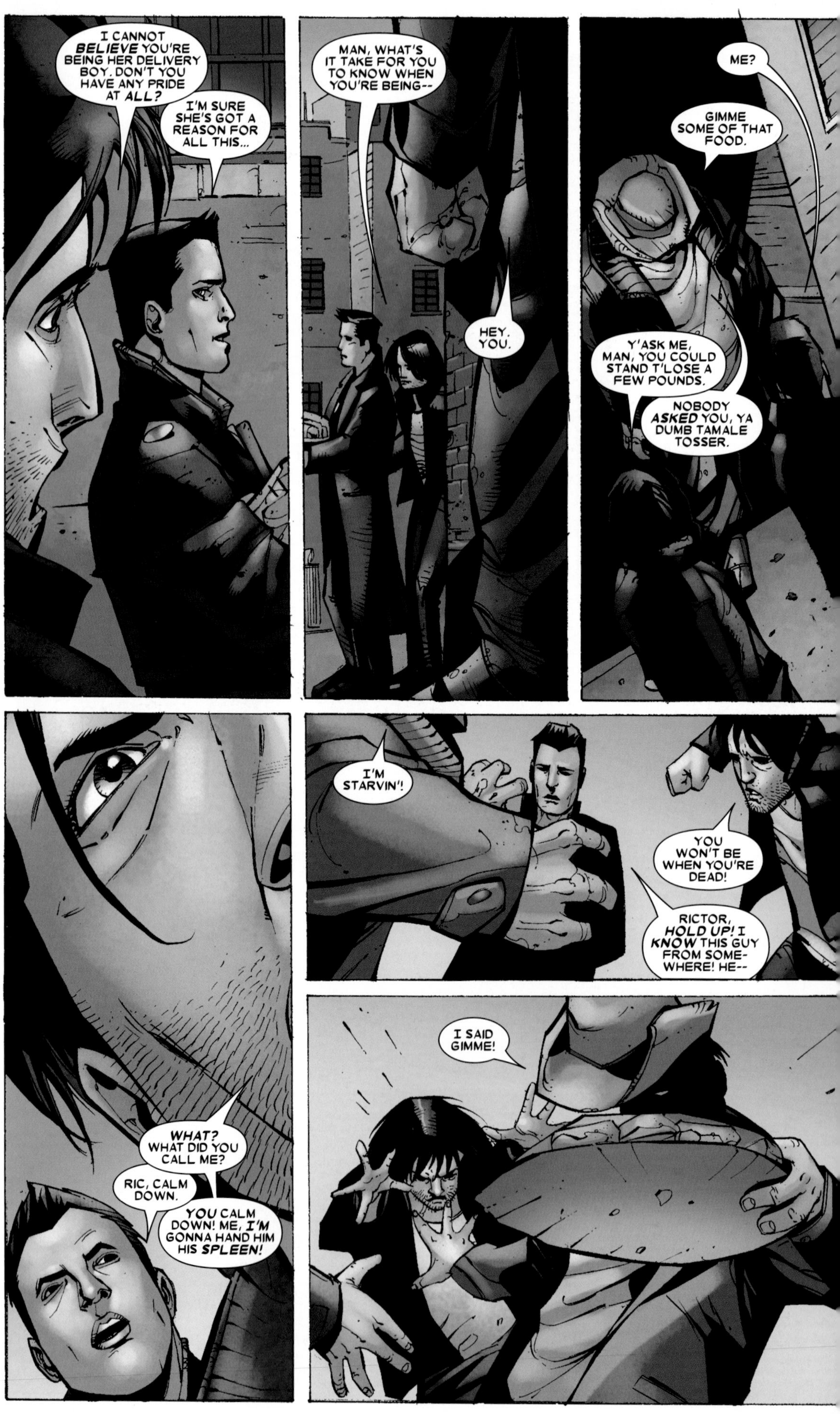

I CANNOT BELIEVE YOU'RE BEING HER DELIVERY BOY. DON'T YOU HAVE ANY PRIDE AT ALL?
I'M SURE SHE'S GOT A REASON FOR ALL THIS...
MAN, WHAT'S IT TAKE FOR YOU TO KNOW WHEN YOU'RE BEING--
HEY. YOU.
ME?
GIMME SOME OF THAT FOOD.
Y'ASK ME, MAN, YOU COULD STAND T'LOSE A FEW POUNDS.
NOBODY ASKED YOU, YA DUMB TAMALE TOSSER.
WHAT? WHAT DID YOU CALL ME?
RIC, CALM DOWN.
YOU CALM DOWN! ME, I'M GONNA HAND HIM HIS SPLEEN!
I'M STARVIN'!
YOU WON'T BE WHEN YOU'RE DEAD!
RICTOR, HOLD UP! I KNOW THIS GUY FROM SOME-WHERE! HE--
I SAID GIMME!

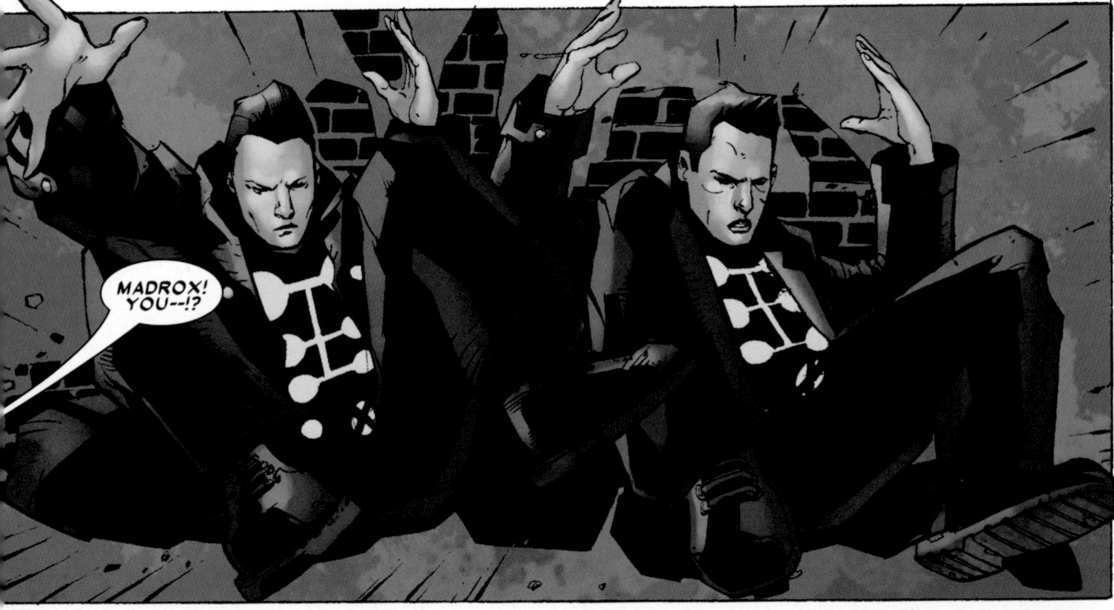
MADROX! YOU--!?
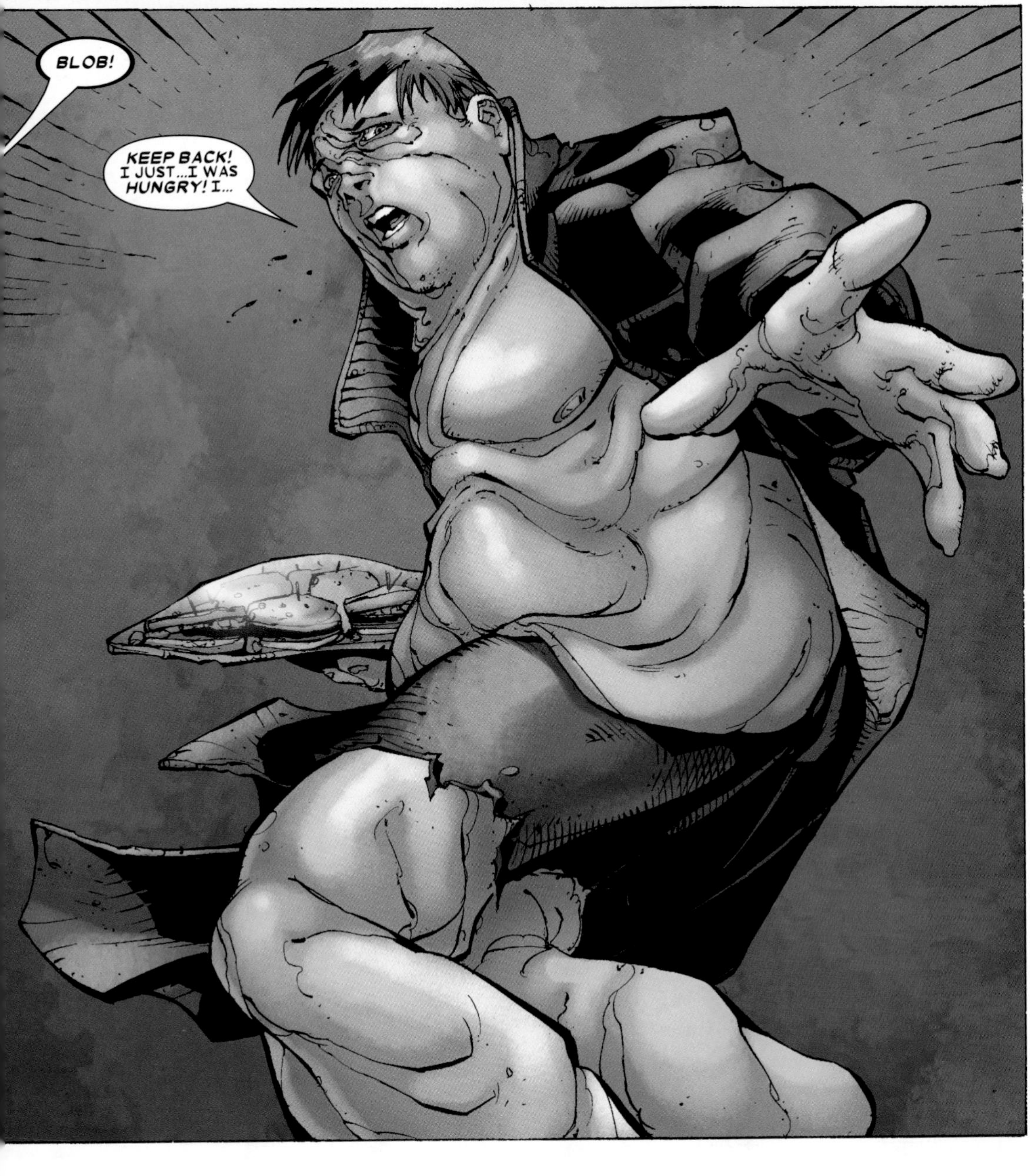
BLOB!
KEEP BACK! I JUST...I WAS HUNGRY! I...

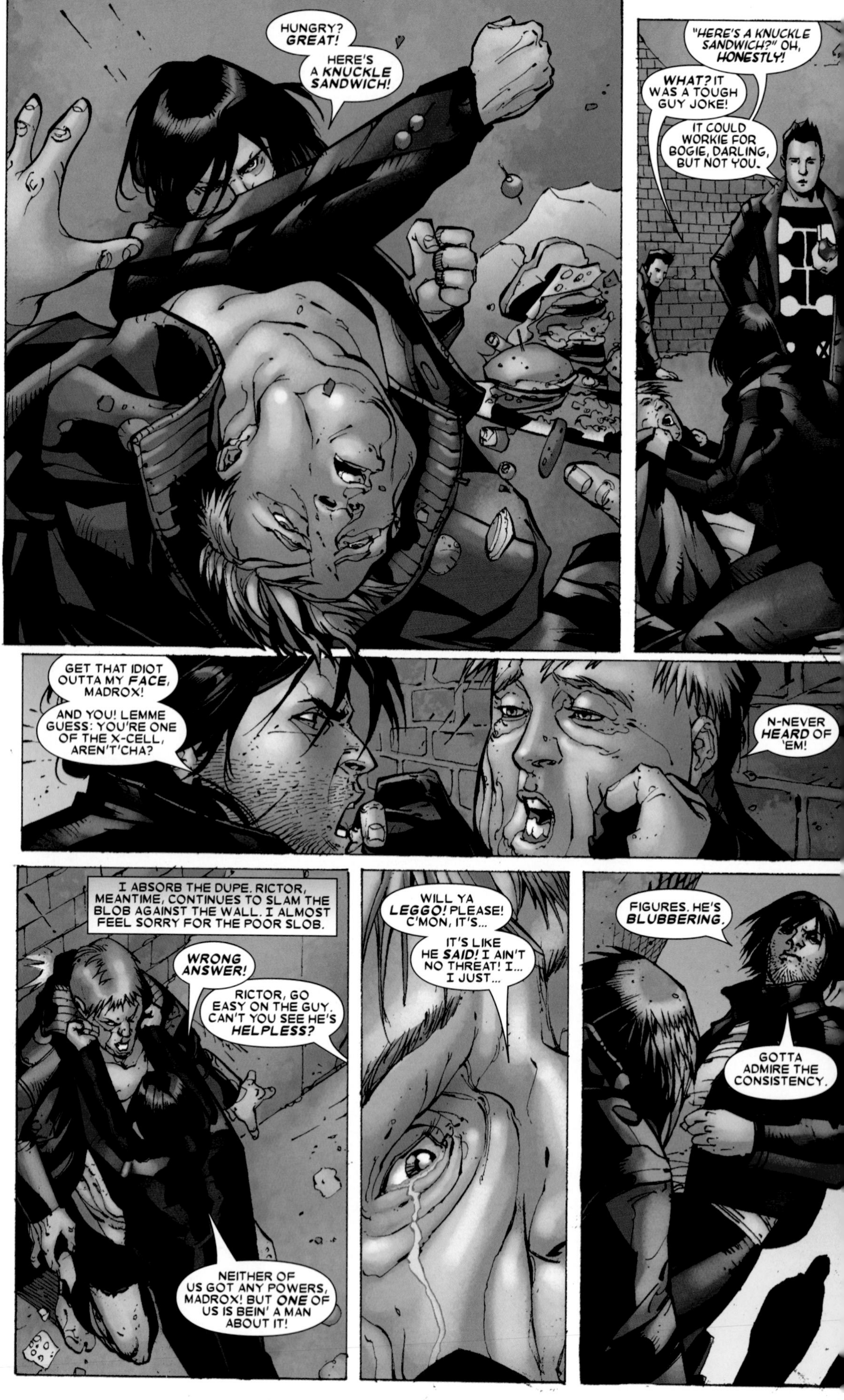
HUNGRY? GREAT!
HERE'S A KNUCKLE SANDWICH!
"HERE'S A KNUCKLE SANDWICH?" OH, HONESTLY!
WHAT? IT WAS A TOUGH GUY JOKE!
IT COULD WORKIE FOR BOGIE, DARLING, BUT NOT YOU.
GET THAT IDIOT OUTTA MY FACE, MADROX!
AND YOU! LEMME GUESS: YOU'RE ONE OF THE X-CELL, AREN'T'CHA?
N-NEVER HEARD OF 'EM!
I ABSORB THE DUPE. RICTOR, MEANTIME, CONTINUES TO SLAM THE BLOB AGAINST THE WALL. I ALMOST FEEL SORRY FOR THE POOR SLOB.
WRONG ANSWER!
RICTOR, GO EASY ON THE GUY. CAN'T YOU SEE HE'S HELPLESS?
NEITHER OF US GOT ANY POWERS, MADROX! BUT ONE OF US IS BEIN' A MAN ABOUT IT!
WILL YA LEGGO! PLEASE! C'MON, IT'S...
IT'S LIKE HE SAID! I AIN'T NO THREAT! I... I JUST...
FIGURES. HE'S BLUBBERING.
GOTTA ADMIRE THE CONSISTENCY.

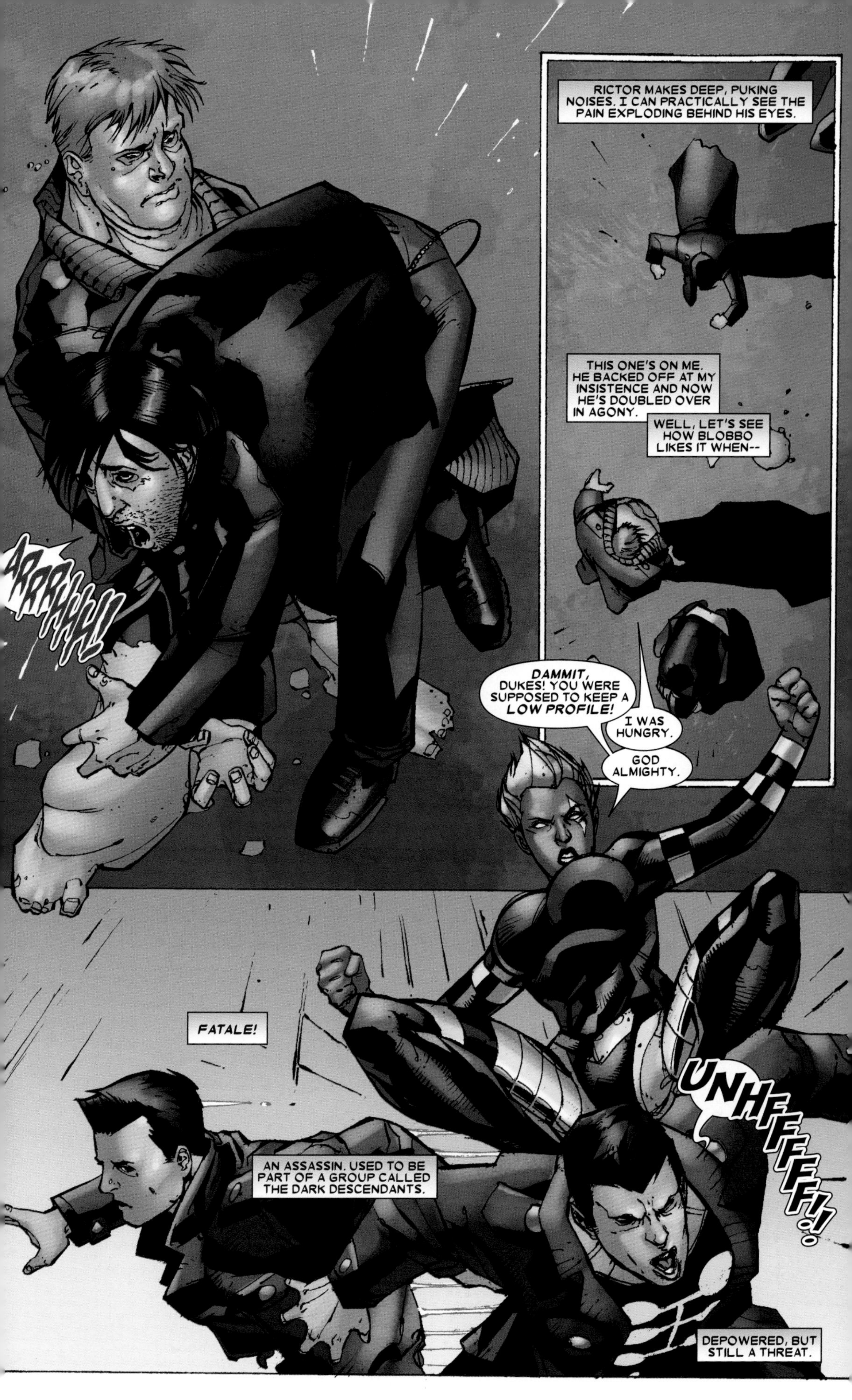

RICTOR MAKES DEEP, PUKING NOISES. I CAN PRACTICALLY SEE THE PAIN EXPLODING BEHIND HIS EYES.
ARRRAHHH!!
THIS ONE'S ON ME. HE BACKED OFF AT MY INSISTENCE AND NOW HE'S DOUBLED OVER IN AGONY.
WELL, LET'S SEE HOW BLOBBO LIKES IT WHEN--
DAMMIT, DUKES! YOU WERE SUPPOSED TO KEEP A LOW PROFILE!
I WAS HUNGRY.
GOD ALMIGHTY.
FATALE!
UNHFFFFF!!
AN ASSASSIN. USED TO BE PART OF A GROUP CALLED THE DARK DESCENDANTS.
DEPOWERED, BUT STILL A THREAT.

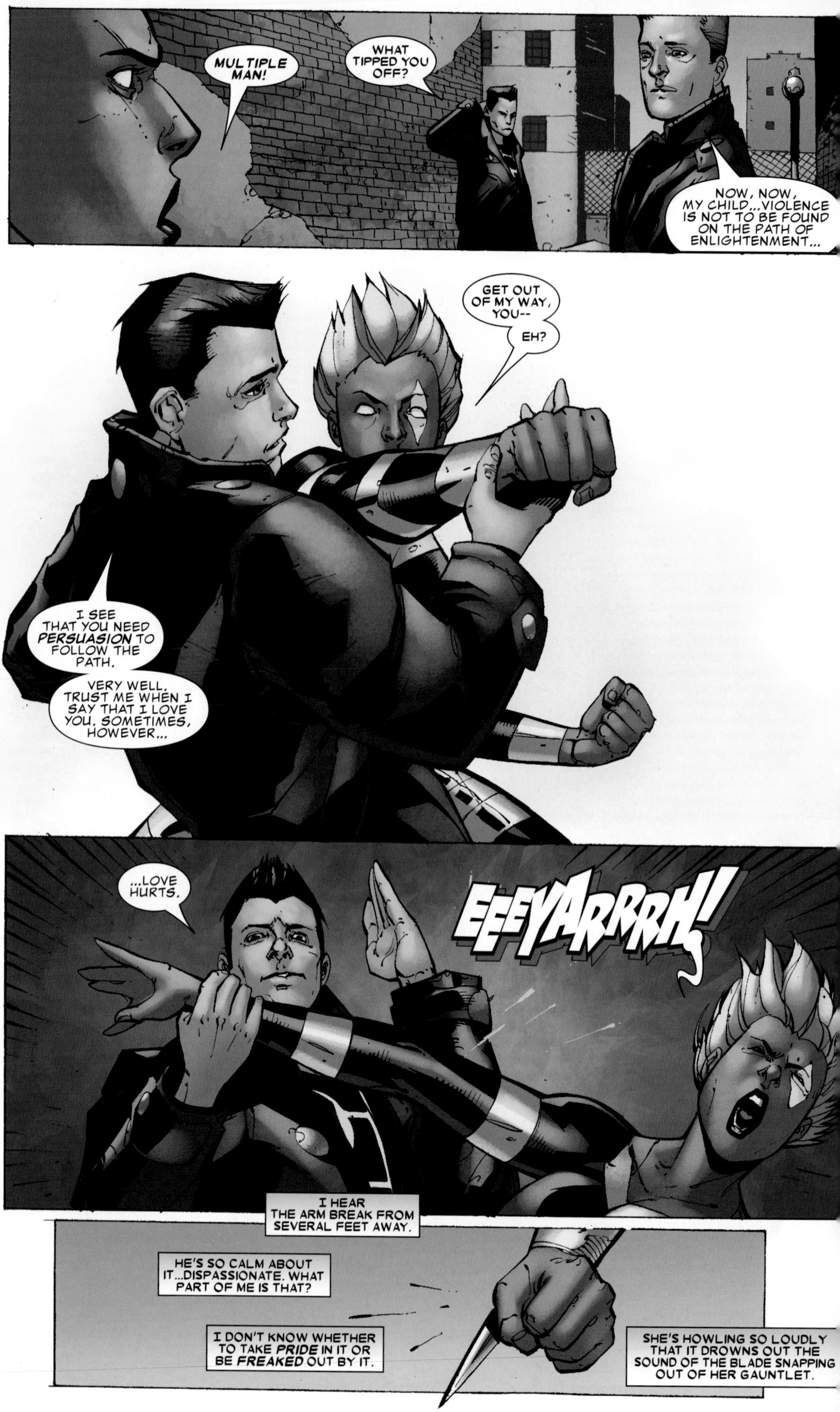
MULTIPLE MAN!
WHAT TIPPED YOU OFF?
NOW, NOW, MY CHILD...VIOLENCE IS NOT TO BE FOUND ON THE PATH OF ENLIGHTENMENT...
GET OUT OF MY WAY, YOU--
EH?
I SEE THAT YOU NEED PERSUASION TO FOLLOW THE PATH.
VERY WELL. TRUST ME WHEN I SAY THAT I LOVE YOU. SOMETIMES, HOWEVER...
...LOVE HURTS.
EEEYARRRH!
I HEAR THE ARM BREAK FROM SEVERAL FEET AWAY.
HE'S SO CALM ABOUT IT...DISPASSIONATE. WHAT PART OF ME IS THAT?
I DON'T KNOW WHETHER TO TAKE PRIDE IN IT OR BE FREAKED OUT BY IT.
SHE'S HOWLING SO LOUDLY THAT IT DROWNS OUT THE SOUND OF THE BLADE SNAPPING OUT OF HER GAUNTLET.

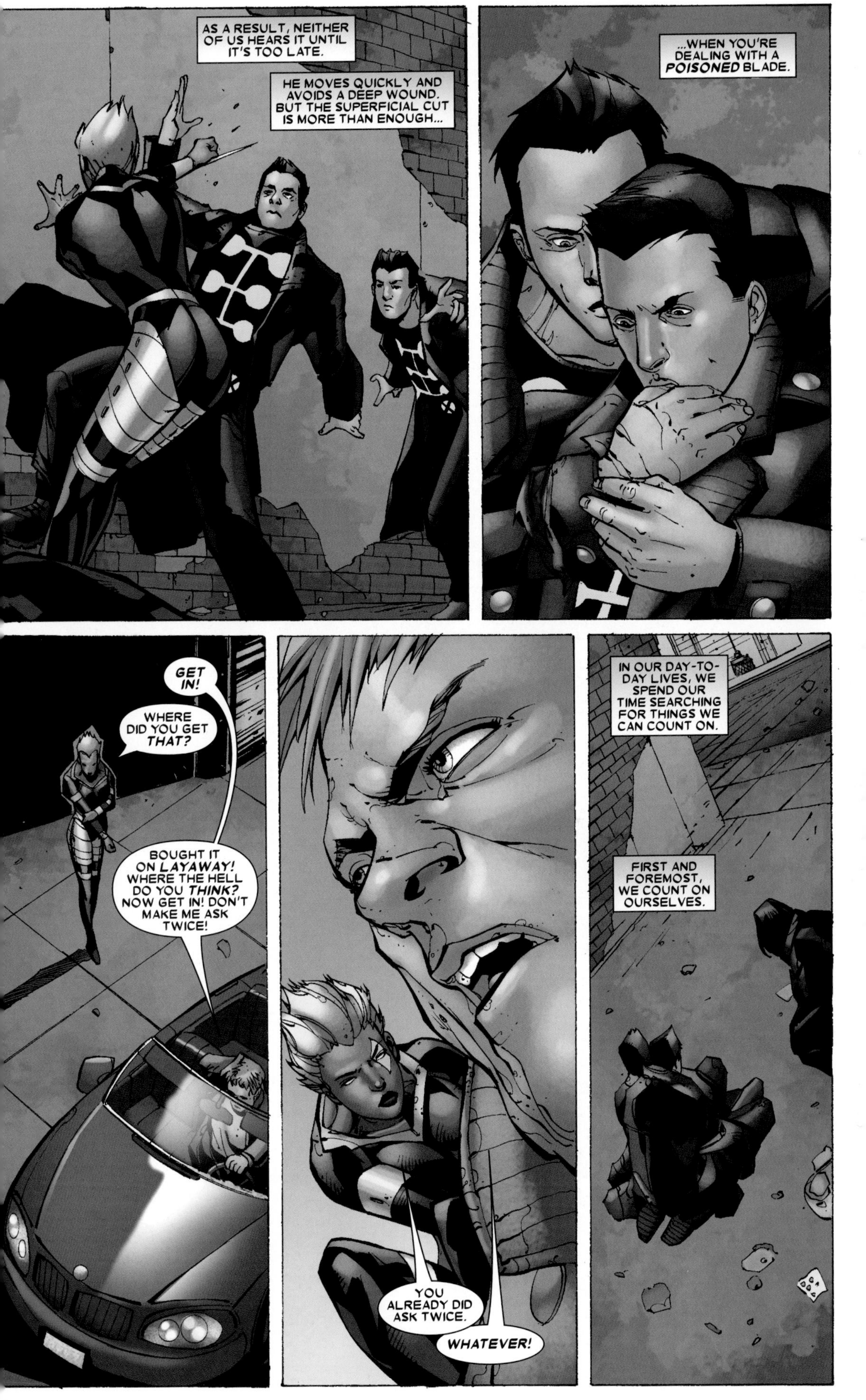
AS A RESULT, NEITHER OF US HEARS IT UNTIL IT'S TOO LATE.
HE MOVES QUICKLY AND AVOIDS A DEEP WOUND. BUT THE SUPERFICIAL CUT IS MORE THAN ENOUGH...
...WHEN YOU'RE DEALING WITH A *POISONED* BLADE.
GET IN!
WHERE DID YOU GET *THAT?*
BOUGHT IT ON *LAYAWAY!* WHERE THE HELL DO YOU *THINK?* NOW GET IN! DON'T MAKE ME ASK TWICE!
YOU ALREADY DID ASK TWICE.
WHATEVER!
IN OUR DAY-TO-DAY LIVES, WE SPEND OUR TIME SEARCHING FOR THINGS WE CAN COUNT ON.
FIRST AND FOREMOST, WE COUNT ON OURSELVES.

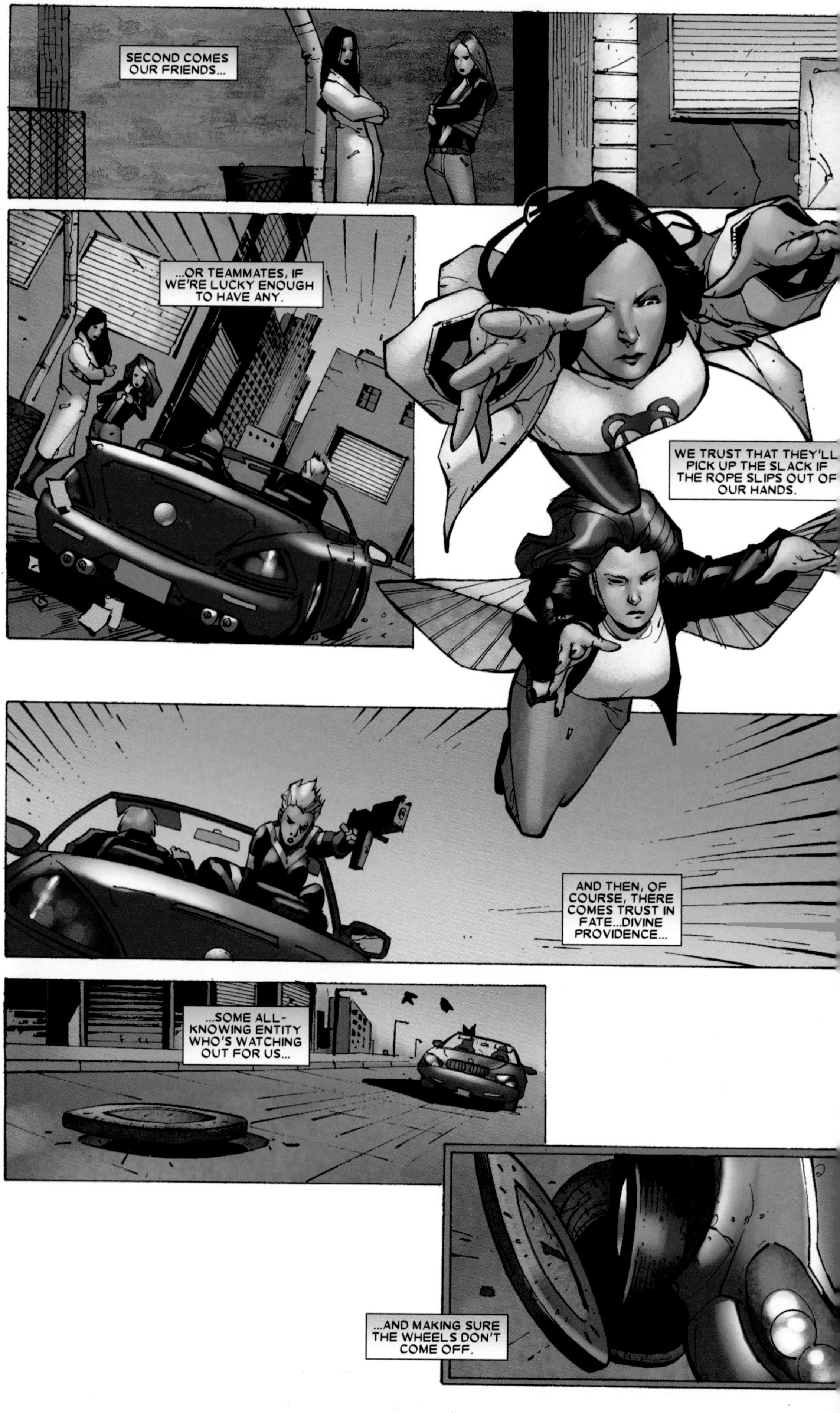
SECOND COMES OUR FRIENDS...
...OR TEAMMATES, IF WE'RE LUCKY ENOUGH TO HAVE ANY.
WE TRUST THAT THEY'LL PICK UP THE SLACK IF THE ROPE SLIPS OUT OF OUR HANDS.
AND THEN, OF COURSE, THERE COMES TRUST IN FATE...DIVINE PROVIDENCE...
...SOME ALL-KNOWING ENTITY WHO'S WATCHING OUT FOR US...
...AND MAKING SURE THE WHEELS DON'T COME OFF.

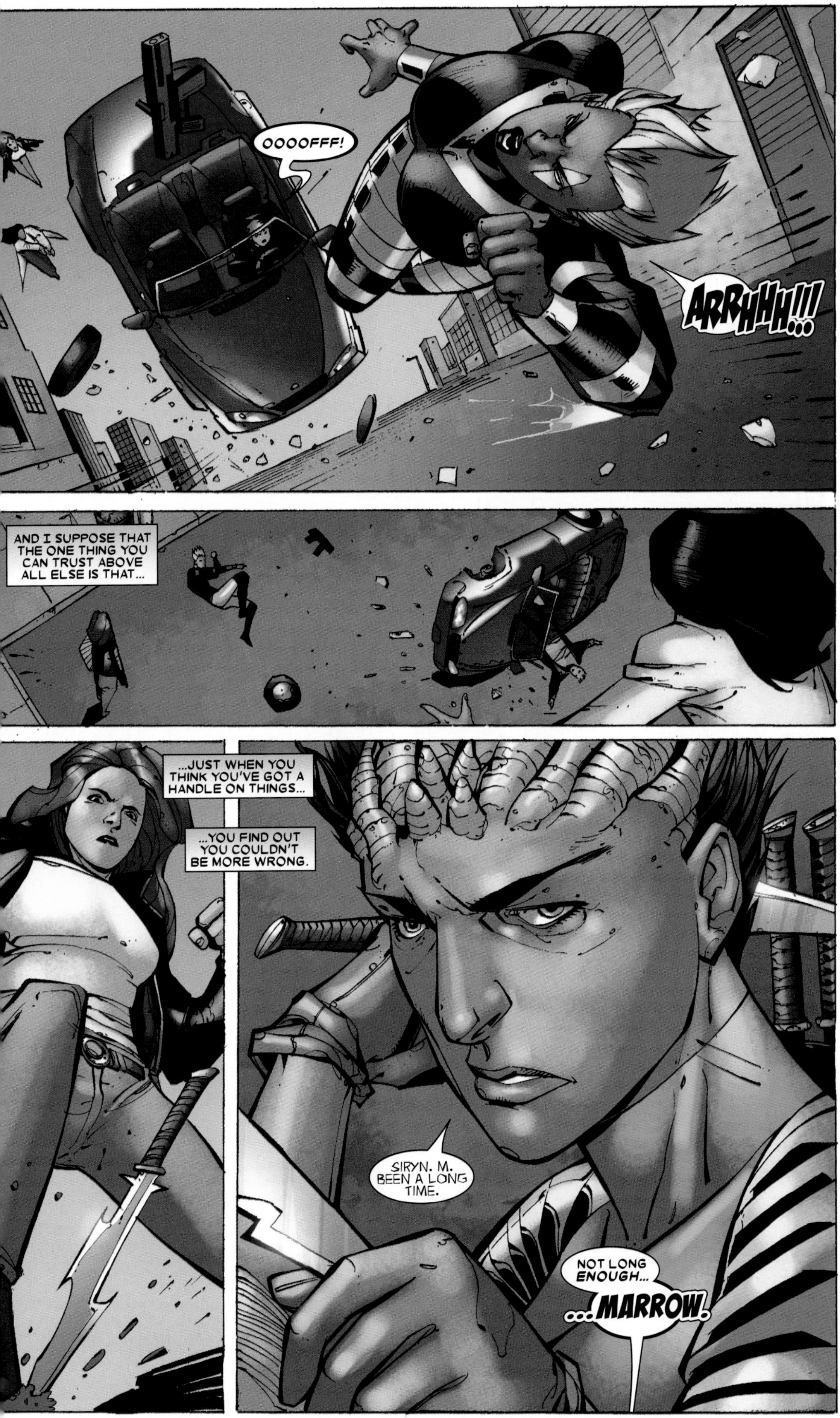
OOOOFFF!
ARRHHH!!!
AND I SUPPOSE THAT THE ONE THING YOU CAN TRUST ABOVE ALL ELSE IS THAT...
...JUST WHEN YOU THINK YOU'VE GOT A HANDLE ON THINGS...
...YOU FIND OUT YOU COULDN'T BE MORE WRONG.
SIRYN. M. BEEN A LONG TIME.
NOT LONG ENOUGH...
...MARROW.

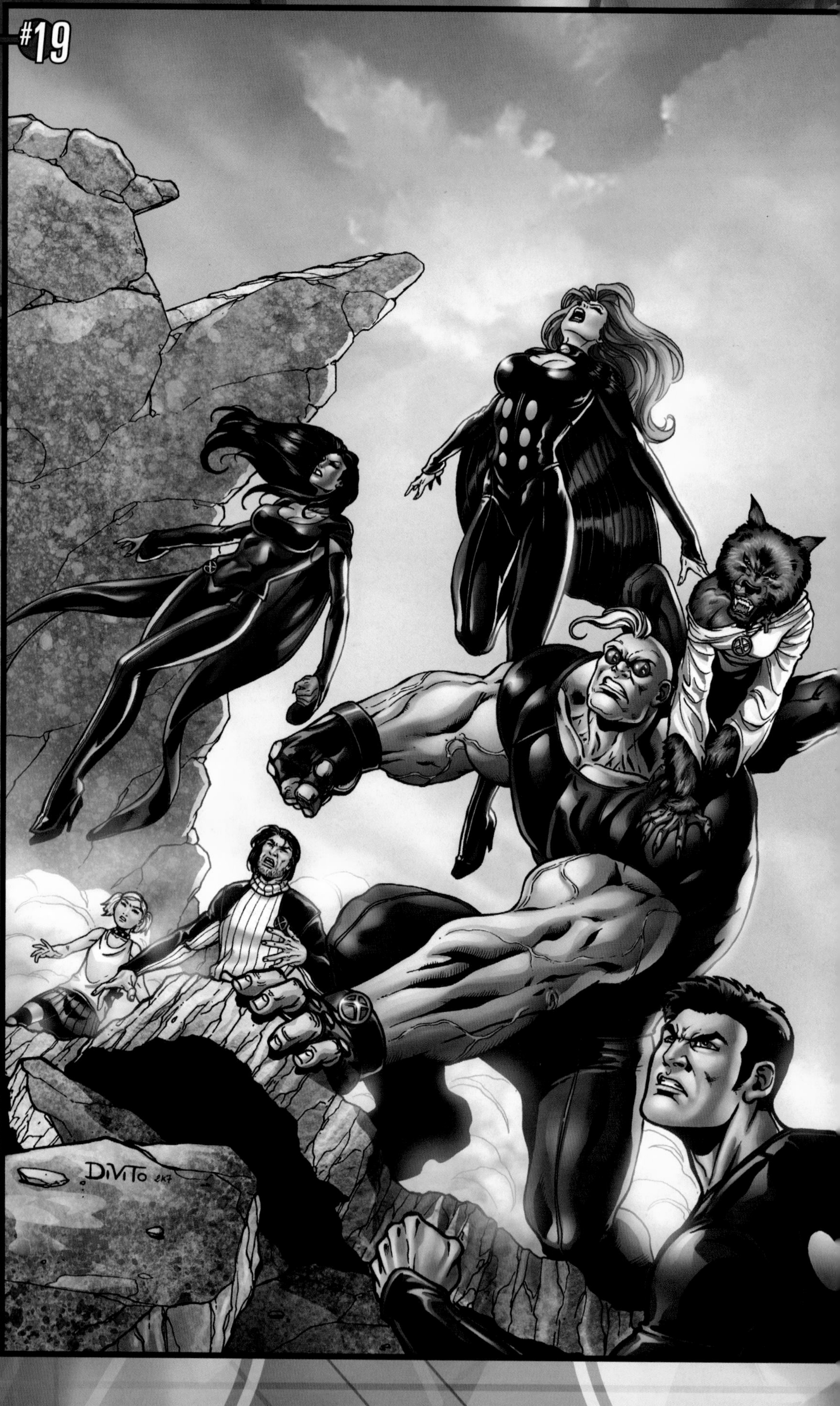
#19
DiViTo

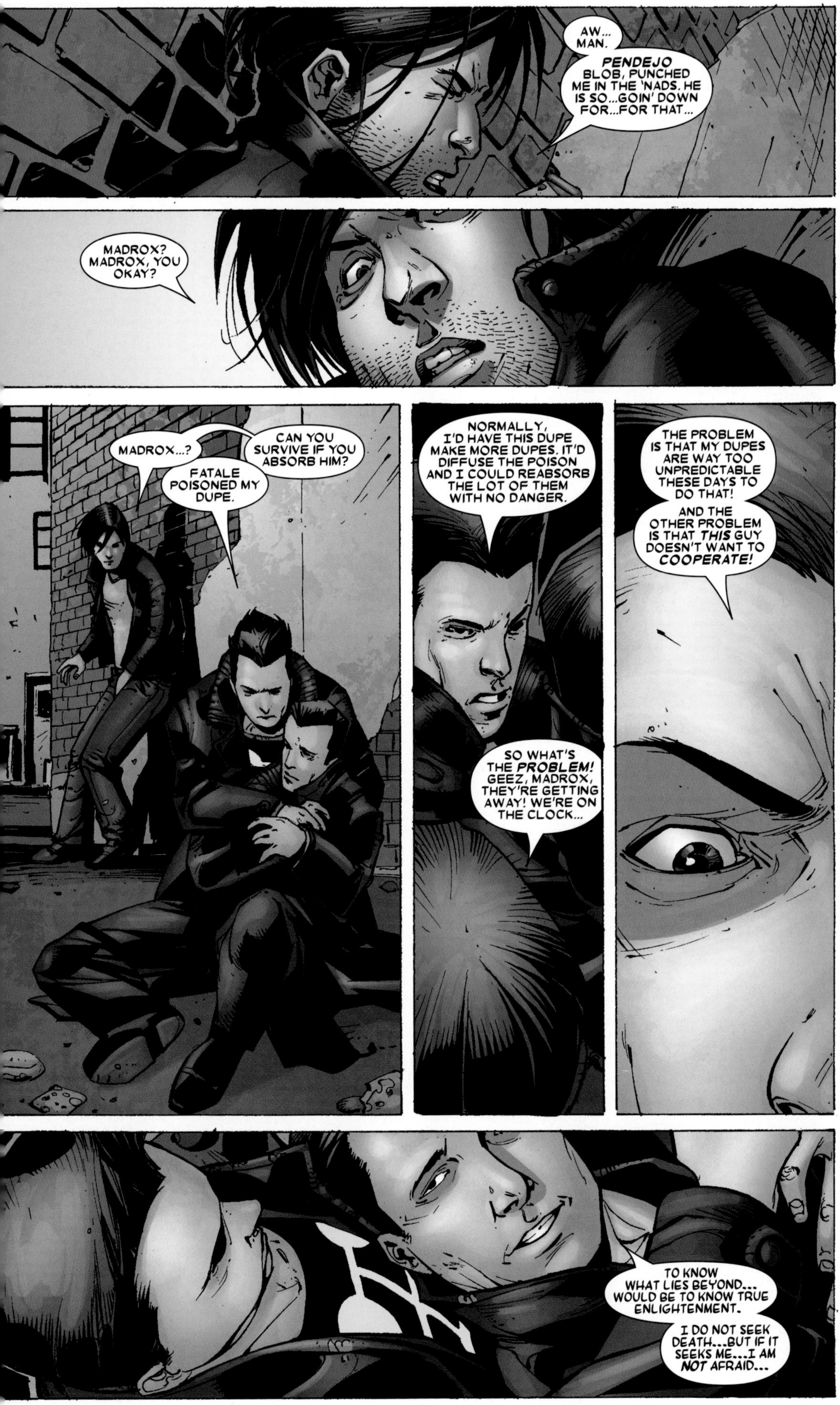
AW... MAN.
PENDEJO BLOB, PUNCHED ME IN THE 'NADS. HE IS SO...GOIN' DOWN FOR...FOR THAT...
MADROX? MADROX, YOU OKAY?
MADROX...?
CAN YOU SURVIVE IF YOU ABSORB HIM?
FATALE POISONED MY DUPE.
NORMALLY, I'D HAVE THIS DUPE MAKE MORE DUPES. IT'D DIFFUSE THE POISON AND I COULD REABSORB THE LOT OF THEM WITH NO DANGER.
SO WHAT'S THE PROBLEM! GEEZ, MADROX, THEY'RE GETTING AWAY! WE'RE ON THE CLOCK...
THE PROBLEM IS THAT MY DUPES ARE WAY TOO UNPREDICTABLE THESE DAYS TO DO THAT!
AND THE OTHER PROBLEM IS THAT THIS GUY DOESN'T WANT TO COOPERATE!
TO KNOW WHAT LIES BEYOND... WOULD BE TO KNOW TRUE ENLIGHTENMENT.
I DO NOT SEEK DEATH...BUT IF IT SEEKS ME...I AM NOT AFRAID...

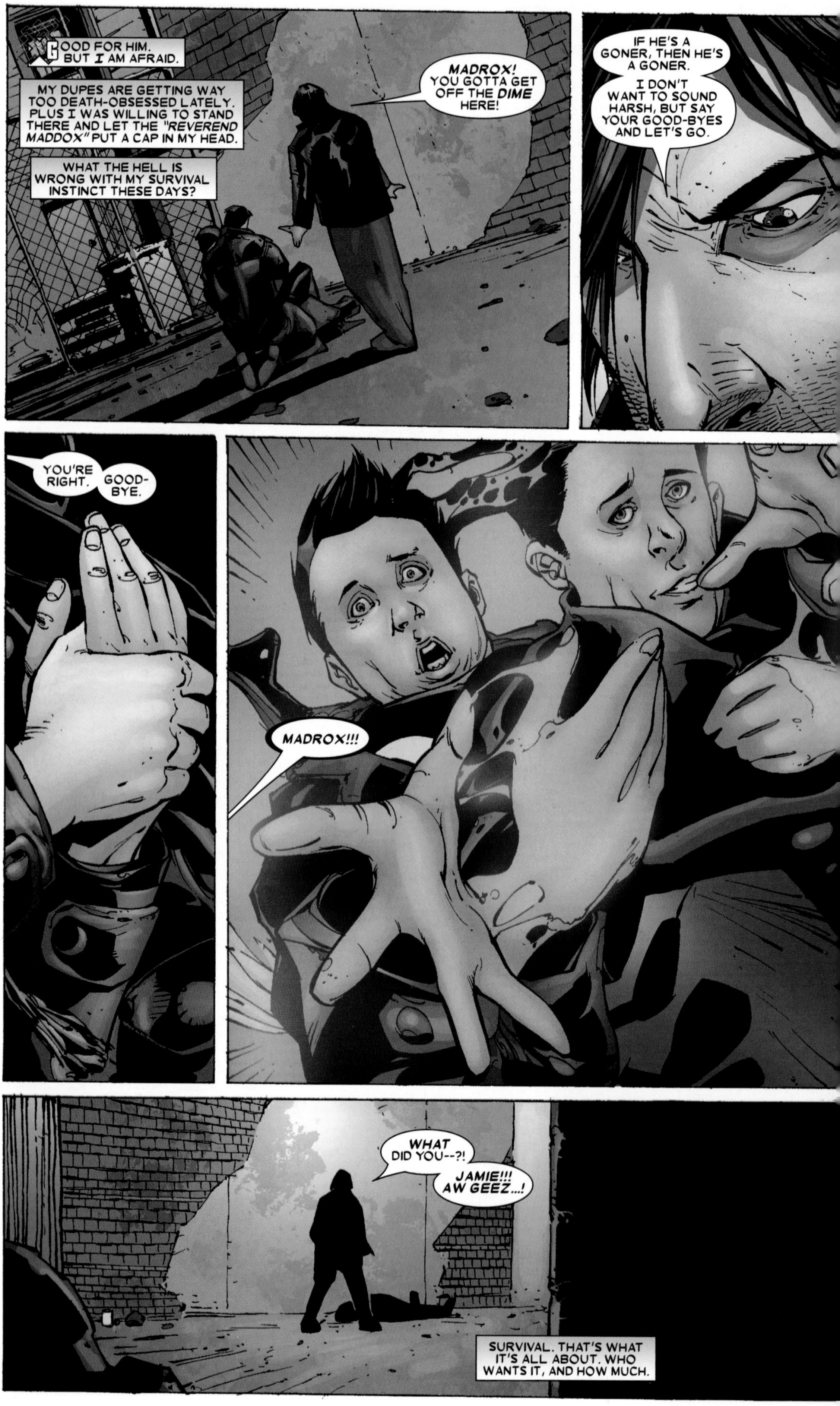
GOOD FOR HIM. BUT I AM AFRAID.
MY DUPES ARE GETTING WAY TOO DEATH-OBSESSED LATELY. PLUS I WAS WILLING TO STAND THERE AND LET THE "REVEREND MADDOX" PUT A CAP IN MY HEAD.
WHAT THE HELL IS WRONG WITH MY SURVIVAL INSTINCT THESE DAYS?
MADROX! YOU GOTTA GET OFF THE DIME HERE!
IF HE'S A GONER, THEN HE'S A GONER.
I DON'T WANT TO SOUND HARSH, BUT SAY YOUR GOOD-BYES AND LET'S GO.
YOU'RE RIGHT.
GOOD-BYE.
MADROX!!!
WHAT DID YOU--?!
JAMIE!!! AW GEEZ...!
SURVIVAL. THAT'S WHAT IT'S ALL ABOUT. WHO WANTS IT, AND HOW MUCH.

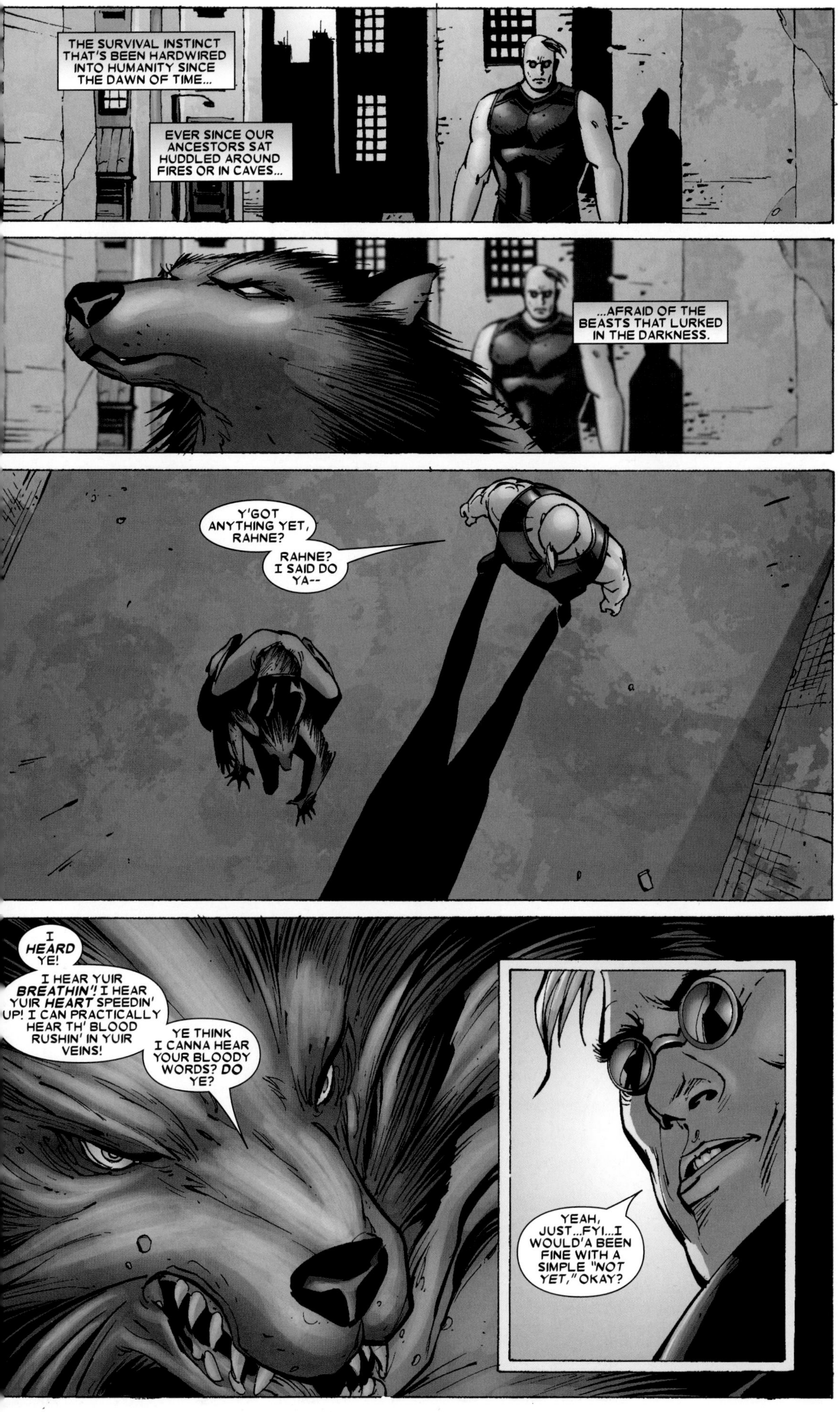
THE SURVIVAL INSTINCT THAT'S BEEN HARDWIRED INTO HUMANITY SINCE THE DAWN OF TIME...
EVER SINCE OUR ANCESTORS SAT HUDDLED AROUND FIRES OR IN CAVES...
...AFRAID OF THE BEASTS THAT LURKED IN THE DARKNESS.
Y'GOT ANYTHING YET, RAHNE?
RAHNE? I SAID DO YA--
I *HEARD* YE!
I HEAR YUIR *BREATHIN'!* I HEAR YUIR *HEART* SPEEDIN' UP! I CAN PRACTICALLY HEAR TH' BLOOD RUSHIN' IN YUIR VEINS!
YE THINK I CANNA HEAR YOUR BLOODY WORDS? *DO* YE?
YEAH, JUST...FYI...I WOULD'A BEEN FINE WITH A SIMPLE *"NOT YET,"* OKAY?

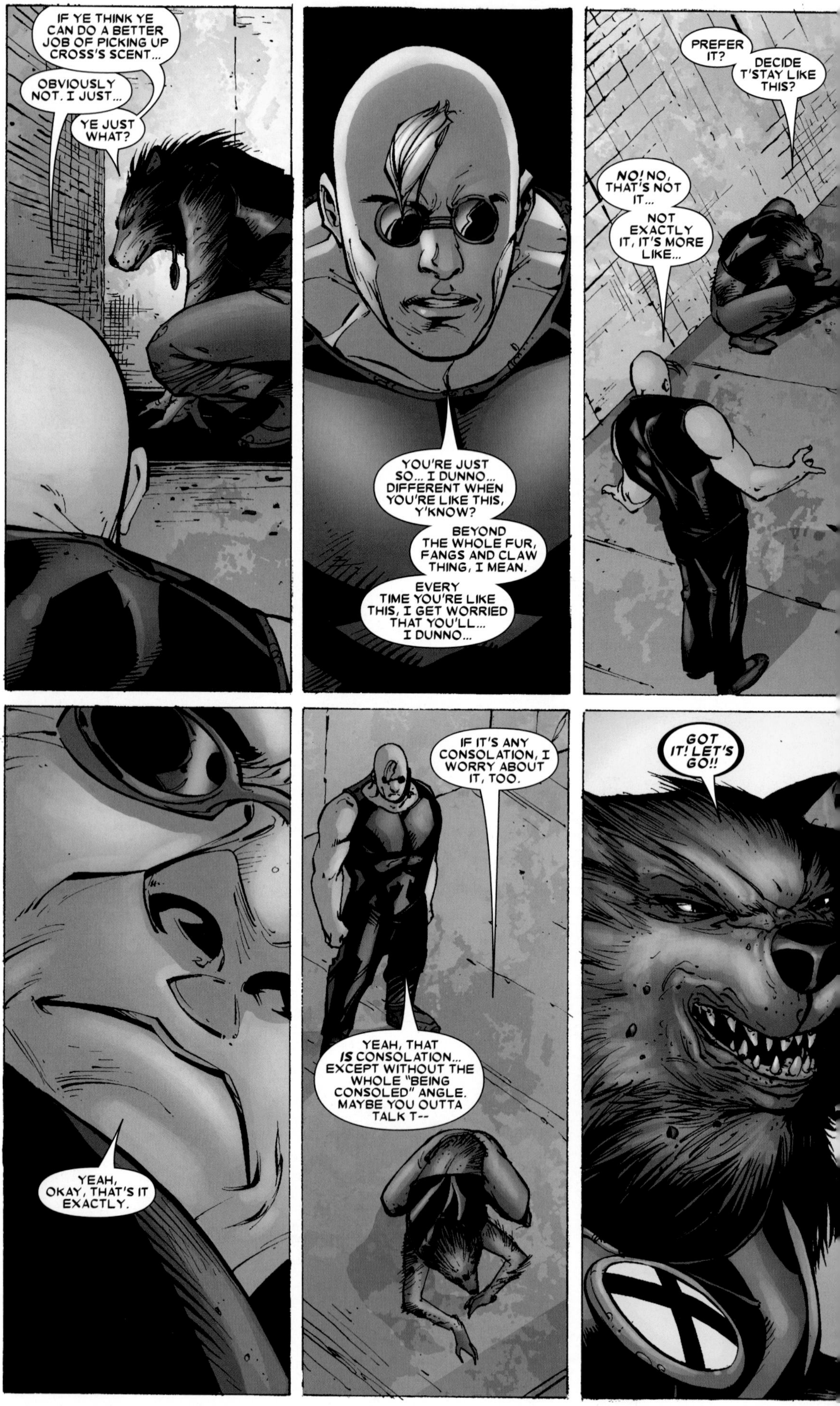
IF YE THINK YE CAN DO A BETTER JOB OF PICKING UP CROSS'S SCENT...
OBVIOUSLY NOT. I JUST...
YE JUST WHAT?
YOU'RE JUST SO... I DUNNO... DIFFERENT WHEN YOU'RE LIKE THIS, Y'KNOW?
BEYOND THE WHOLE FUR, FANGS AND CLAW THING, I MEAN.
EVERY TIME YOU'RE LIKE THIS, I GET WORRIED THAT YOU'LL... I DUNNO...
PREFER IT?
DECIDE T'STAY LIKE THIS?
NO! NO, THAT'S NOT IT...
NOT EXACTLY IT, IT'S MORE LIKE...
YEAH, OKAY, THAT'S IT EXACTLY.
IF IT'S ANY CONSOLATION, I WORRY ABOUT IT, TOO.
YEAH, THAT IS CONSOLATION... EXCEPT WITHOUT THE WHOLE "BEING CONSOLED" ANGLE. MAYBE YOU OUTTA TALK T--
GOT IT! LET'S GO!!

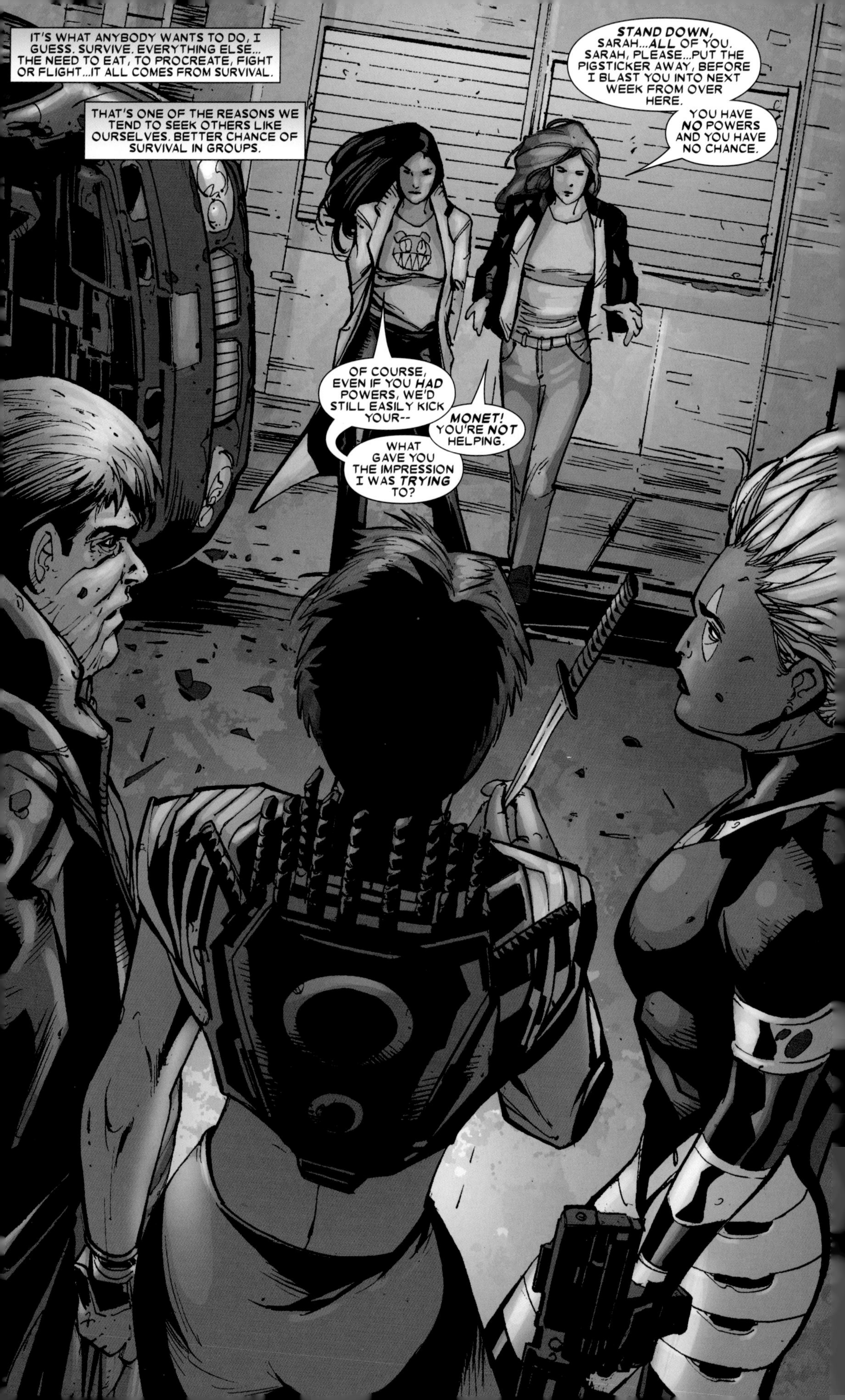
IT'S WHAT ANYBODY WANTS TO DO, I GUESS. SURVIVE. EVERYTHING ELSE... THE NEED TO EAT, TO PROCREATE, FIGHT OR FLIGHT...IT ALL COMES FROM SURVIVAL.
THAT'S ONE OF THE REASONS WE TEND TO SEEK OTHERS LIKE OURSELVES. BETTER CHANCE OF SURVIVAL IN GROUPS.
STAND DOWN, SARAH...ALL OF YOU. SARAH, PLEASE...PUT THE PIGSTICKER AWAY, BEFORE I BLAST YOU INTO NEXT WEEK FROM OVER HERE.
YOU HAVE NO POWERS AND YOU HAVE NO CHANCE.
OF COURSE, EVEN IF YOU HAD POWERS, WE'D STILL EASILY KICK YOUR--
MONET! YOU'RE NOT HELPING.
WHAT GAVE YOU THE IMPRESSION I WAS TRYING TO?

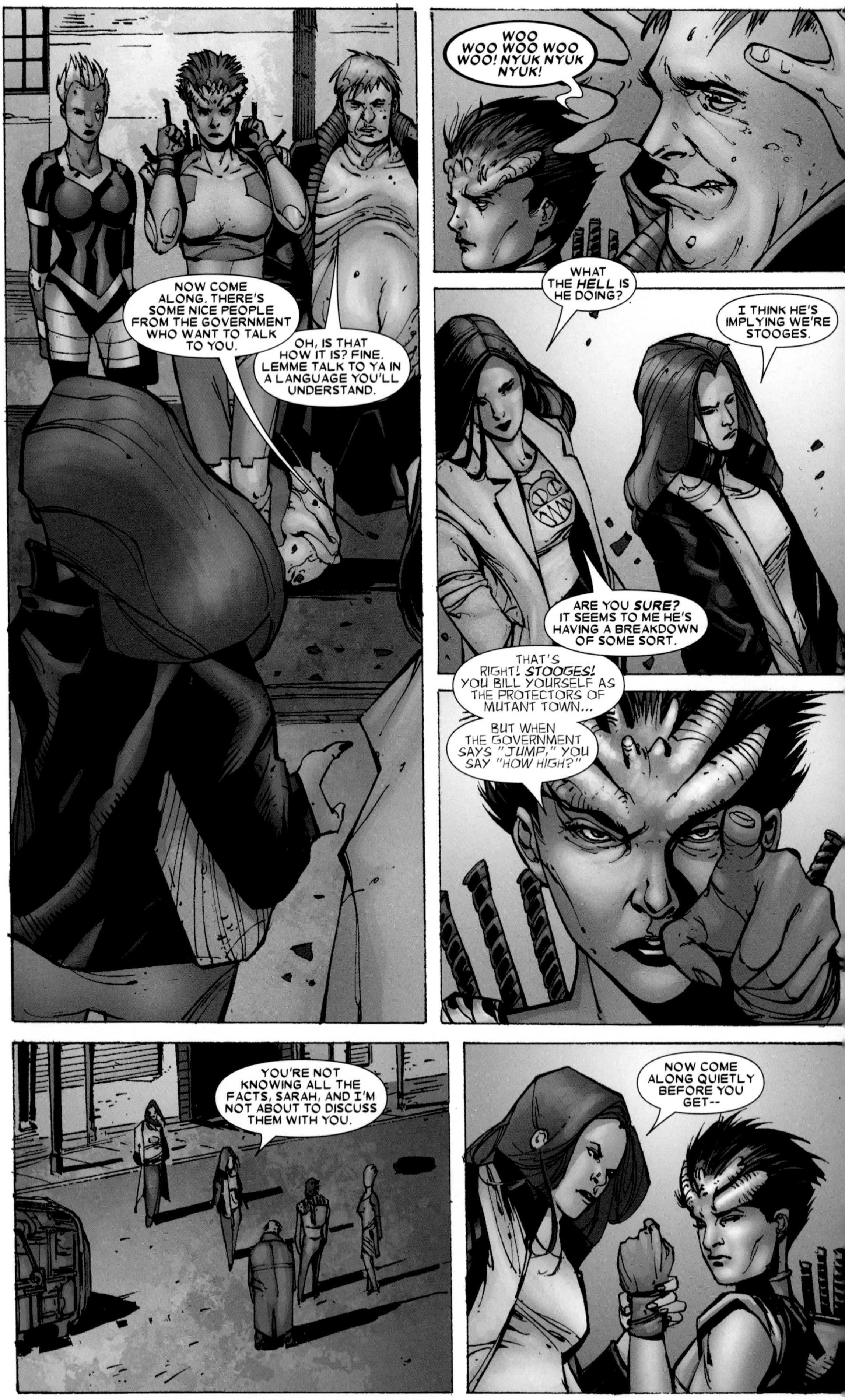
NOW COME ALONG. THERE'S SOME NICE PEOPLE FROM THE GOVERNMENT WHO WANT TO TALK TO YOU.
OH, IS THAT HOW IT IS? FINE. LEMME TALK TO YA IN A LANGUAGE YOU'LL UNDERSTAND.
WOO WOO WOO WOO WOO! NYUK NYUK NYUK!
WHAT THE HELL IS HE DOING?
I THINK HE'S IMPLYING WE'RE STOOGES.
ARE YOU SURE? IT SEEMS TO ME HE'S HAVING A BREAKDOWN OF SOME SORT.
THAT'S RIGHT! STOOGES! YOU BILL YOURSELF AS THE PROTECTORS OF MUTANT TOWN...
BUT WHEN THE GOVERNMENT SAYS "JUMP," YOU SAY "HOW HIGH?"
YOU'RE NOT KNOWING ALL THE FACTS, SARAH, AND I'M NOT ABOUT TO DISCUSS THEM WITH YOU.
NOW COME ALONG QUIETLY BEFORE YOU GET--

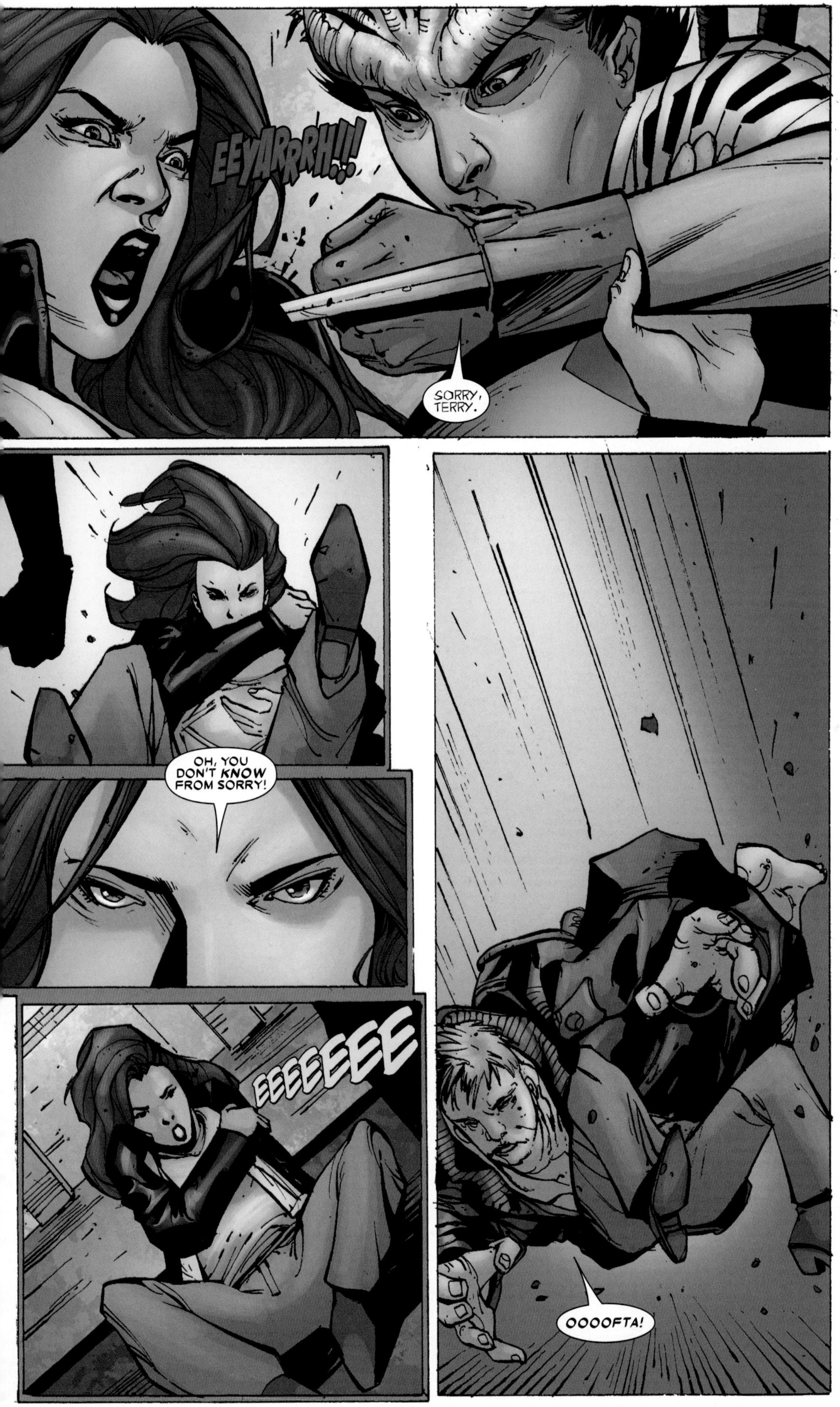
EEYARRRH!!!
SORRY, TERRY.
OH, YOU DON'T KNOW FROM SORRY!
EEEEEEEE
OOOOFTA!

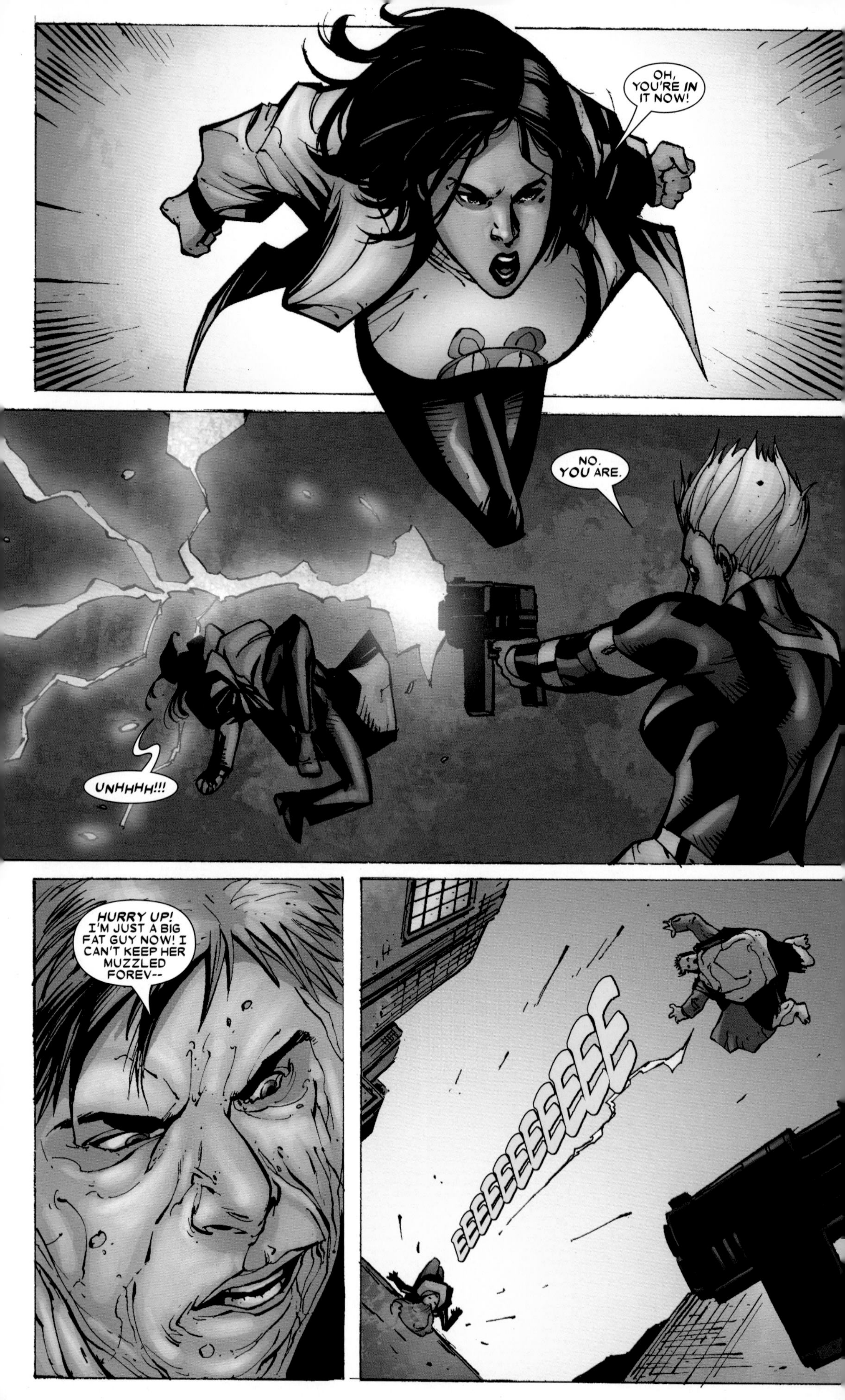
OH, YOU'RE *IN* IT NOW!
NO. *YOU* ARE.
UNHHHH!!!
HURRY UP! I'M JUST A BIG FAT GUY NOW! I CAN'T KEEP HER MUZZLED FOREV--
EEEEEEEEEEEE

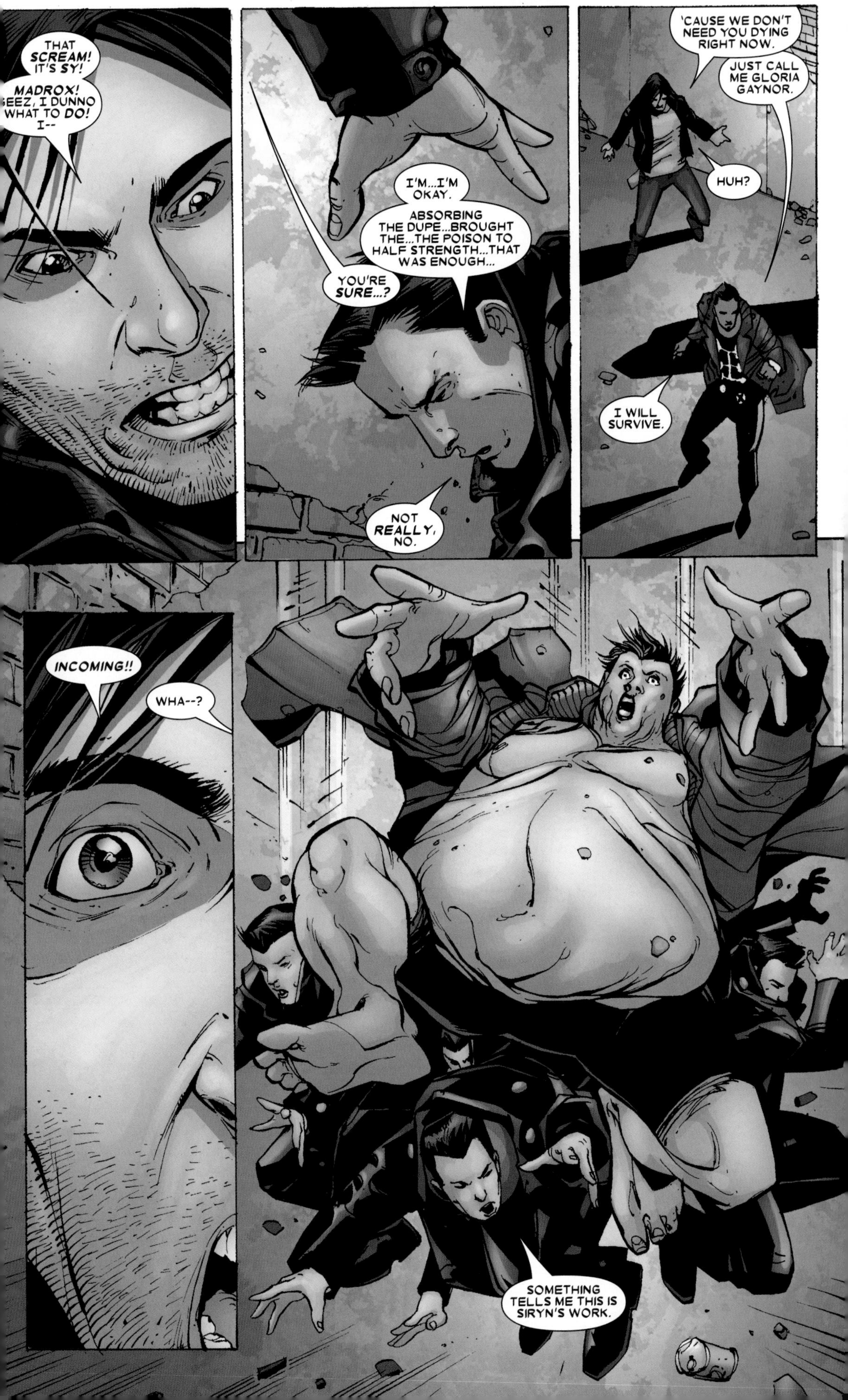

THAT SCREAM! IT'S SY!
MADROX! JEEZ, I DUNNO WHAT TO DO! I--
I'M...I'M OKAY.
ABSORBING THE DUPE...BROUGHT THE...THE POISON TO HALF STRENGTH...THAT WAS ENOUGH...
YOU'RE SURE...?
NOT REALLY, NO.
'CAUSE WE DON'T NEED YOU DYING RIGHT NOW.
JUST CALL ME GLORIA GAYNOR.
HUH?
I WILL SURVIVE.
INCOMING!!
WHA--?
SOMETHING TELLS ME THIS IS SIRYN'S WORK.

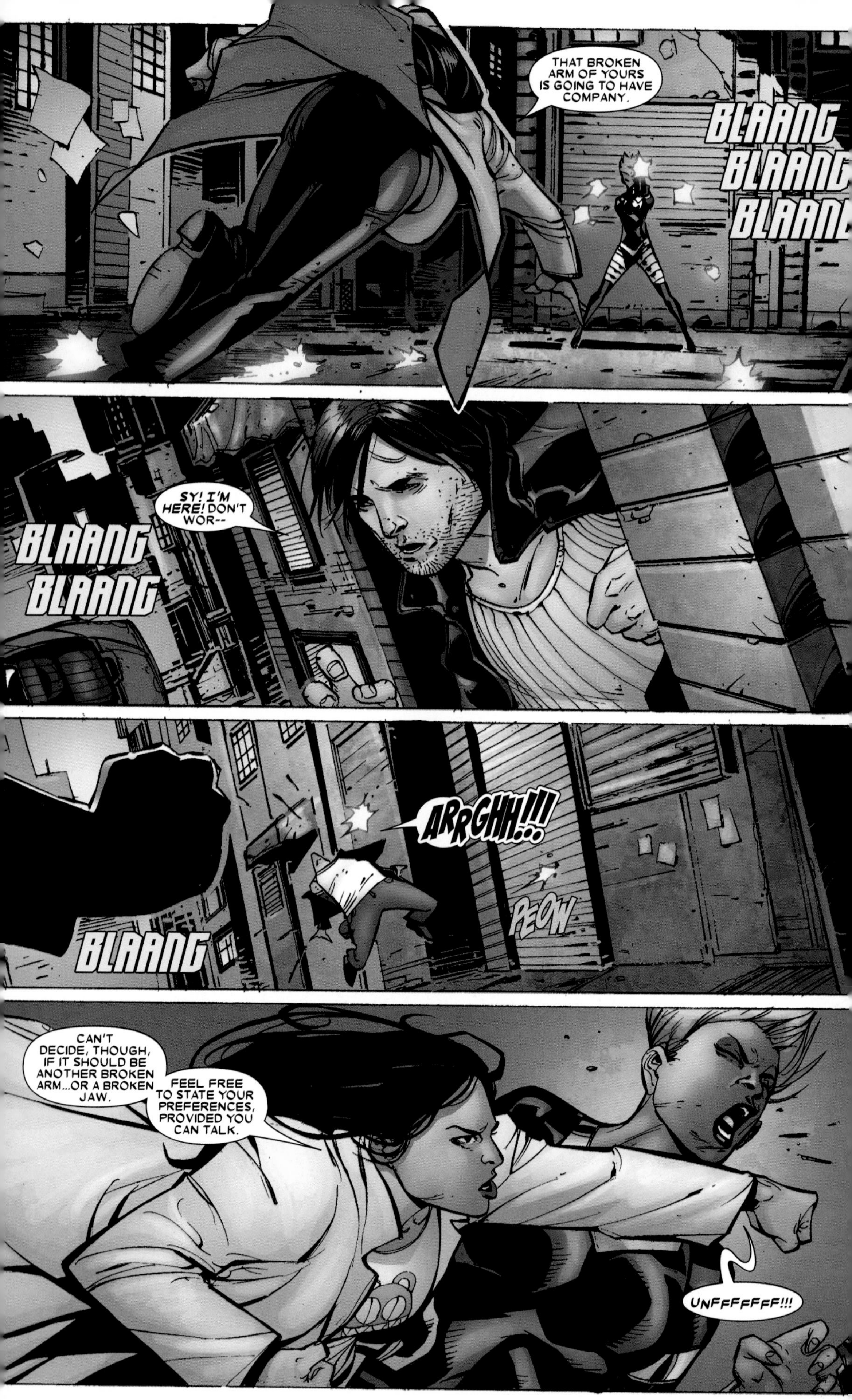
THAT BROKEN ARM OF YOURS IS GOING TO HAVE COMPANY.
BLAAANG
BLAAANG
BLAAANG
SY! I'M HERE! DON'T WOR--
BLAAANG
BLAAANG
ARRGHH!!!
PEOW
BLAAANG
CAN'T DECIDE, THOUGH, IF IT SHOULD BE ANOTHER BROKEN ARM...OR A BROKEN JAW.
FEEL FREE TO STATE YOUR PREFERENCES, PROVIDED YOU CAN TALK.
UNFFFFFFF!!!

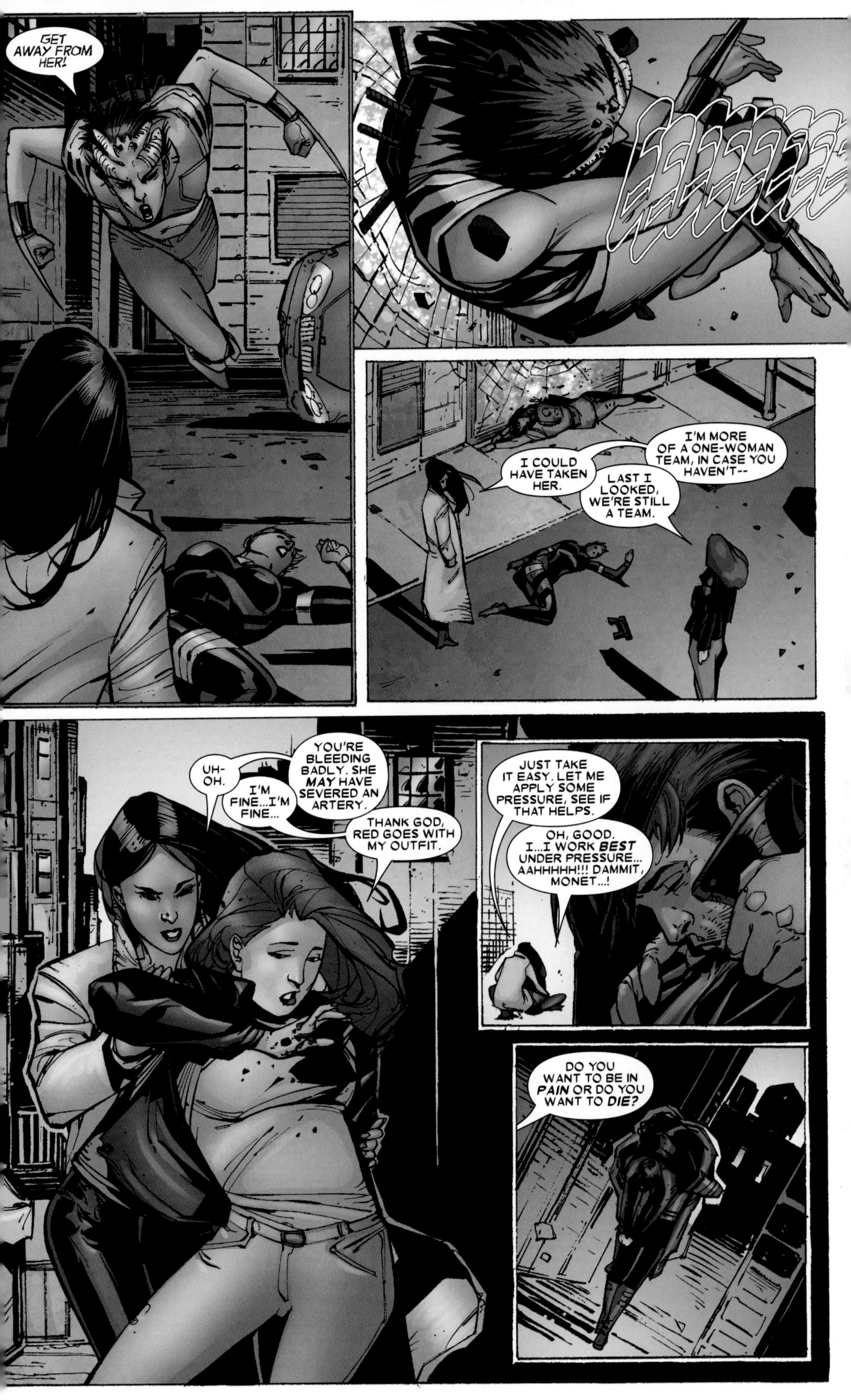

GET AWAY FROM HER!
I'M MORE OF A ONE-WOMAN TEAM, IN CASE YOU HAVEN'T--
I COULD HAVE TAKEN HER.
LAST I LOOKED, WE'RE STILL A TEAM.
UH-OH.
YOU'RE BLEEDING BADLY. SHE MAY HAVE SEVERED AN ARTERY.
I'M FINE...I'M FINE...
THANK GOD, RED GOES WITH MY OUTFIT.
JUST TAKE IT EASY. LET ME APPLY SOME PRESSURE, SEE IF THAT HELPS.
OH, GOOD. I...I WORK BEST UNDER PRESSURE... AAHHHHH!!! DAMMIT, MONET...!
DO YOU WANT TO BE IN PAIN OR DO YOU WANT TO DIE?

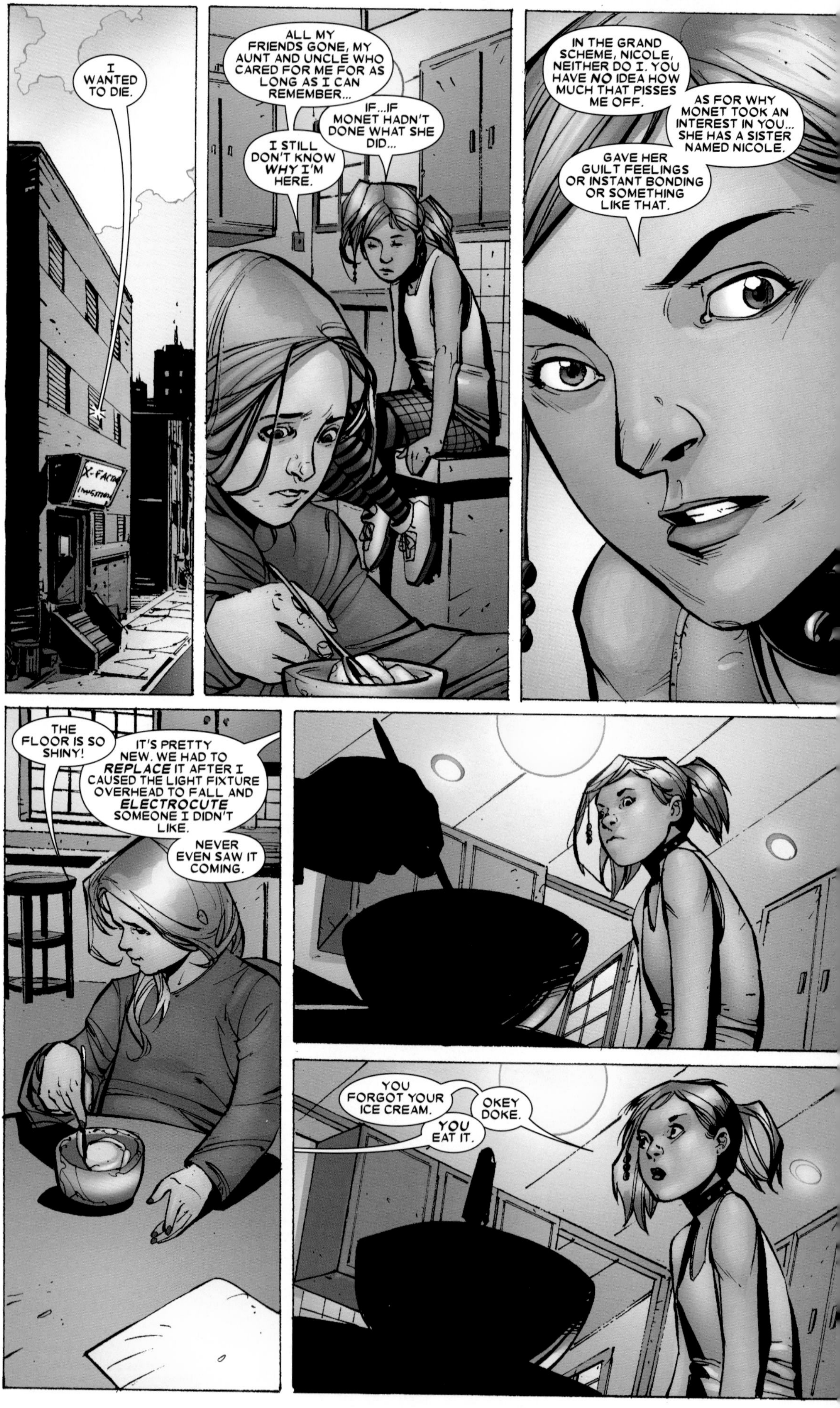

I WANTED TO DIE.
X-FACTOR INVESTIGATIONS
ALL MY FRIENDS GONE, MY AUNT AND UNCLE WHO CARED FOR ME FOR AS LONG AS I CAN REMEMBER...
IF...IF MONET HADN'T DONE WHAT SHE DID...
I STILL DON'T KNOW WHY I'M HERE.
IN THE GRAND SCHEME, NICOLE, NEITHER DO I. YOU HAVE NO IDEA HOW MUCH THAT PISSES ME OFF.
AS FOR WHY MONET TOOK AN INTEREST IN YOU... SHE HAS A SISTER NAMED NICOLE.
GAVE HER GUILT FEELINGS OR INSTANT BONDING OR SOMETHING LIKE THAT.
THE FLOOR IS SO SHINY!
IT'S PRETTY NEW. WE HAD TO REPLACE IT AFTER I CAUSED THE LIGHT FIXTURE OVERHEAD TO FALL AND ELECTROCUTE SOMEONE I DIDN'T LIKE.
NEVER EVEN SAW IT COMING.
YOU FORGOT YOUR ICE CREAM.
OKEY DOKE.
YOU EAT IT.

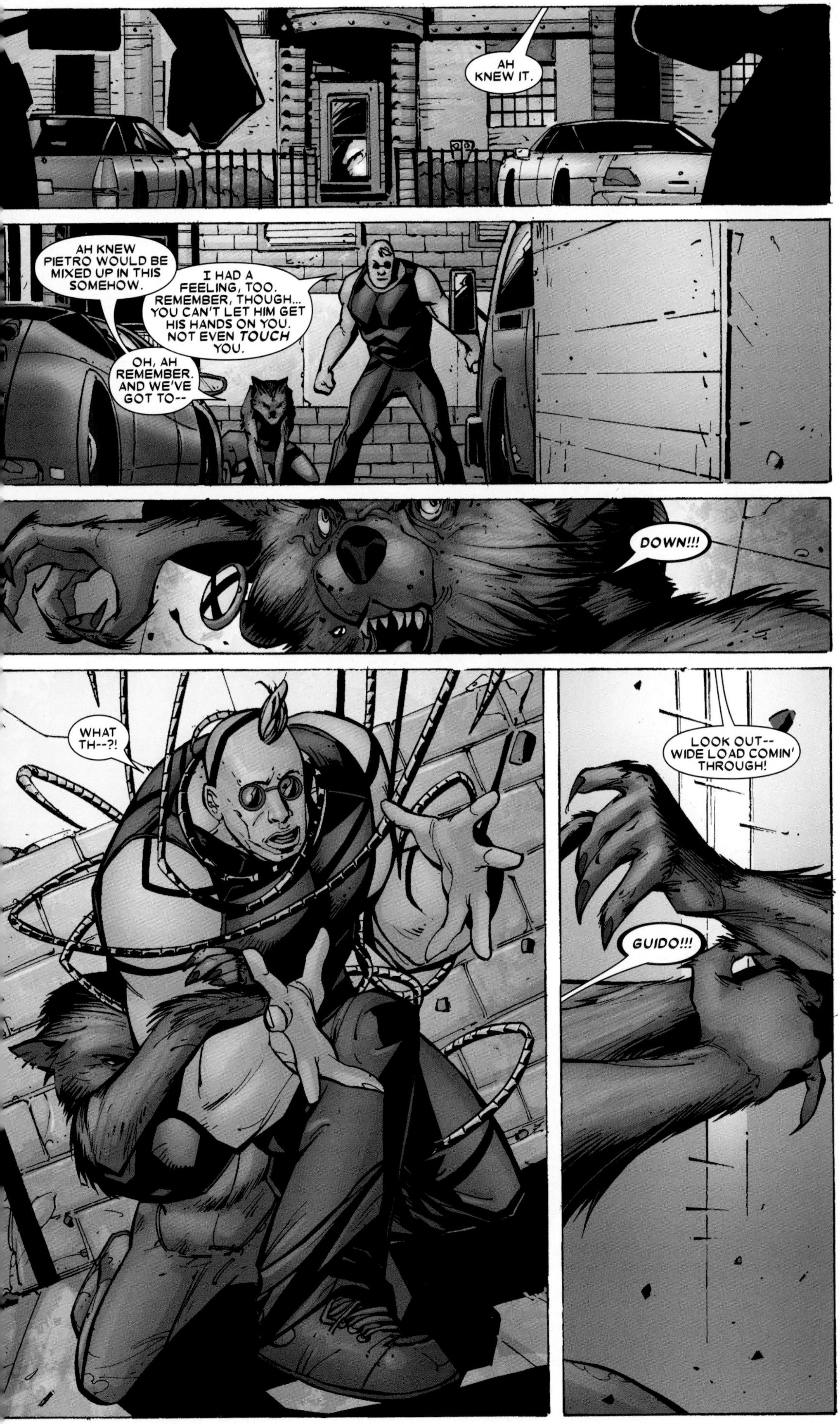
AH KNEW IT.
AH KNEW PIETRO WOULD BE MIXED UP IN THIS SOMEHOW.
I HAD A FEELING, TOO. REMEMBER, THOUGH... YOU CAN'T LET HIM GET HIS HANDS ON YOU. NOT EVEN TOUCH YOU.
OH, AH REMEMBER. AND WE'VE GOT TO--
DOWN!!!
WHAT TH--?!
LOOK OUT-- WIDE LOAD COMIN' THROUGH!
GUIDO!!!

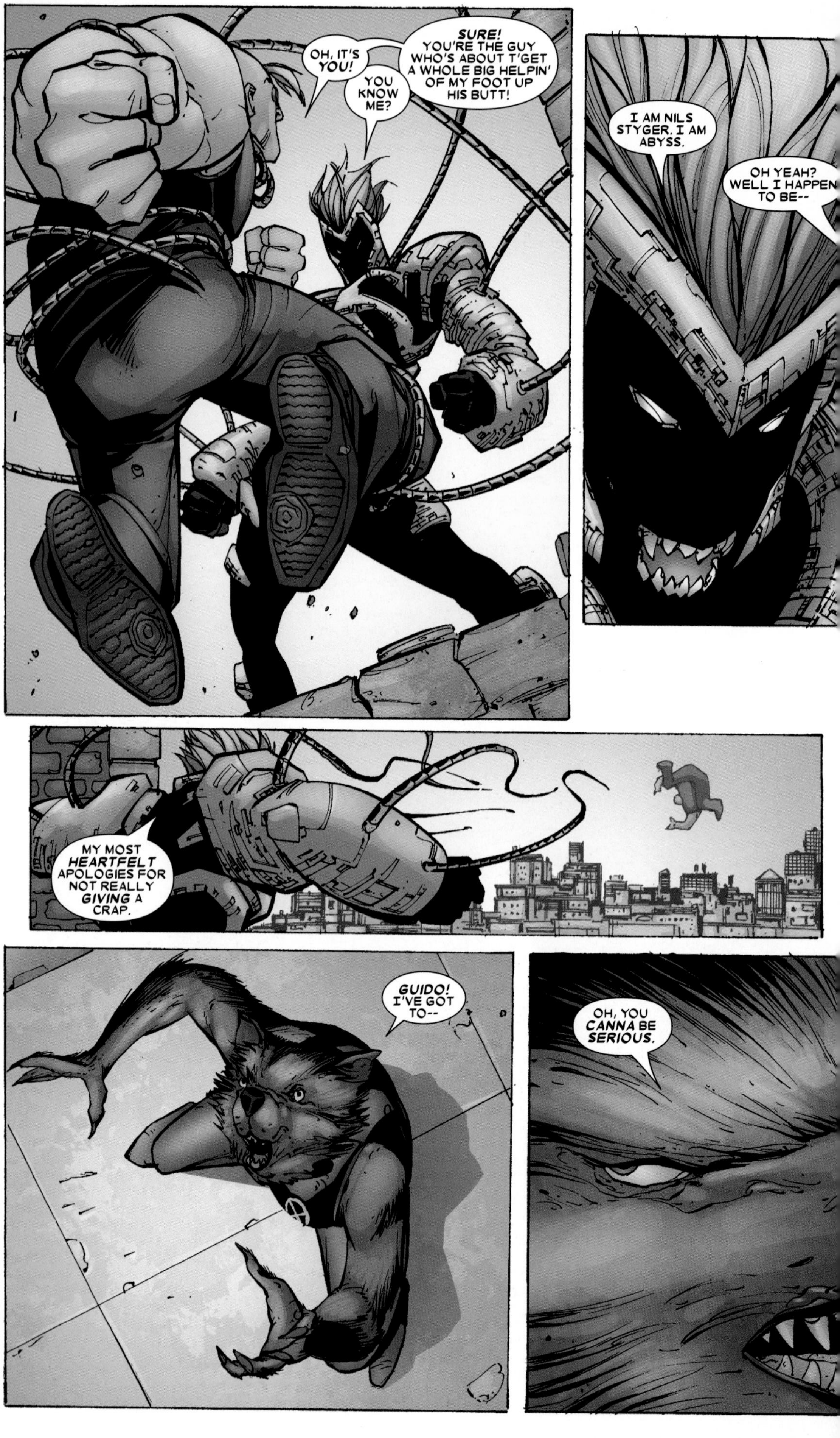
OH, IT'S YOU!
SURE! YOU'RE THE GUY WHO'S ABOUT T'GET A WHOLE BIG HELPIN' OF MY FOOT UP HIS BUTT!
YOU KNOW ME?
I AM NILS STYGER. I AM ABYSS.
OH YEAH? WELL I HAPPEN TO BE--
MY MOST HEARTFELT APOLOGIES FOR NOT REALLY GIVING A CRAP.
GUIDO! I'VE GOT TO--
OH, YOU CANNA BE SERIOUS.

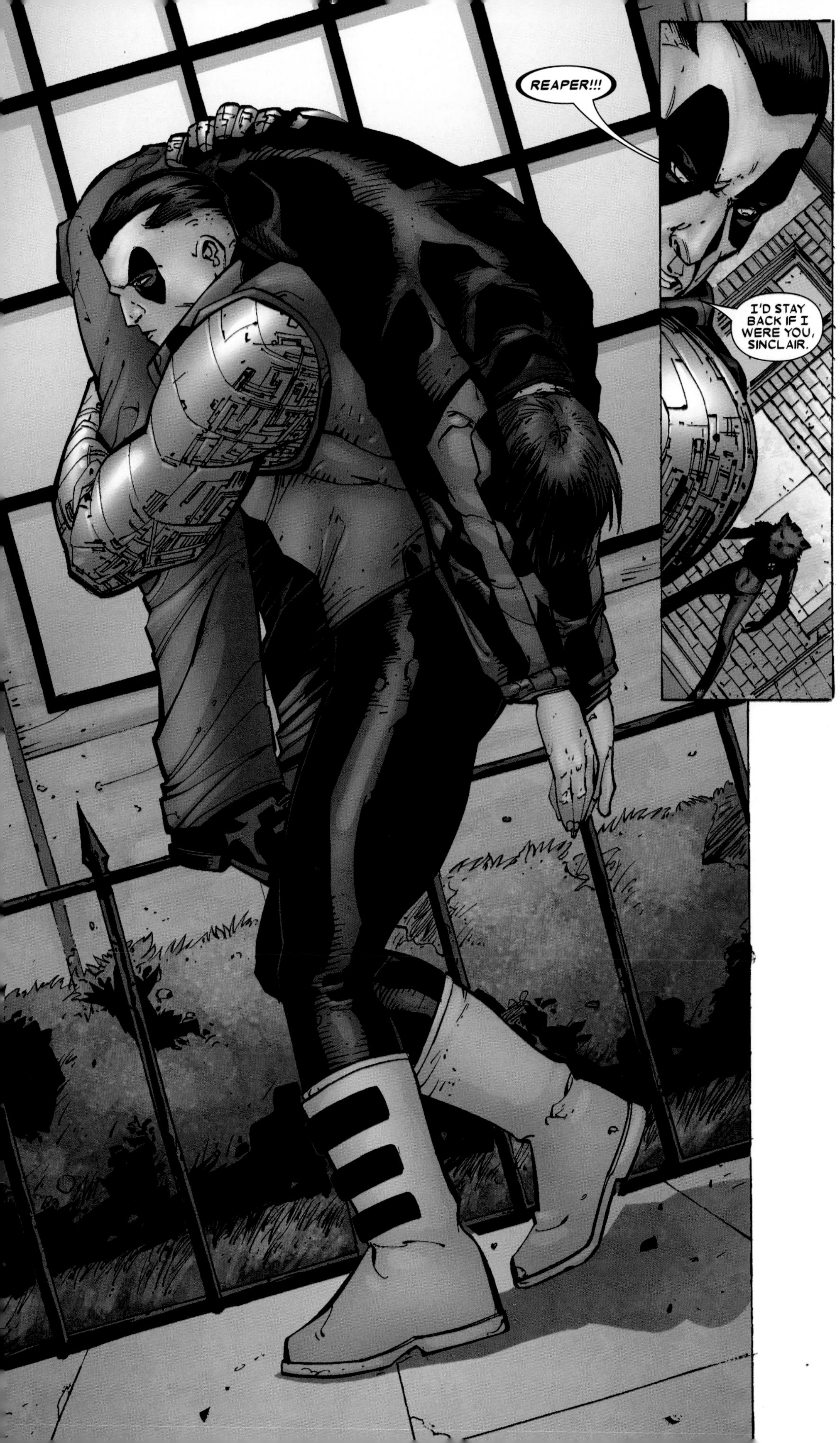
REAPER!!!
I'D STAY BACK IF I WERE YOU, SINCLAIR.

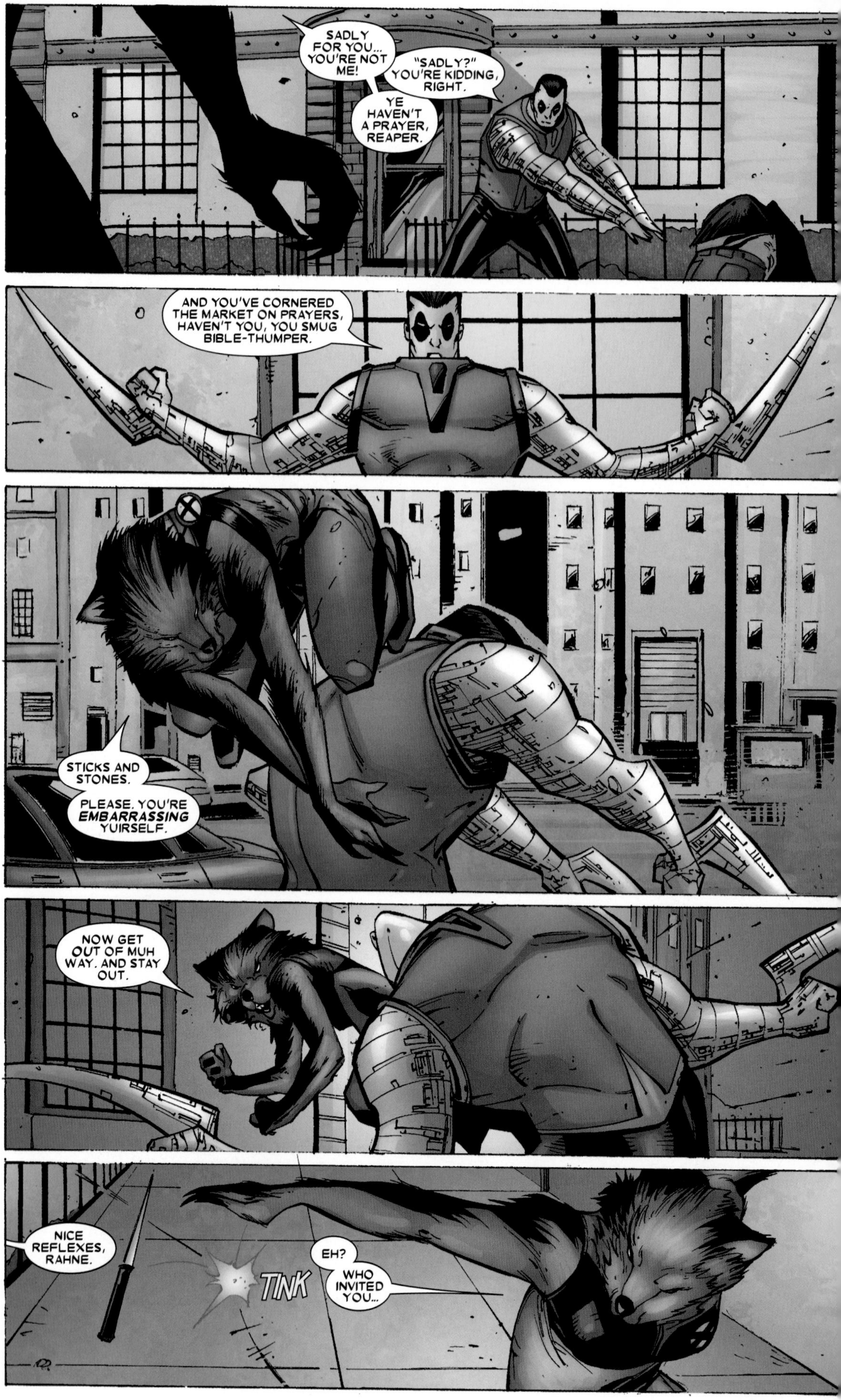
SADLY FOR YOU... YOU'RE NOT ME!
"SADLY?" YOU'RE KIDDING, RIGHT.
YE HAVEN'T A PRAYER, REAPER.
AND YOU'VE CORNERED THE MARKET ON PRAYERS, HAVEN'T YOU, YOU SMUG BIBLE-THUMPER.
STICKS AND STONES.
PLEASE. YOU'RE EMBARRASSING YUIRSELF.
NOW GET OUT OF MUH WAY. AND STAY OUT.
NICE REFLEXES, RAHNE.
TINK
EH?
WHO INVITED YOU...

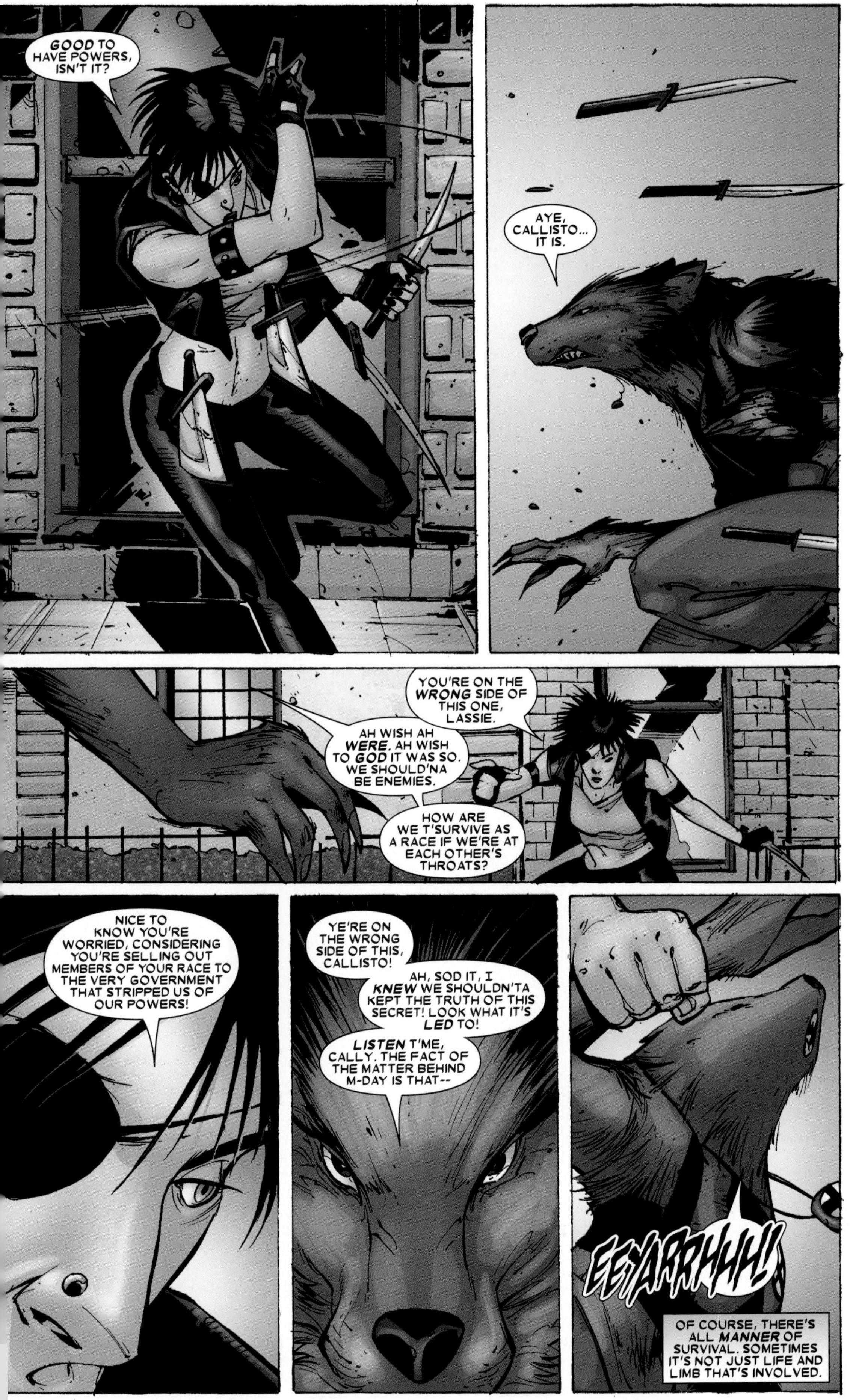

GOOD TO HAVE POWERS, ISN'T IT?
AYE, CALLISTO... IT IS.
YOU'RE ON THE WRONG SIDE OF THIS ONE, LASSIE.
AH WISH AH WERE. AH WISH TO GOD IT WAS SO. WE SHOULD'NA BE ENEMIES.
HOW ARE WE T'SURVIVE AS A RACE IF WE'RE AT EACH OTHER'S THROATS?
NICE TO KNOW YOU'RE WORRIED, CONSIDERING YOU'RE SELLING OUT MEMBERS OF YOUR RACE TO THE VERY GOVERNMENT THAT STRIPPED US OF OUR POWERS!
YE'RE ON THE WRONG SIDE OF THIS, CALLISTO!
AH, SOD IT, I KNEW WE SHOULDN'TA KEPT THE TRUTH OF THIS SECRET! LOOK WHAT IT'S LED TO!
LISTEN T'ME, CALLY. THE FACT OF THE MATTER BEHIND M-DAY IS THAT--
EEYARRHHH!
OF COURSE, THERE'S ALL MANNER OF SURVIVAL. SOMETIMES IT'S NOT JUST LIFE AND LIMB THAT'S INVOLVED.

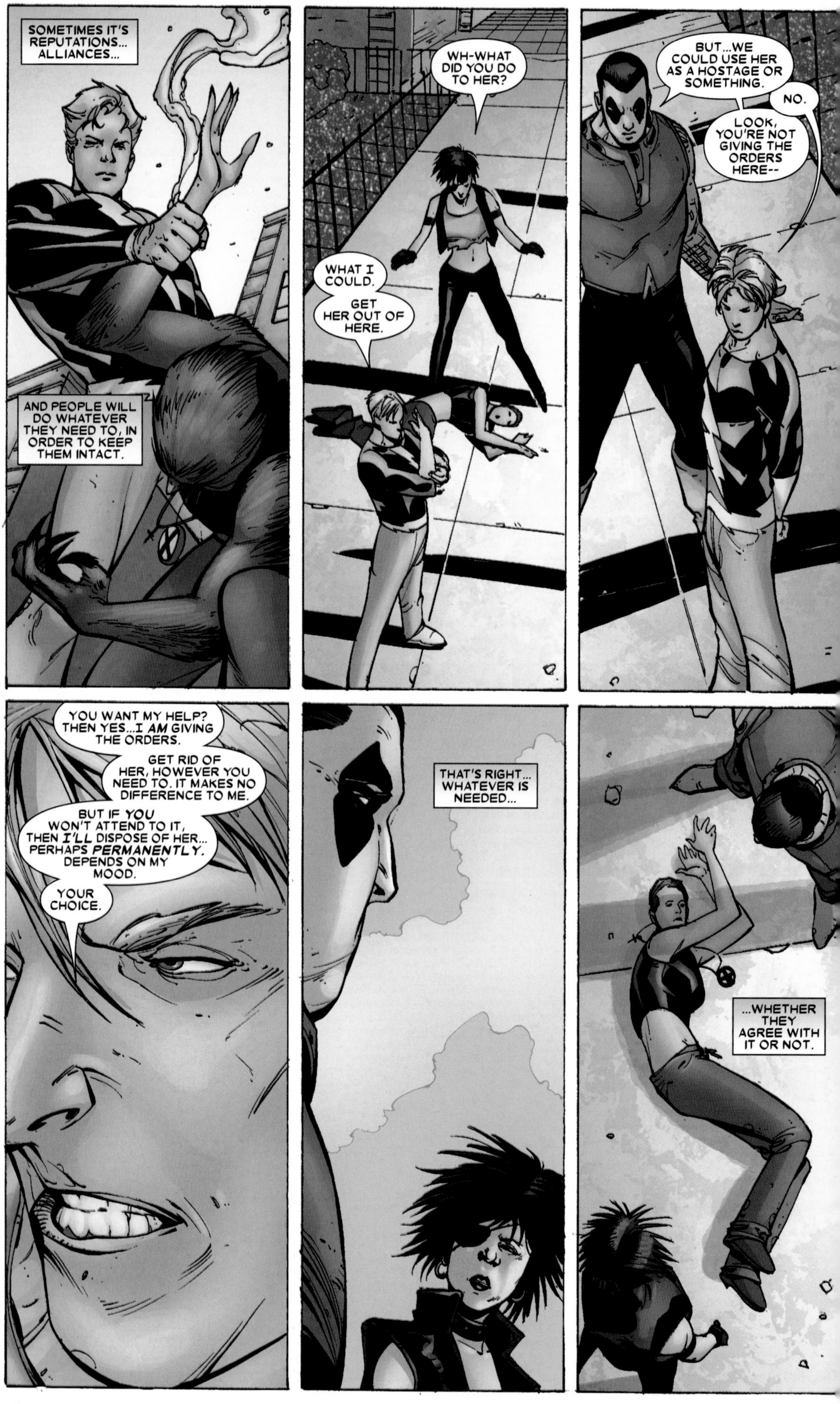
SOMETIMES IT'S REPUTATIONS... ALLIANCES...
AND PEOPLE WILL DO WHATEVER THEY NEED TO, IN ORDER TO KEEP THEM INTACT.
WH-WHAT DID YOU DO TO HER?
WHAT I COULD.
GET HER OUT OF HERE.
BUT...WE COULD USE HER AS A HOSTAGE OR SOMETHING.
NO.
LOOK, YOU'RE NOT GIVING THE ORDERS HERE--
YOU WANT MY HELP? THEN YES...I AM GIVING THE ORDERS.
GET RID OF HER, HOWEVER YOU NEED TO. IT MAKES NO DIFFERENCE TO ME.
BUT IF YOU WON'T ATTEND TO IT, THEN I'LL DISPOSE OF HER... PERHAPS PERMANENTLY. DEPENDS ON MY MOOD.
YOUR CHOICE.
THAT'S RIGHT... WHATEVER IS NEEDED...
...WHETHER THEY AGREE WITH IT OR NOT.

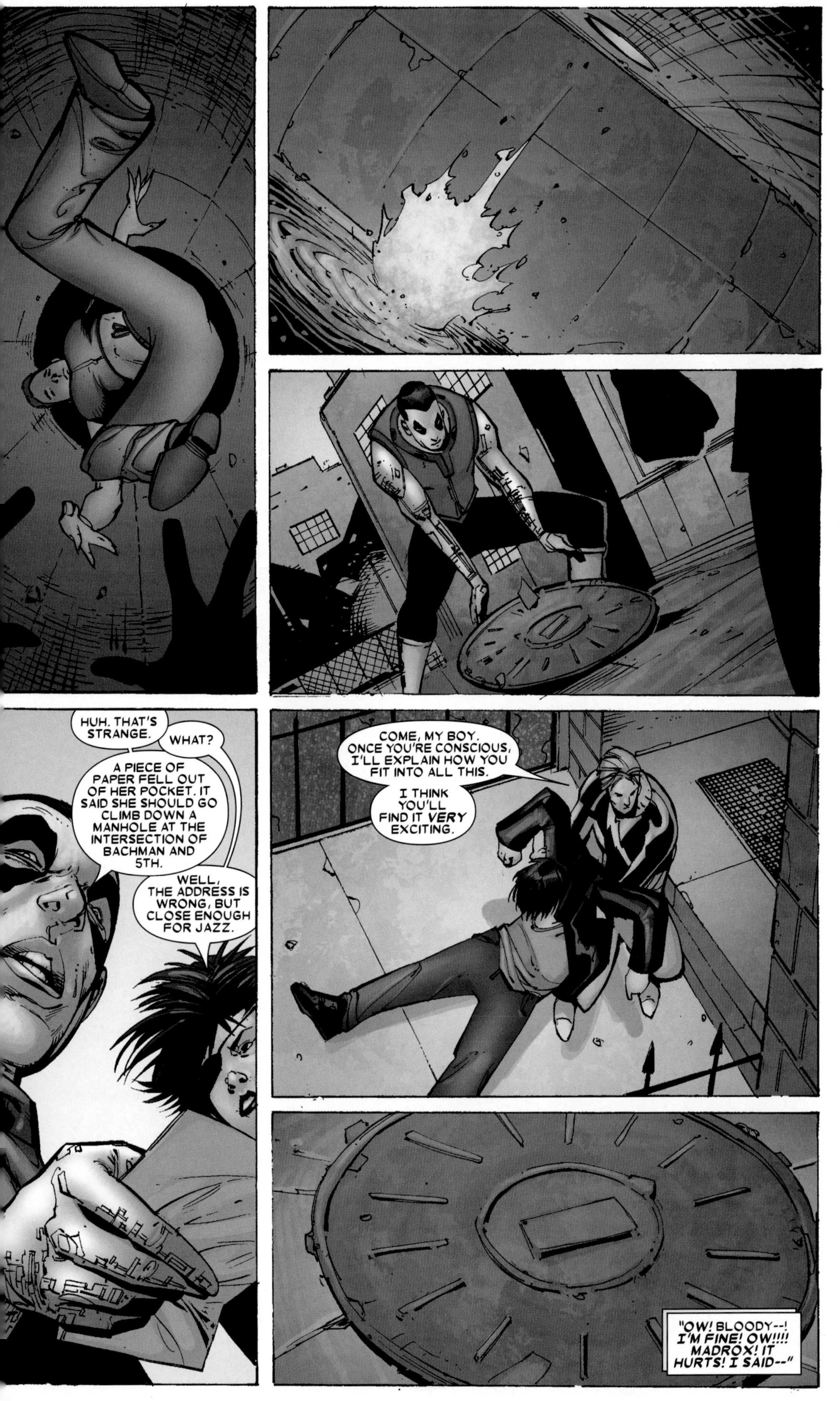
HUH. THAT'S STRANGE.
WHAT?
A PIECE OF PAPER FELL OUT OF HER POCKET. IT SAID SHE SHOULD GO CLIMB DOWN A MANHOLE AT THE INTERSECTION OF BACHMAN AND 5TH.
WELL, THE ADDRESS IS WRONG, BUT CLOSE ENOUGH FOR JAZZ.
COME, MY BOY. ONCE YOU'RE CONSCIOUS, I'LL EXPLAIN HOW YOU FIT INTO ALL THIS.
I THINK YOU'LL FIND IT VERY EXCITING.
"OW! BLOODY--! I'M FINE! OW!!!! MADROX! IT HURTS! I SAID--"

IT HURTS!
WELL, IF YOU'D GIVEN IT ENOUGH TIME FOR THE NOVOCAINE TO KICK IN...
WE DON'T HAVE TIME! THEY GOT AWAY BECAUSE OF ME!
NOT ALL OF THEM.
I'M NOT TELLING YOU JACK!
OH, PLEASE DON'T, CHER. I'M HOPING YOU WON'T. I'M PRAYING YOU WON'T.
BECAUSE WHEN YOU DON'T, MADROX HERE IS GOING TO TURN ME LOOSE ON YOUR MIND. WON'T YOU, MADROX?
NO CHOICE BUT TO.
HEAR THAT? NO CHOICE.
AND I'M GOING TO PULL THE INFORMATION FROM YOUR MIND. BUT I DON'T HAVE TIME TO DELICATELY PLUMB YOUR DEPTHS.
SO IT'LL BE MORE LIKE STRIP-MINING. I'LL GO THROUGH YOUR BRAIN AND JUST MENTALLY RIP OUT EVERYTHING THAT LOOKS INTERESTING.
SCORCHED EARTH, BLOBBO. THERE WILL JUST BE SMOKING RUINS IN YOUR SKULL... UNLESS YOU TELL ME THE X-CELL'S LOCATION, WHERE YOU GOT THE WEAPONS... EVERYTHING I WANT TO KNOW.
IS IT... ALWAYS LIKE THIS AROUND HERE?
ACTUALLY, THIS IS A SLOW DAY.

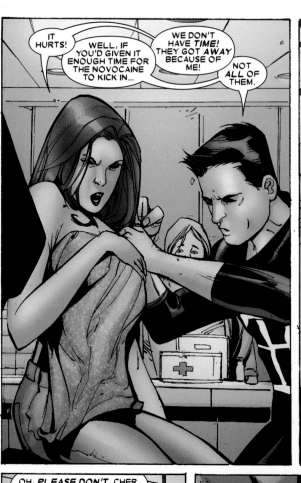

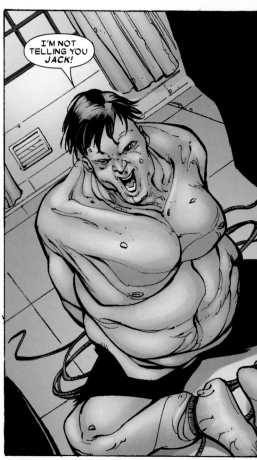

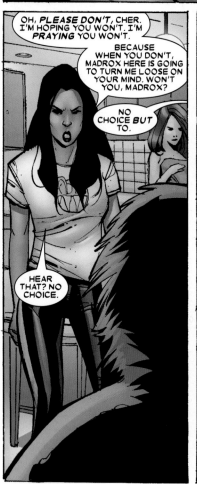

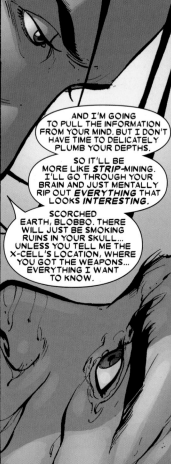

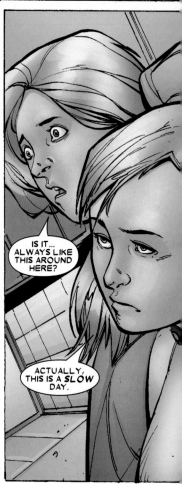

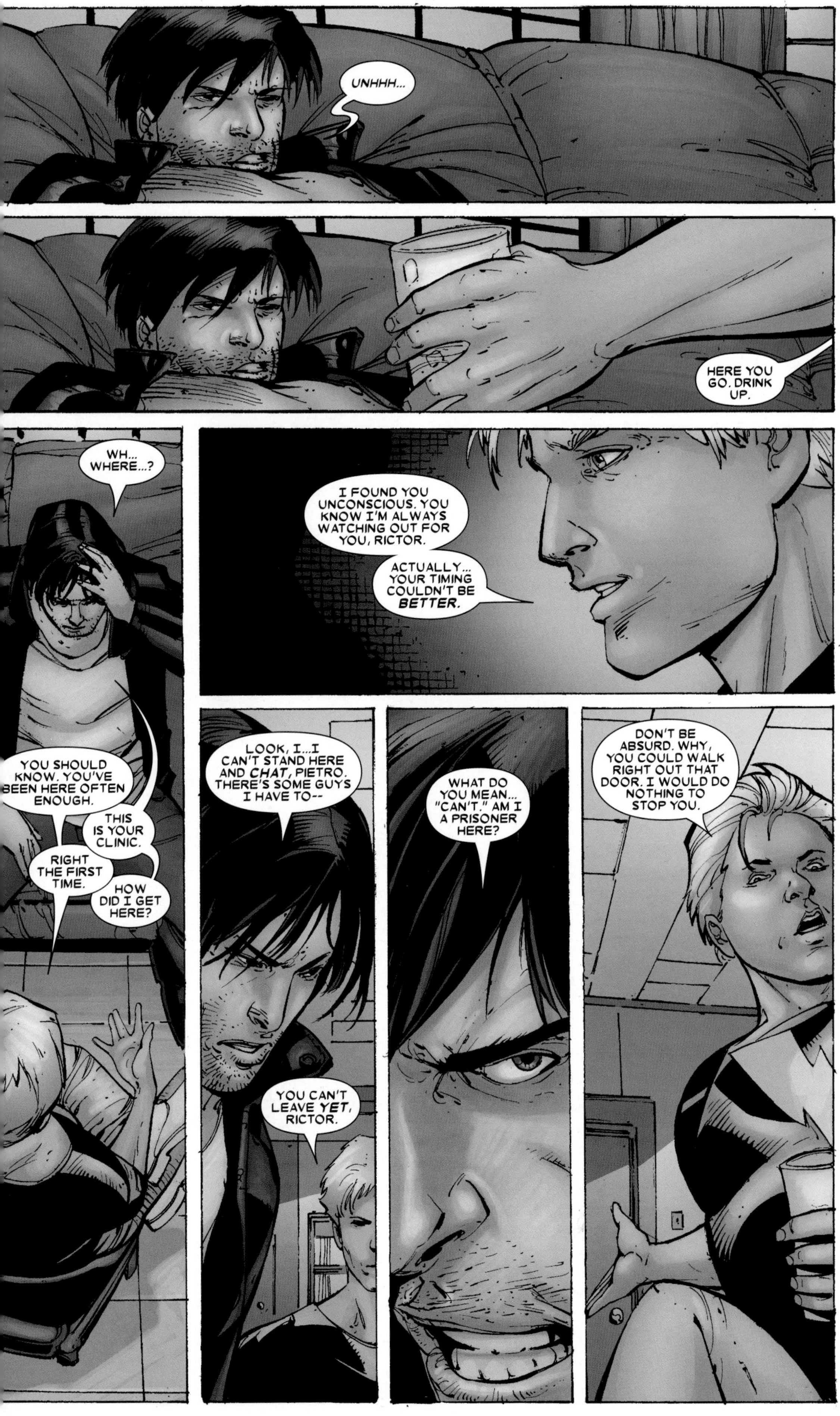
UNHHH...
HERE YOU GO. DRINK UP.
WH... WHERE...?
YOU SHOULD KNOW. YOU'VE BEEN HERE OFTEN ENOUGH.
THIS IS YOUR CLINIC.
RIGHT THE FIRST TIME.
HOW DID I GET HERE?
I FOUND YOU UNCONSCIOUS. YOU KNOW I'M ALWAYS WATCHING OUT FOR YOU, RICTOR.
ACTUALLY... YOUR TIMING COULDN'T BE BETTER.
LOOK, I...I CAN'T STAND HERE AND CHAT, PIETRO. THERE'S SOME GUYS I HAVE TO--
YOU CAN'T LEAVE YET, RICTOR.
WHAT DO YOU MEAN... "CAN'T." AM I A PRISONER HERE?
DON'T BE ABSURD. WHY, YOU COULD WALK RIGHT OUT THAT DOOR. I WOULD DO NOTHING TO STOP YOU.

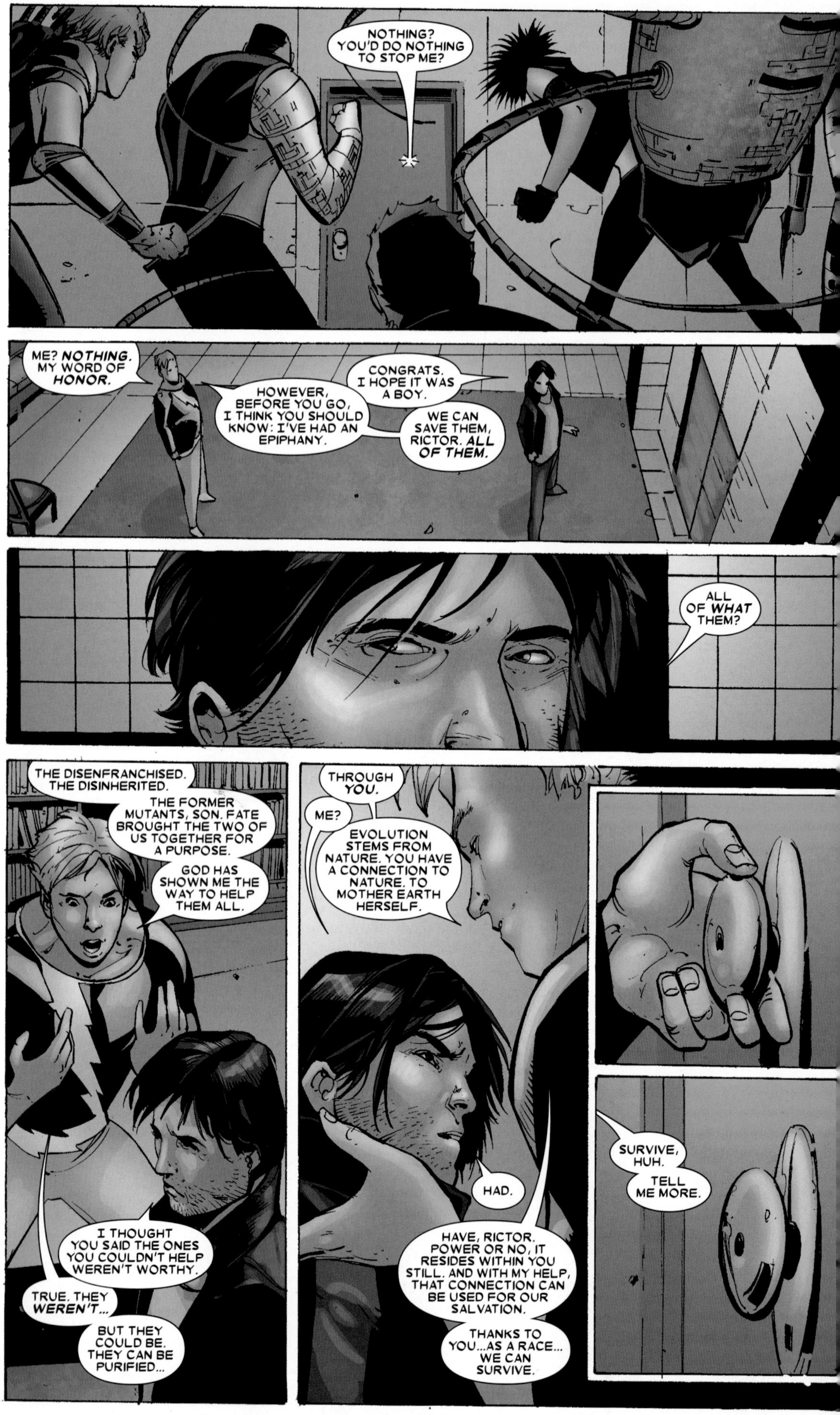
NOTHING? YOU'D DO NOTHING TO STOP ME?
ME? NOTHING. MY WORD OF HONOR.
HOWEVER, BEFORE YOU GO, I THINK YOU SHOULD KNOW: I'VE HAD AN EPIPHANY.
CONGRATS. I HOPE IT WAS A BOY.
WE CAN SAVE THEM, RICTOR. ALL OF THEM.
ALL OF WHAT THEM?
THE DISENFRANCHISED. THE DISINHERITED.
THE FORMER MUTANTS, SON. FATE BROUGHT THE TWO OF US TOGETHER FOR A PURPOSE.
GOD HAS SHOWN ME THE WAY TO HELP THEM ALL.
I THOUGHT YOU SAID THE ONES YOU COULDN'T HELP WEREN'T WORTHY.
TRUE. THEY WEREN'T...
BUT THEY COULD BE. THEY CAN BE PURIFIED...
THROUGH YOU.
ME?
EVOLUTION STEMS FROM NATURE. YOU HAVE A CONNECTION TO NATURE. TO MOTHER EARTH HERSELF.
HAD.
HAVE, RICTOR. POWER OR NO, IT RESIDES WITHIN YOU STILL. AND WITH MY HELP, THAT CONNECTION CAN BE USED FOR OUR SALVATION.
THANKS TO YOU...AS A RACE... WE CAN SURVIVE.
SURVIVE, HUH.
TELL ME MORE.

#20

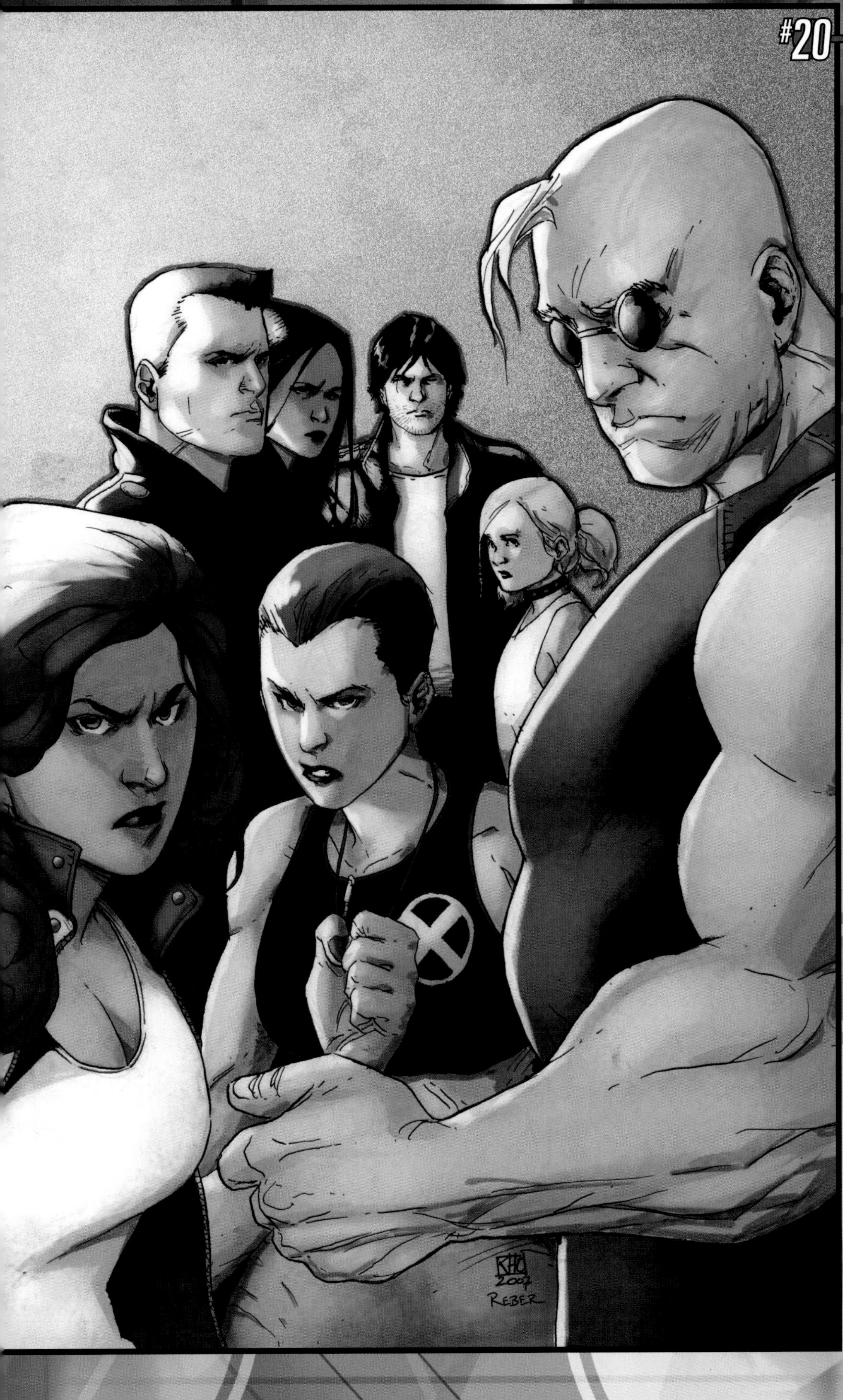
REBER

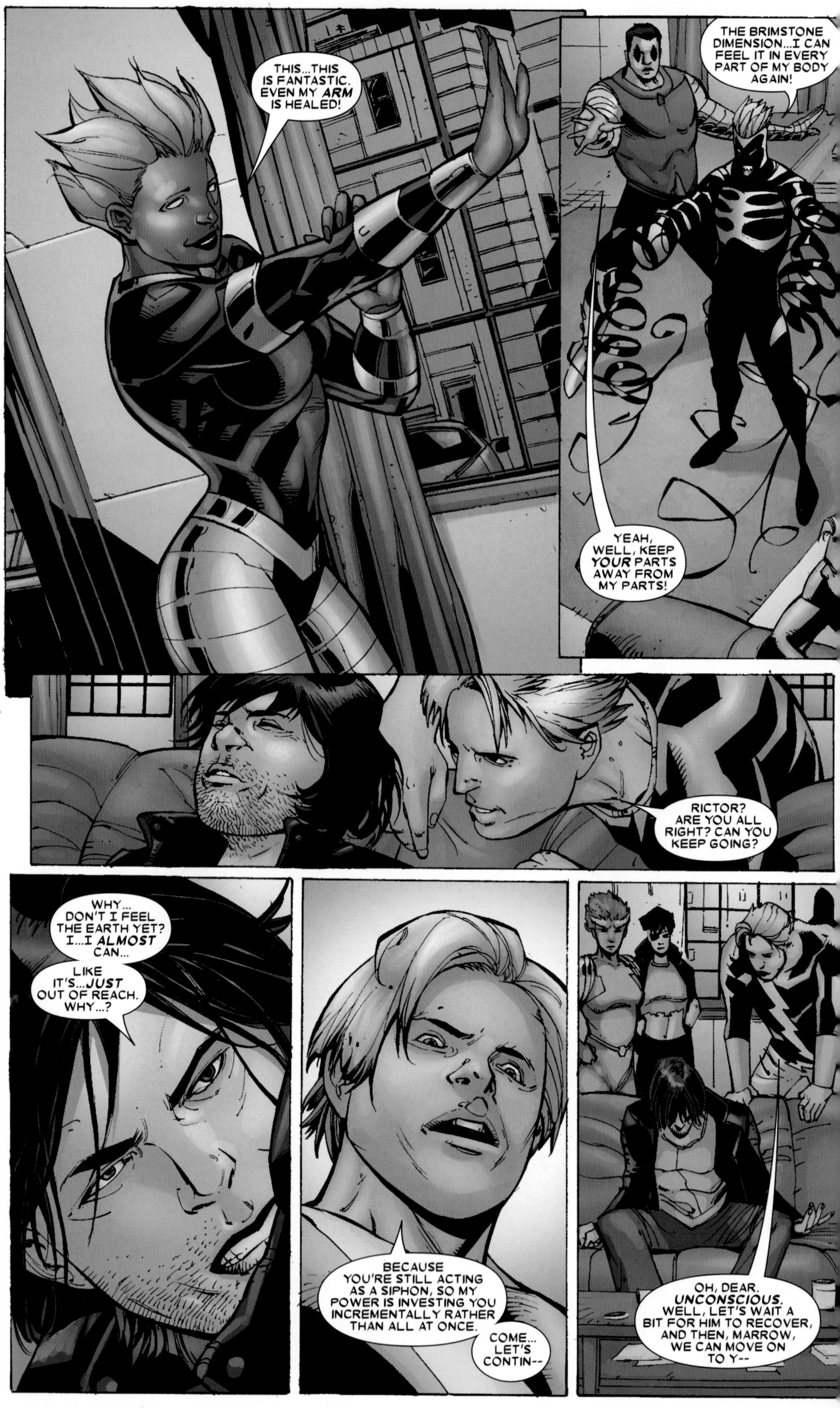
THIS...THIS IS FANTASTIC. EVEN MY *ARM* IS HEALED!
THE BRIMSTONE DIMENSION...I CAN FEEL IT IN EVERY PART OF MY BODY AGAIN!
YEAH, WELL, KEEP *YOUR* PARTS AWAY FROM MY PARTS!
RICTOR? ARE YOU ALL RIGHT? CAN YOU KEEP GOING?
WHY... DON'T I FEEL THE EARTH YET? I...I *ALMOST* CAN...
LIKE IT'S...*JUST* OUT OF REACH. WHY...?
BECAUSE YOU'RE STILL ACTING AS A SIPHON, SO MY POWER IS INVESTING YOU INCREMENTALLY RATHER THAN ALL AT ONCE.
COME... LET'S CONTIN--
OH, DEAR. *UNCONSCIOUS.* WELL, LET'S WAIT A BIT FOR HIM TO RECOVER, AND THEN, MARROW, WE CAN MOVE ON TO Y--

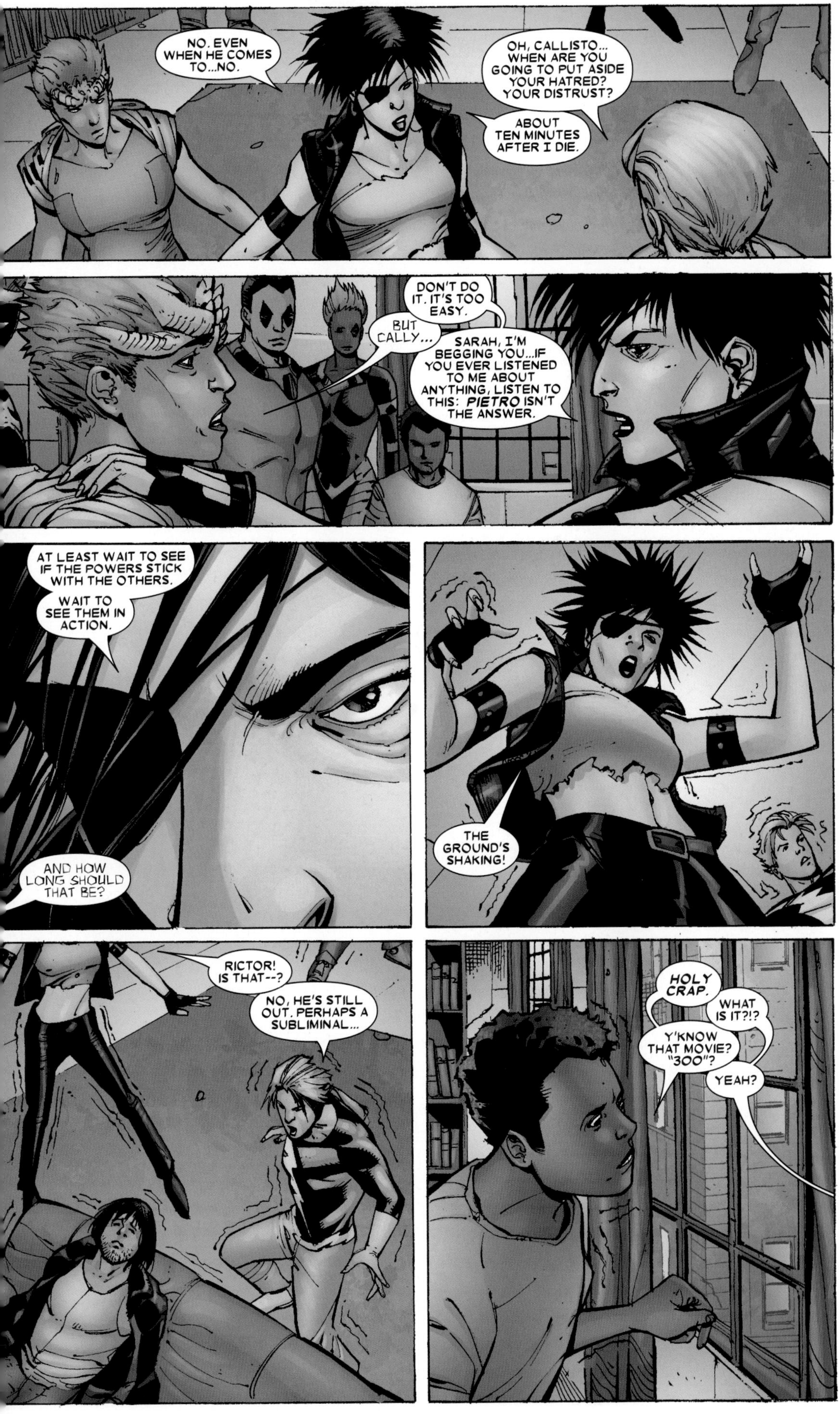

NO. EVEN WHEN HE COMES TO...NO.
OH, CALLISTO... WHEN ARE YOU GOING TO PUT ASIDE YOUR HATRED? YOUR DISTRUST?
ABOUT TEN MINUTES AFTER I DIE.
DON'T DO IT. IT'S TOO EASY.
BUT CALLY...
SARAH, I'M BEGGING YOU...IF YOU EVER LISTENED TO ME ABOUT ANYTHING, LISTEN TO THIS: PIETRO ISN'T THE ANSWER.
AT LEAST WAIT TO SEE IF THE POWERS STICK WITH THE OTHERS.
WAIT TO SEE THEM IN ACTION.
AND HOW LONG SHOULD THAT BE?
THE GROUND'S SHAKING!
RICTOR! IS THAT--?
NO, HE'S STILL OUT. PERHAPS A SUBLIMINAL...
HOLY CRAP.
WHAT IS IT?!?
Y'KNOW THAT MOVIE? "300"?
YEAH?

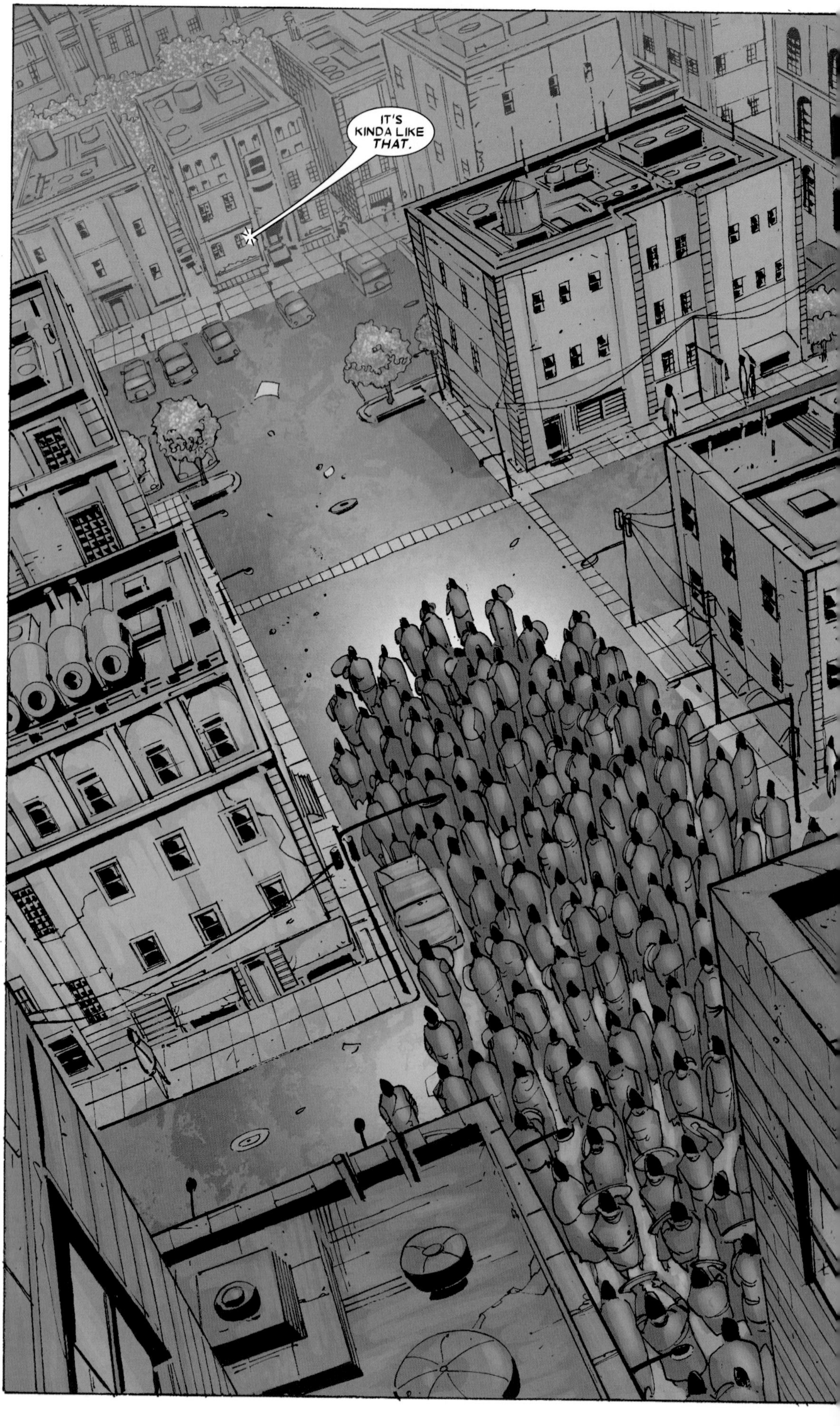
IT'S KINDA LIKE THAT.

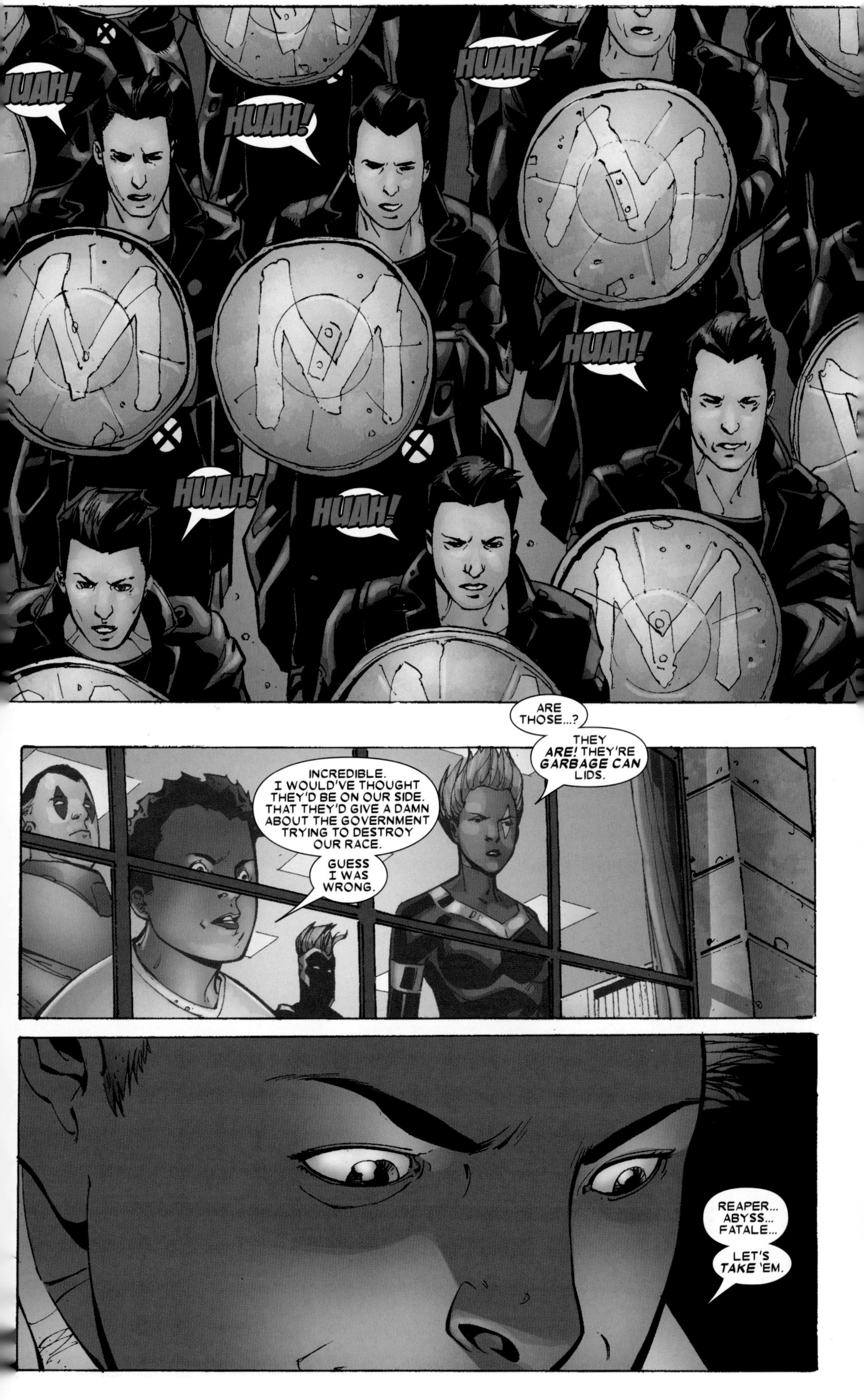
UAH!
HUAH!
HUAH!
HUAH!
HUAH!
HUAH!
ARE THOSE...?
THEY *ARE!* THEY'RE *GARBAGE CAN* LIDS.
INCREDIBLE. I WOULD'VE THOUGHT THEY'D BE ON OUR SIDE. THAT THEY'D GIVE A DAMN ABOUT THE GOVERNMENT TRYING TO DESTROY OUR RACE.
GUESS I WAS WRONG.
REAPER... ABYSS... FATALE...
LET'S *TAKE* 'EM.

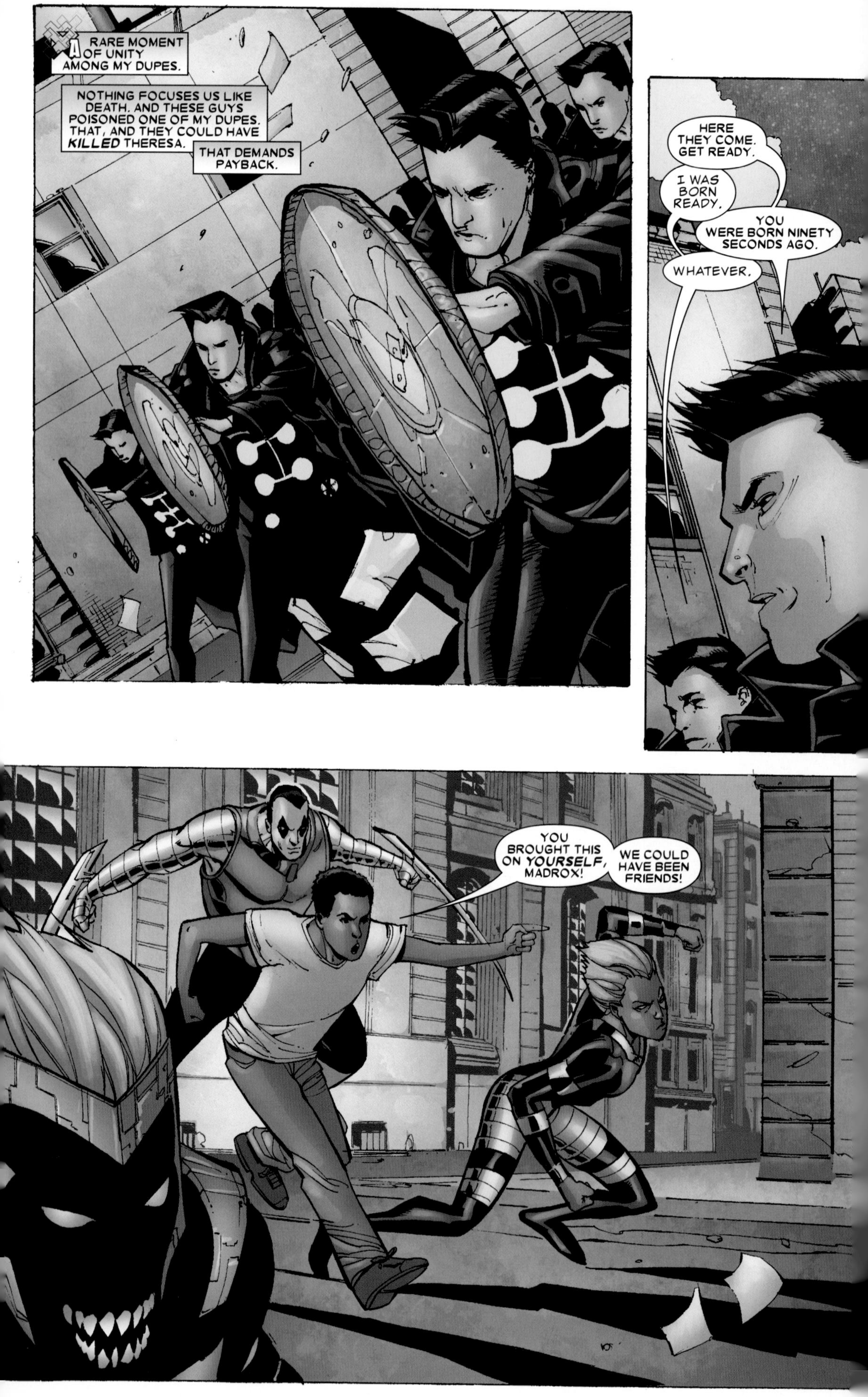
A RARE MOMENT OF UNITY AMONG MY DUPES.
NOTHING FOCUSES US LIKE DEATH. AND THESE GUYS POISONED ONE OF MY DUPES. THAT, AND THEY COULD HAVE *KILLED* THERESA.
THAT DEMANDS PAYBACK.
HERE THEY COME. GET READY.
I WAS BORN READY.
YOU WERE BORN NINETY SECONDS AGO.
WHATEVER.
YOU BROUGHT THIS ON *YOURSELF*, MADROX!
WE COULD HAVE BEEN FRIENDS!

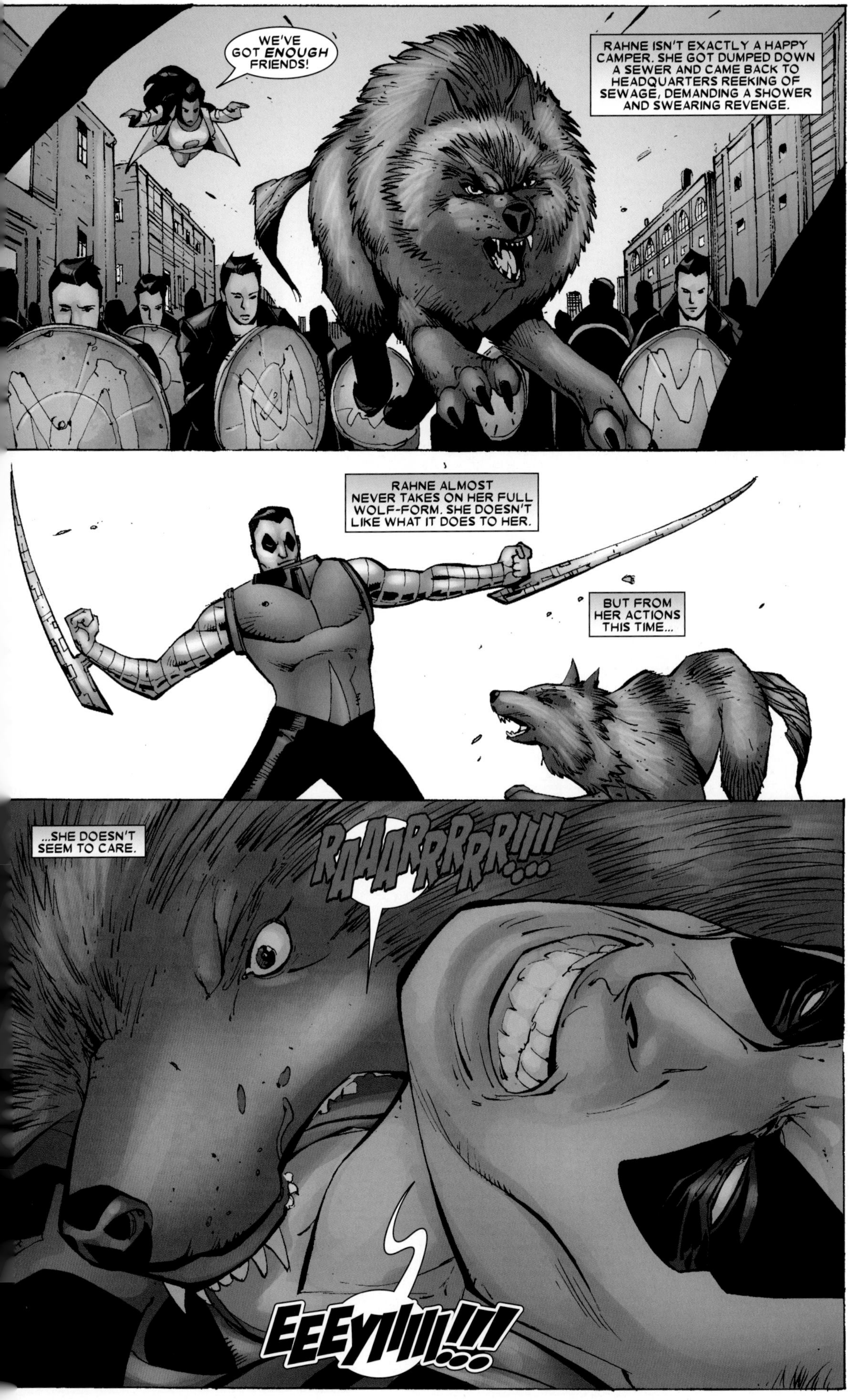
WE'VE GOT ENOUGH FRIENDS!
RAHNE ISN'T EXACTLY A HAPPY CAMPER. SHE GOT DUMPED DOWN A SEWER AND CAME BACK TO HEADQUARTERS REEKING OF SEWAGE, DEMANDING A SHOWER AND SWEARING REVENGE.
RAHNE ALMOST NEVER TAKES ON HER FULL WOLF-FORM. SHE DOESN'T LIKE WHAT IT DOES TO HER.
BUT FROM HER ACTIONS THIS TIME...
...SHE DOESN'T SEEM TO CARE.
RAAARRRRR!!!!...
EEEYIIIII!!!...

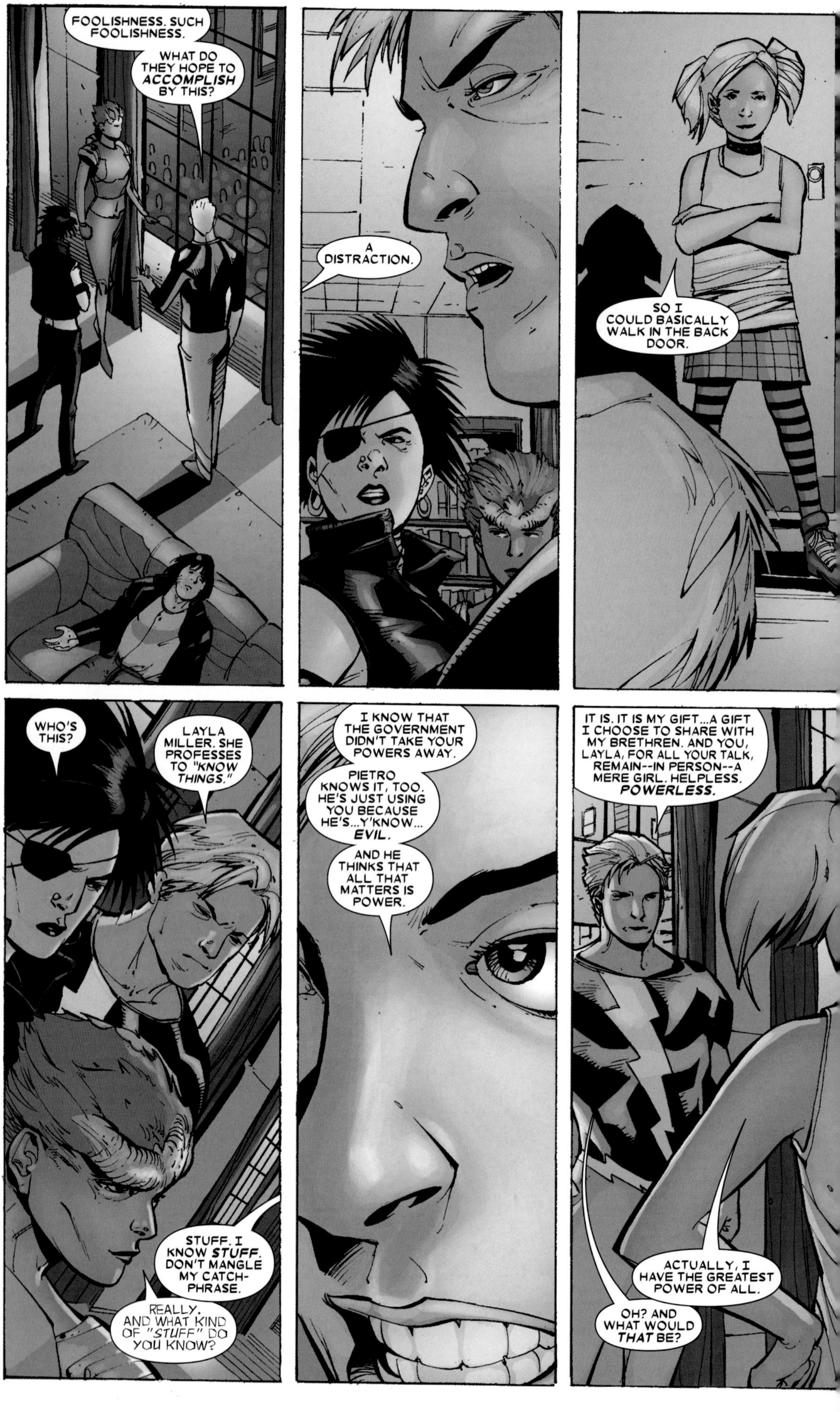
FOOLISHNESS. SUCH FOOLISHNESS.
WHAT DO THEY HOPE TO *ACCOMPLISH* BY THIS?
A DISTRACTION.
SO I COULD BASICALLY WALK IN THE BACK DOOR.
WHO'S THIS?
LAYLA MILLER. SHE PROFESSES TO *"KNOW THINGS."*
STUFF. I KNOW *STUFF*. DON'T MANGLE MY CATCH-PHRASE.
REALLY. AND WHAT KIND OF *"STUFF"* DO YOU KNOW?
I KNOW THAT THE GOVERNMENT DIDN'T TAKE YOUR POWERS AWAY.
PIETRO KNOWS IT, TOO. HE'S JUST USING YOU BECAUSE HE'S...Y'KNOW... ***EVIL.***
AND HE THINKS THAT ALL THAT MATTERS IS POWER.
IT IS. IT IS MY GIFT...A GIFT I CHOOSE TO SHARE WITH MY BRETHREN. AND YOU, LAYLA, FOR ALL YOUR TALK, REMAIN--IN PERSON--A MERE GIRL. HELPLESS. ***POWERLESS.***
ACTUALLY, I HAVE THE GREATEST POWER OF ALL.
OH? AND WHAT WOULD *THAT* BE?

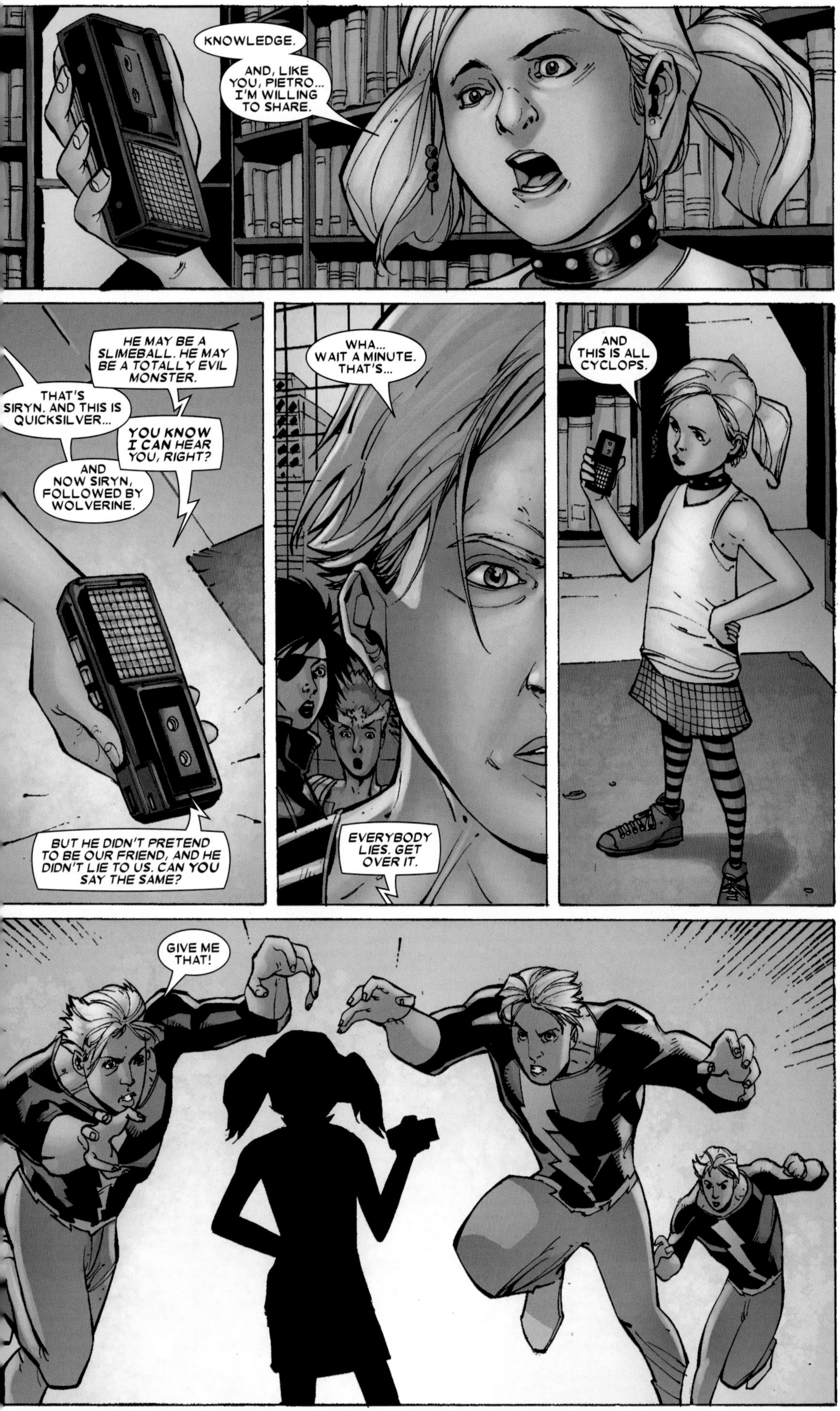
KNOWLEDGE.
AND, LIKE YOU, PIETRO... I'M WILLING TO SHARE.
THAT'S SIRYN. AND THIS IS QUICKSILVER...
HE MAY BE A SLIMEBALL. HE MAY BE A TOTALLY EVIL MONSTER.
YOU KNOW I CAN HEAR YOU, RIGHT?
AND NOW SIRYN, FOLLOWED BY WOLVERINE.
BUT HE DIDN'T PRETEND TO BE OUR FRIEND, AND HE DIDN'T LIE TO US. CAN YOU SAY THE SAME?
WHA... WAIT A MINUTE. THAT'S...
EVERYBODY LIES. GET OVER IT.
AND THIS IS ALL CYCLOPS.
GIVE ME THAT!
!

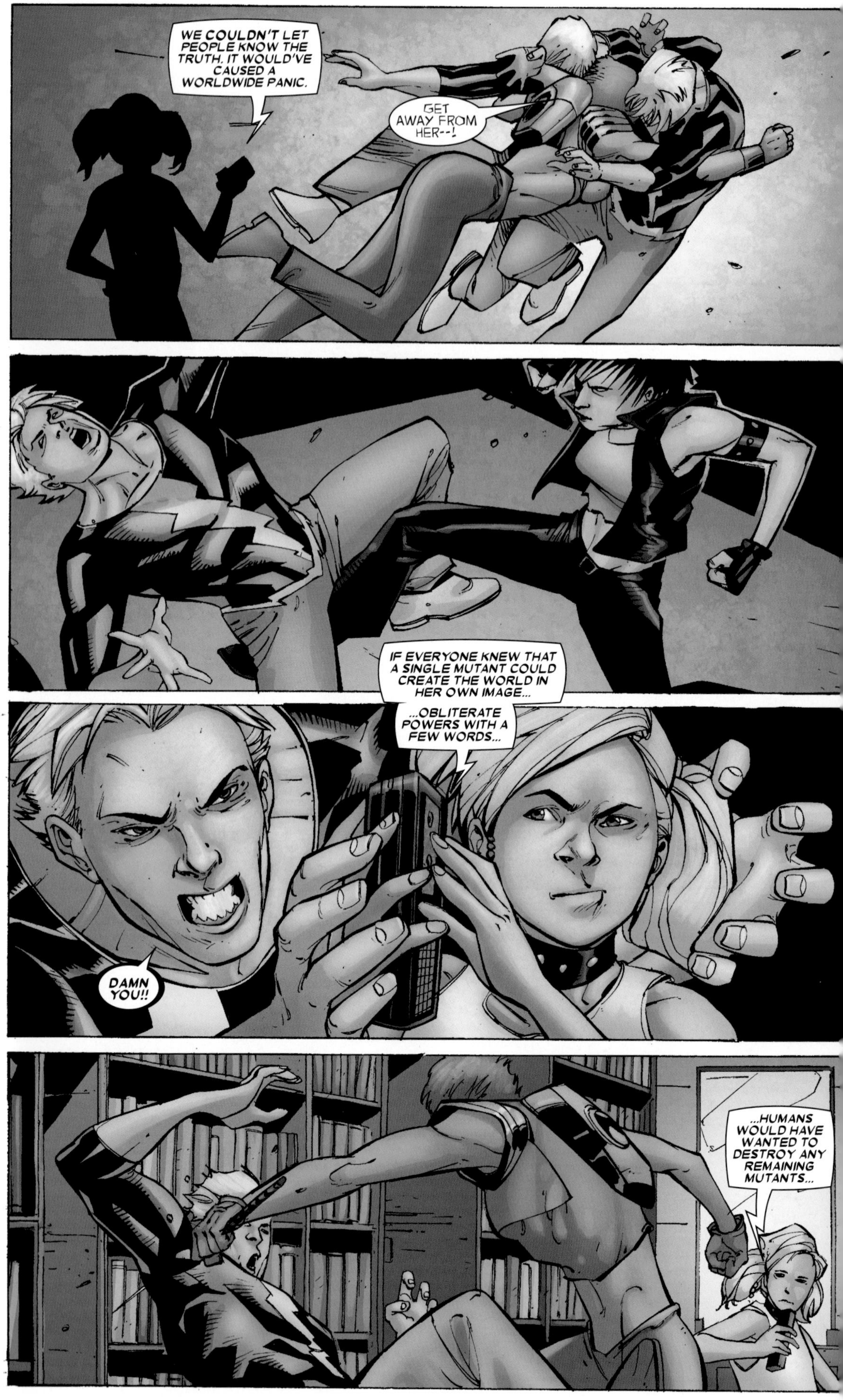
WE COULDN'T LET PEOPLE KNOW THE TRUTH. IT WOULD'VE CAUSED A WORLDWIDE PANIC.
GET AWAY FROM HER--!
IF EVERYONE KNEW THAT A SINGLE MUTANT COULD CREATE THE WORLD IN HER OWN IMAGE...
...OBLITERATE POWERS WITH A FEW WORDS...
DAMN YOU!!
...HUMANS WOULD HAVE WANTED TO DESTROY ANY REMAINING MUTANTS...

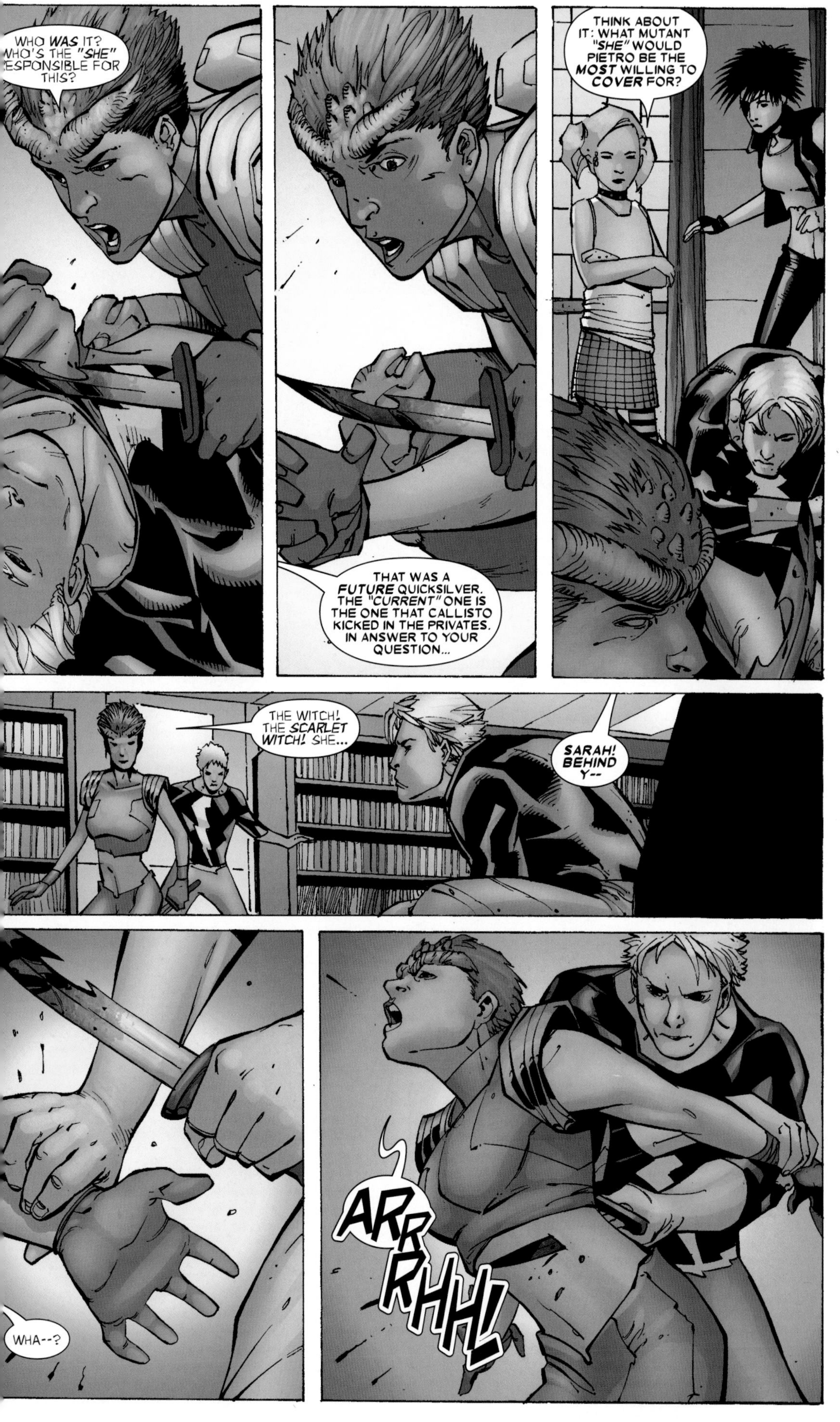

WHO WAS IT? WHO'S THE "SHE" RESPONSIBLE FOR THIS?
THAT WAS A FUTURE QUICKSILVER. THE "CURRENT" ONE IS THE ONE THAT CALLISTO KICKED IN THE PRIVATES. IN ANSWER TO YOUR QUESTION...
THINK ABOUT IT: WHAT MUTANT "SHE" WOULD PIETRO BE THE MOST WILLING TO COVER FOR?
THE WITCH! THE SCARLET WITCH! SHE...
SARAH! BEHIND Y--
WHA--?
ARRRHH!

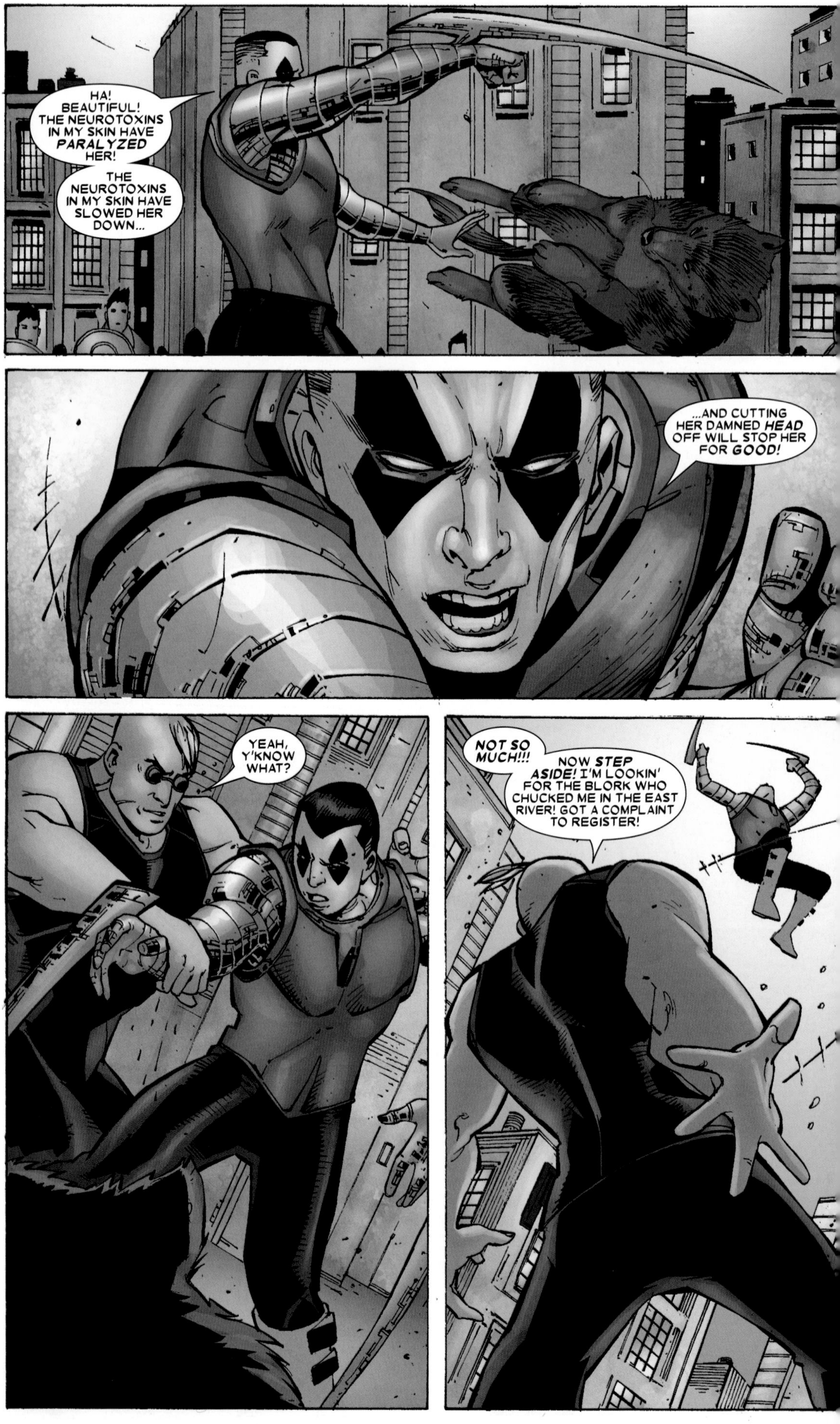

HA! BEAUTIFUL! THE NEUROTOXINS IN MY SKIN HAVE PARALYZED HER!
THE NEUROTOXINS IN MY SKIN HAVE SLOWED HER DOWN...
...AND CUTTING HER DAMNED HEAD OFF WILL STOP HER FOR GOOD!
YEAH, Y'KNOW WHAT?
NOT SO MUCH!!!
NOW STEP ASIDE! I'M LOOKIN' FOR THE BLORK WHO CHUCKED ME IN THE EAST RIVER! GOT A COMPLAINT TO REGISTER!

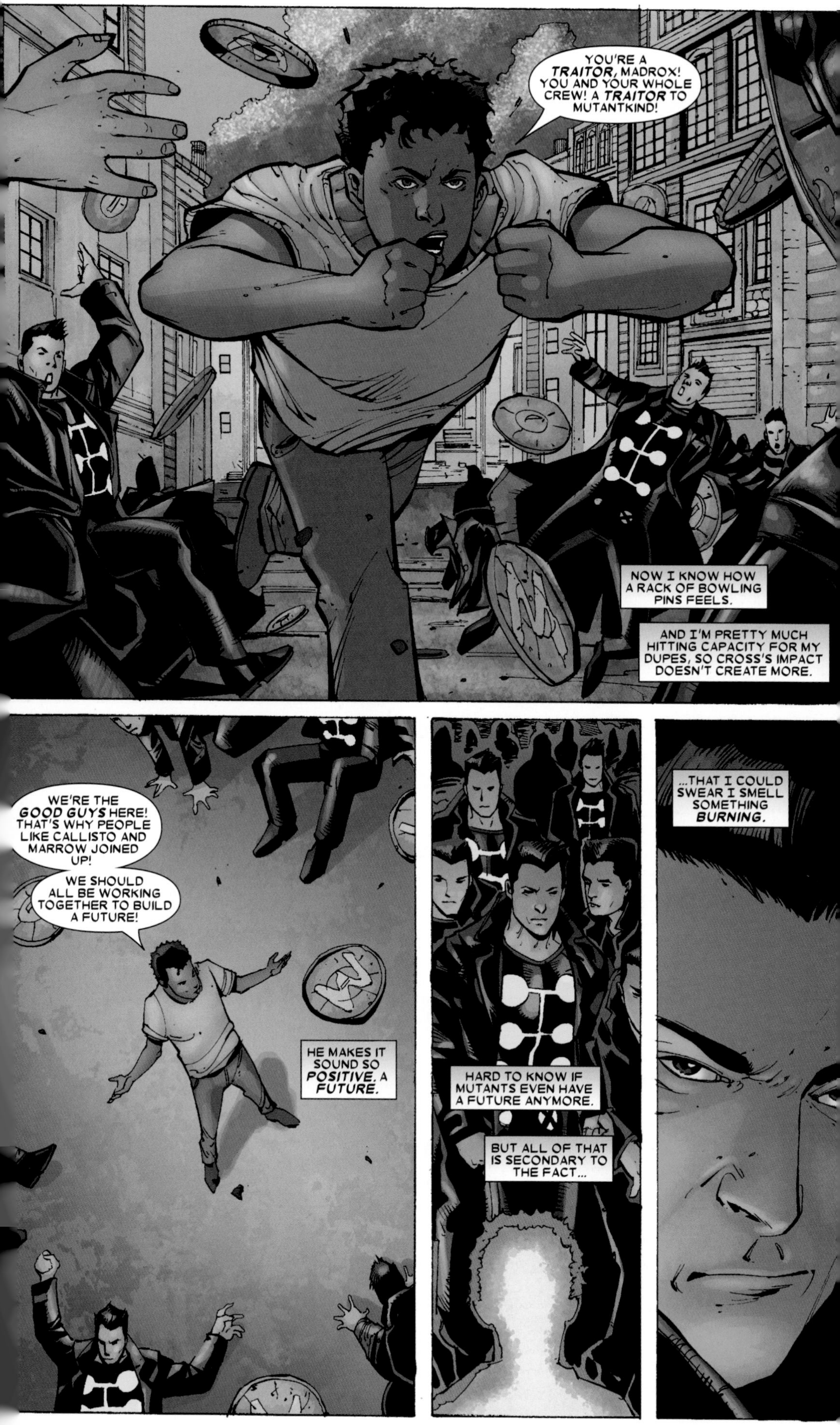
YOU'RE A TRAITOR, MADROX! YOU AND YOUR WHOLE CREW! A TRAITOR TO MUTANTKIND!
NOW I KNOW HOW A RACK OF BOWLING PINS FEELS.
AND I'M PRETTY MUCH HITTING CAPACITY FOR MY DUPES, SO CROSS'S IMPACT DOESN'T CREATE MORE.
WE'RE THE GOOD GUYS HERE! THAT'S WHY PEOPLE LIKE CALLISTO AND MARROW JOINED UP!
WE SHOULD ALL BE WORKING TOGETHER TO BUILD A FUTURE!
HE MAKES IT SOUND SO POSITIVE. A FUTURE.
HARD TO KNOW IF MUTANTS EVEN HAVE A FUTURE ANYMORE.
BUT ALL OF THAT IS SECONDARY TO THE FACT...
...THAT I COULD SWEAR I SMELL SOMETHING BURNING.

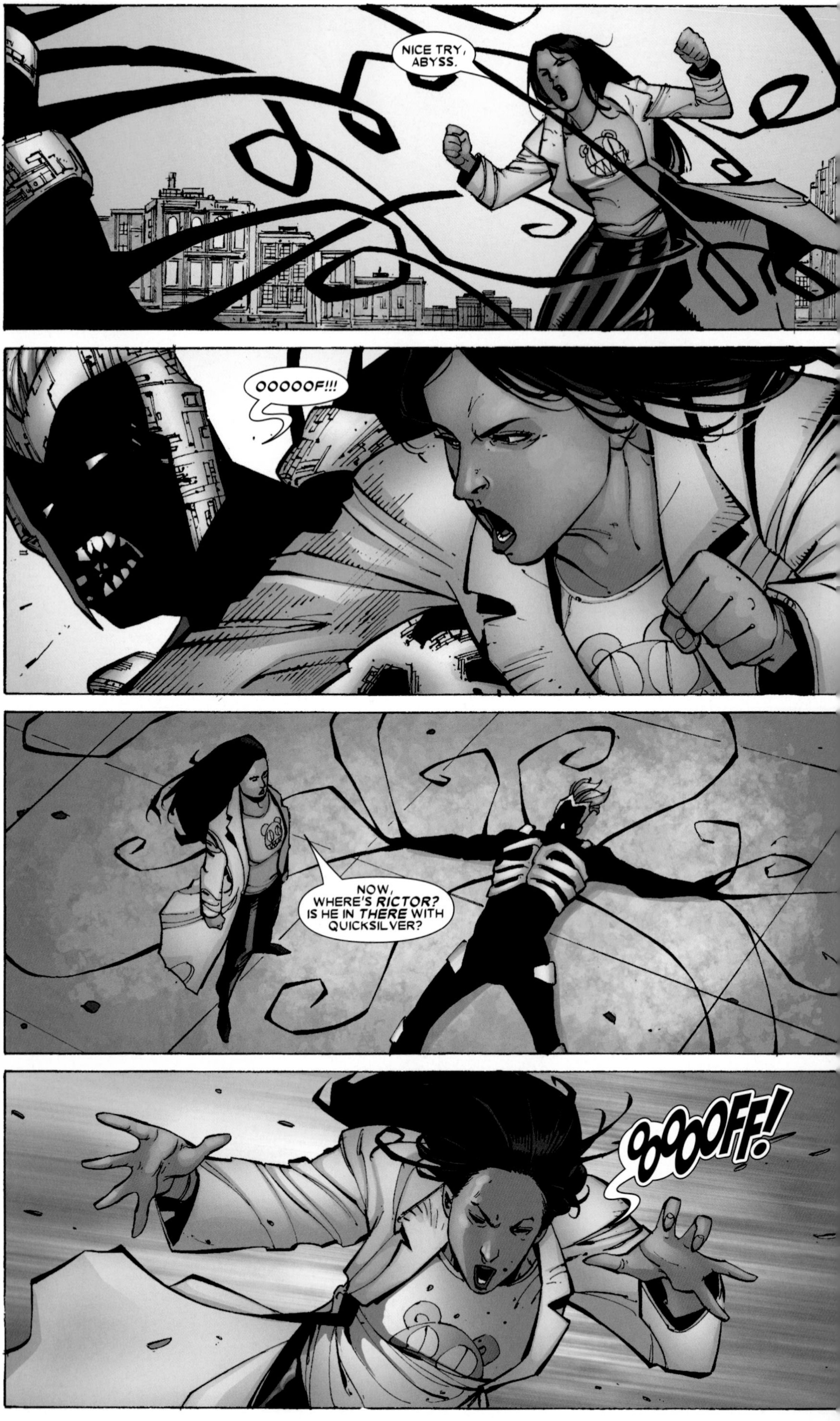
NICE TRY, ABYSS.
OOOOOF!!!
NOW, WHERE'S RICTOR? IS HE IN THERE WITH QUICKSILVER?
OOOOFF!

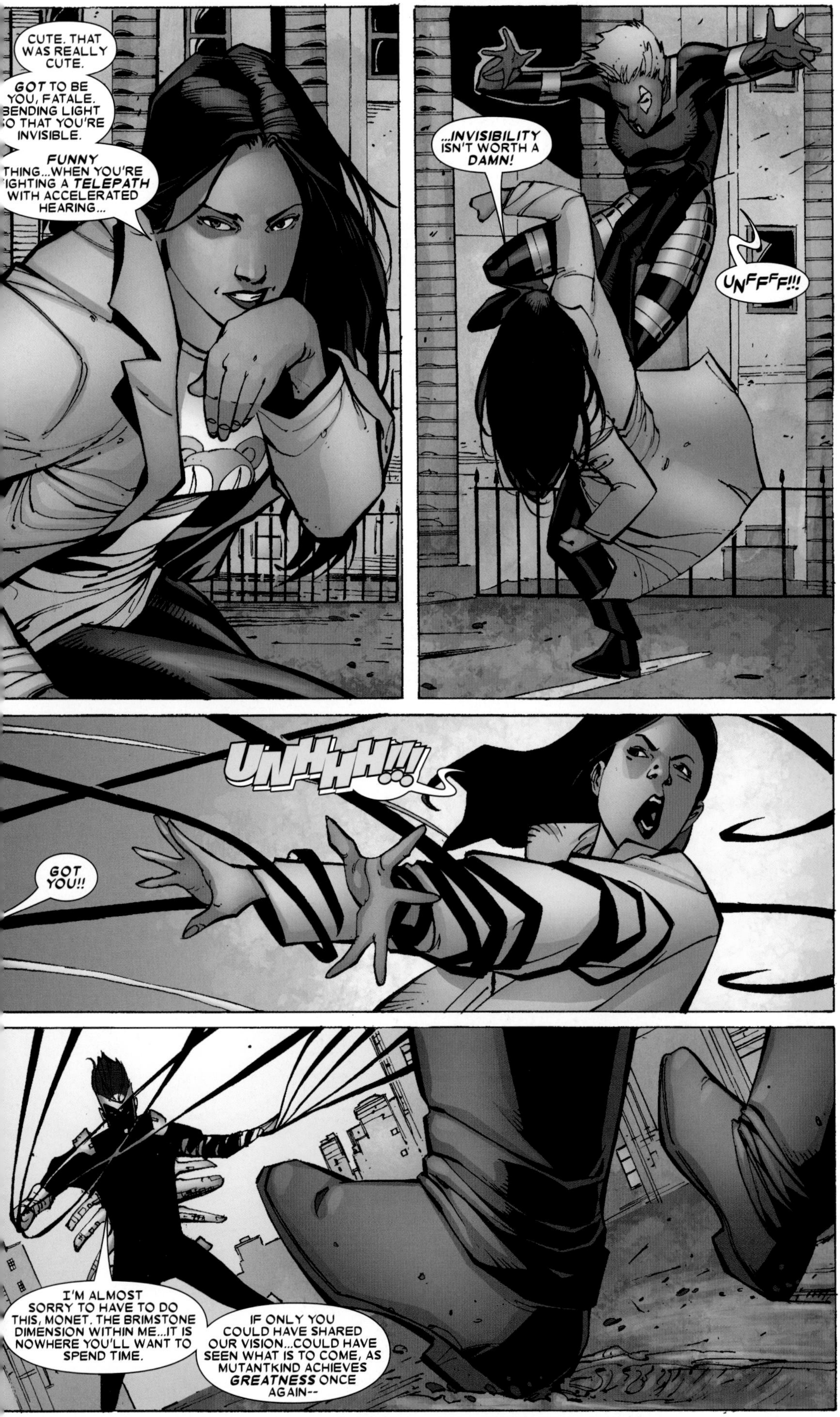
CUTE. THAT WAS REALLY CUTE.
GOT TO BE YOU, FATALE. BENDING LIGHT SO THAT YOU'RE INVISIBLE.
FUNNY THING...WHEN YOU'RE FIGHTING A TELEPATH WITH ACCELERATED HEARING...
...INVISIBILITY ISN'T WORTH A DAMN!
UNFFFF!!!
UNHHHH!!!
GOT YOU!!
I'M ALMOST SORRY TO HAVE TO DO THIS, MONET. THE BRIMSTONE DIMENSION WITHIN ME...IT IS NOWHERE YOU'LL WANT TO SPEND TIME.
IF ONLY YOU COULD HAVE SHARED OUR VISION...COULD HAVE SEEN WHAT IS TO COME, AS MUTANTKIND ACHIEVES GREATNESS ONCE AGAIN--

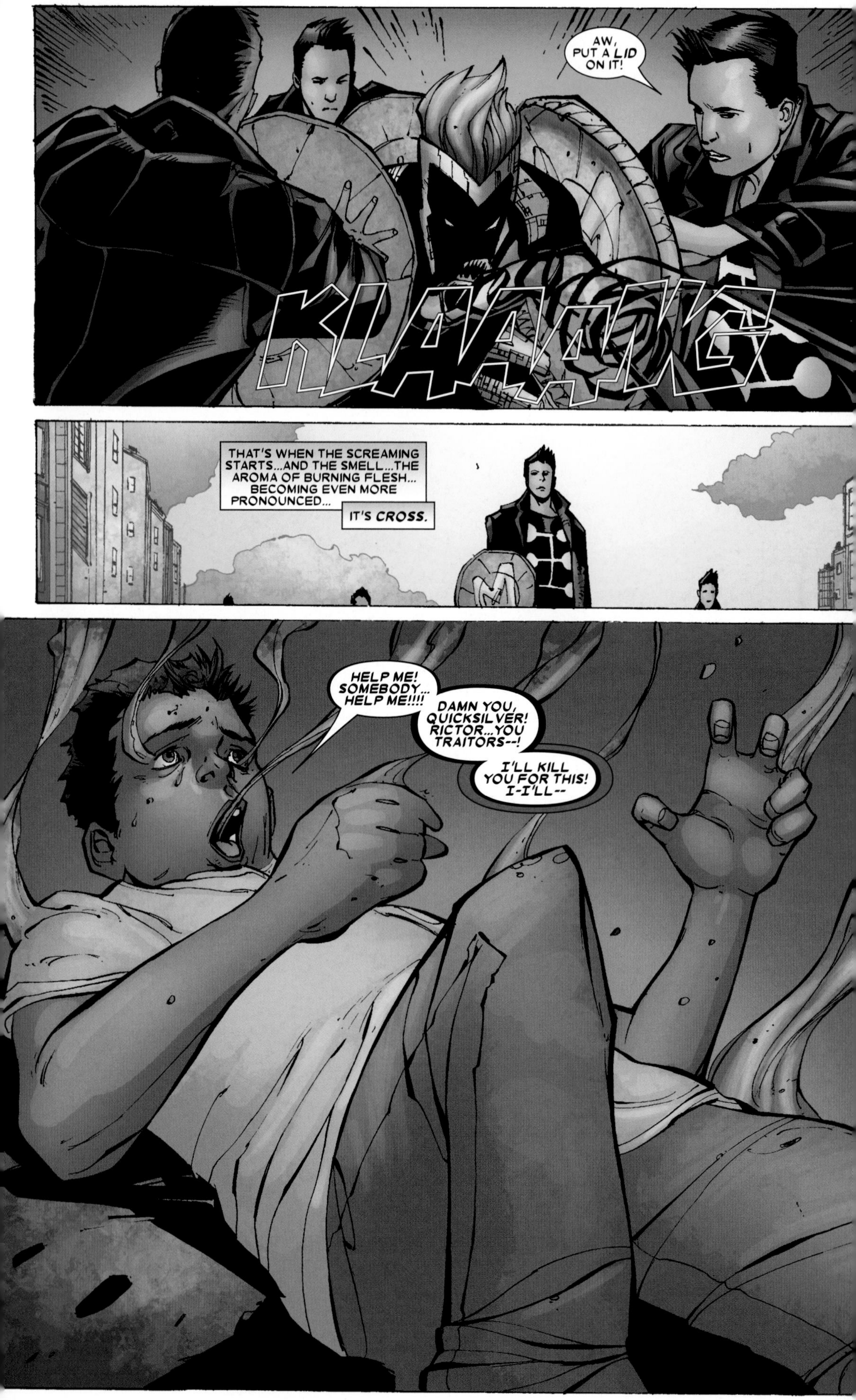
AW, PUT A LID ON IT!
KLAAANG!
THAT'S WHEN THE SCREAMING STARTS...AND THE SMELL...THE AROMA OF BURNING FLESH... BECOMING EVEN MORE PRONOUNCED...
IT'S CROSS.
HELP ME! SOMEBODY... HELP ME!!!!
DAMN YOU, QUICKSILVER! RICTOR...YOU TRAITORS--!
I'LL KILL YOU FOR THIS! I-I'LL--

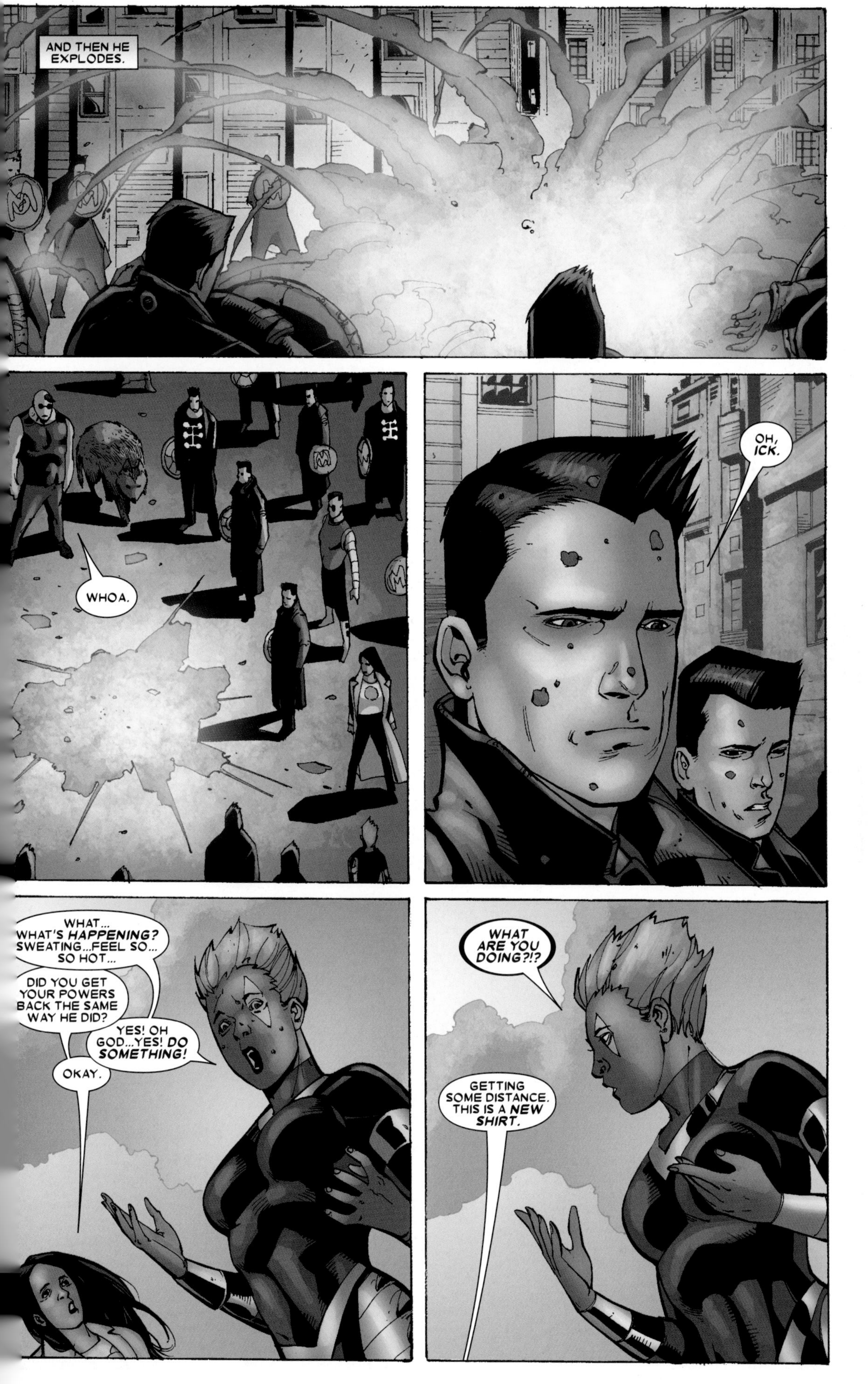
AND THEN HE EXPLODES.
WHOA.
OH, *ICK.*
WHAT... WHAT'S *HAPPENING?* SWEATING...FEEL SO... SO HOT...
DID YOU GET YOUR POWERS BACK THE SAME WAY HE DID?
YES! OH GOD...YES! *DO SOMETHING!*
OKAY.
WHAT ARE YOU DOING?!?
GETTING SOME DISTANCE. THIS IS A *NEW SHIRT.*

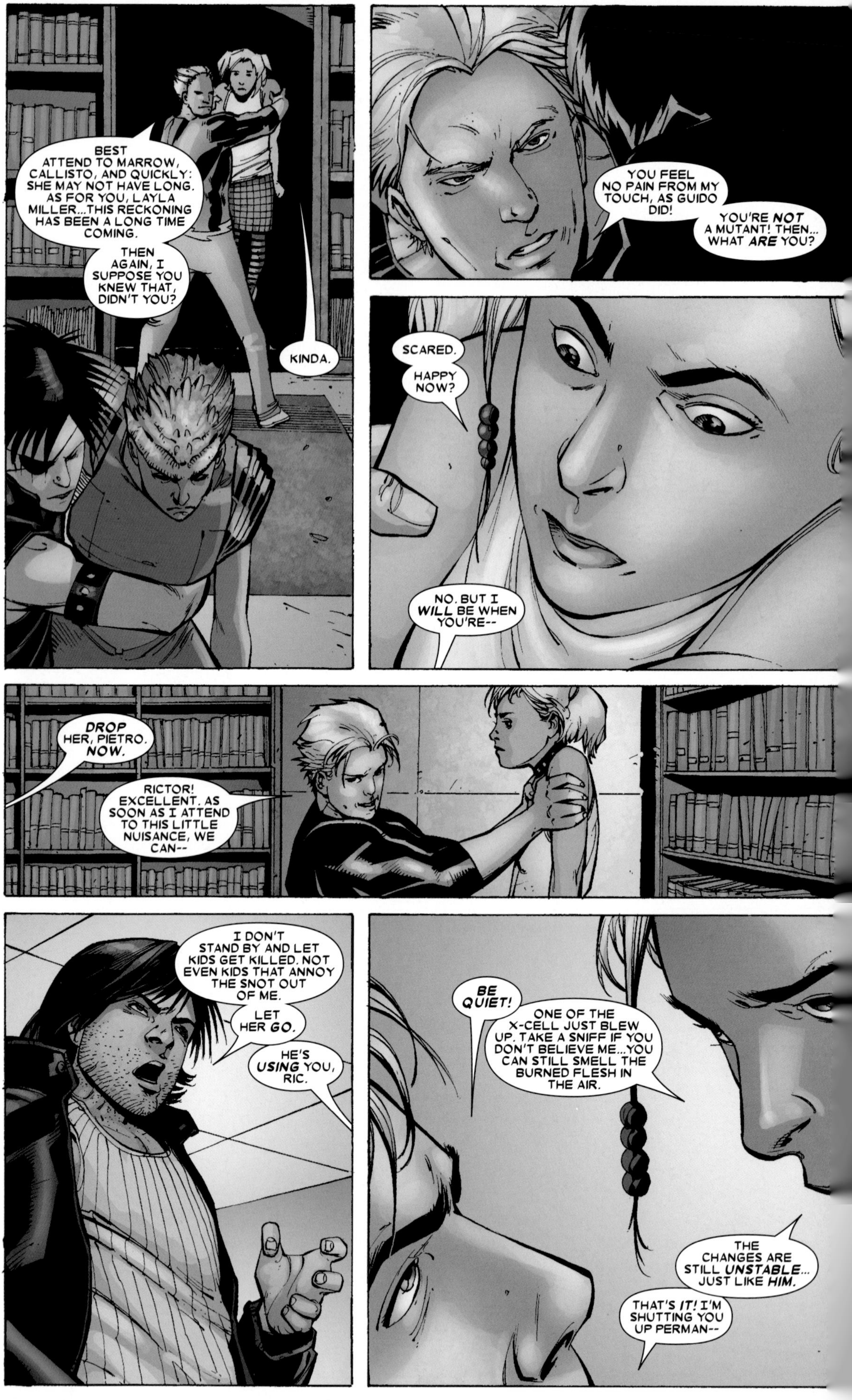
BEST ATTEND TO MARROW, CALLISTO, AND QUICKLY: SHE MAY NOT HAVE LONG. AS FOR YOU, LAYLA MILLER...THIS RECKONING HAS BEEN A LONG TIME COMING.
THEN AGAIN, I SUPPOSE YOU KNEW THAT, DIDN'T YOU?
KINDA.
YOU FEEL NO PAIN FROM MY TOUCH, AS GUIDO DID!
YOU'RE NOT A MUTANT! THEN... WHAT ARE YOU?
SCARED.
HAPPY NOW?
NO. BUT I WILL BE WHEN YOU'RE--
DROP HER, PIETRO. NOW.
RICTOR! EXCELLENT. AS SOON AS I ATTEND TO THIS LITTLE NUISANCE, WE CAN--
I DON'T STAND BY AND LET KIDS GET KILLED. NOT EVEN KIDS THAT ANNOY THE SNOT OUT OF ME.
LET HER GO.
HE'S USING YOU, RIC.
BE QUIET!
ONE OF THE X-CELL JUST BLEW UP. TAKE A SNIFF IF YOU DON'T BELIEVE ME...YOU CAN STILL SMELL THE BURNED FLESH IN THE AIR.
THE CHANGES ARE STILL UNSTABLE... JUST LIKE HIM.
THAT'S IT! I'M SHUTTING YOU UP PERMAN--

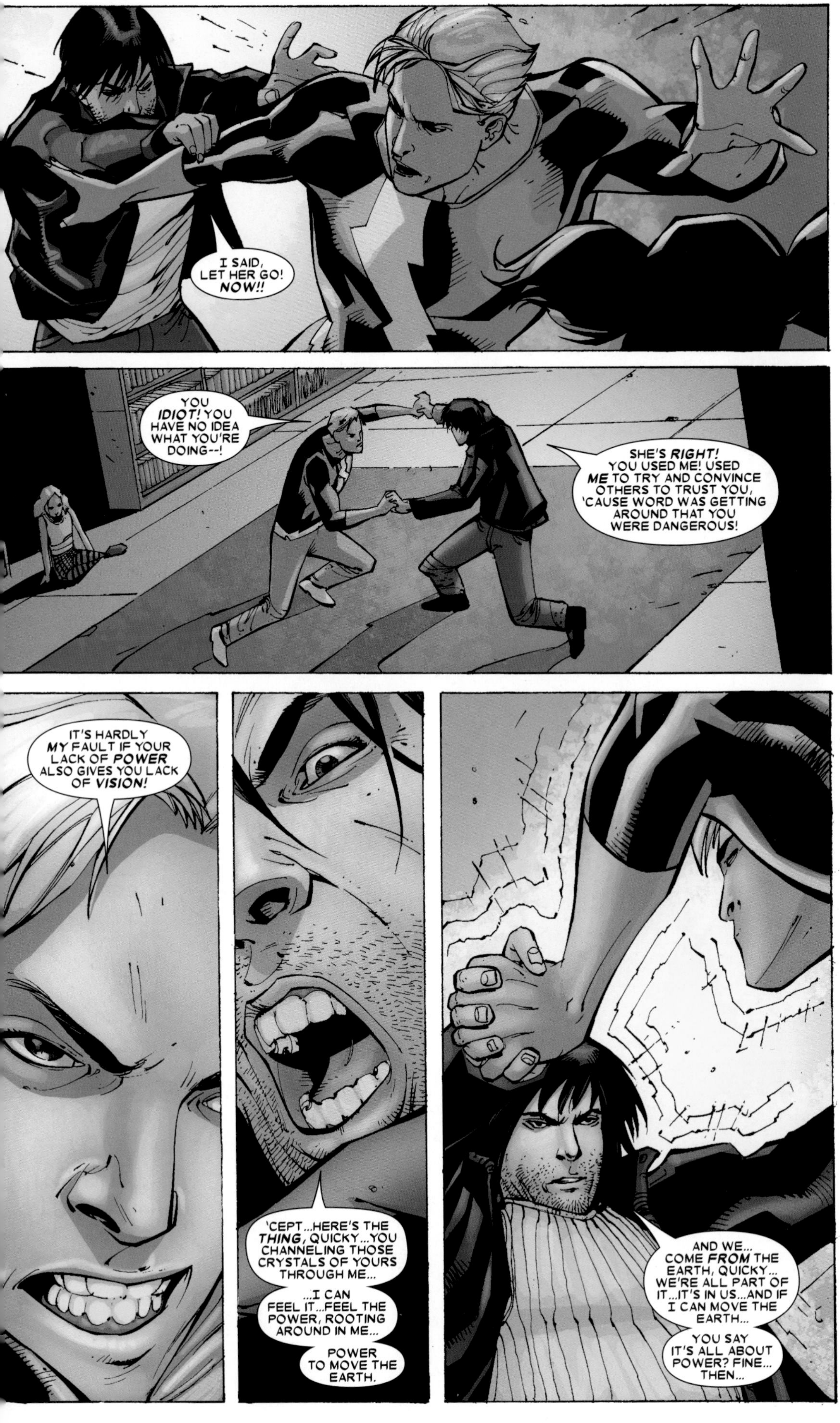

I SAID, LET HER GO! NOW!!
YOU IDIOT! YOU HAVE NO IDEA WHAT YOU'RE DOING--!
SHE'S RIGHT! YOU USED ME! USED ME TO TRY AND CONVINCE OTHERS TO TRUST YOU, 'CAUSE WORD WAS GETTING AROUND THAT YOU WERE DANGEROUS!
IT'S HARDLY MY FAULT IF YOUR LACK OF POWER ALSO GIVES YOU LACK OF VISION!
'CEPT...HERE'S THE THING, QUICKY...YOU CHANNELING THOSE CRYSTALS OF YOURS THROUGH ME...
...I CAN FEEL IT...FEEL THE POWER, ROOTING AROUND IN ME...
POWER TO MOVE THE EARTH.
AND WE... COME FROM THE EARTH, QUICKY... WE'RE ALL PART OF IT...IT'S IN US...AND IF I CAN MOVE THE EARTH...
YOU SAY IT'S ALL ABOUT POWER? FINE... THEN...

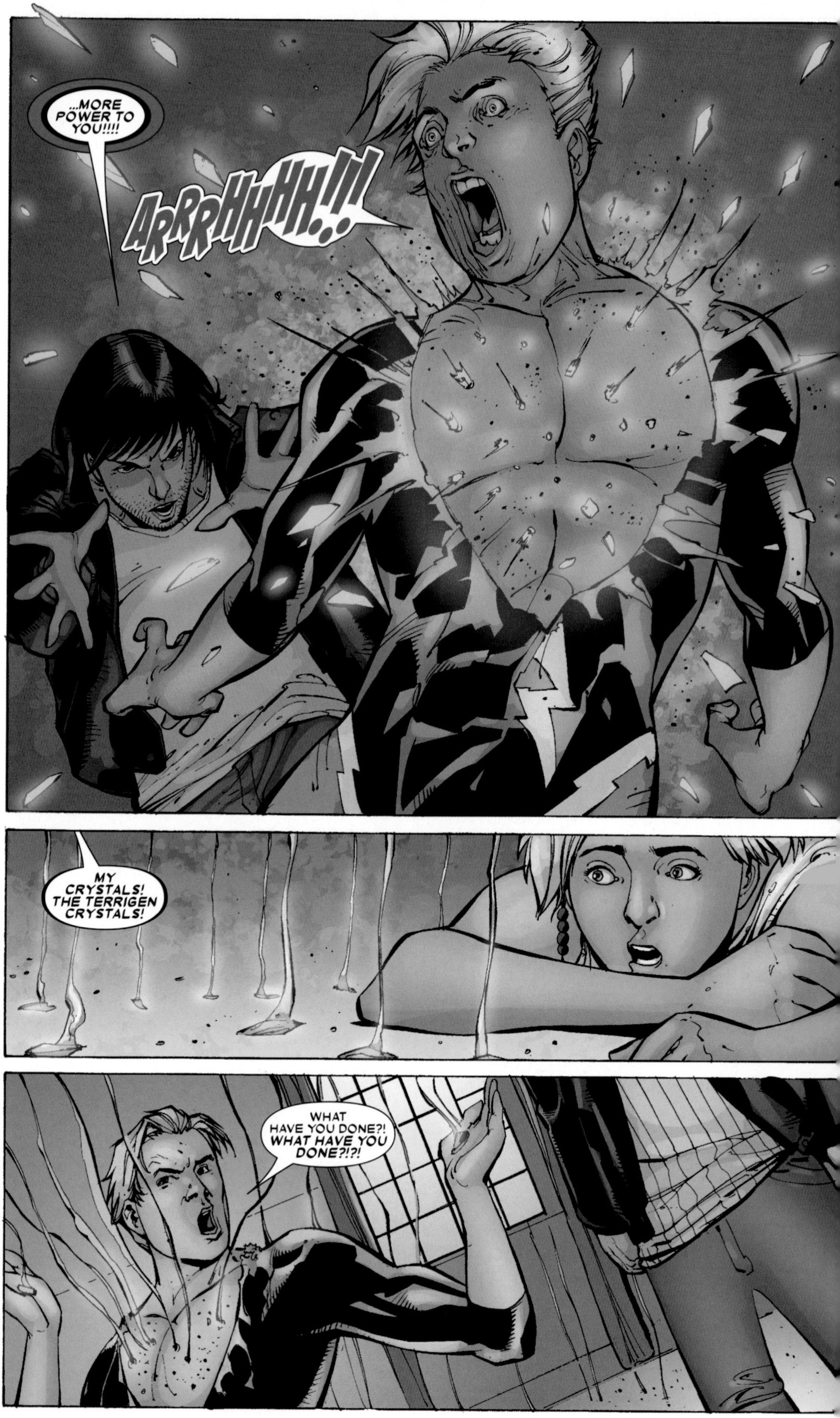
...MORE POWER TO YOU!!!!
ARRRHHHHH..!!!
MY CRYSTALS! THE TERRIGEN CRYSTALS!
WHAT HAVE YOU DONE?! WHAT HAVE YOU DONE?!?!

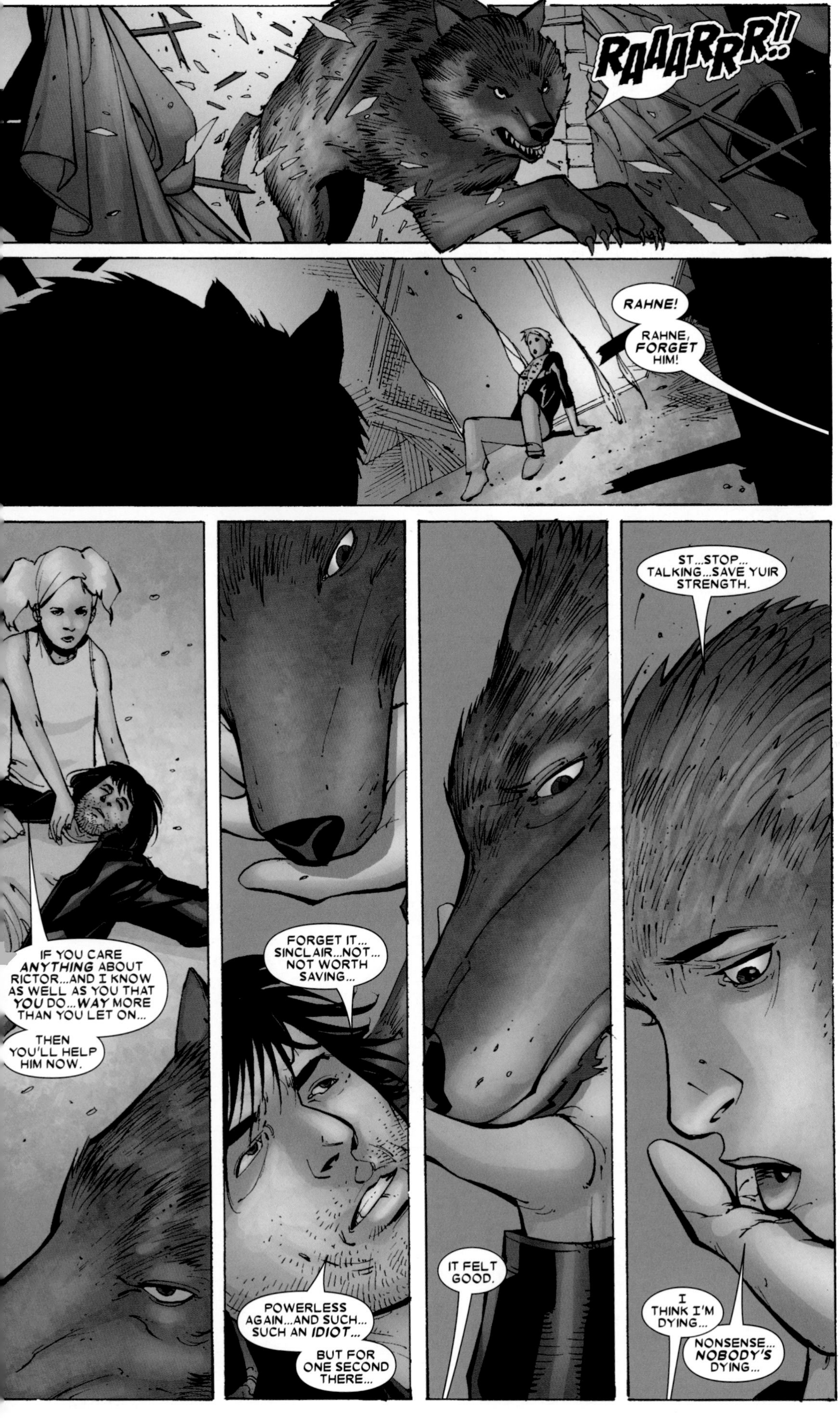
RAAARRR!!
RAHNE!
RAHNE, FORGET HIM!
IF YOU CARE ANYTHING ABOUT RICTOR...AND I KNOW AS WELL AS YOU THAT YOU DO...WAY MORE THAN YOU LET ON...
THEN YOU'LL HELP HIM NOW.
FORGET IT... SINCLAIR...NOT... NOT WORTH SAVING...
POWERLESS AGAIN...AND SUCH... SUCH AN IDIOT...
BUT FOR ONE SECOND THERE...
IT FELT GOOD.
ST...STOP... TALKING...SAVE YUIR STRENGTH.
I THINK I'M DYING...
NONSENSE... NOBODY'S DYING...

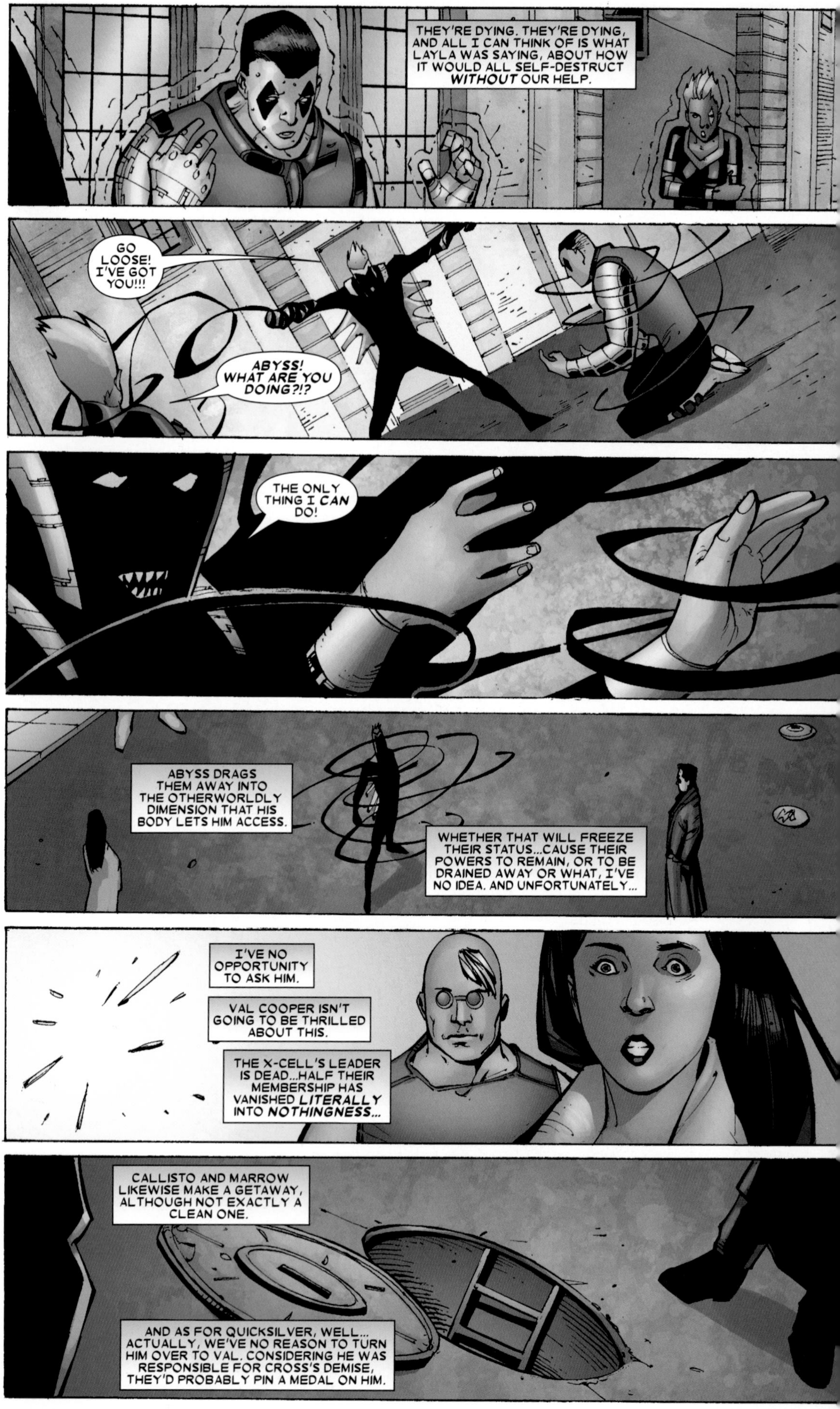
THEY'RE DYING. THEY'RE DYING, AND ALL I CAN THINK OF IS WHAT LAYLA WAS SAYING, ABOUT HOW IT WOULD ALL SELF-DESTRUCT WITHOUT OUR HELP.
GO LOOSE! I'VE GOT YOU!!!
ABYSS! WHAT ARE YOU DOING?!?
THE ONLY THING I CAN DO!
ABYSS DRAGS THEM AWAY INTO THE OTHERWORLDLY DIMENSION THAT HIS BODY LETS HIM ACCESS.
WHETHER THAT WILL FREEZE THEIR STATUS...CAUSE THEIR POWERS TO REMAIN, OR TO BE DRAINED AWAY OR WHAT, I'VE NO IDEA. AND UNFORTUNATELY...
I'VE NO OPPORTUNITY TO ASK HIM.
VAL COOPER ISN'T GOING TO BE THRILLED ABOUT THIS.
THE X-CELL'S LEADER IS DEAD...HALF THEIR MEMBERSHIP HAS VANISHED LITERALLY INTO NOTHINGNESS...
CALLISTO AND MARROW LIKEWISE MAKE A GETAWAY, ALTHOUGH NOT EXACTLY A CLEAN ONE.
AND AS FOR QUICKSILVER, WELL... ACTUALLY, WE'VE NO REASON TO TURN HIM OVER TO VAL. CONSIDERING HE WAS RESPONSIBLE FOR CROSS'S DEMISE, THEY'D PROBABLY PIN A MEDAL ON HIM.

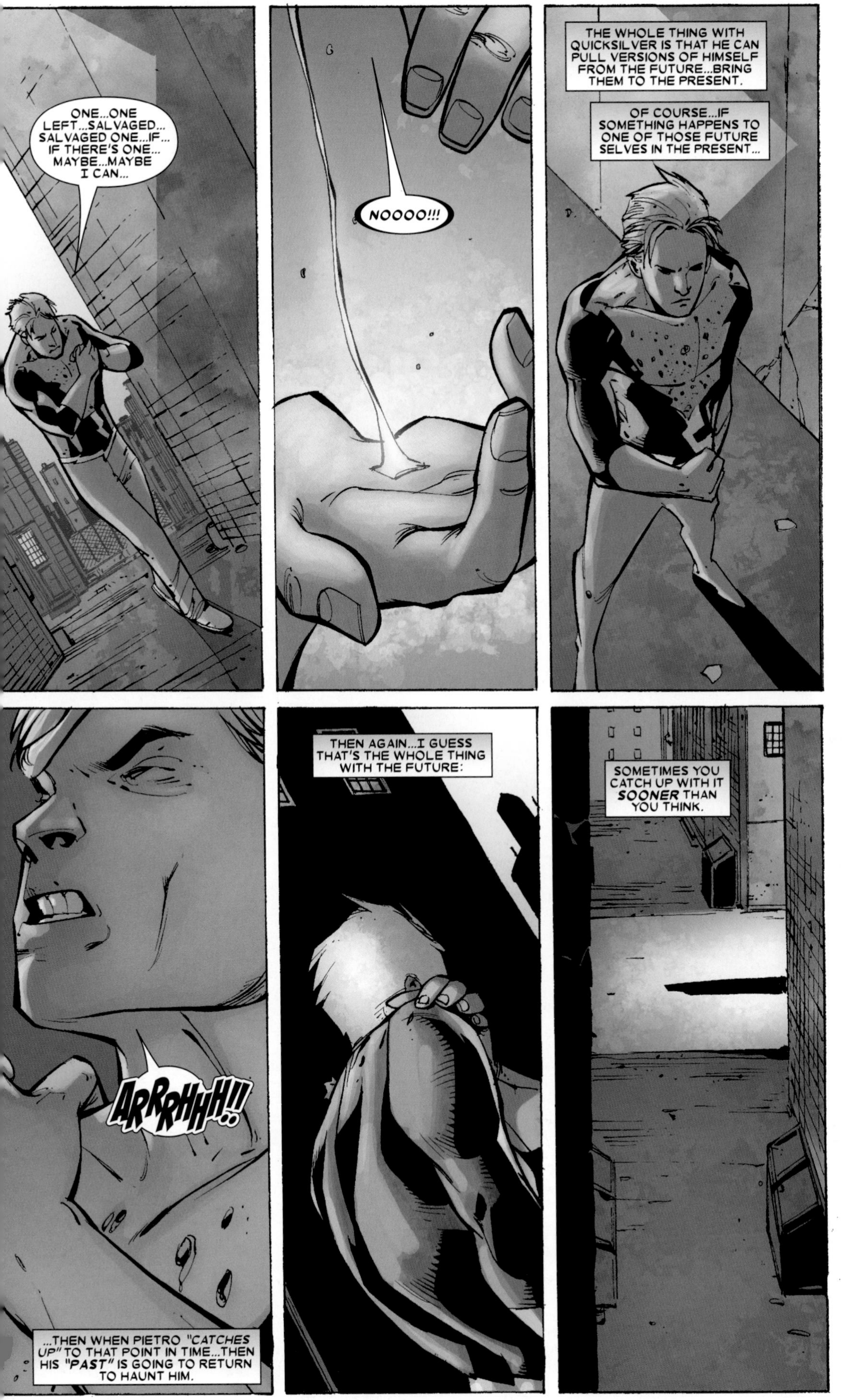
ONE...ONE LEFT...SALVAGED... SALVAGED ONE...IF... IF THERE'S ONE... MAYBE...MAYBE I CAN...
NOOOO!!!
THE WHOLE THING WITH QUICKSILVER IS THAT HE CAN PULL VERSIONS OF HIMSELF FROM THE FUTURE...BRING THEM TO THE PRESENT.
OF COURSE...IF SOMETHING HAPPENS TO ONE OF THOSE FUTURE SELVES IN THE PRESENT...
ARRRHHH!!
...THEN WHEN PIETRO "CATCHES UP" TO THAT POINT IN TIME...THEN HIS "PAST" IS GOING TO RETURN TO HAUNT HIM.
THEN AGAIN...I GUESS THAT'S THE WHOLE THING WITH THE FUTURE:
SOMETIMES YOU CATCH UP WITH IT SOONER THAN YOU THINK.

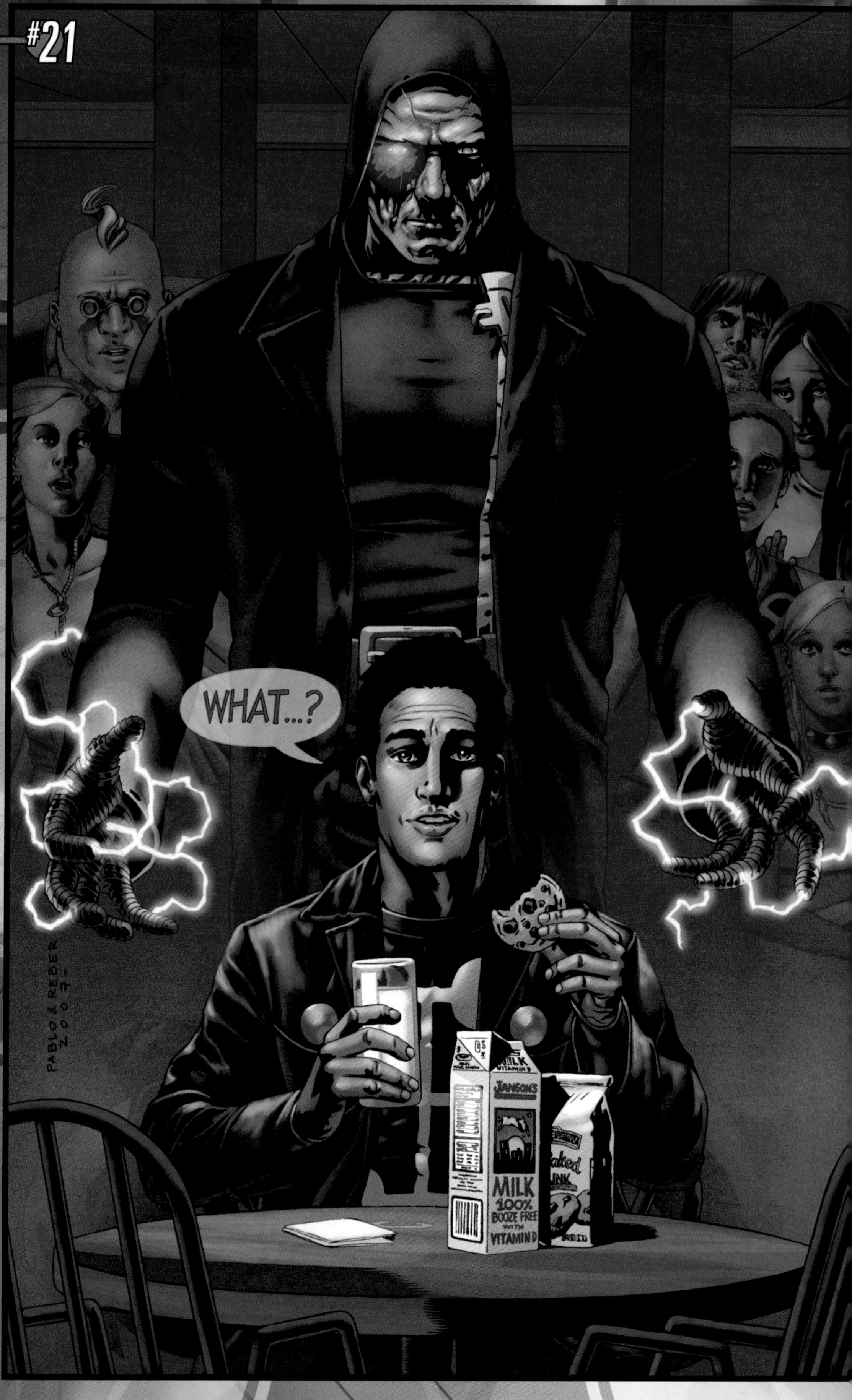
#21
WHAT...?
PABLO & REBER 2007
JANSON'S
MILK
100%
BOOZE FREE
WITH
VITAMIN D

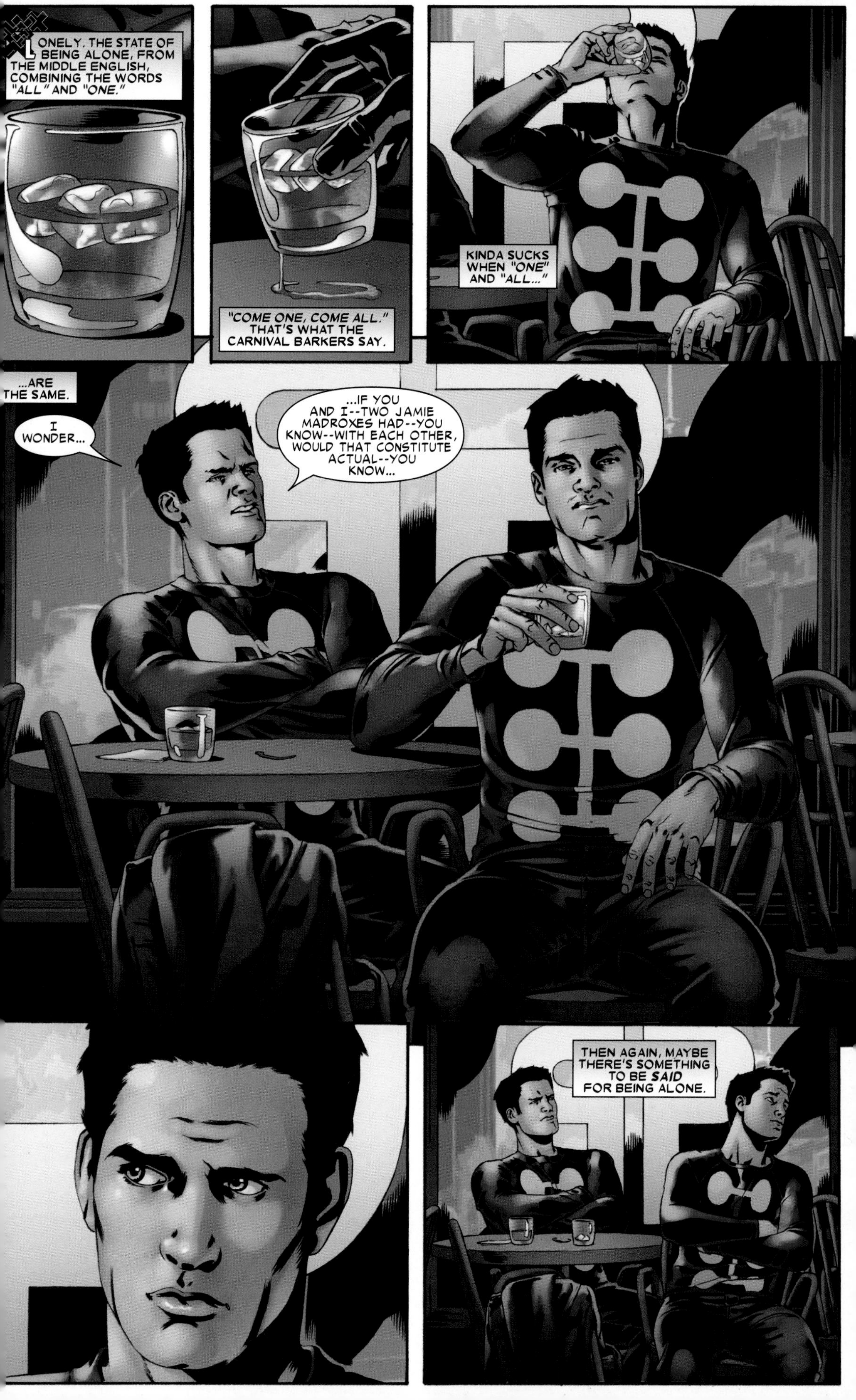
LONELY. THE STATE OF BEING ALONE, FROM THE MIDDLE ENGLISH, COMBINING THE WORDS "ALL" AND "ONE."
"COME ONE, COME ALL." THAT'S WHAT THE CARNIVAL BARKERS SAY.
KINDA SUCKS WHEN "ONE" AND "ALL..."
...ARE THE SAME.
I WONDER...
...IF YOU AND I--TWO JAMIE MADROXES HAD--YOU KNOW--WITH EACH OTHER, WOULD THAT CONSTITUTE ACTUAL--YOU KNOW...
THEN AGAIN, MAYBE THERE'S SOMETHING TO BE SAID FOR BEING ALONE.

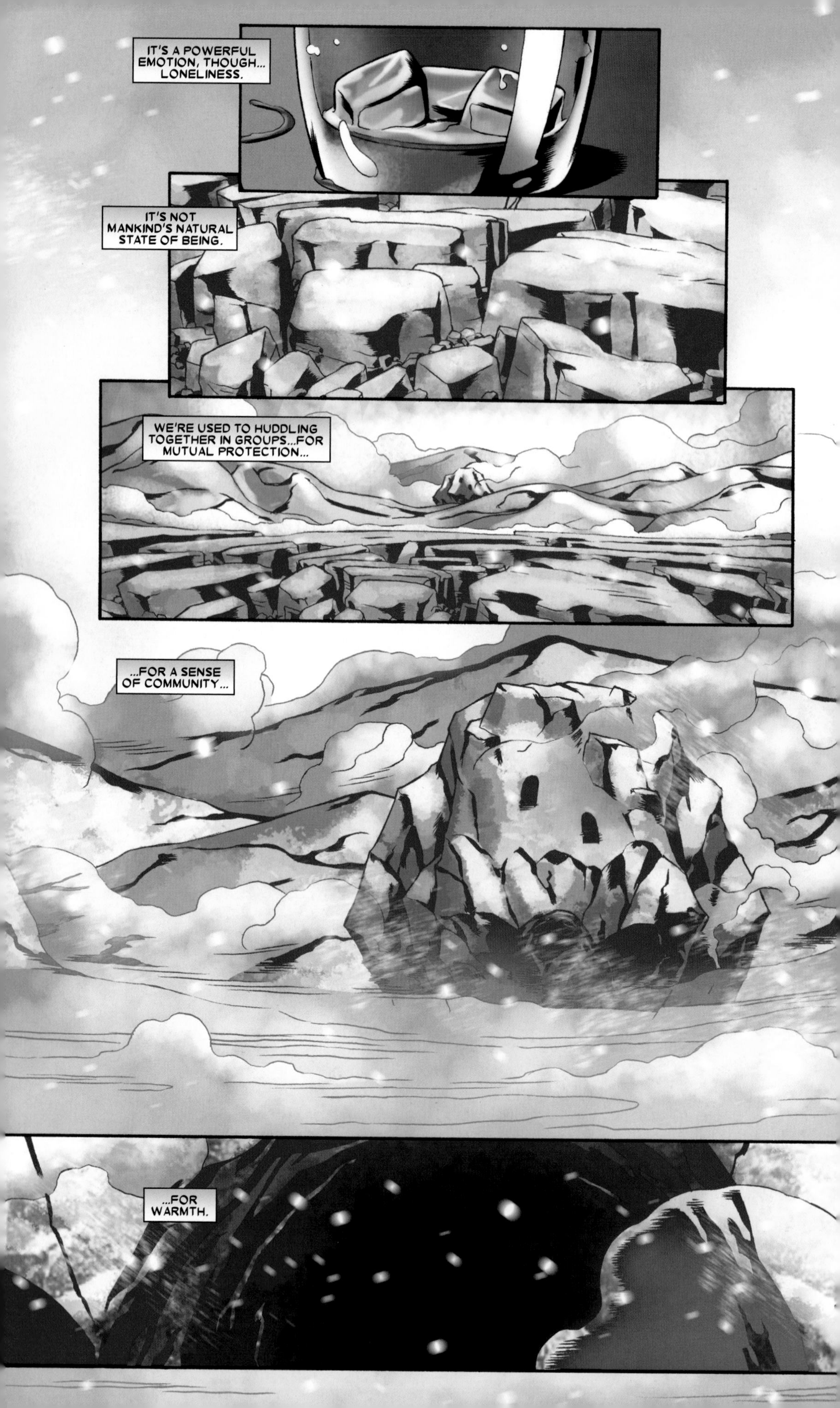
IT'S A POWERFUL EMOTION, THOUGH... LONELINESS.
IT'S NOT MANKIND'S NATURAL STATE OF BEING.
WE'RE USED TO HUDDLING TOGETHER IN GROUPS...FOR MUTUAL PROTECTION...
...FOR A SENSE OF COMMUNITY...
...FOR WARMTH.

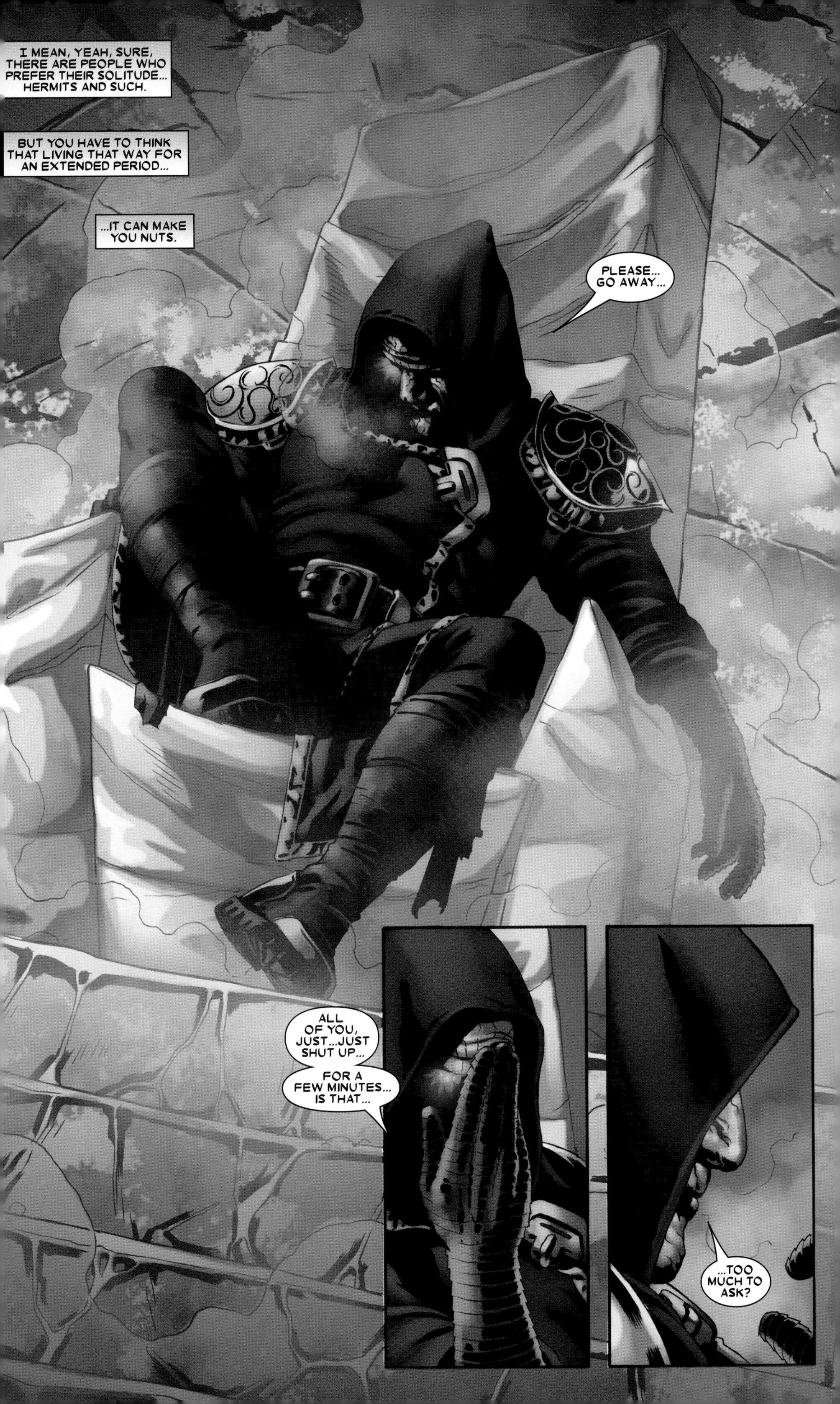
I MEAN, YEAH, SURE, THERE ARE PEOPLE WHO PREFER THEIR SOLITUDE... HERMITS AND SUCH.
BUT YOU HAVE TO THINK THAT LIVING THAT WAY FOR AN EXTENDED PERIOD...
...IT CAN MAKE YOU NUTS.
PLEASE... GO AWAY...
ALL OF YOU, JUST...JUST SHUT UP...
FOR A FEW MINUTES... IS THAT...
...TOO MUCH TO ASK?

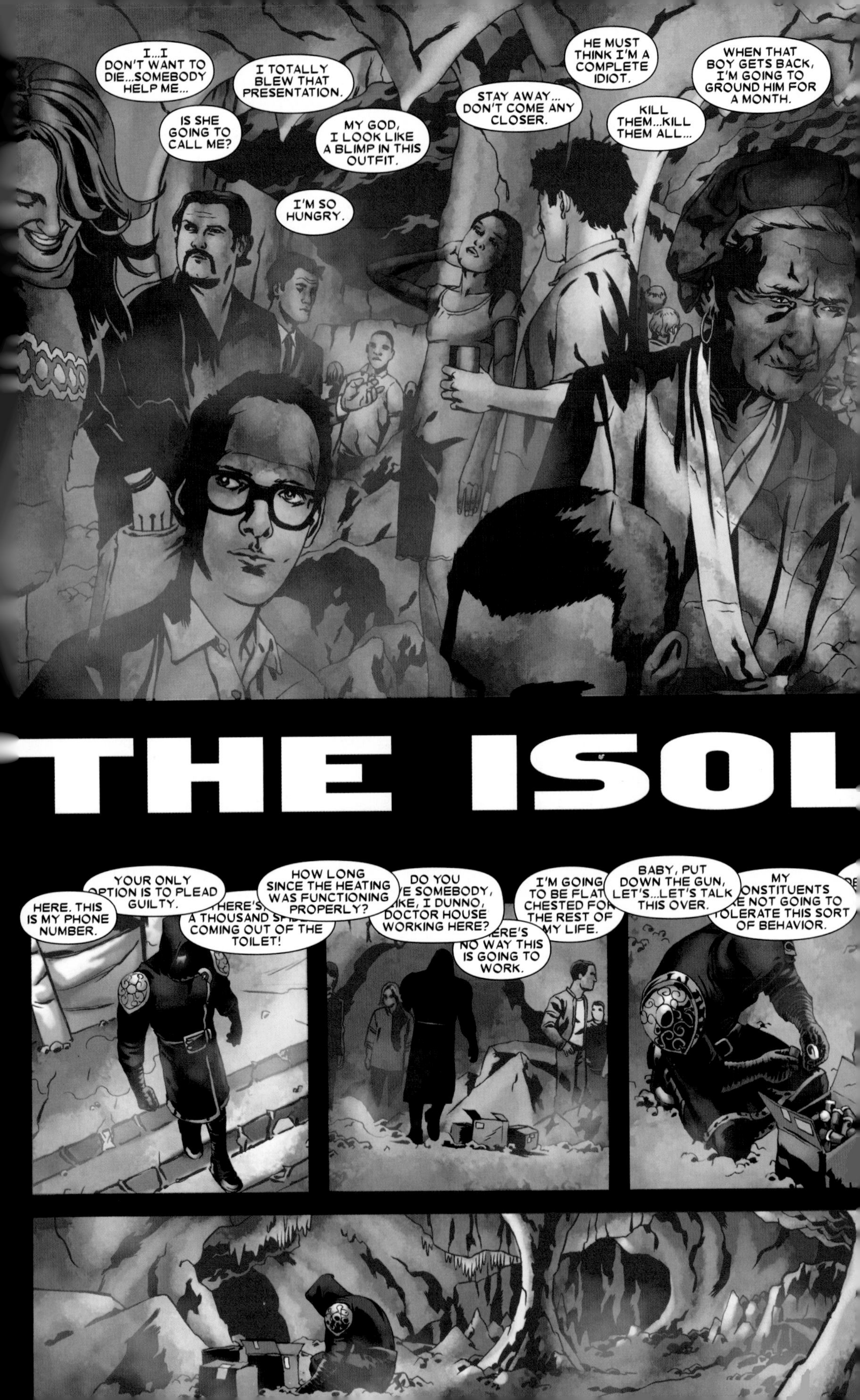
I...I DON'T WANT TO DIE...SOMEBODY HELP ME...
I TOTALLY BLEW THAT PRESENTATION.
IS SHE GOING TO CALL ME?
MY GOD, I LOOK LIKE A BLIMP IN THIS OUTFIT.
I'M SO HUNGRY.
STAY AWAY... DON'T COME ANY CLOSER.
HE MUST THINK I'M A COMPLETE IDIOT.
KILL THEM...KILL THEM ALL...
WHEN THAT BOY GETS BACK, I'M GOING TO GROUND HIM FOR A MONTH.
THE ISOL
HERE. THIS IS MY PHONE NUMBER.
YOUR ONLY OPTION IS TO PLEAD GUILTY.
A THOUSAND COMING OUT OF THE TOILET!
HOW LONG SINCE THE HEATING WAS FUNCTIONING PROPERLY?
DO YOU SOMEBODY, I DUNNO, DOCTOR HOUSE WORKING HERE?
NO WAY THIS IS GOING TO WORK.
I'M GOING TO BE FLAT CHESTED FOR THE REST OF MY LIFE.
BABY, PUT DOWN THE GUN, LET'S...LET'S TALK THIS OVER.
MY NOT GOING TO TOLERATE THIS SORT OF BEHAVIOR.

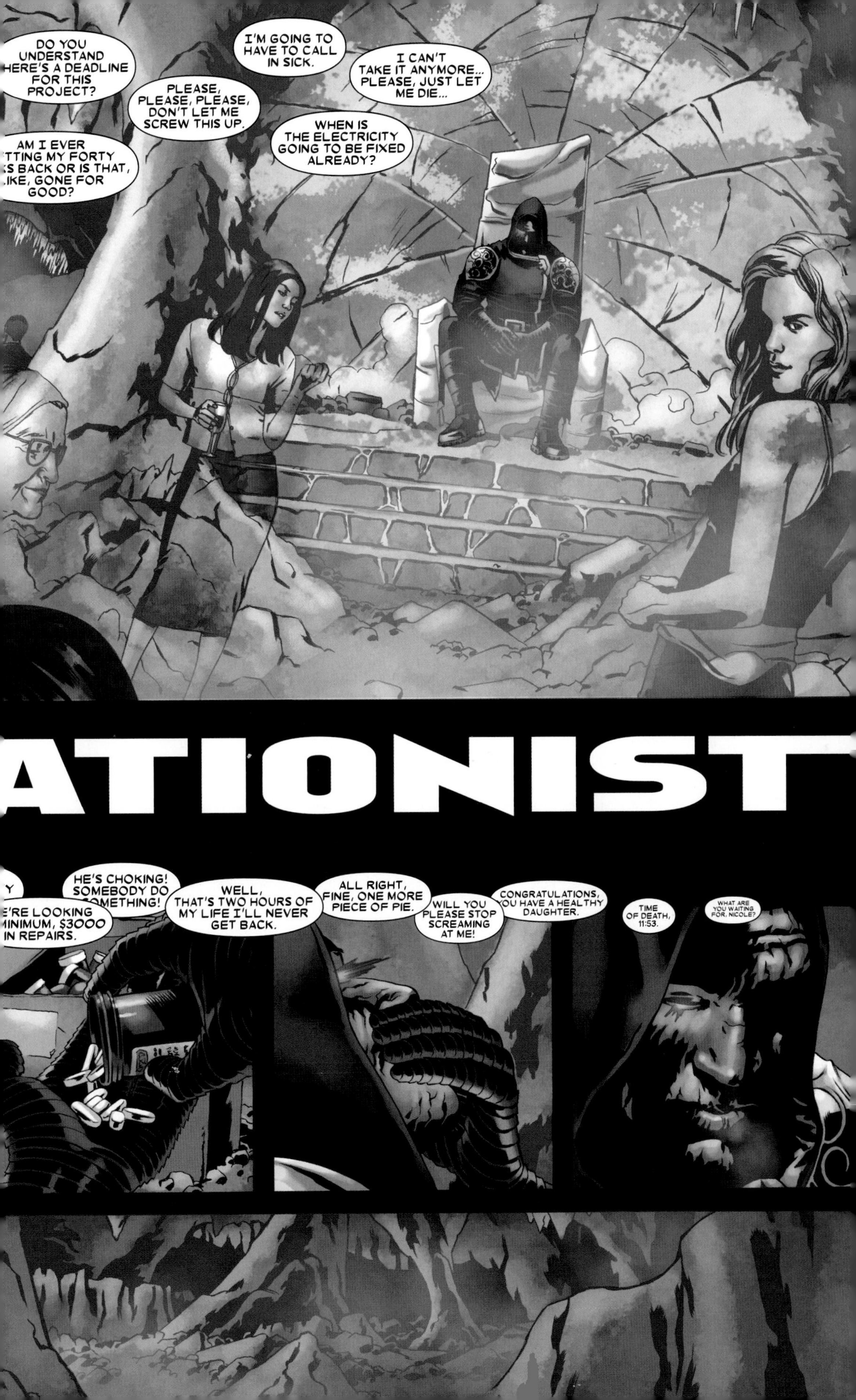
DO YOU UNDERSTAND HERE'S A DEADLINE FOR THIS PROJECT?
AM I EVER TTING MY FORTY S BACK OR IS THAT, IKE, GONE FOR GOOD?
PLEASE, PLEASE, PLEASE, DON'T LET ME SCREW THIS UP.
I'M GOING TO HAVE TO CALL IN SICK.
WHEN IS THE ELECTRICITY GOING TO BE FIXED ALREADY?
I CAN'T TAKE IT ANYMORE... PLEASE, JUST LET ME DIE...
ATIONIST
Y
E'RE LOOKING MINIMUM, $3000 IN REPAIRS.
HE'S CHOKING! SOMEBODY DO OMETHING!
WELL, THAT'S TWO HOURS OF MY LIFE I'LL NEVER GET BACK.
ALL RIGHT, FINE, ONE MORE PIECE OF PIE.
WILL YOU PLEASE STOP SCREAMING AT ME!
CONGRATULATIONS, YOU HAVE A HEALTHY DAUGHTER.
TIME OF DEATH, 11:53.
WHAT ARE YOU WAITING FOR, NICOLE?

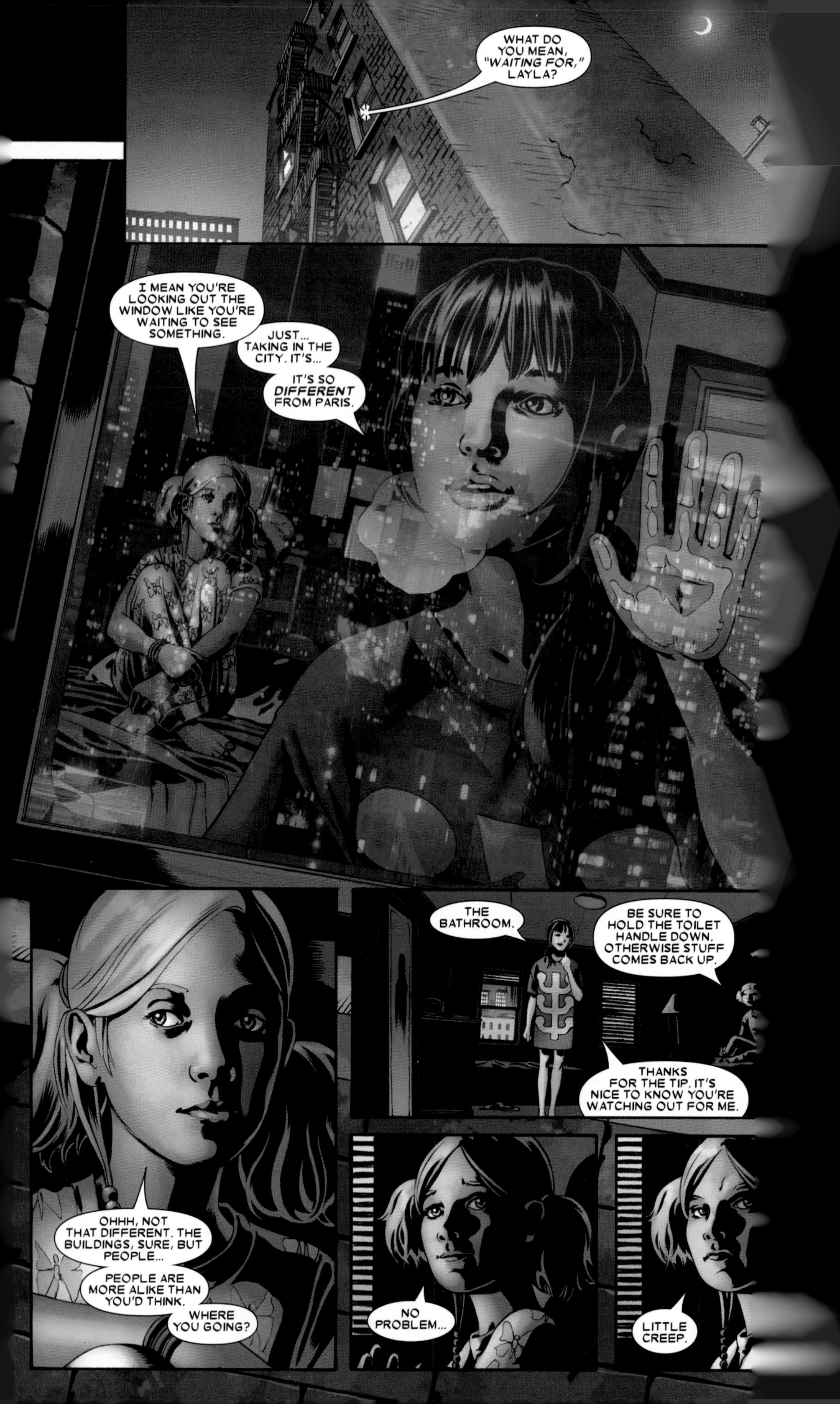
WHAT DO YOU MEAN, "WAITING FOR," LAYLA?
I MEAN YOU'RE LOOKING OUT THE WINDOW LIKE YOU'RE WAITING TO SEE SOMETHING.
JUST... TAKING IN THE CITY. IT'S...
IT'S SO DIFFERENT FROM PARIS.
OHHH, NOT THAT DIFFERENT. THE BUILDINGS, SURE, BUT PEOPLE...
PEOPLE ARE MORE ALIKE THAN YOU'D THINK.
WHERE YOU GOING?
THE BATHROOM.
BE SURE TO HOLD THE TOILET HANDLE DOWN. OTHERWISE STUFF COMES BACK UP.
THANKS FOR THE TIP. IT'S NICE TO KNOW YOU'RE WATCHING OUT FOR ME.
NO PROBLEM...
LITTLE CREEP.

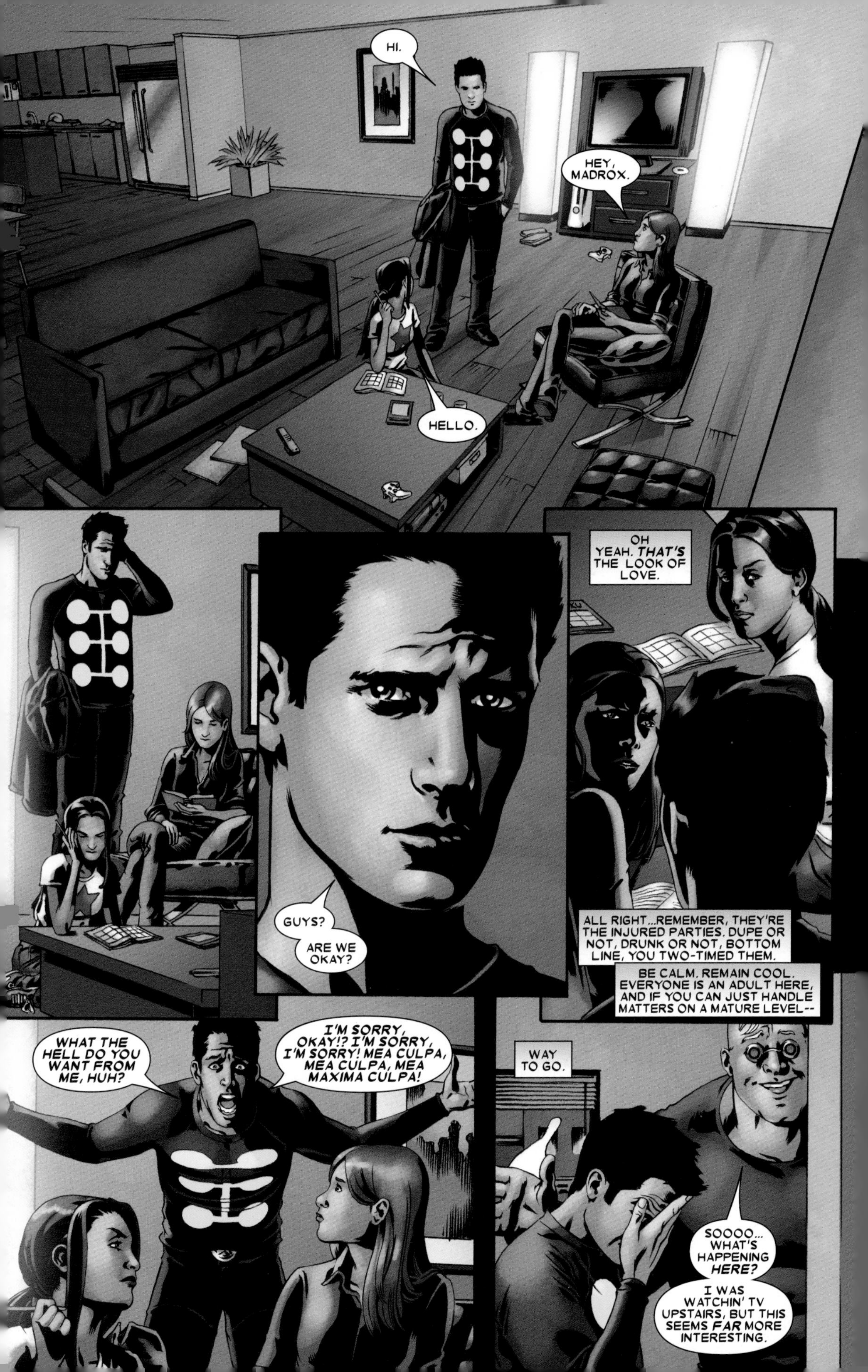
HI.
HEY, MADROX.
HELLO.
GUYS?
ARE WE OKAY?
OH YEAH. *THAT'S* THE LOOK OF LOVE.
ALL RIGHT...REMEMBER, THEY'RE THE INJURED PARTIES. DUPE OR NOT, DRUNK OR NOT, BOTTOM LINE, YOU TWO-TIMED THEM.
BE CALM. REMAIN COOL. EVERYONE IS AN ADULT HERE, AND IF YOU CAN JUST HANDLE MATTERS ON A MATURE LEVEL--
WHAT THE HELL DO YOU WANT FROM ME, HUH?
I'M SORRY, OKAY!? I'M SORRY, I'M SORRY! MEA CULPA, MEA CULPA, MEA MAXIMA CULPA!
WAY TO GO.
SOOOO... WHAT'S HAPPENING *HERE?*
I WAS WATCHIN' TV UPSTAIRS, BUT THIS SEEMS *FAR* MORE INTERESTING.

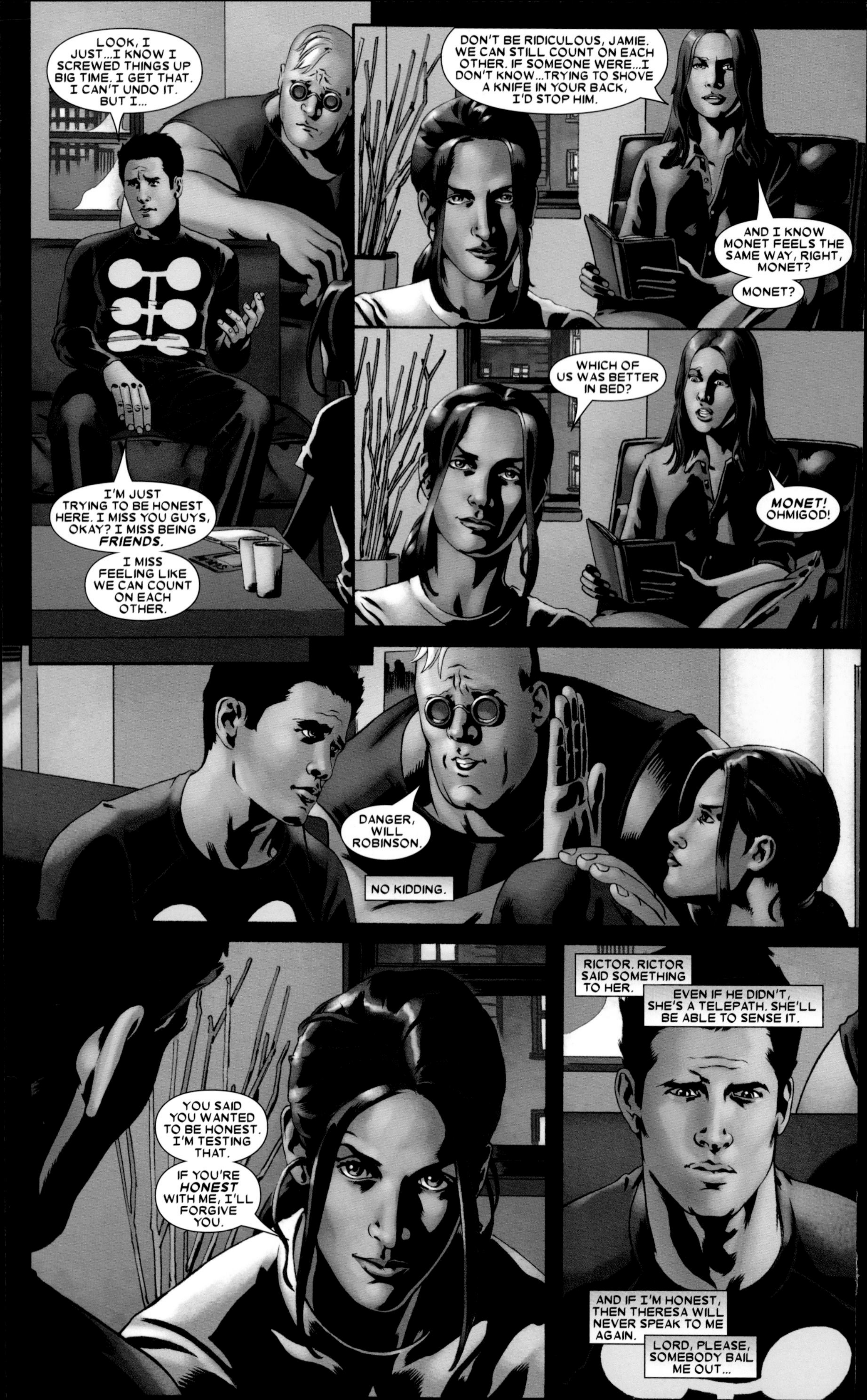
LOOK, I JUST...I KNOW I SCREWED THINGS UP BIG TIME. I GET THAT. I CAN'T UNDO IT. BUT I...
I'M JUST TRYING TO BE HONEST HERE. I MISS YOU GUYS, OKAY? I MISS BEING *FRIENDS.*
I MISS FEELING LIKE WE CAN COUNT ON EACH OTHER.
DON'T BE RIDICULOUS, JAMIE. WE CAN STILL COUNT ON EACH OTHER. IF SOMEONE WERE...I DON'T KNOW...TRYING TO SHOVE A KNIFE IN YOUR BACK, I'D STOP HIM.
AND I KNOW MONET FEELS THE SAME WAY, RIGHT, MONET?
MONET?
WHICH OF US WAS BETTER IN BED?
MONET! OHMIGOD!
DANGER, WILL ROBINSON.
NO KIDDING.
YOU SAID YOU WANTED TO BE HONEST. I'M TESTING THAT.
IF YOU'RE *HONEST* WITH ME, I'LL FORGIVE YOU.
RICTOR. RICTOR SAID SOMETHING TO HER.
EVEN IF HE DIDN'T, SHE'S A TELEPATH. SHE'LL BE ABLE TO SENSE IT.
AND IF I'M HONEST, THEN THERESA WILL NEVER SPEAK TO ME AGAIN.
LORD, PLEASE, SOMEBODY BAIL ME OUT...

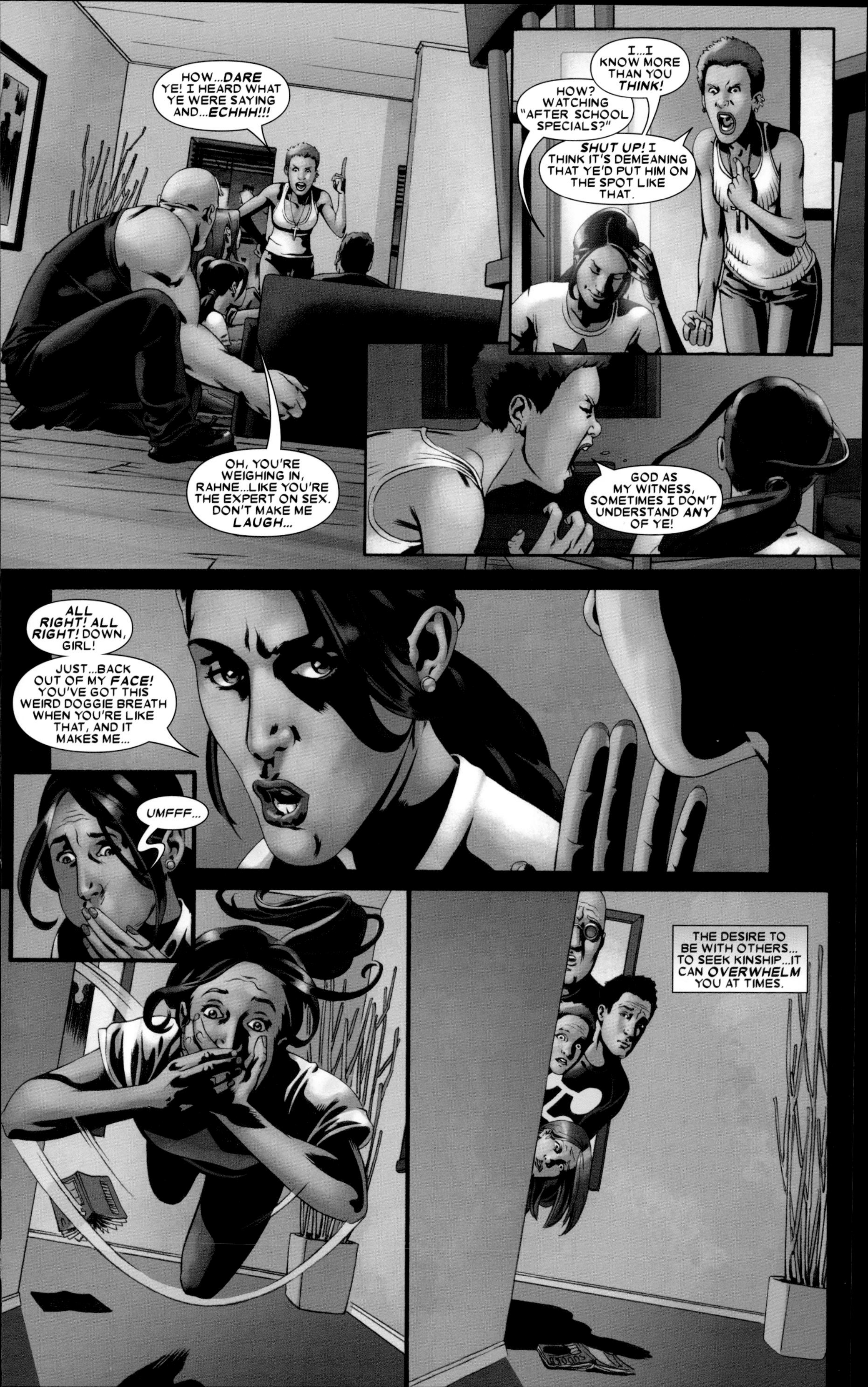

HOW...DARE YE! I HEARD WHAT YE WERE SAYING AND...ECHHH!!!
OH, YOU'RE WEIGHING IN, RAHNE...LIKE YOU'RE THE EXPERT ON SEX. DON'T MAKE ME LAUGH...
I...I KNOW MORE THAN YOU THINK!
HOW? WATCHING "AFTER SCHOOL SPECIALS?"
SHUT UP! I THINK IT'S DEMEANING THAT YE'D PUT HIM ON THE SPOT LIKE THAT.
GOD AS MY WITNESS, SOMETIMES I DON'T UNDERSTAND ANY OF YE!
ALL RIGHT! ALL RIGHT! DOWN, GIRL!
JUST...BACK OUT OF MY FACE! YOU'VE GOT THIS WEIRD DOGGIE BREATH WHEN YOU'RE LIKE THAT, AND IT MAKES ME...
UMFFF...
THE DESIRE TO BE WITH OTHERS... TO SEEK KINSHIP...IT CAN OVERWHELM YOU AT TIMES.

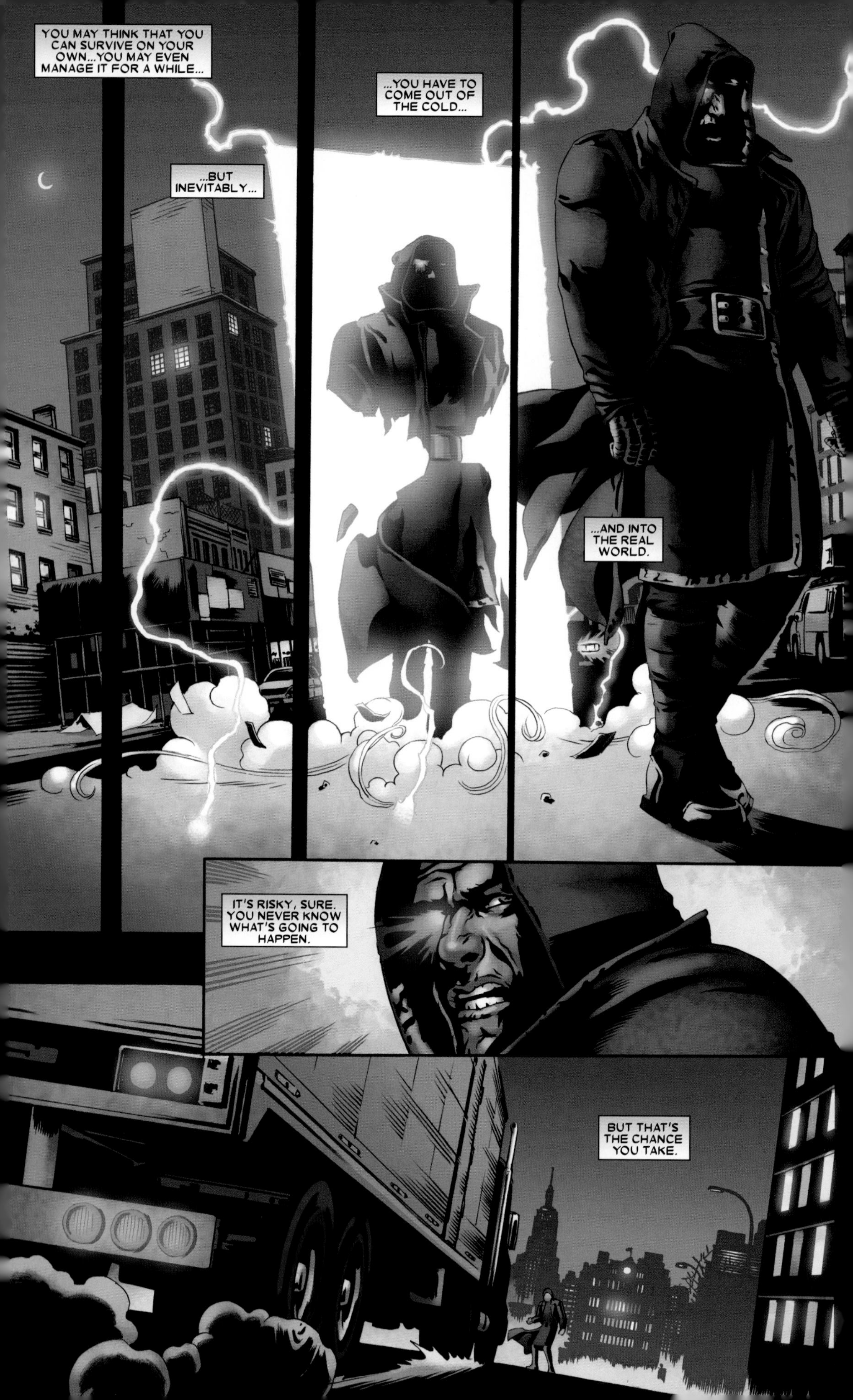
YOU MAY THINK THAT YOU CAN SURVIVE ON YOUR OWN...YOU MAY EVEN MANAGE IT FOR A WHILE...
...BUT INEVITABLY...
...YOU HAVE TO COME OUT OF THE COLD...
...AND INTO THE REAL WORLD.
IT'S RISKY, SURE. YOU NEVER KNOW WHAT'S GOING TO HAPPEN.
BUT THAT'S THE CHANCE YOU TAKE.

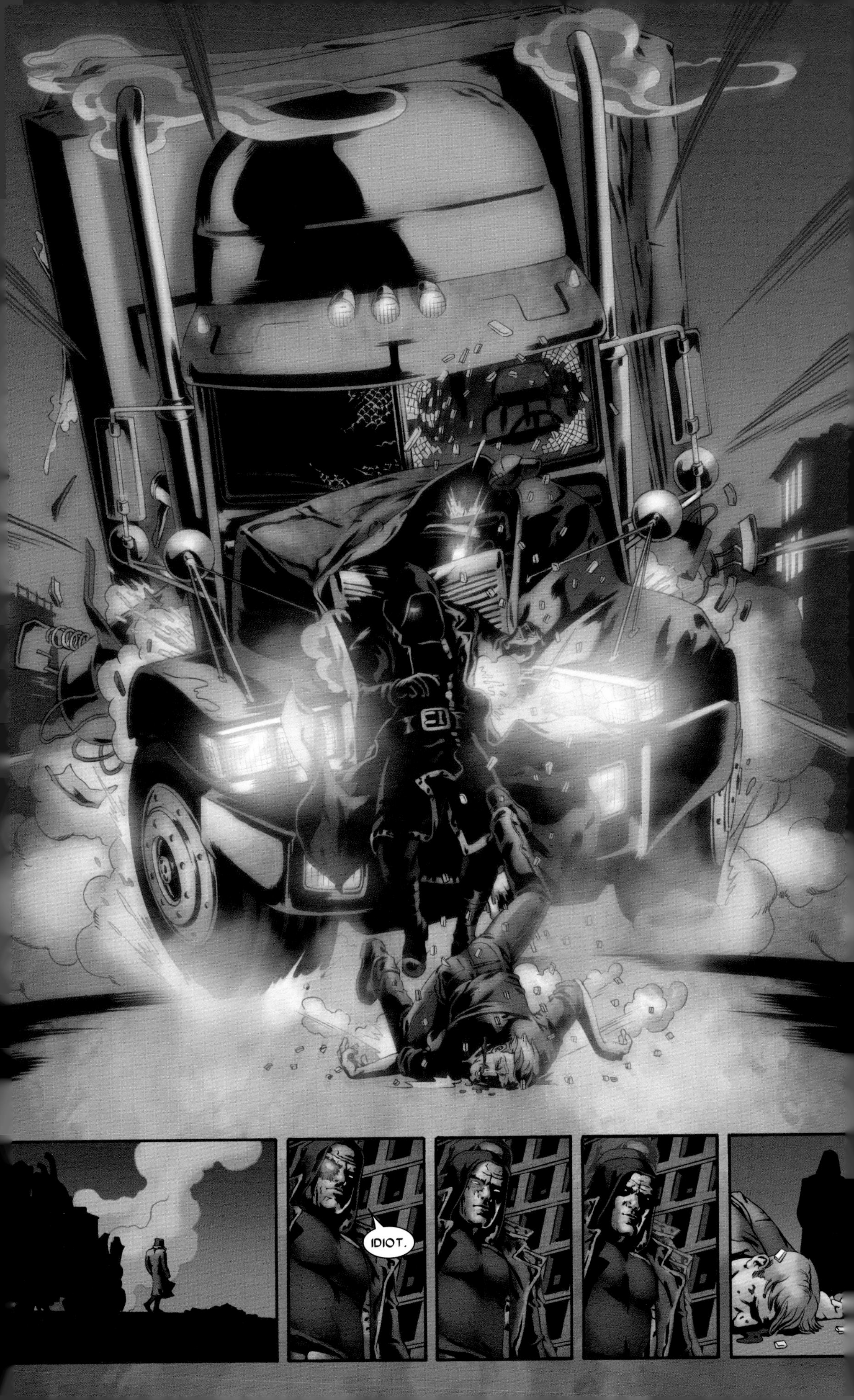
IDIOT.

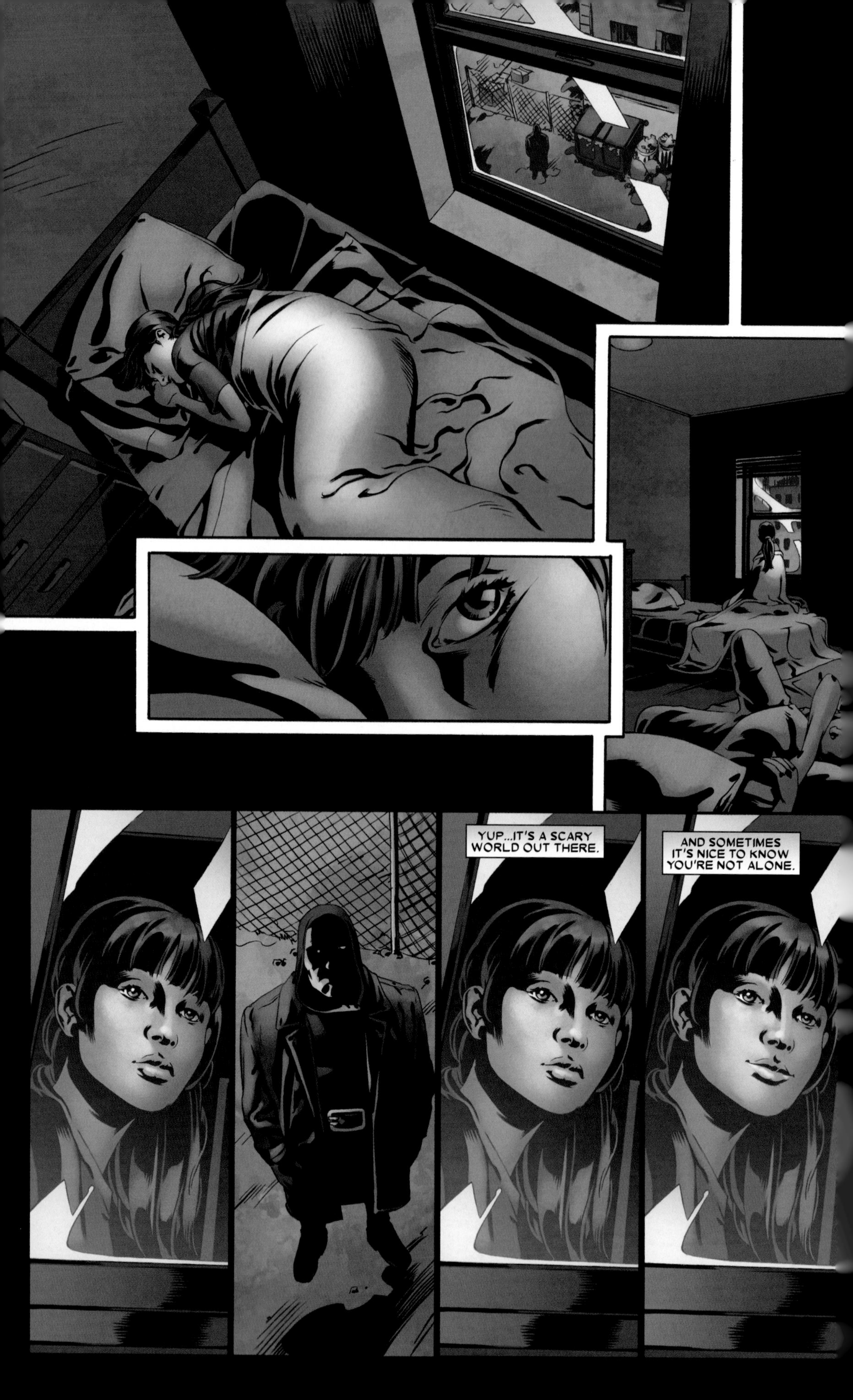
YUP...IT'S A SCARY WORLD OUT THERE.
AND SOMETIMES IT'S NICE TO KNOW YOU'RE NOT ALONE.

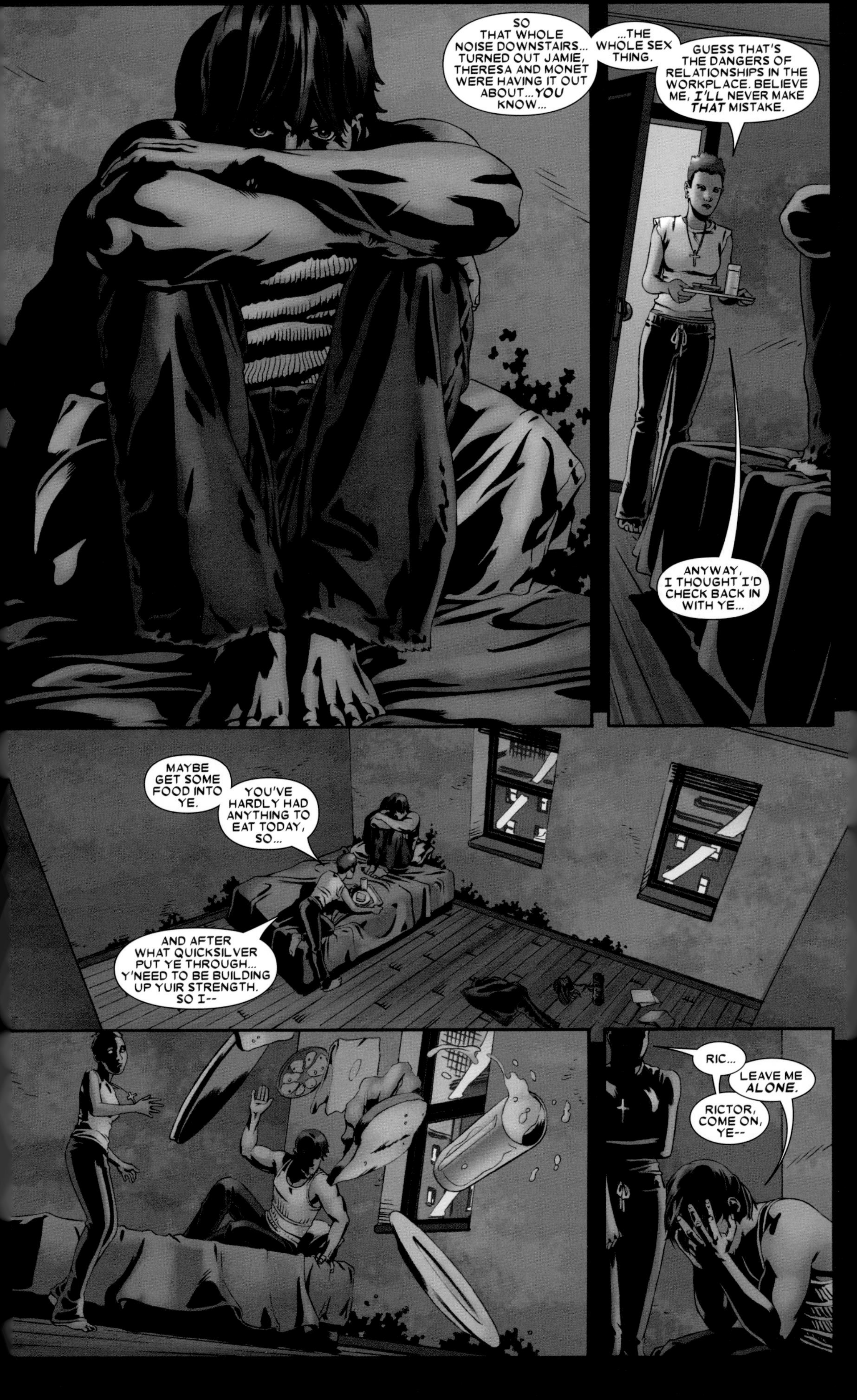
SO THAT WHOLE NOISE DOWNSTAIRS... TURNED OUT JAMIE, THERESA AND MONET WERE HAVING IT OUT ABOUT... YOU KNOW...
...THE WHOLE SEX THING.
GUESS THAT'S THE DANGERS OF RELATIONSHIPS IN THE WORKPLACE. BELIEVE ME, I'LL NEVER MAKE THAT MISTAKE.
ANYWAY, I THOUGHT I'D CHECK BACK IN WITH YE...
MAYBE GET SOME FOOD INTO YE.
YOU'VE HARDLY HAD ANYTHING TO EAT TODAY, SO...
AND AFTER WHAT QUICKSILVER PUT YE THROUGH... Y'NEED TO BE BUILDING UP YUIR STRENGTH. SO I--
RIC...
LEAVE ME ALONE.
RICTOR, COME ON, YE--

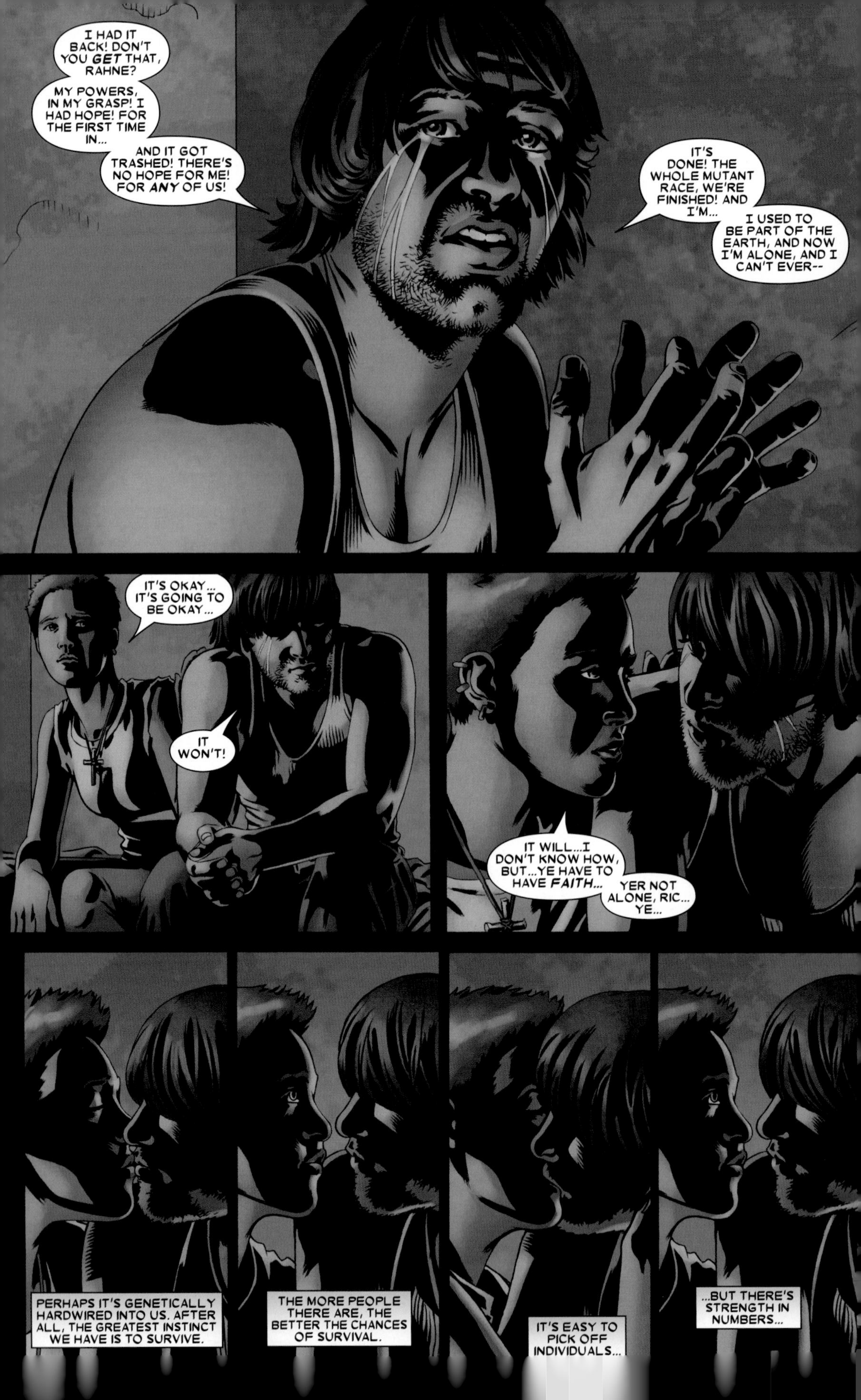
I HAD IT BACK! DON'T YOU GET THAT, RAHNE?
MY POWERS, IN MY GRASP! I HAD HOPE! FOR THE FIRST TIME IN...
AND IT GOT TRASHED! THERE'S NO HOPE FOR ME! FOR ANY OF US!
IT'S DONE! THE WHOLE MUTANT RACE, WE'RE FINISHED! AND I'M...
I USED TO BE PART OF THE EARTH, AND NOW I'M ALONE, AND I CAN'T EVER--
IT'S OKAY... IT'S GOING TO BE OKAY...
IT WON'T!
IT WILL...I DON'T KNOW HOW, BUT...YE HAVE TO HAVE FAITH...
YER NOT ALONE, RIC... YE...
PERHAPS IT'S GENETICALLY HARDWIRED INTO US. AFTER ALL, THE GREATEST INSTINCT WE HAVE IS TO SURVIVE.
THE MORE PEOPLE THERE ARE, THE BETTER THE CHANCES OF SURVIVAL.
IT'S EASY TO PICK OFF INDIVIDUALS...
...BUT THERE'S STRENGTH IN NUMBERS...

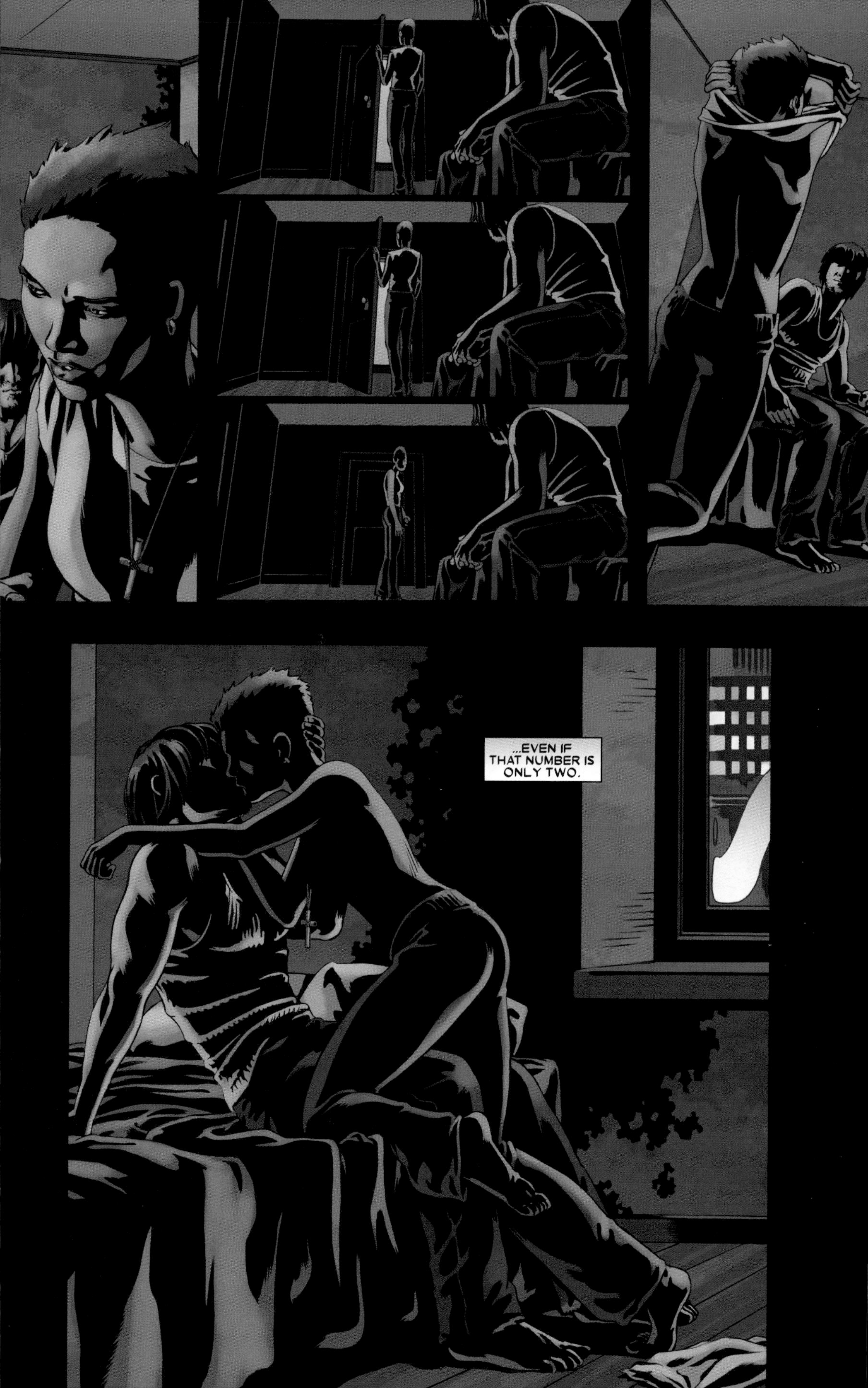
...EVEN IF THAT NUMBER IS ONLY TWO.

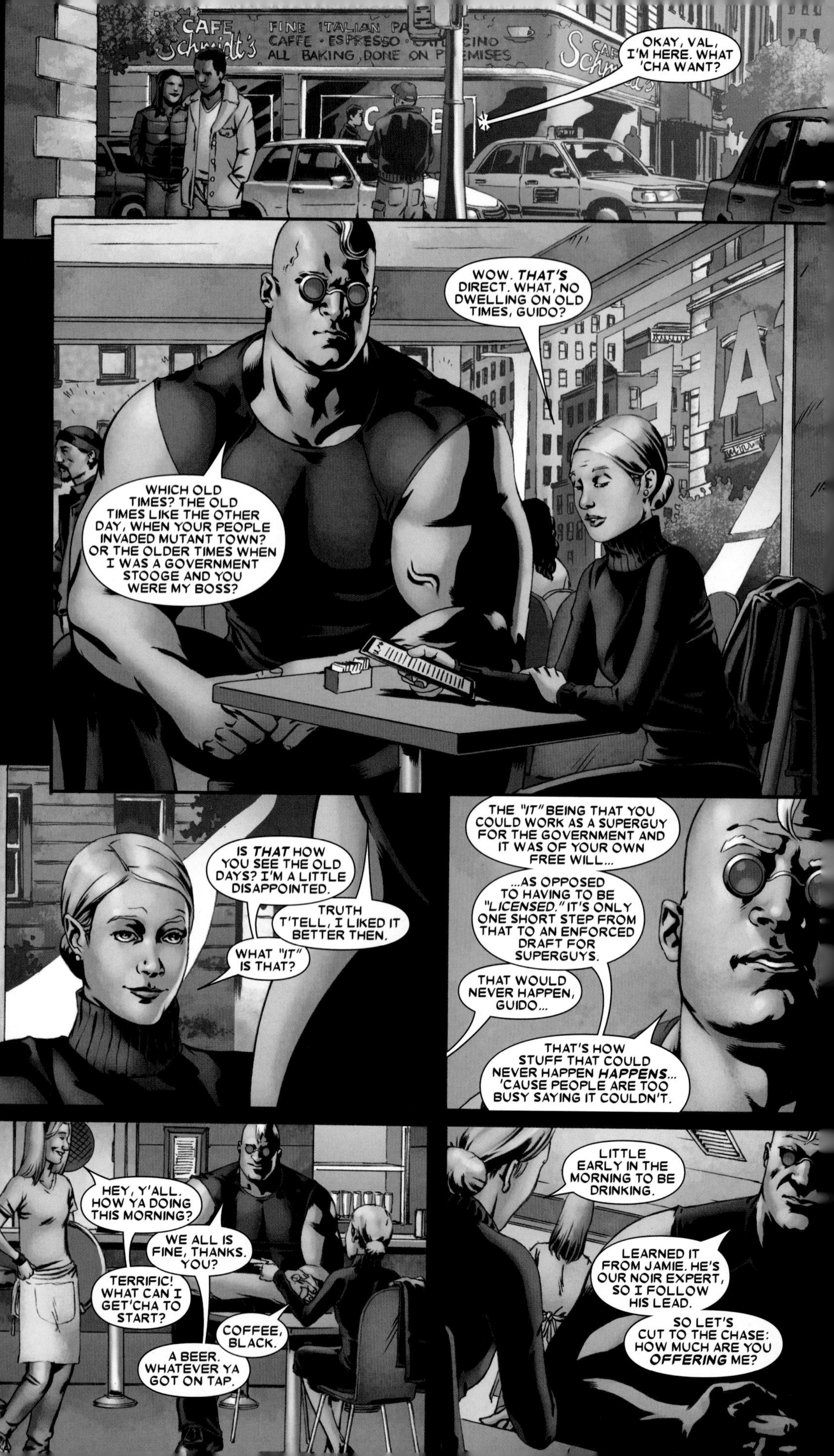
CAFE Schmidt's
FINE ITALIAN PA S
CAFFE · ESPRESSO · CINO
ALL BAKING DONE ON P EMISES
OKAY, VAL, I'M HERE. WHAT 'CHA WANT?
WOW. THAT'S DIRECT. WHAT, NO DWELLING ON OLD TIMES, GUIDO?
WHICH OLD TIMES? THE OLD TIMES LIKE THE OTHER DAY, WHEN YOUR PEOPLE INVADED MUTANT TOWN? OR THE OLDER TIMES WHEN I WAS A GOVERNMENT STOOGE AND YOU WERE MY BOSS?
IS THAT HOW YOU SEE THE OLD DAYS? I'M A LITTLE DISAPPOINTED.
TRUTH T'TELL, I LIKED IT BETTER THEN.
WHAT "IT" IS THAT?
THE "IT" BEING THAT YOU COULD WORK AS A SUPERGUY FOR THE GOVERNMENT AND IT WAS OF YOUR OWN FREE WILL...
...AS OPPOSED TO HAVING TO BE "LICENSED." IT'S ONLY ONE SHORT STEP FROM THAT TO AN ENFORCED DRAFT FOR SUPERGUYS.
THAT WOULD NEVER HAPPEN, GUIDO...
THAT'S HOW STUFF THAT COULD NEVER HAPPEN HAPPENS... 'CAUSE PEOPLE ARE TOO BUSY SAYING IT COULDN'T.
HEY, Y'ALL. HOW YA DOING THIS MORNING?
WE ALL IS FINE, THANKS. YOU?
TERRIFIC! WHAT CAN I GET'CHA TO START?
COFFEE, BLACK.
A BEER. WHATEVER YA GOT ON TAP.
LITTLE EARLY IN THE MORNING TO BE DRINKING.
LEARNED IT FROM JAMIE. HE'S OUR NOIR EXPERT, SO I FOLLOW HIS LEAD.
SO LET'S CUT TO THE CHASE: HOW MUCH ARE YOU OFFERING ME?

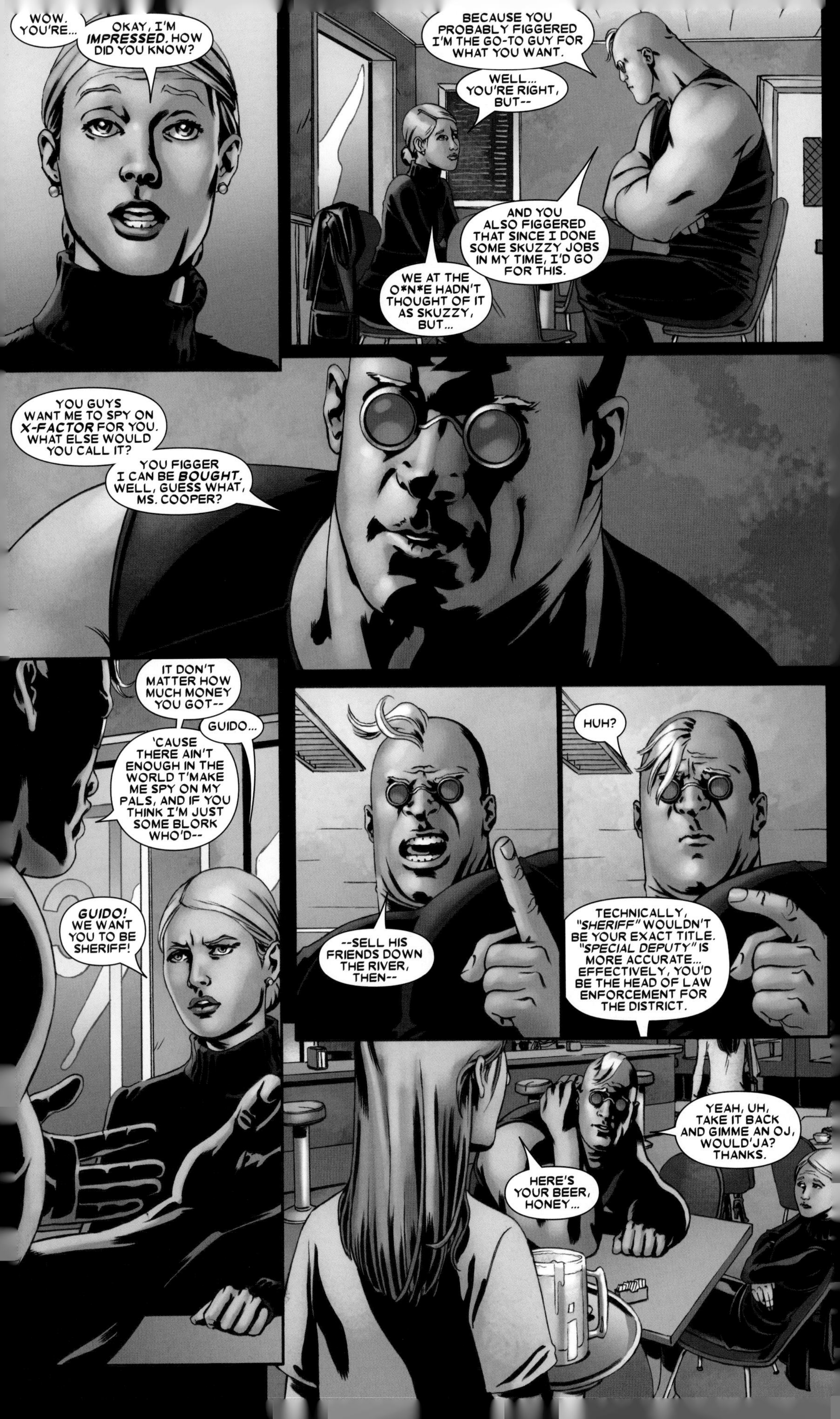
WOW. YOU'RE...
OKAY, I'M *IMPRESSED.* HOW DID YOU KNOW?
BECAUSE YOU PROBABLY FIGGERED I'M THE GO-TO GUY FOR WHAT YOU WANT.
WELL... YOU'RE RIGHT, BUT--
AND YOU ALSO FIGGERED THAT SINCE I DONE SOME SKUZZY JOBS IN MY TIME, I'D GO FOR THIS.
WE AT THE O*N*E HADN'T THOUGHT OF IT AS SKUZZY, BUT...
YOU GUYS WANT ME TO SPY ON *X-FACTOR* FOR YOU. WHAT ELSE WOULD YOU CALL IT?
YOU FIGGER I CAN BE *BOUGHT.* WELL, GUESS WHAT, MS. COOPER?
IT DON'T MATTER HOW MUCH MONEY YOU GOT--
GUIDO...
'CAUSE THERE AIN'T ENOUGH IN THE WORLD T'MAKE ME SPY ON MY PALS, AND IF YOU THINK I'M JUST SOME BLORK WHO'D--
GUIDO! WE WANT YOU TO BE SHERIFF!
--SELL HIS FRIENDS DOWN THE RIVER, THEN--
HUH?
TECHNICALLY, *"SHERIFF"* WOULDN'T BE YOUR EXACT TITLE. *"SPECIAL DEPUTY"* IS MORE ACCURATE... EFFECTIVELY, YOU'D BE THE HEAD OF LAW ENFORCEMENT FOR THE DISTRICT.
HERE'S YOUR BEER, HONEY...
YEAH, UH, TAKE IT BACK AND GIMME AN OJ, WOULD'JA? THANKS.

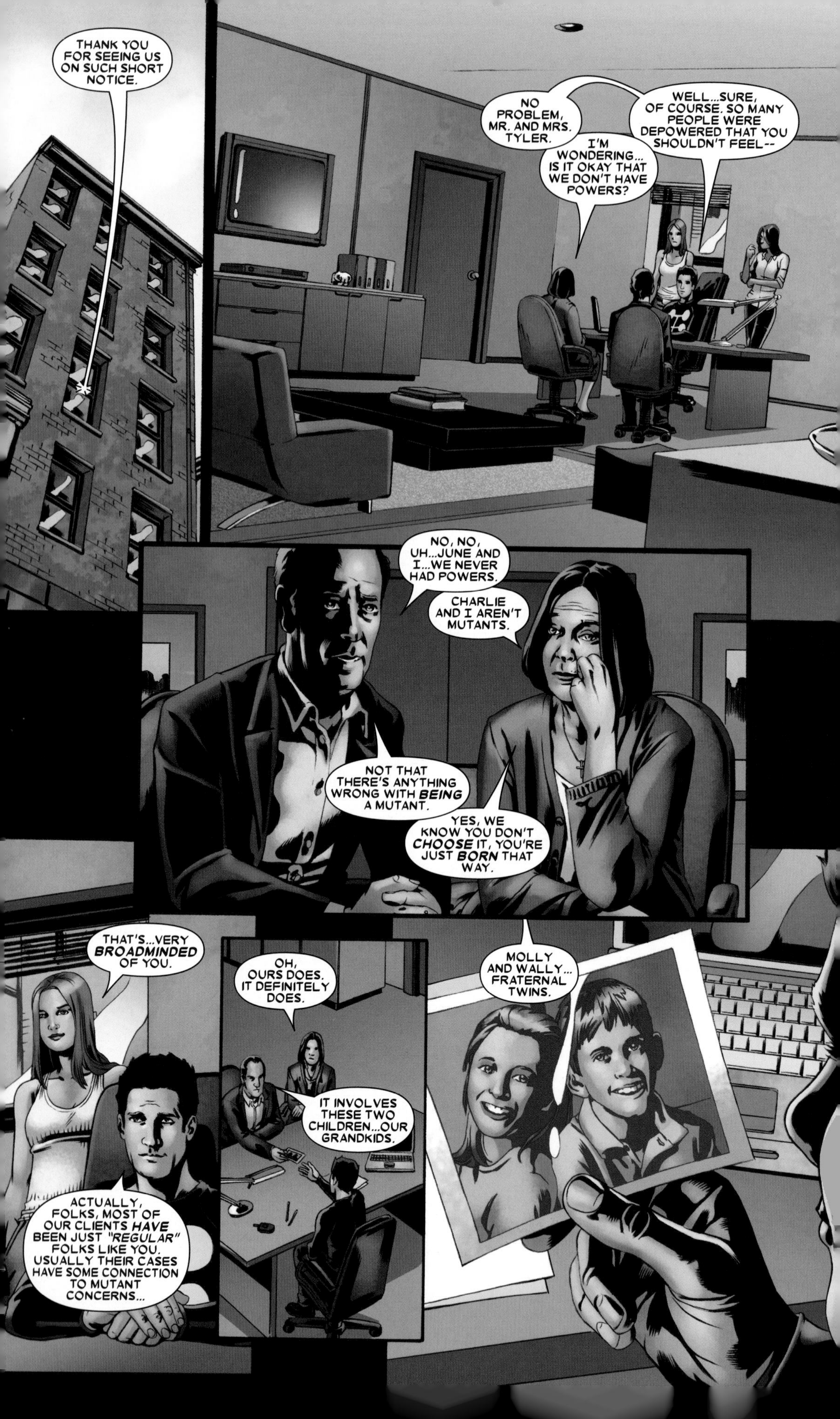
THANK YOU FOR SEEING US ON SUCH SHORT NOTICE.
NO PROBLEM, MR. AND MRS. TYLER.
WELL...SURE, OF COURSE. SO MANY PEOPLE WERE DEPOWERED THAT YOU SHOULDN'T FEEL--
I'M WONDERING... IS IT OKAY THAT WE DON'T HAVE POWERS?
NO, NO, UH...JUNE AND I...WE NEVER HAD POWERS.
CHARLIE AND I AREN'T MUTANTS.
NOT THAT THERE'S ANYTHING WRONG WITH *BEING* A MUTANT.
YES, WE KNOW YOU DON'T *CHOOSE* IT, YOU'RE JUST *BORN* THAT WAY.
THAT'S...VERY *BROADMINDED* OF YOU.
ACTUALLY, FOLKS, MOST OF OUR CLIENTS *HAVE* BEEN JUST *"REGULAR"* FOLKS LIKE YOU. USUALLY THEIR CASES HAVE SOME CONNECTION TO MUTANT CONCERNS...
OH, OURS DOES. IT DEFINITELY DOES.
IT INVOLVES THESE TWO CHILDREN...OUR GRANDKIDS.
MOLLY AND WALLY... FRATERNAL TWINS.

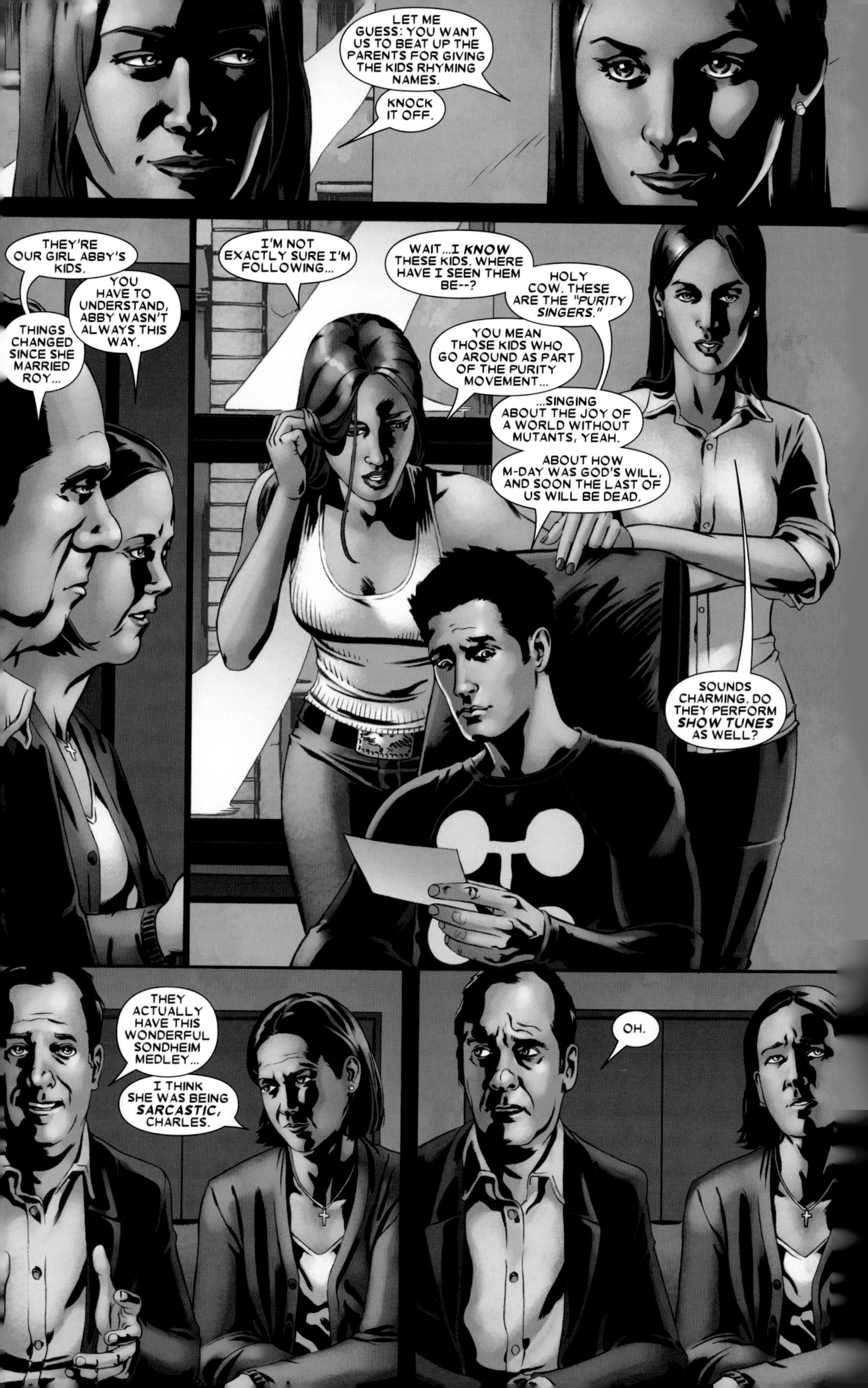
LET ME GUESS: YOU WANT US TO BEAT UP THE PARENTS FOR GIVING THE KIDS RHYMING NAMES.
KNOCK IT OFF.
THEY'RE OUR GIRL ABBY'S KIDS.
THINGS CHANGED SINCE SHE MARRIED ROY...
YOU HAVE TO UNDERSTAND, ABBY WASN'T ALWAYS THIS WAY.
I'M NOT EXACTLY SURE I'M FOLLOWING...
WAIT...I KNOW THESE KIDS. WHERE HAVE I SEEN THEM BE--?
HOLY COW. THESE ARE THE "PURITY SINGERS."
YOU MEAN THOSE KIDS WHO GO AROUND AS PART OF THE PURITY MOVEMENT...
...SINGING ABOUT THE JOY OF A WORLD WITHOUT MUTANTS, YEAH.
ABOUT HOW M-DAY WAS GOD'S WILL, AND SOON THE LAST OF US WILL BE DEAD.
SOUNDS CHARMING. DO THEY PERFORM SHOW TUNES AS WELL?
THEY ACTUALLY HAVE THIS WONDERFUL SONDHEIM MEDLEY...
I THINK SHE WAS BEING SARCASTIC, CHARLES.
OH.

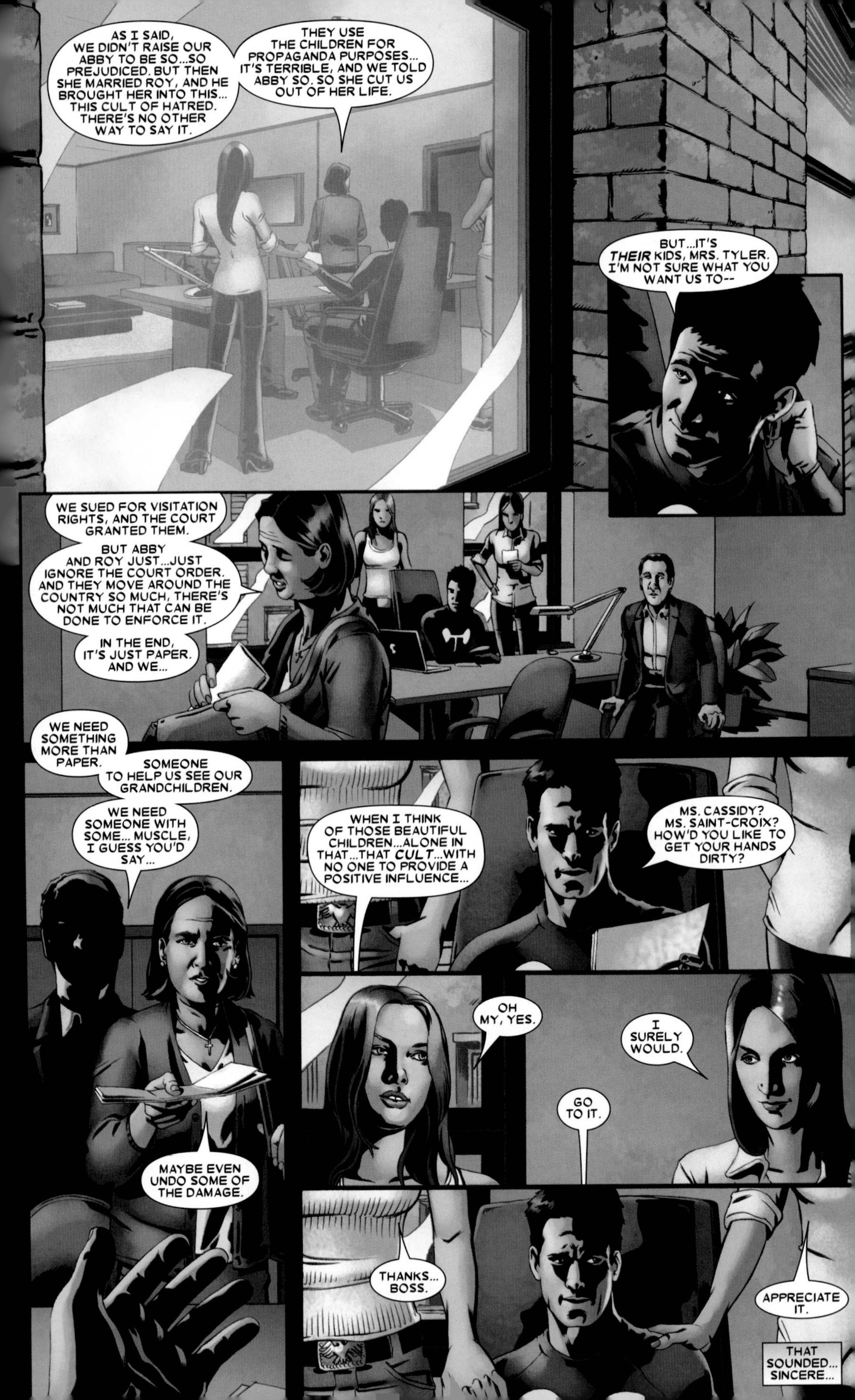
AS I SAID, WE DIDN'T RAISE OUR ABBY TO BE SO...SO PREJUDICED. BUT THEN SHE MARRIED ROY, AND HE BROUGHT HER INTO THIS... THIS CULT OF HATRED. THERE'S NO OTHER WAY TO SAY IT.
THEY USE THE CHILDREN FOR PROPAGANDA PURPOSES... IT'S TERRIBLE, AND WE TOLD ABBY SO. SO SHE CUT US OUT OF HER LIFE.
BUT...IT'S THEIR KIDS, MRS. TYLER. I'M NOT SURE WHAT YOU WANT US TO--
WE SUED FOR VISITATION RIGHTS, AND THE COURT GRANTED THEM.
BUT ABBY AND ROY JUST...JUST IGNORE THE COURT ORDER. AND THEY MOVE AROUND THE COUNTRY SO MUCH, THERE'S NOT MUCH THAT CAN BE DONE TO ENFORCE IT.
IN THE END, IT'S JUST PAPER. AND WE...
WE NEED SOMETHING MORE THAN PAPER.
SOMEONE TO HELP US SEE OUR GRANDCHILDREN.
WE NEED SOMEONE WITH SOME... MUSCLE, I GUESS YOU'D SAY...
MAYBE EVEN UNDO SOME OF THE DAMAGE.
WHEN I THINK OF THOSE BEAUTIFUL CHILDREN...ALONE IN THAT...THAT CULT...WITH NO ONE TO PROVIDE A POSITIVE INFLUENCE...
MS. CASSIDY? MS. SAINT-CROIX? HOW'D YOU LIKE TO GET YOUR HANDS DIRTY?
OH MY, YES.
I SURELY WOULD.
GO TO IT.
THANKS... BOSS.
APPRECIATE IT.
THAT SOUNDED... SINCERE...

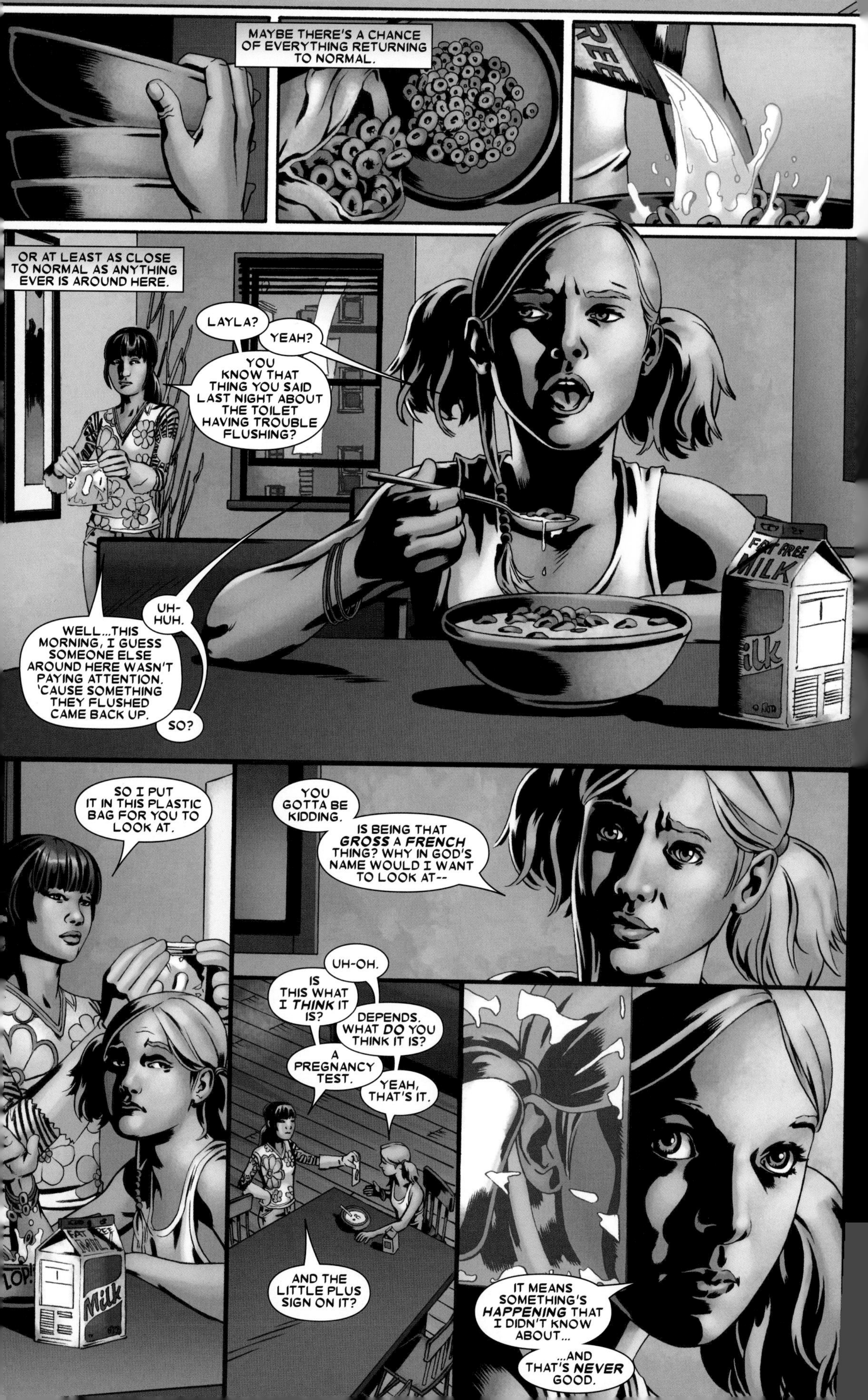

MAYBE THERE'S A CHANCE OF EVERYTHING RETURNING TO NORMAL.
OR AT LEAST AS CLOSE TO NORMAL AS ANYTHING EVER IS AROUND HERE.
LAYLA?
YEAH?
YOU KNOW THAT THING YOU SAID LAST NIGHT ABOUT THE TOILET HAVING TROUBLE FLUSHING?
UH-HUH.
WELL...THIS MORNING, I GUESS SOMEONE ELSE AROUND HERE WASN'T PAYING ATTENTION. 'CAUSE SOMETHING THEY FLUSHED CAME BACK UP.
SO?
FAT FREE MILK
SO I PUT IT IN THIS PLASTIC BAG FOR YOU TO LOOK AT.
YOU GOTTA BE KIDDING.
IS BEING THAT GROSS A FRENCH THING? WHY IN GOD'S NAME WOULD I WANT TO LOOK AT--
UH-OH.
IS THIS WHAT I THINK IT IS?
DEPENDS. WHAT DO YOU THINK IT IS?
A PREGNANCY TEST.
YEAH, THAT'S IT.
AND THE LITTLE PLUS SIGN ON IT?
IT MEANS SOMETHING'S HAPPENING THAT I DIDN'T KNOW ABOUT...
...AND THAT'S NEVER GOOD.

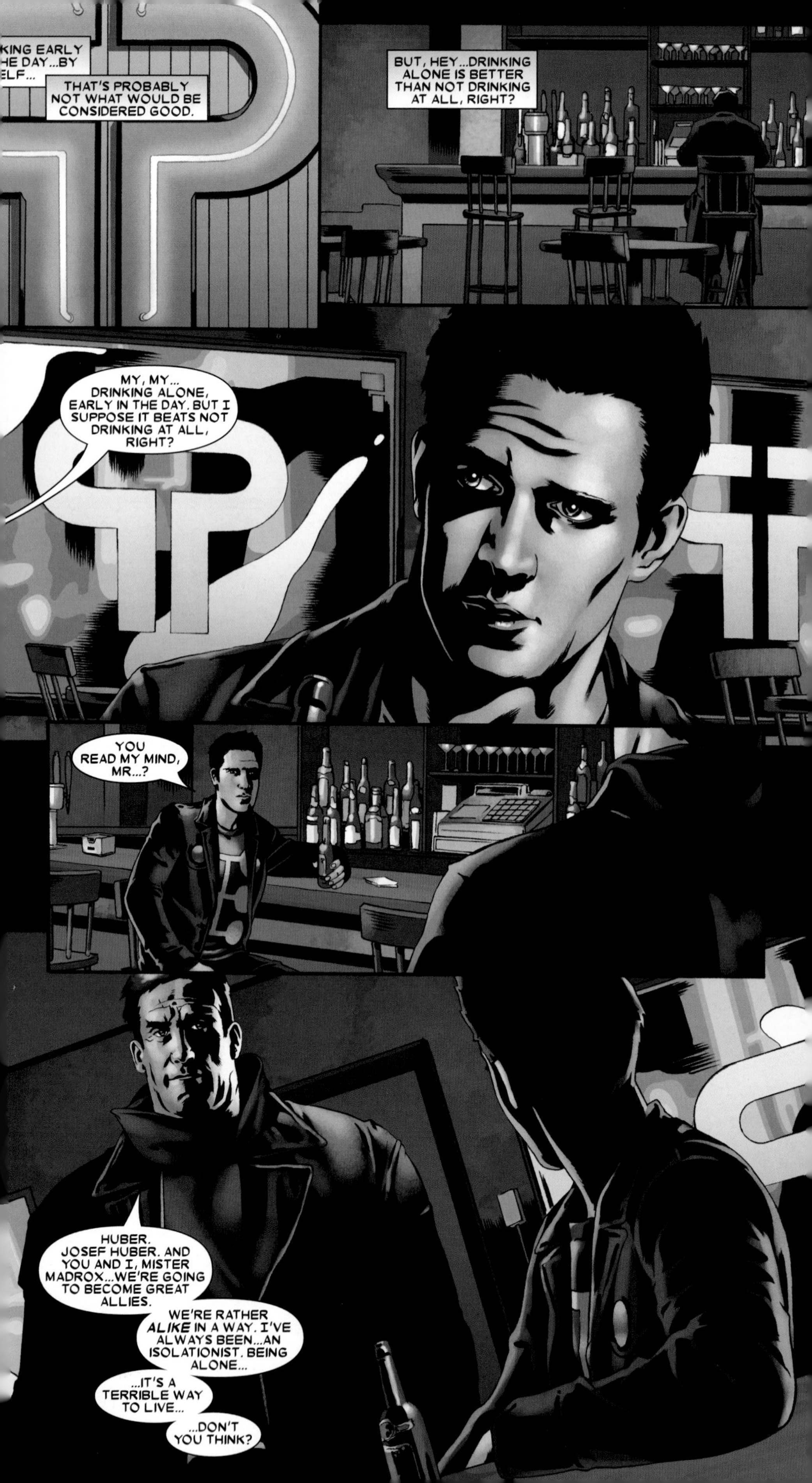

KING EARLY
HE DAY...BY
ELF...
THAT'S PROBABLY NOT WHAT WOULD BE CONSIDERED GOOD.
BUT, HEY...DRINKING ALONE IS BETTER THAN NOT DRINKING AT ALL, RIGHT?
MY, MY... DRINKING ALONE, EARLY IN THE DAY. BUT I SUPPOSE IT BEATS NOT DRINKING AT ALL, RIGHT?
YOU READ MY MIND, MR...?
HUBER. JOSEF HUBER. AND YOU AND I, MISTER MADROX...WE'RE GOING TO BECOME GREAT ALLIES.
WE'RE RATHER *ALIKE* IN A WAY. I'VE ALWAYS BEEN...AN ISOLATIONIST. BEING ALONE...
...IT'S A TERRIBLE WAY TO LIVE...
...DON'T YOU THINK?

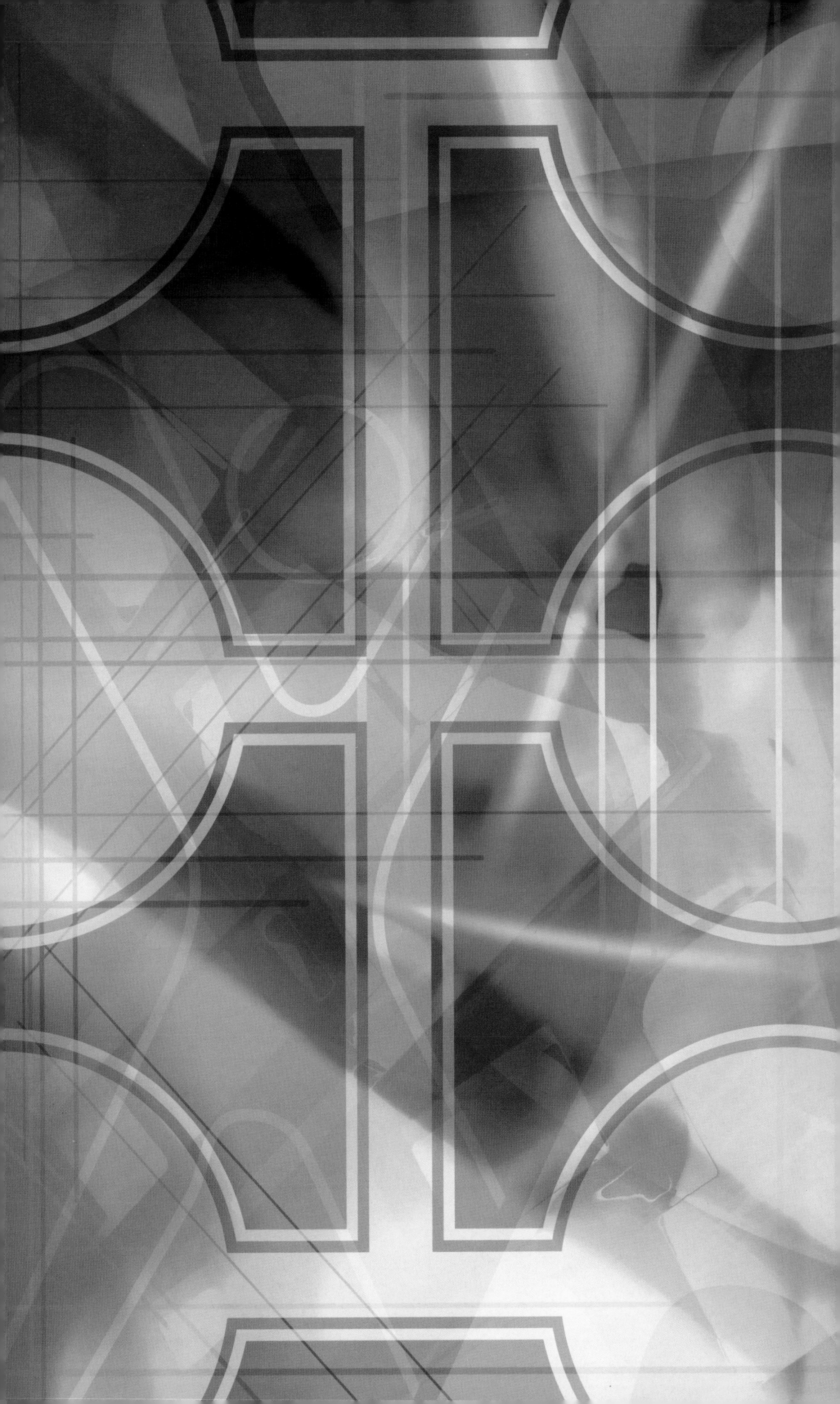

#22

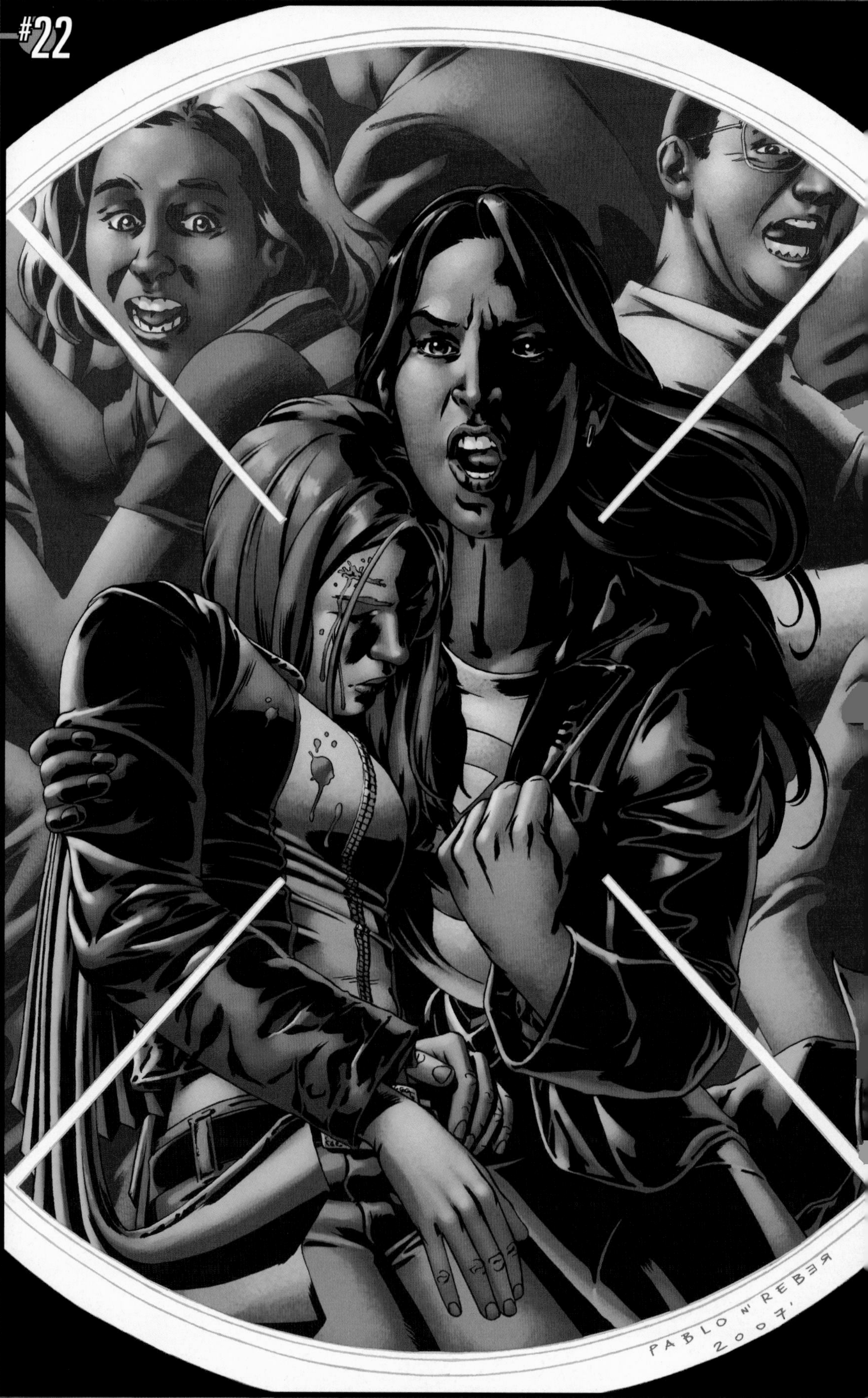

PABLO N' REBER
2007

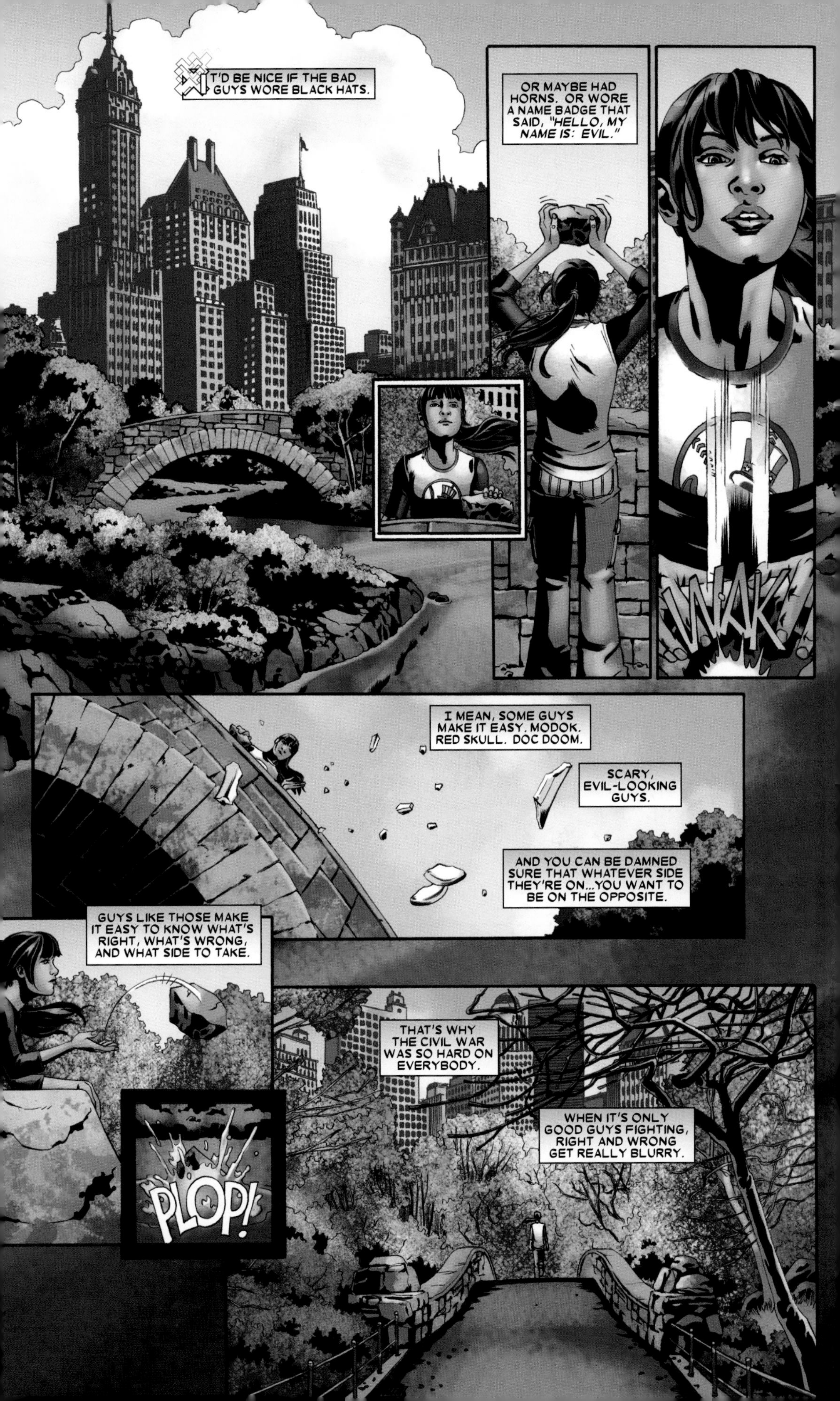
IT'D BE NICE IF THE BAD GUYS WORE BLACK HATS.
OR MAYBE HAD HORNS. OR WORE A NAME BADGE THAT SAID, "HELLO, MY NAME IS: EVIL."
WAK!
I MEAN, SOME GUYS MAKE IT EASY. MODOK. RED SKULL. DOC DOOM.
SCARY, EVIL-LOOKING GUYS.
AND YOU CAN BE DAMNED SURE THAT WHATEVER SIDE THEY'RE ON...YOU WANT TO BE ON THE OPPOSITE.
GUYS LIKE THOSE MAKE IT EASY TO KNOW WHAT'S RIGHT, WHAT'S WRONG, AND WHAT SIDE TO TAKE.
PLOP!
THAT'S WHY THE CIVIL WAR WAS SO HARD ON EVERYBODY.
WHEN IT'S ONLY GOOD GUYS FIGHTING, RIGHT AND WRONG GET REALLY BLURRY.

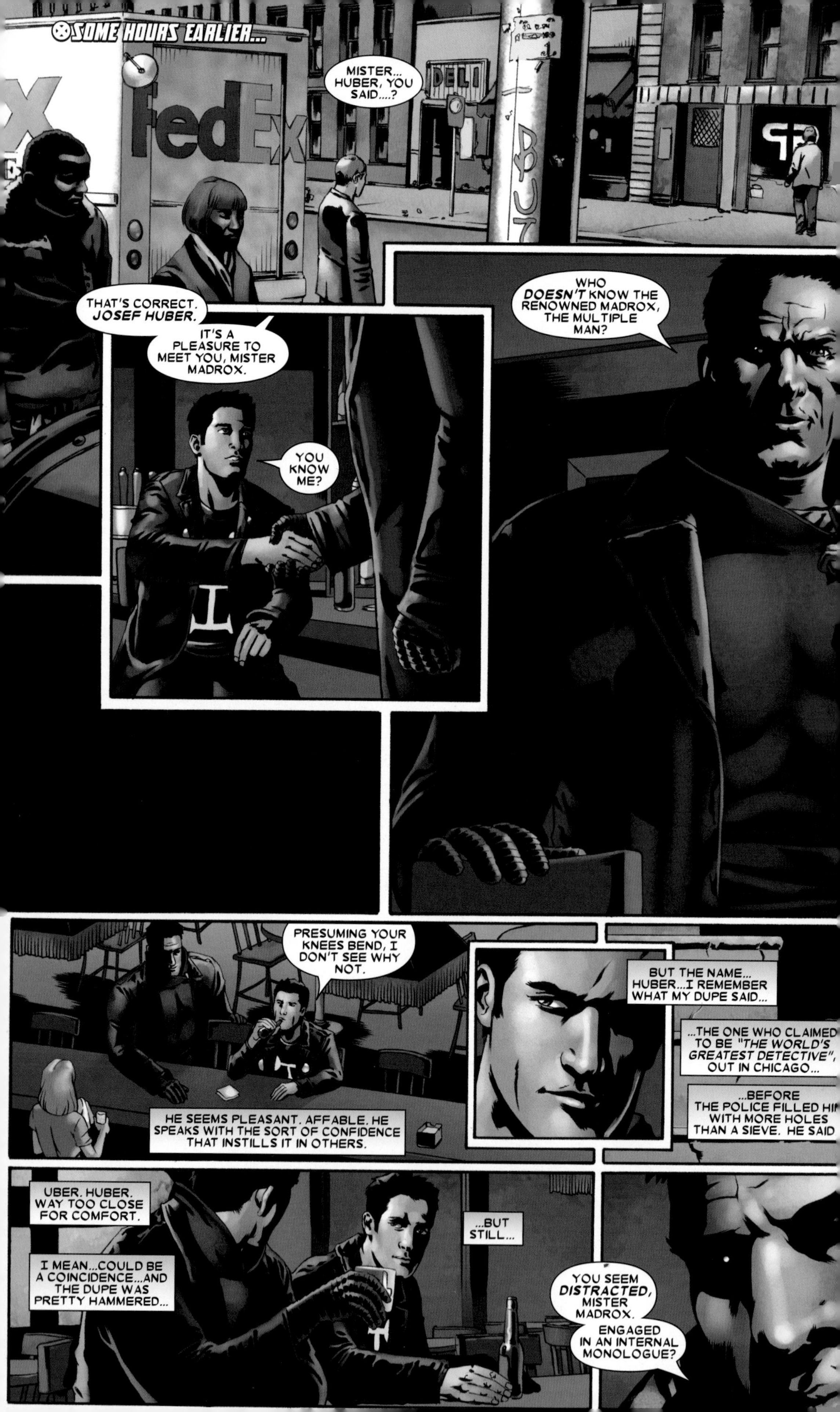
SOME HOURS EARLIER...
MISTER... HUBER, YOU SAID....?
DELI
FedEx
THAT'S CORRECT. *JOSEF HUBER.*
IT'S A PLEASURE TO MEET YOU, MISTER MADROX.
YOU KNOW ME?
WHO *DOESN'T* KNOW THE RENOWNED MADROX, THE MULTIPLE MAN?
PRESUMING YOUR KNEES BEND, I DON'T SEE WHY NOT.
HE SEEMS PLEASANT. AFFABLE. HE SPEAKS WITH THE SORT OF CONFIDENCE THAT INSTILLS IT IN OTHERS.
BUT THE NAME... HUBER...I REMEMBER WHAT MY DUPE SAID...
...THE ONE WHO CLAIMED TO BE *"THE WORLD'S GREATEST DETECTIVE"*, OUT IN CHICAGO...
...BEFORE THE POLICE FILLED HI WITH MORE HOLES THAN A SIEVE. HE SAID
UBER. HUBER. WAY TOO CLOSE FOR COMFORT.
I MEAN...COULD BE A COINCIDENCE...AND THE DUPE WAS PRETTY HAMMERED...
...BUT STILL...
YOU SEEM *DISTRACTED,* MISTER MADROX.
ENGAGED IN AN INTERNAL MONOLOGUE?

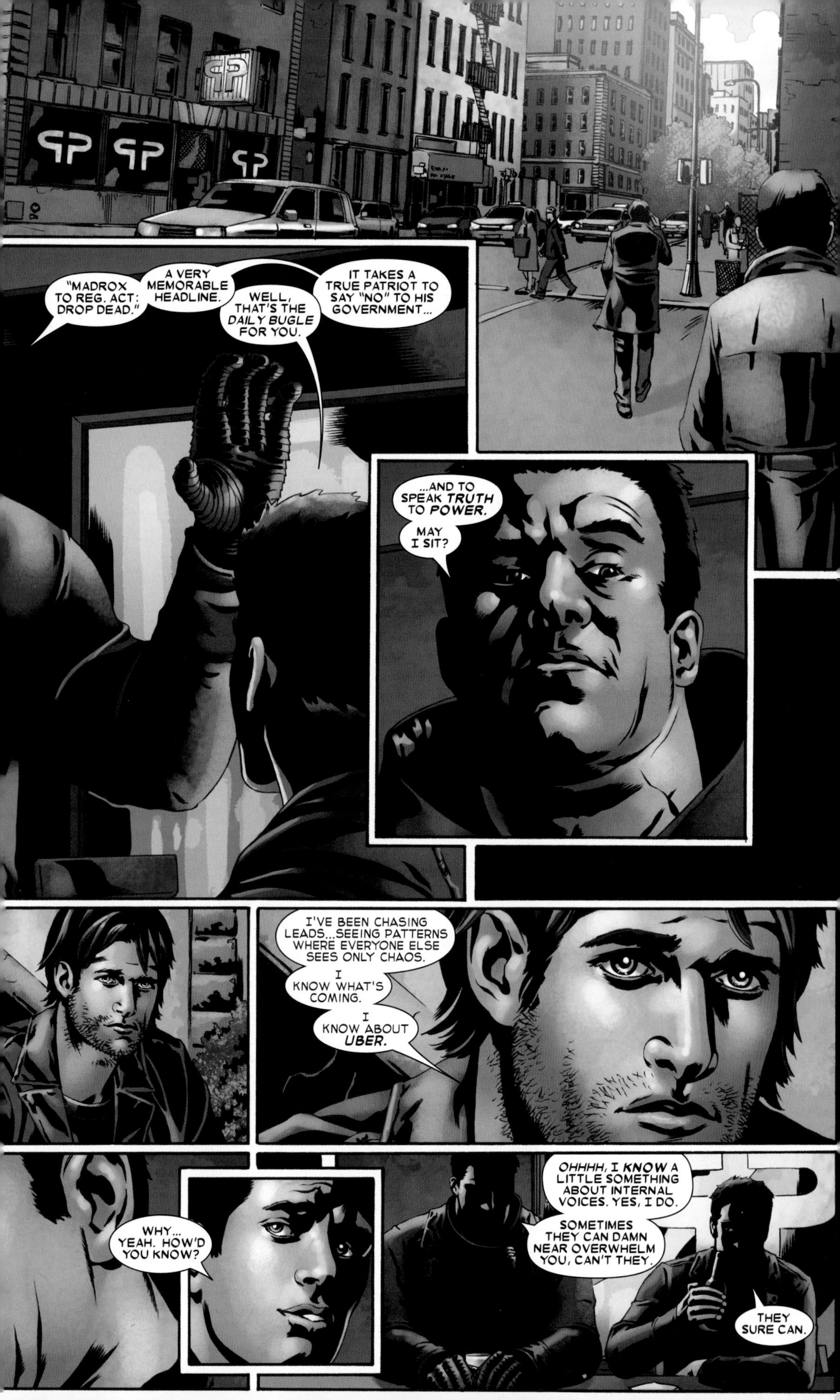
"MADROX TO REG. ACT: DROP DEAD."
A VERY MEMORABLE HEADLINE.
WELL, THAT'S THE *DAILY BUGLE* FOR YOU.
IT TAKES A TRUE PATRIOT TO SAY "NO" TO HIS GOVERNMENT...
...AND TO SPEAK *TRUTH* TO *POWER.*
MAY I SIT?
I'VE BEEN CHASING LEADS...SEEING PATTERNS WHERE EVERYONE ELSE SEES ONLY CHAOS.
I KNOW WHAT'S COMING.
I KNOW ABOUT *UBER.*
WHY... YEAH. HOW'D YOU KNOW?
OHHHH, I *KNOW* A LITTLE SOMETHING ABOUT INTERNAL VOICES. YES, I DO.
SOMETIMES THEY CAN DAMN NEAR OVERWHELM YOU, CAN'T THEY.
THEY SURE CAN.

SO, MISTER HUBER...WHAT BRINGS YOU TO OUR LITTLE SECTION OF HELL?

YOU'RE NOT EXACTLY FROM AROUND HERE, I TAKE IT?

I'M GERMAN, ACTUALLY.

BUT I AM ALSO...IN MY OWN HUMBLE WAY...RATHER INFLUENTIAL.

I HAVE A GOOD DEAL OF MONEY, MISTER MADROX. MY FAMILY IS QUITE RICH. ALWAYS HAS BEEN.

BUT I ALSO HAVE...AND THIS WILL NOT SOUND HUMBLE AT ALL...A FINELY HONED SENSE OF MORALITY. OF RIGHT AND WRONG.

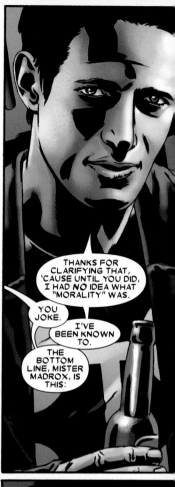

THANKS FOR CLARIFYING THAT, 'CAUSE UNTIL YOU DID, I HAD NO IDEA WHAT "MORALITY" WAS.

YOU JOKE.

I'VE BEEN KNOWN TO.

THE BOTTOM LINE, MISTER MADROX, IS THIS:

THE MUTANT POPULATION NEEDS A LOBBY.

ARE WE BUILDING A HOTEL?

MORE LIKE A FOUNDATION. MUTANTS HAVE LOST THEIR POWER... BUT THAT DOESN'T MEAN THEY CAN'T HAVE A POWER BASE.

WE ARE GOING TO MAKE THE VERY SAME GOVERNMENT THAT HAS ABANDONED YOU...BERATED YOU...INVADED YOUR PRIVACY...

WE'RE GOING TO MAKE THE GOVERNMENT MUTANTKIND'S GREATEST ALLY.

REALLY. HOW, EXACTLY?

SIMPLICITY ITSELF: THE E.S.A. OF 1973.

THAT'S...THE ENDANGERED SPECIES ACT...

THAT'S RIGHT, MISTER MADROX.

WE'RE GOING TO HAVE HOMO SUPERIOR DECLARED AN ENDANGERED SPECIES.

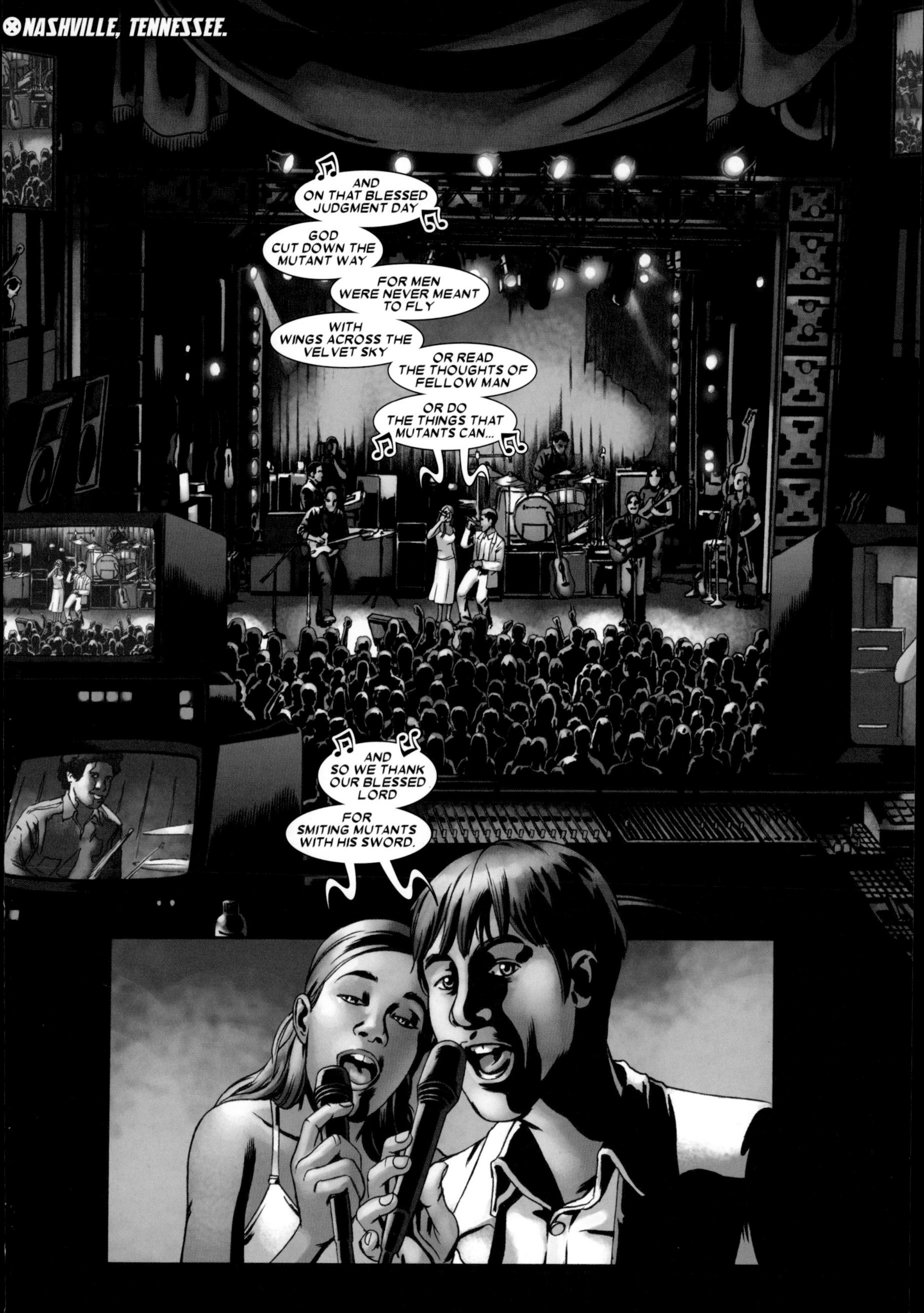
NASHVILLE, TENNESSEE.
AND ON THAT BLESSED JUDGMENT DAY
GOD CUT DOWN THE MUTANT WAY
FOR MEN WERE NEVER MEANT TO FLY
WITH WINGS ACROSS THE VELVET SKY
OR READ THE THOUGHTS OF FELLOW MAN
OR DO THE THINGS THAT MUTANTS CAN...
AND SO WE THANK OUR BLESSED LORD
FOR SMITING MUTANTS WITH HIS SWORD.

"THE ISOLATIONIST, PART II: NATURAL ORDER"

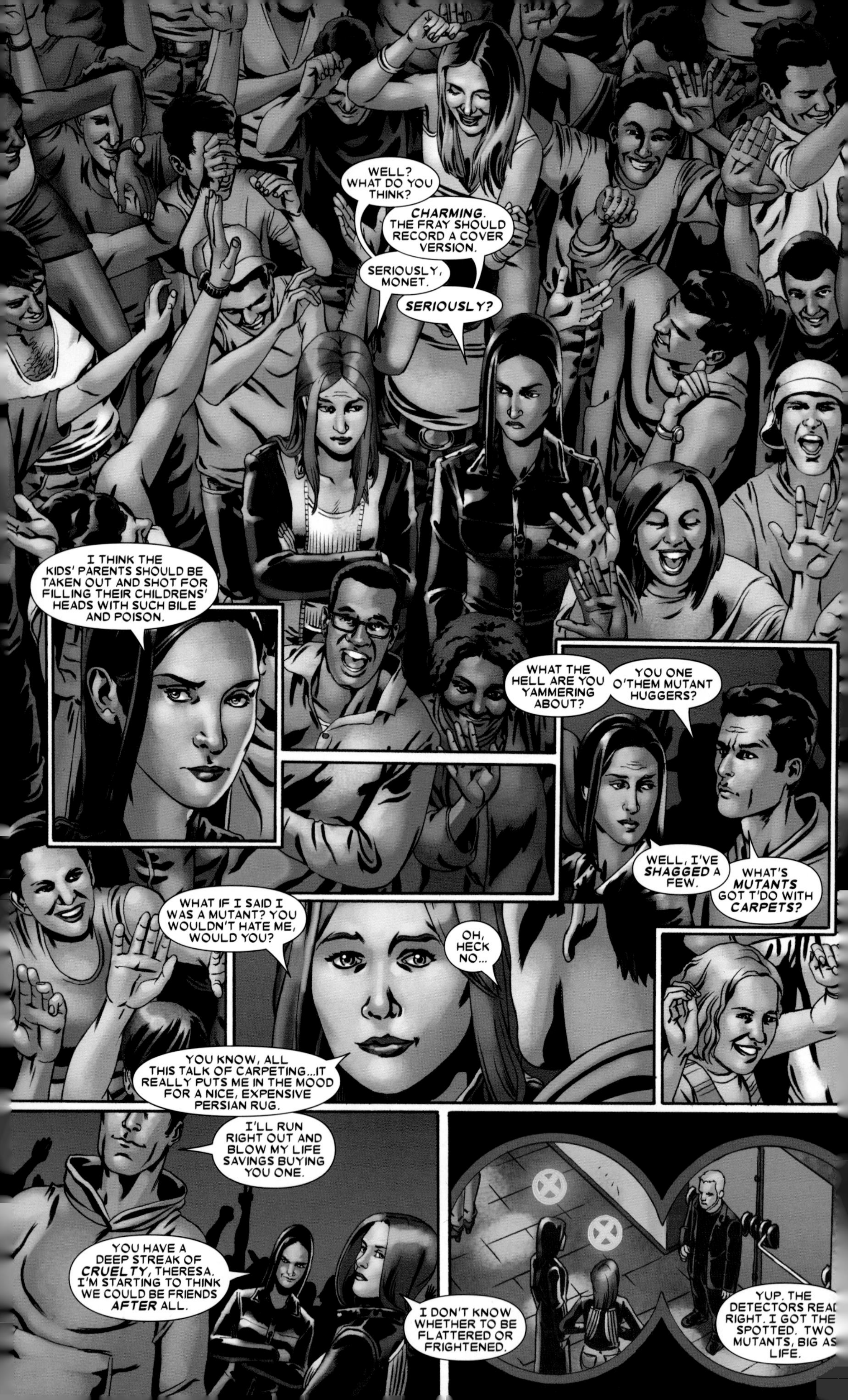

WELL? WHAT DO YOU THINK?
CHARMING. THE FRAY SHOULD RECORD A COVER VERSION.
SERIOUSLY, MONET.
SERIOUSLY?
I THINK THE KIDS' PARENTS SHOULD BE TAKEN OUT AND SHOT FOR FILLING THEIR CHILDRENS' HEADS WITH SUCH BILE AND POISON.
WHAT THE HELL ARE YOU YAMMERING ABOUT?
YOU ONE O'THEM MUTANT HUGGERS?
WELL, I'VE SHAGGED A FEW.
WHAT'S MUTANTS GOT T'DO WITH CARPETS?
WHAT IF I SAID I WAS A MUTANT? YOU WOULDN'T HATE ME, WOULD YOU?
OH, HECK NO...
YOU KNOW, ALL THIS TALK OF CARPETING...IT REALLY PUTS ME IN THE MOOD FOR A NICE, EXPENSIVE PERSIAN RUG.
I'LL RUN RIGHT OUT AND BLOW MY LIFE SAVINGS BUYING YOU ONE.
YOU HAVE A DEEP STREAK OF CRUELTY, THERESA. I'M STARTING TO THINK WE COULD BE FRIENDS AFTER ALL.
I DON'T KNOW WHETHER TO BE FLATTERED OR FRIGHTENED.
YUP. THE DETECTORS READ RIGHT. I GOT THE SPOTTED. TWO MUTANTS, BIG AS LIFE.

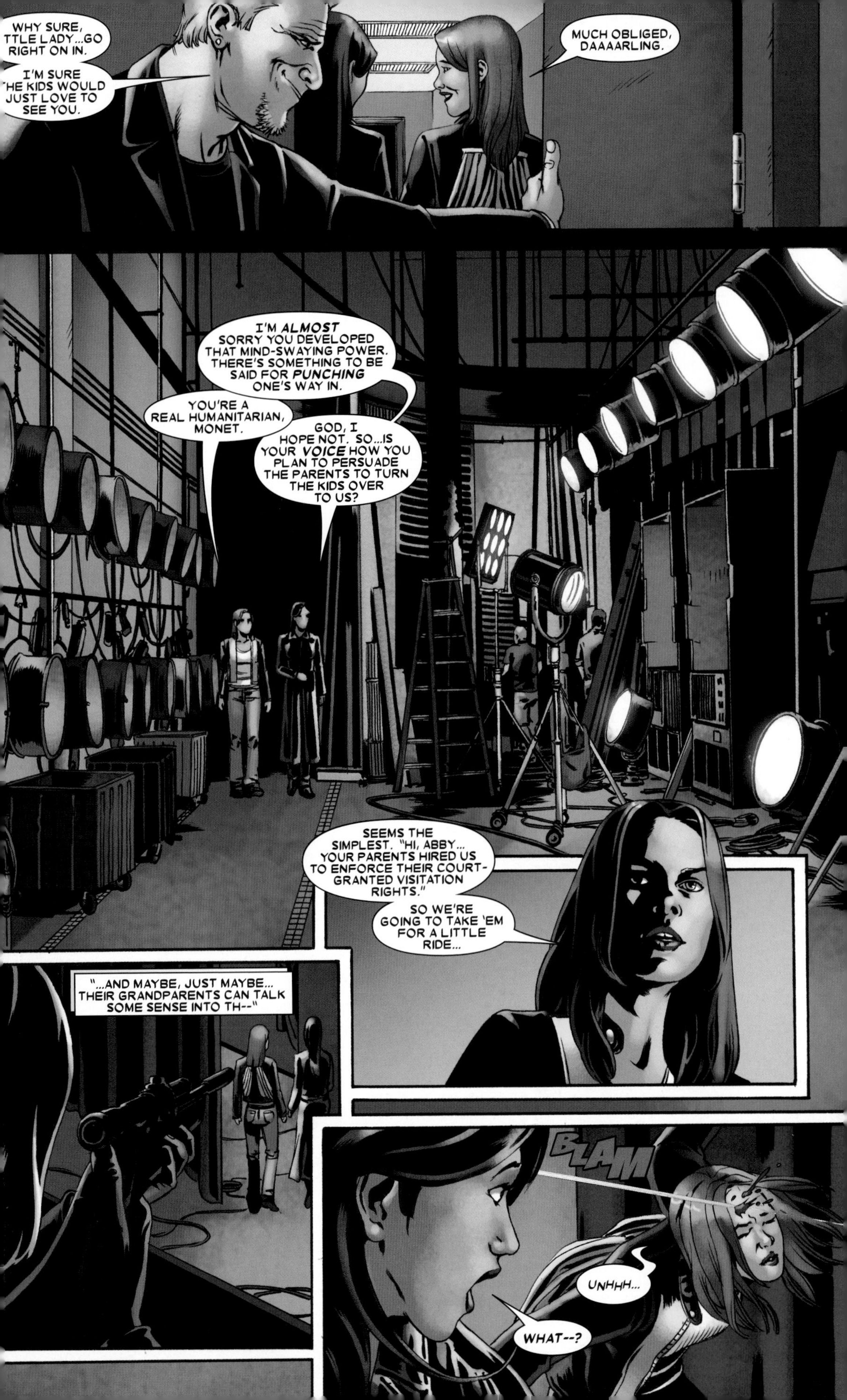

WHY SURE, TTLE LADY...GO RIGHT ON IN.
I'M SURE HE KIDS WOULD JUST LOVE TO SEE YOU.
MUCH OBLIGED, DAAAARLING.
I'M ALMOST SORRY YOU DEVELOPED THAT MIND-SWAYING POWER. THERE'S SOMETHING TO BE SAID FOR PUNCHING ONE'S WAY IN.
YOU'RE A REAL HUMANITARIAN, MONET.
GOD, I HOPE NOT. SO...IS YOUR VOICE HOW YOU PLAN TO PERSUADE THE PARENTS TO TURN THE KIDS OVER TO US?
SEEMS THE SIMPLEST. "HI, ABBY... YOUR PARENTS HIRED US TO ENFORCE THEIR COURT-GRANTED VISITATION RIGHTS."
SO WE'RE GOING TO TAKE 'EM FOR A LITTLE RIDE...
"...AND MAYBE, JUST MAYBE... THEIR GRANDPARENTS CAN TALK SOME SENSE INTO TH--"
BLAM
UNHHH...
WHAT--?

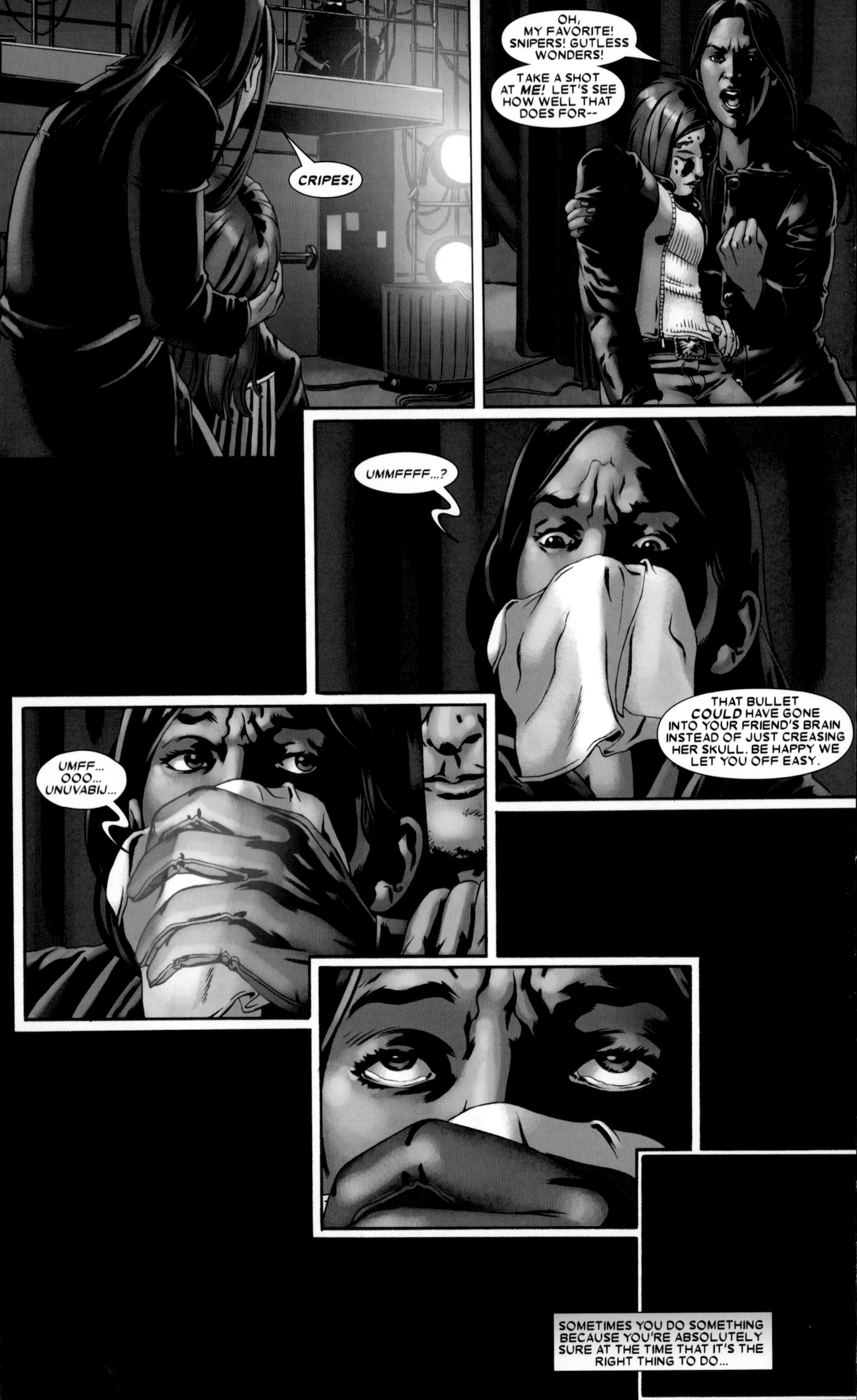
CRIPES!
OH, MY FAVORITE! SNIPERS! GUTLESS WONDERS!
TAKE A SHOT AT ME! LET'S SEE HOW WELL THAT DOES FOR--
UMMFFFF...?
THAT BULLET COULD HAVE GONE INTO YOUR FRIEND'S BRAIN INSTEAD OF JUST CREASING HER SKULL. BE HAPPY WE LET YOU OFF EASY.
UMFF... OOO... UNUVABIJ...
SOMETIMES YOU DO SOMETHING BECAUSE YOU'RE ABSOLUTELY SURE AT THE TIME THAT IT'S THE RIGHT THING TO DO...

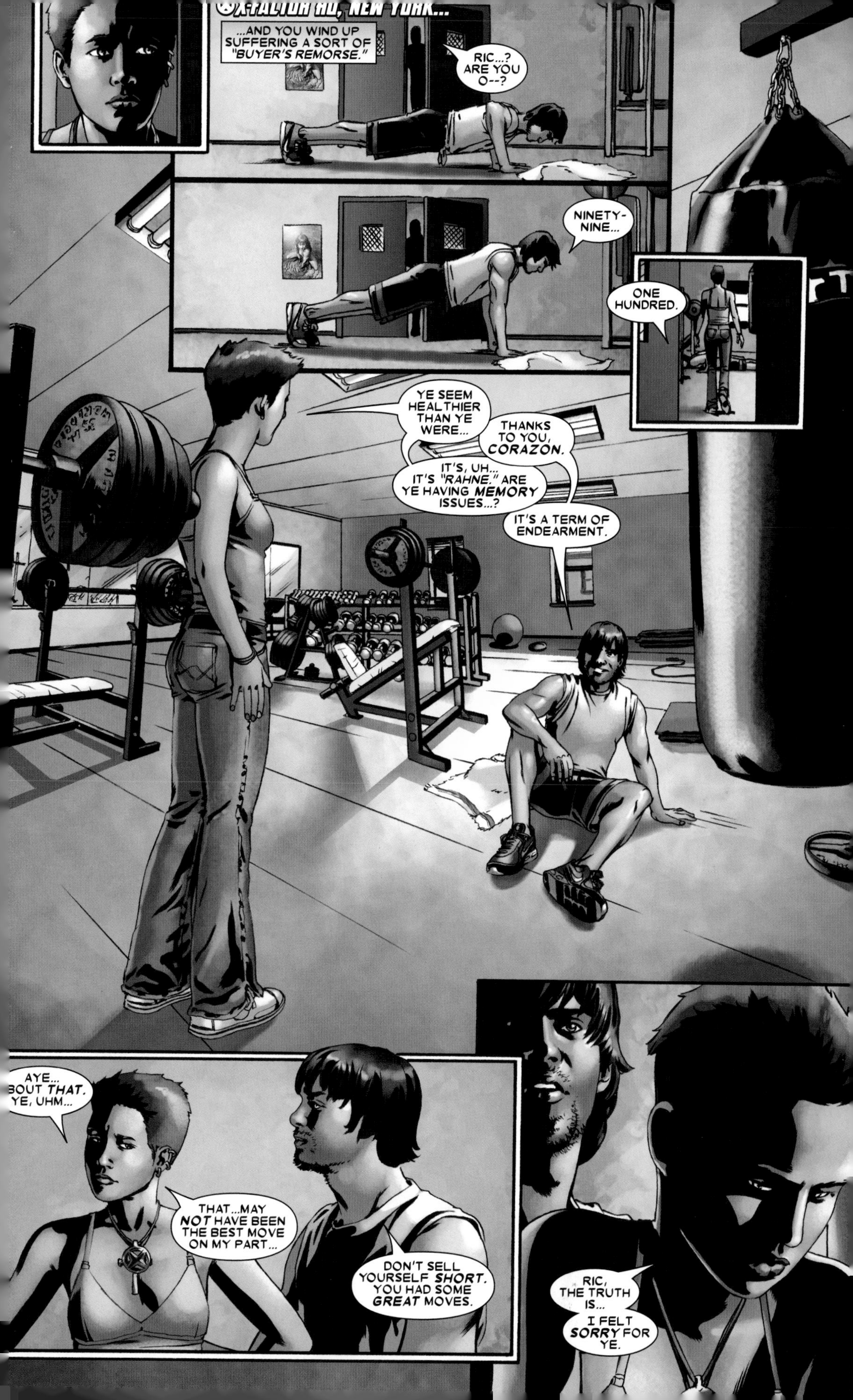
X-FACTOR HQ, NEW YORK...
...AND YOU WIND UP SUFFERING A SORT OF "BUYER'S REMORSE."
RIC...? ARE YOU O--?
NINETY-NINE...
ONE HUNDRED.
YE SEEM HEALTHIER THAN YE WERE...
THANKS TO YOU, CORAZON.
IT'S, UH... IT'S "RAHNE." ARE YE HAVING MEMORY ISSUES...?
IT'S A TERM OF ENDEARMENT.
AYE... BOUT THAT. YE, UHM...
THAT...MAY NOT HAVE BEEN THE BEST MOVE ON MY PART...
DON'T SELL YOURSELF SHORT. YOU HAD SOME GREAT MOVES.
RIC, THE TRUTH IS...
I FELT SORRY FOR YE.

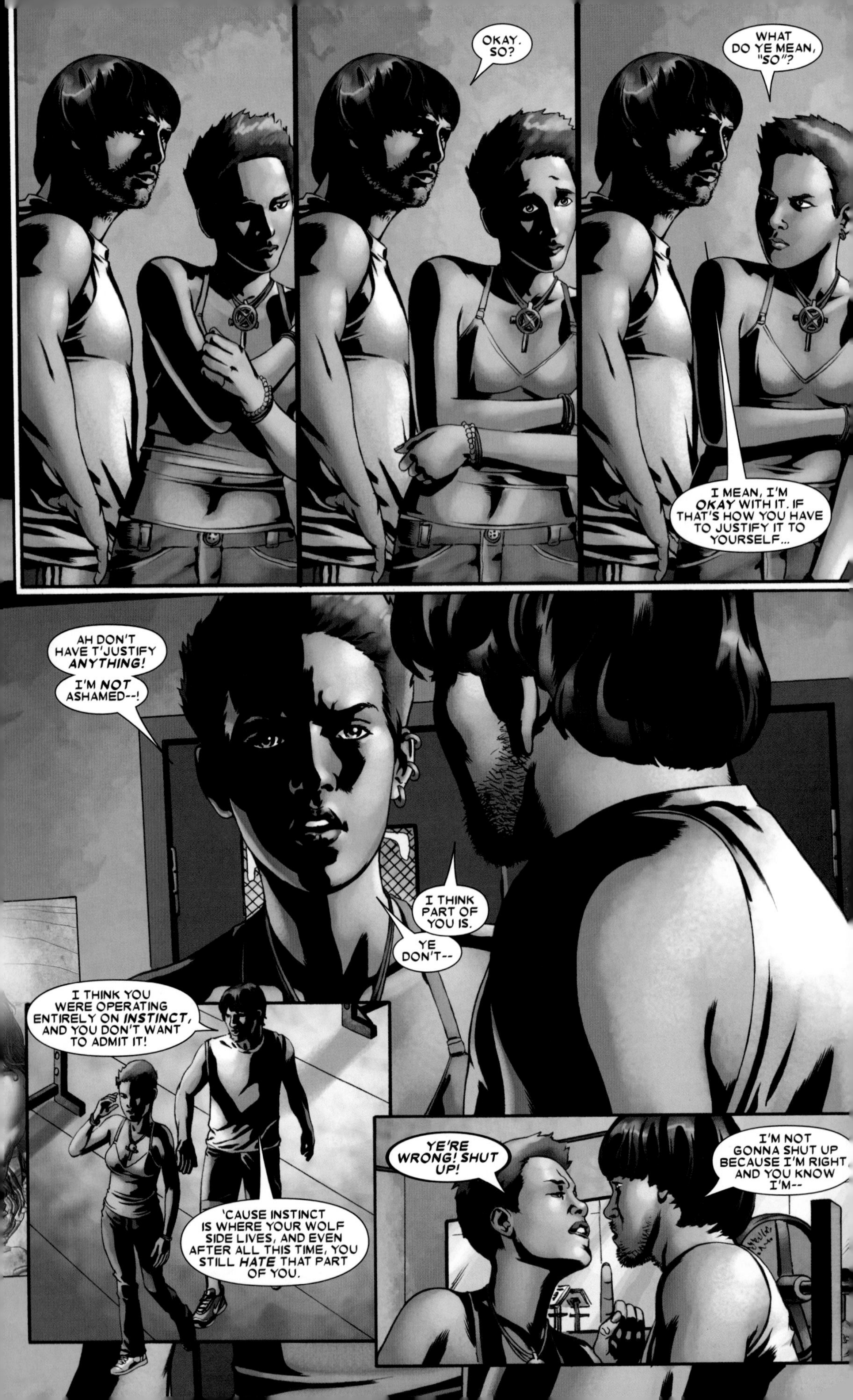
OKAY. SO?
WHAT DO YE MEAN, "SO"?
I MEAN, I'M OKAY WITH IT. IF THAT'S HOW YOU HAVE TO JUSTIFY IT TO YOURSELF...
AH DON'T HAVE T'JUSTIFY ANYTHING!
I'M NOT ASHAMED--!
I THINK PART OF YOU IS.
YE DON'T--
I THINK YOU WERE OPERATING ENTIRELY ON INSTINCT, AND YOU DON'T WANT TO ADMIT IT!
'CAUSE INSTINCT IS WHERE YOUR WOLF SIDE LIVES, AND EVEN AFTER ALL THIS TIME, YOU STILL HATE THAT PART OF YOU.
YE'RE WRONG! SHUT UP!
I'M NOT GONNA SHUT UP BECAUSE I'M RIGHT AND YOU KNOW I'M--

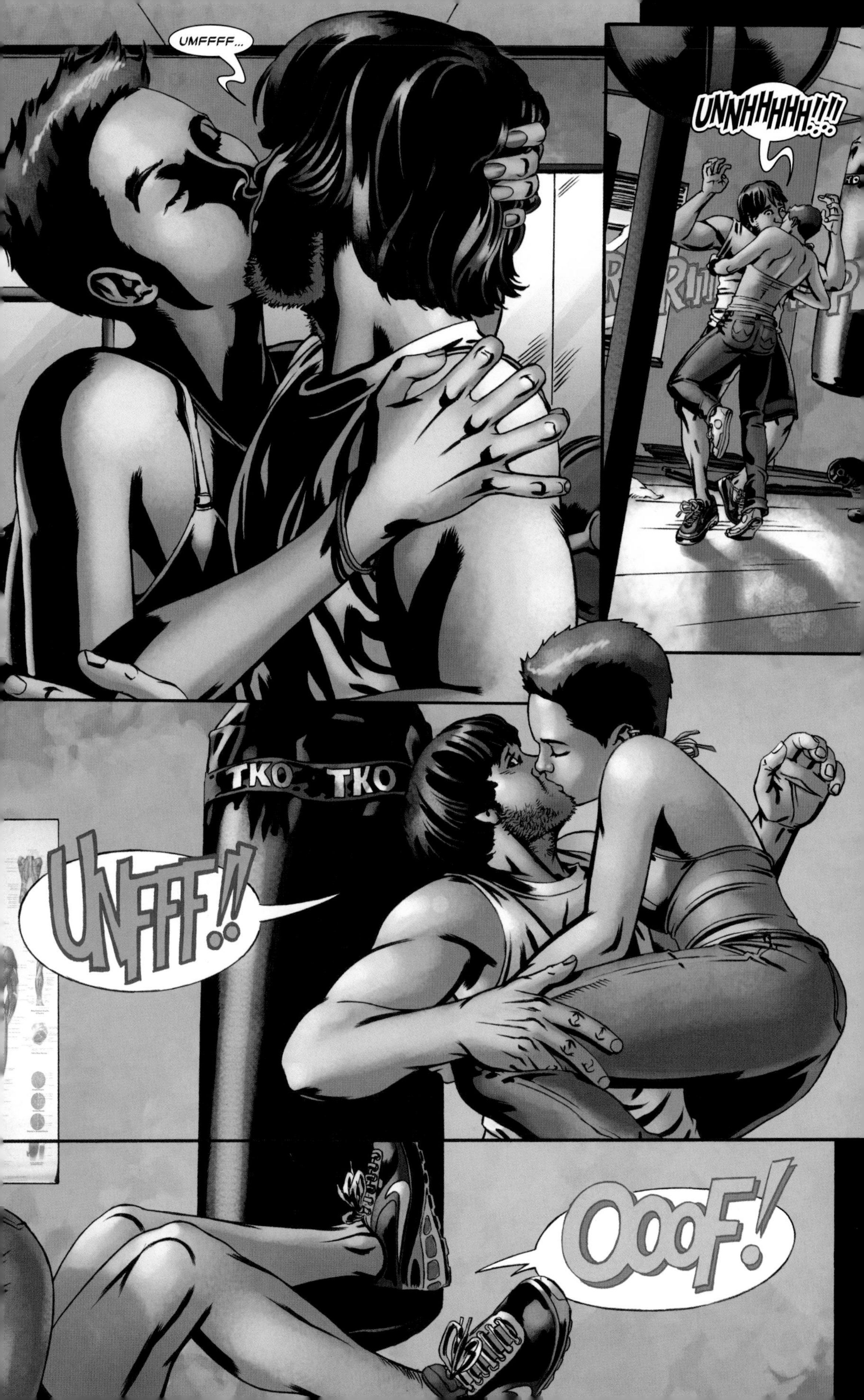
UMFFFF...
UNNHHHHH!!!!
TKO TKO
UNFFF!!
OOOF!

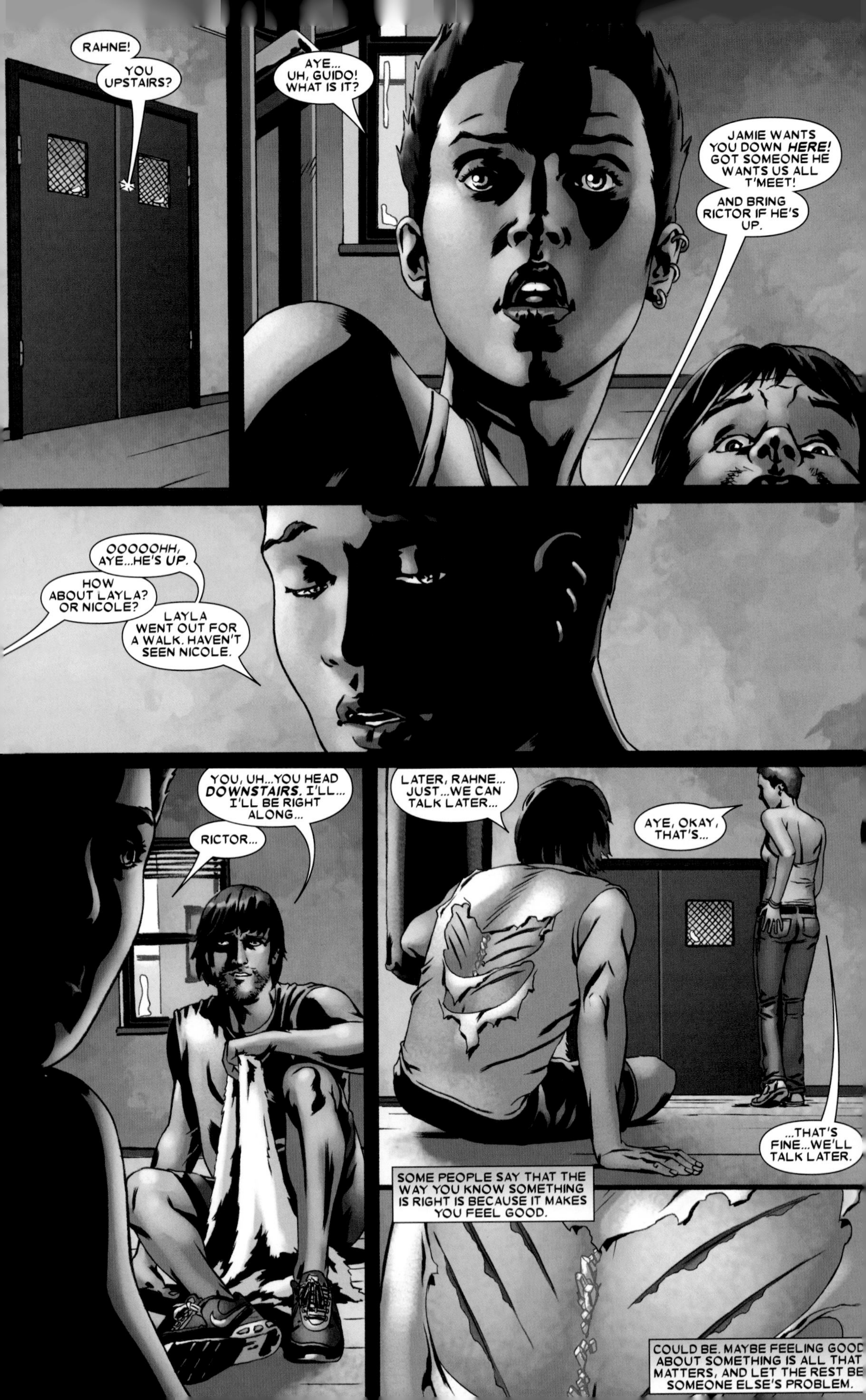
RAHNE!
YOU UPSTAIRS?
AYE... UH, GUIDO! WHAT IS IT?
JAMIE WANTS YOU DOWN HERE! GOT SOMEONE HE WANTS US ALL T'MEET!
AND BRING RICTOR IF HE'S UP.
OOOOOHH, AYE...HE'S UP.
HOW ABOUT LAYLA? OR NICOLE?
LAYLA WENT OUT FOR A WALK. HAVEN'T SEEN NICOLE.
YOU, UH...YOU HEAD DOWNSTAIRS. I'LL... I'LL BE RIGHT ALONG...
RICTOR...
LATER, RAHNE... JUST...WE CAN TALK LATER...
AYE, OKAY, THAT'S...
...THAT'S FINE...WE'LL TALK LATER.
SOME PEOPLE SAY THAT THE WAY YOU KNOW SOMETHING IS RIGHT IS BECAUSE IT MAKES YOU FEEL GOOD.
COULD BE. MAYBE FEELING GOOD ABOUT SOMETHING IS ALL THAT MATTERS, AND LET THE REST BE SOMEONE ELSE'S PROBLEM.

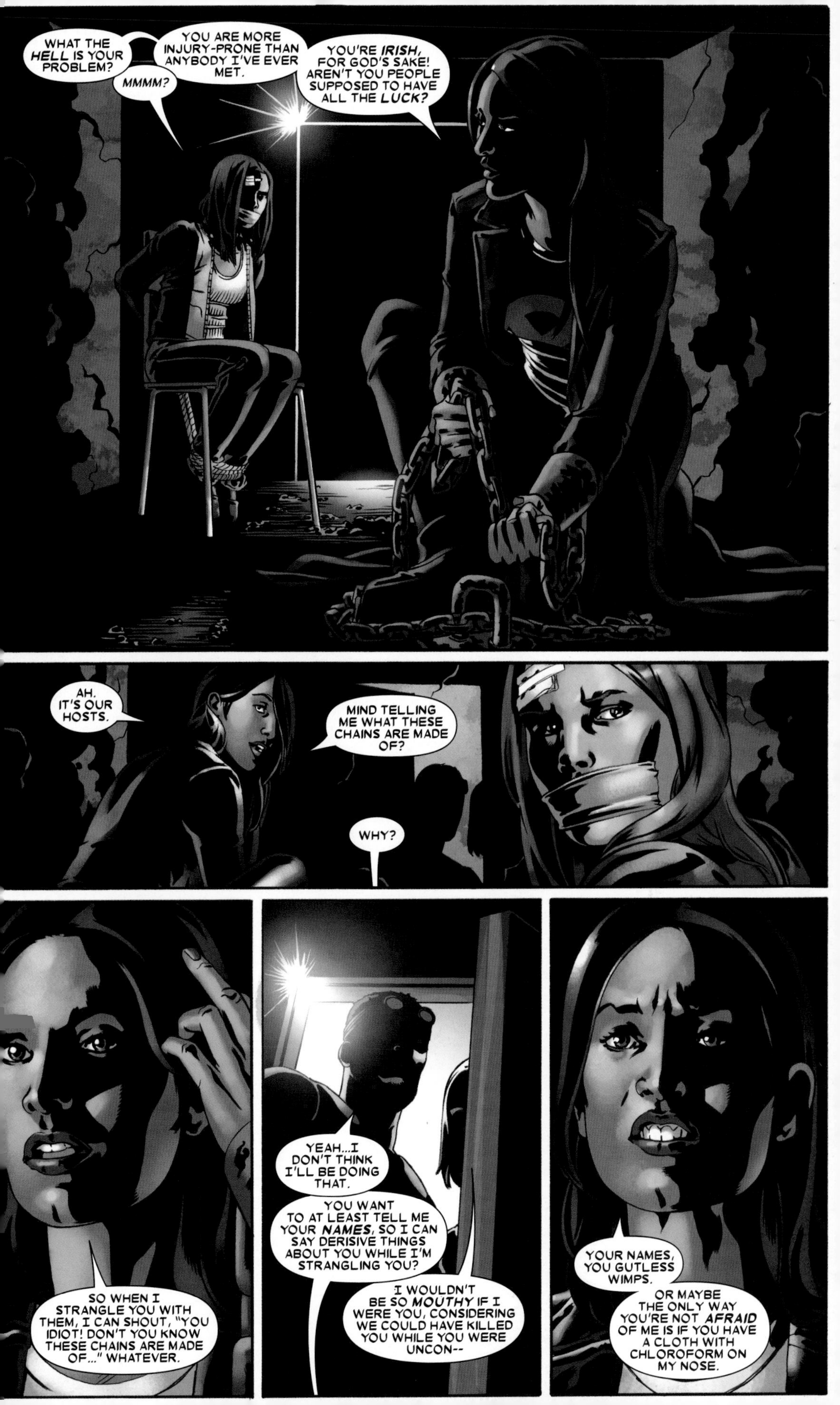

WHAT THE HELL IS YOUR PROBLEM?
YOU ARE MORE INJURY-PRONE THAN ANYBODY I'VE EVER MET.
MMMM?
YOU'RE IRISH, FOR GOD'S SAKE! AREN'T YOU PEOPLE SUPPOSED TO HAVE ALL THE LUCK?
AH. IT'S OUR HOSTS.
MIND TELLING ME WHAT THESE CHAINS ARE MADE OF?
WHY?
SO WHEN I STRANGLE YOU WITH THEM, I CAN SHOUT, "YOU IDIOT! DON'T YOU KNOW THESE CHAINS ARE MADE OF..." WHATEVER.
YEAH...I DON'T THINK I'LL BE DOING THAT.
YOU WANT TO AT LEAST TELL ME YOUR NAMES, SO I CAN SAY DERISIVE THINGS ABOUT YOU WHILE I'M STRANGLING YOU?
I WOULDN'T BE SO MOUTHY IF I WERE YOU, CONSIDERING WE COULD HAVE KILLED YOU WHILE YOU WERE UNCON--
YOUR NAMES, YOU GUTLESS WIMPS.
OR MAYBE THE ONLY WAY YOU'RE NOT AFRAID OF ME IS IF YOU HAVE A CLOTH WITH CHLOROFORM ON MY NOSE.

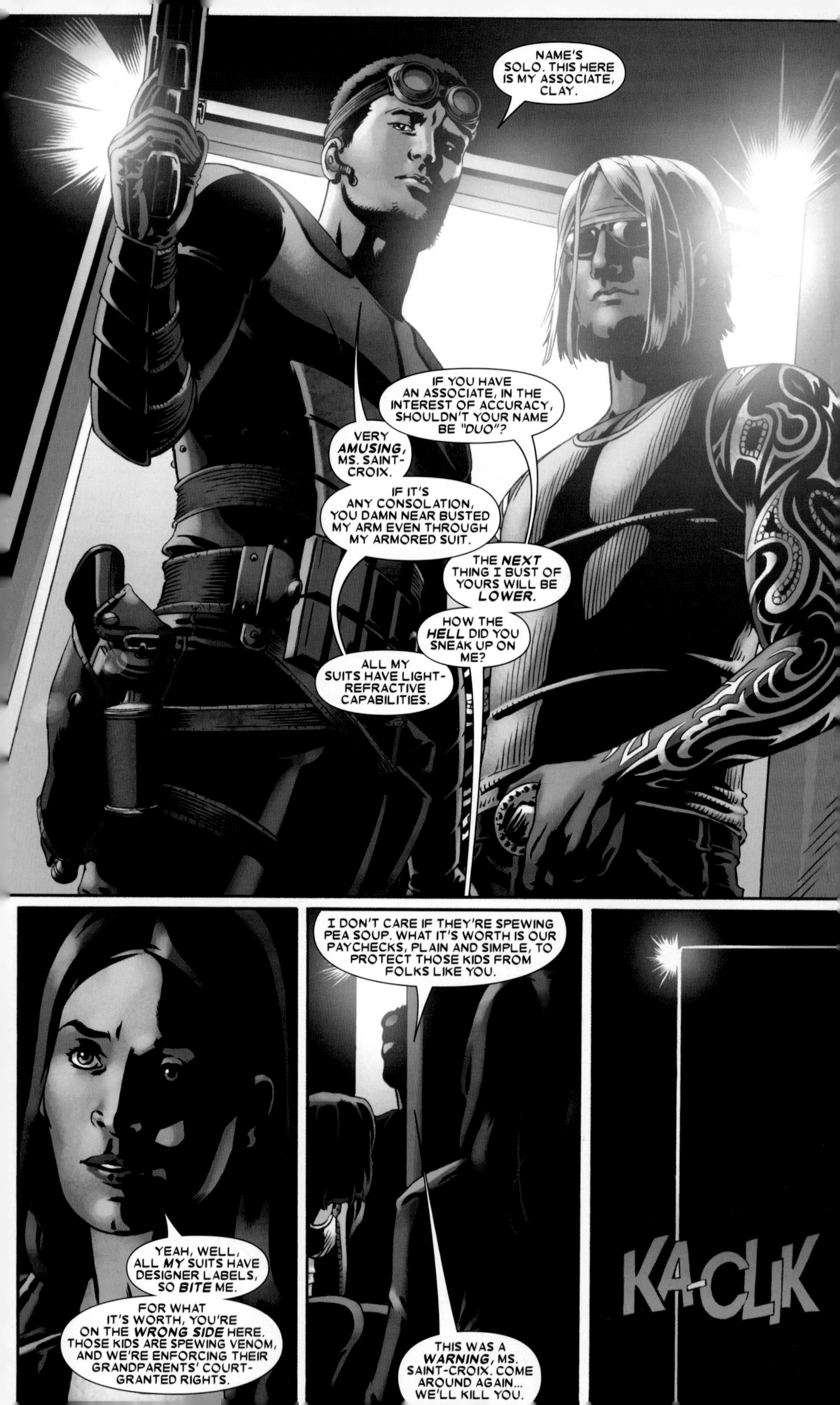
NAME'S SOLO. THIS HERE IS MY ASSOCIATE, CLAY.
IF YOU HAVE AN ASSOCIATE, IN THE INTEREST OF ACCURACY, SHOULDN'T YOUR NAME BE "DUO"?
VERY AMUSING, MS. SAINT-CROIX.
IF IT'S ANY CONSOLATION, YOU DAMN NEAR BUSTED MY ARM EVEN THROUGH MY ARMORED SUIT.
THE NEXT THING I BUST OF YOURS WILL BE LOWER.
HOW THE HELL DID YOU SNEAK UP ON ME?
ALL MY SUITS HAVE LIGHT-REFRACTIVE CAPABILITIES.
YEAH, WELL, ALL MY SUITS HAVE DESIGNER LABELS, SO BITE ME.
FOR WHAT IT'S WORTH, YOU'RE ON THE WRONG SIDE HERE. THOSE KIDS ARE SPEWING VENOM, AND WE'RE ENFORCING THEIR GRANDPARENTS' COURT-GRANTED RIGHTS.
I DON'T CARE IF THEY'RE SPEWING PEA SOUP. WHAT IT'S WORTH IS OUR PAYCHECKS, PLAIN AND SIMPLE, TO PROTECT THOSE KIDS FROM FOLKS LIKE YOU.
THIS WAS A WARNING, MS. SAINT-CROIX. COME AROUND AGAIN... WE'LL KILL YOU.
KA-CLIK

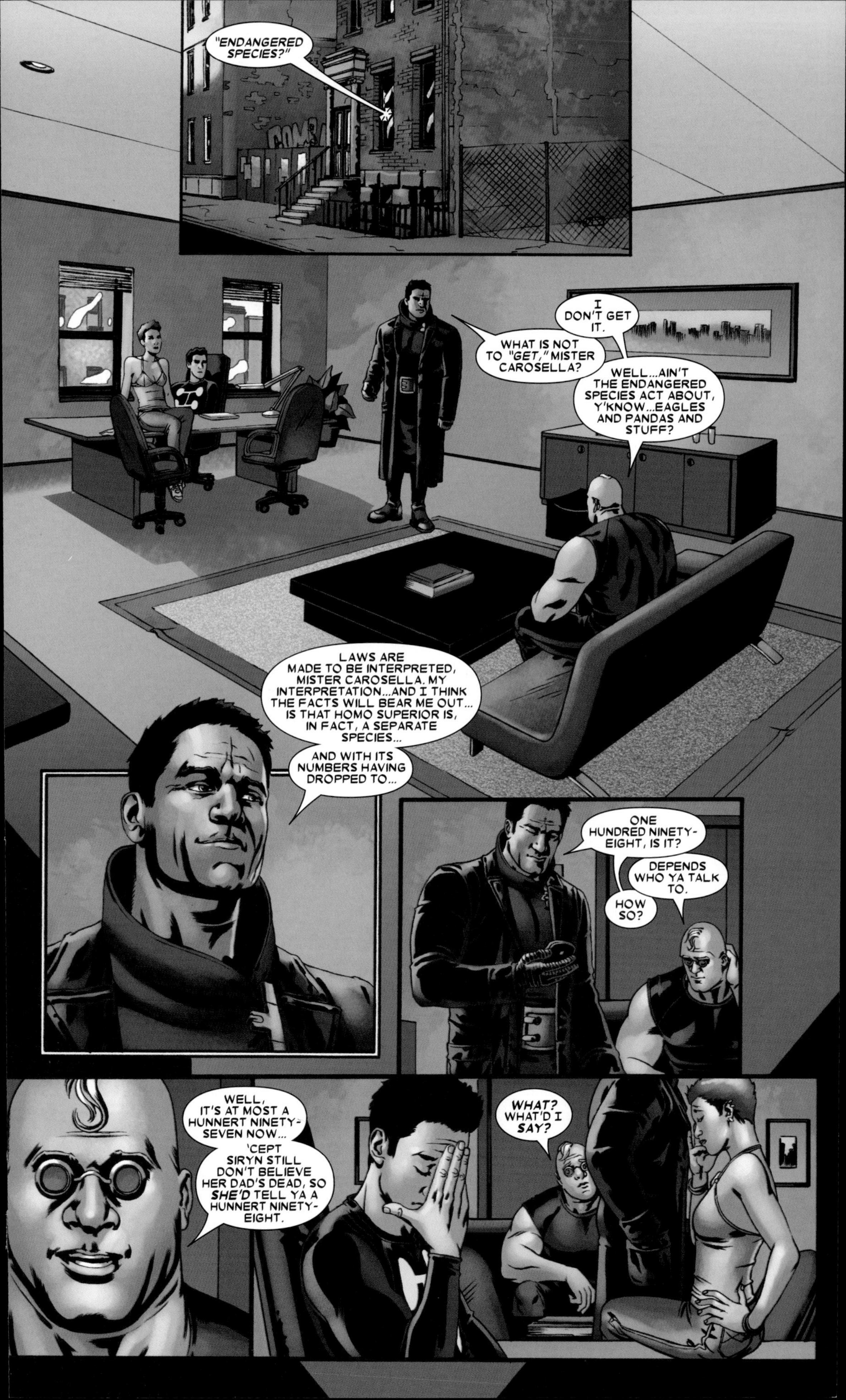
"ENDANGERED SPECIES?"
I DON'T GET IT.
WHAT IS NOT TO "*GET*," MISTER CAROSELLA?
WELL...AIN'T THE ENDANGERED SPECIES ACT ABOUT, Y'KNOW...EAGLES AND PANDAS AND STUFF?
LAWS ARE MADE TO BE INTERPRETED, MISTER CAROSELLA. MY INTERPRETATION...AND I THINK THE FACTS WILL BEAR ME OUT... IS THAT HOMO SUPERIOR IS, IN FACT, A SEPARATE SPECIES...
AND WITH ITS NUMBERS HAVING DROPPED TO...
ONE HUNDRED NINETY-EIGHT, IS IT?
DEPENDS WHO YA TALK TO.
HOW SO?
WELL, IT'S AT MOST A HUNNERT NINETY-SEVEN NOW...
'CEPT SIRYN STILL DON'T BELIEVE HER DAD'S DEAD, SO *SHE'D* TELL YA A HUNNERT NINETY-EIGHT.
WHAT? WHAT'D I *SAY?*

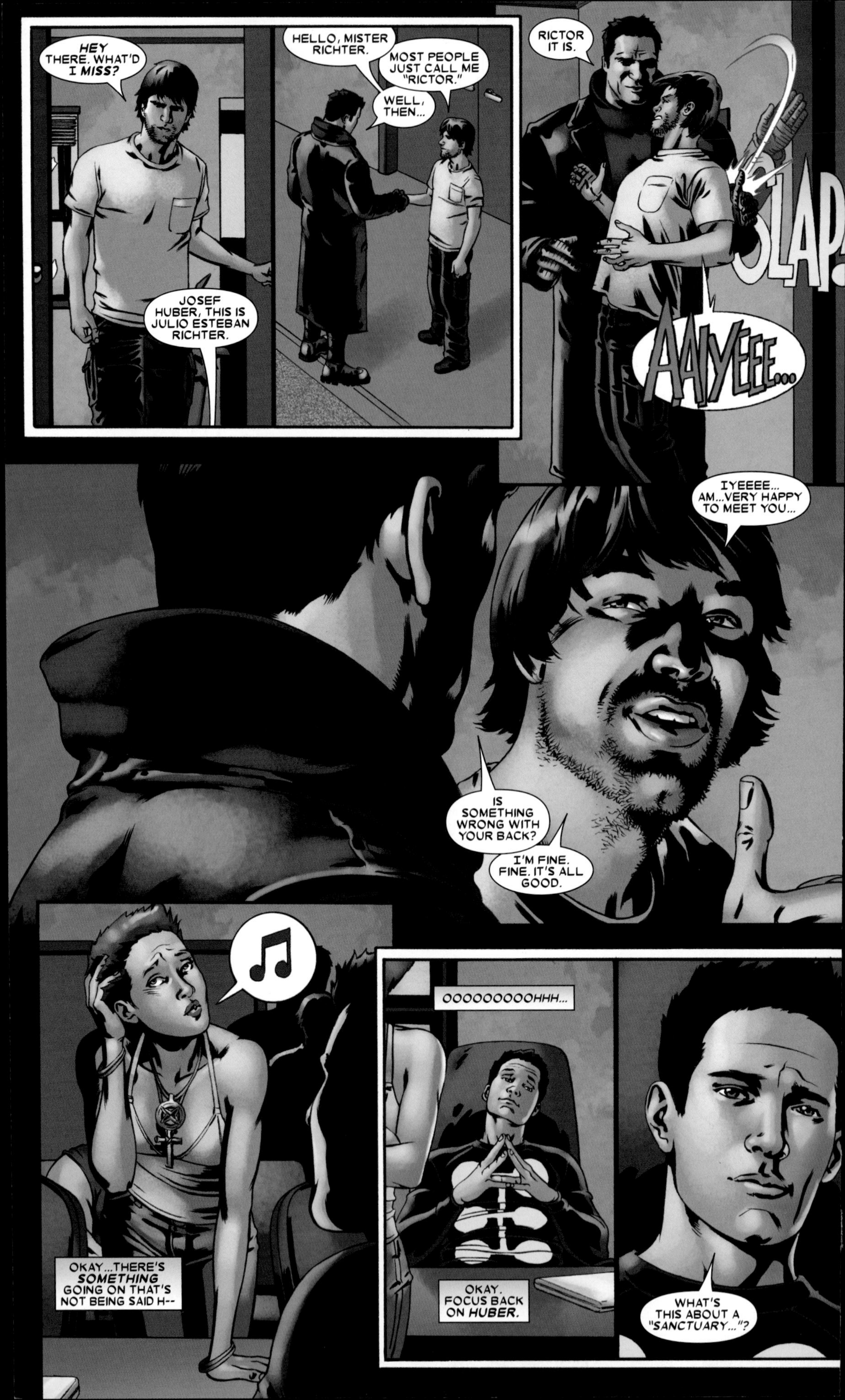
HEY THERE. WHAT'D I MISS?
JOSEF HUBER, THIS IS JULIO ESTEBAN RICHTER.
HELLO, MISTER RICHTER.
MOST PEOPLE JUST CALL ME "RICTOR."
WELL, THEN...
RICTOR IT IS.
SLAP!
AAIYEEE...
IYEEEE... AM...VERY HAPPY TO MEET YOU...
IS SOMETHING WRONG WITH YOUR BACK?
I'M FINE. FINE. IT'S ALL GOOD.
♫
OKAY...THERE'S SOMETHING GOING ON THAT'S NOT BEING SAID H--
OOOOOOOOHHH...
OKAY. FOCUS BACK ON HUBER.
WHAT'S THIS ABOUT A "SANCTUARY..."?

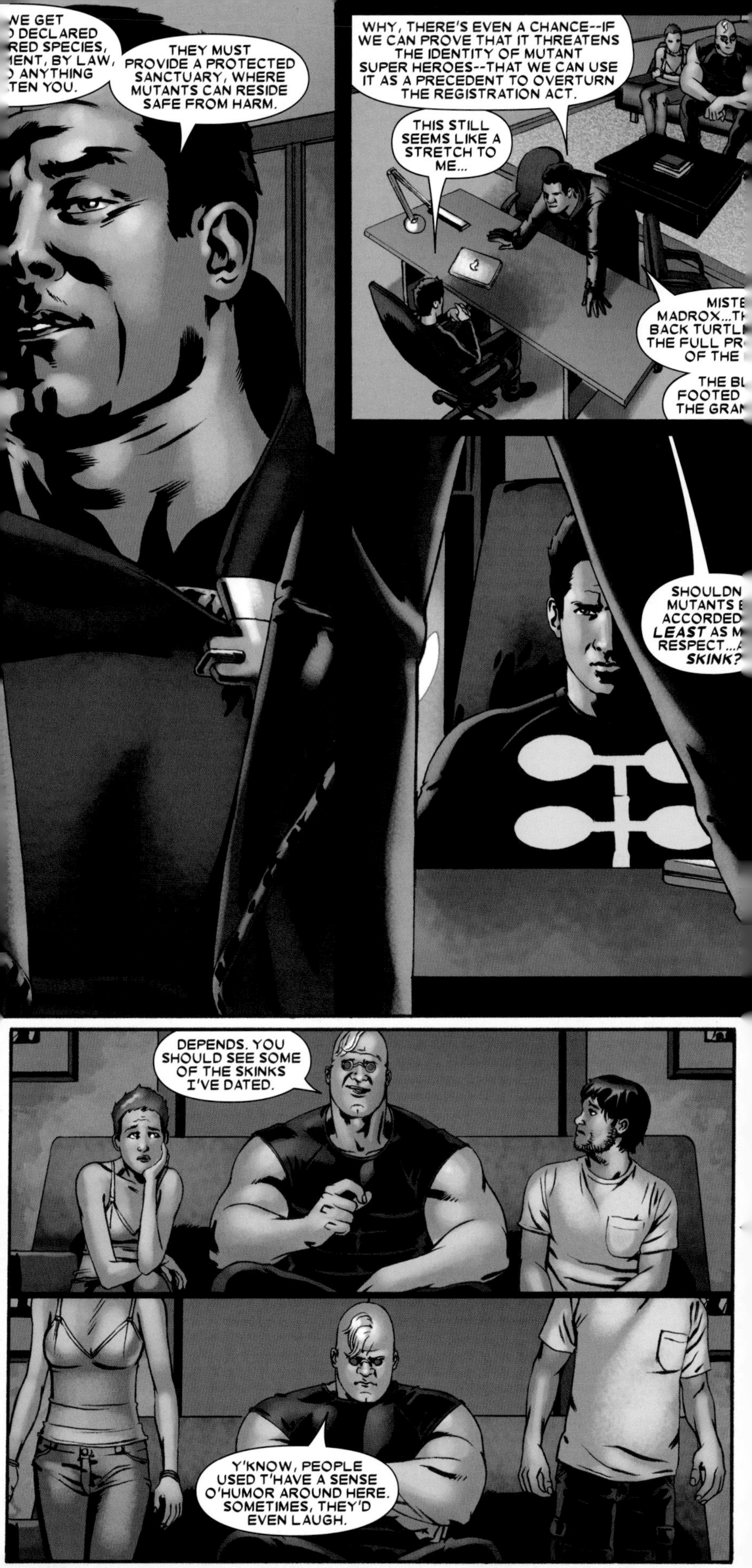
WE GET
D DECLARED
RED SPECIES,
MENT, BY LAW,
D ANYTHING
TEN YOU.
THEY MUST PROVIDE A PROTECTED SANCTUARY, WHERE MUTANTS CAN RESIDE SAFE FROM HARM.
WHY, THERE'S EVEN A CHANCE--IF WE CAN PROVE THAT IT THREATENS THE IDENTITY OF MUTANT SUPER HEROES--THAT WE CAN USE IT AS A PRECEDENT TO OVERTURN THE REGISTRATION ACT.
THIS STILL SEEMS LIKE A STRETCH TO ME...
MISTE
MADROX...TH
BACK TURTLE
THE FULL PR
OF THE
THE BL
FOOTED
THE GRA
SHOULDN
MUTANTS B
ACCORDED
LEAST AS M
RESPECT...A
SKINK?
DEPENDS. YOU SHOULD SEE SOME OF THE SKINKS I'VE DATED.
Y'KNOW, PEOPLE USED T'HAVE A SENSE O'HUMOR AROUND HERE. SOMETIMES, THEY'D EVEN LAUGH.

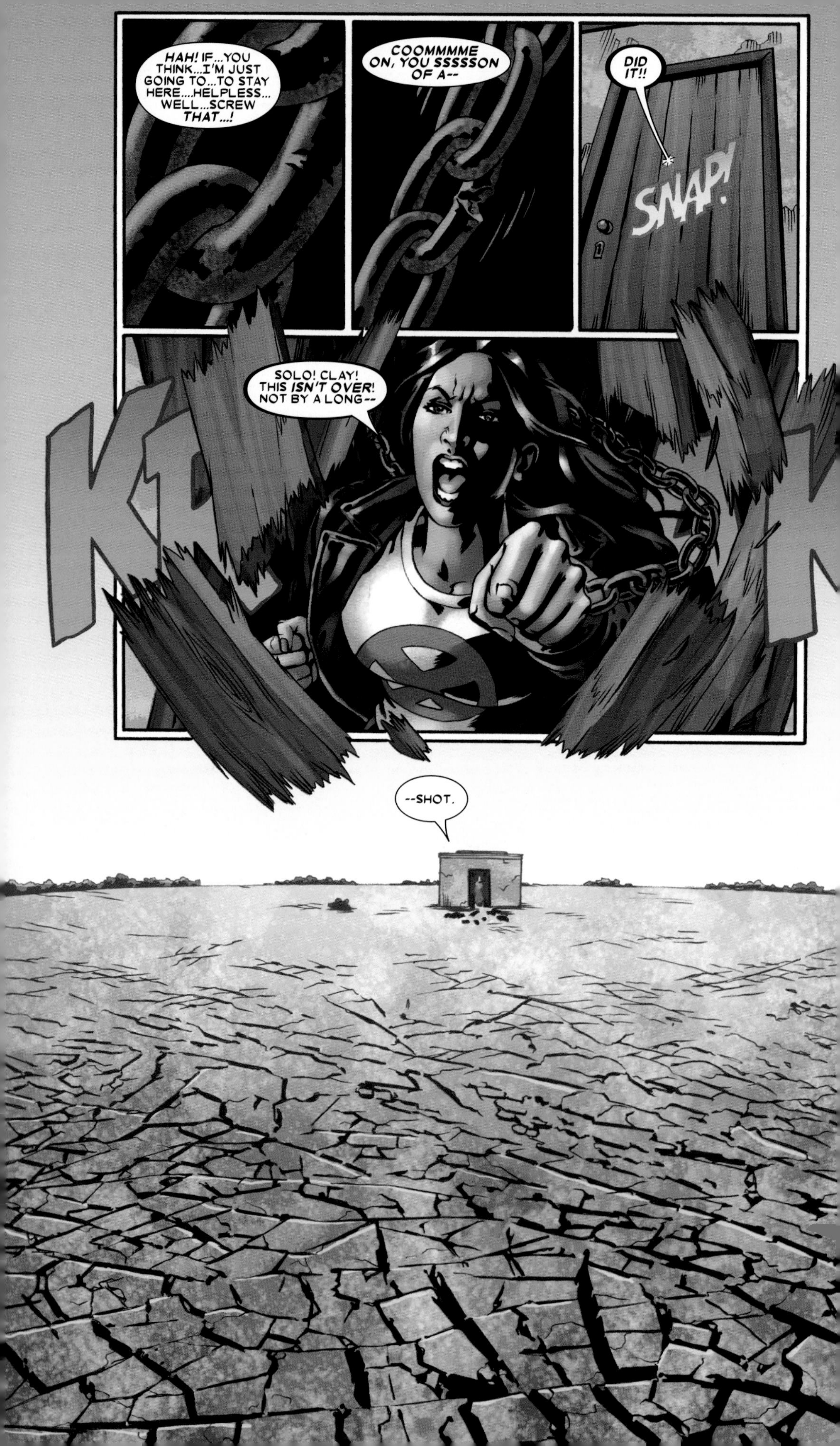
HAH! IF...YOU THINK...I'M JUST GOING TO...TO STAY HERE....HELPLESS... WELL...SCREW THAT...!
COOMMMME ON, YOU SSSSSON OF A--
DID IT!!
SNAP!
SOLO! CLAY! THIS ISN'T OVER! NOT BY A LONG--
--SHOT.

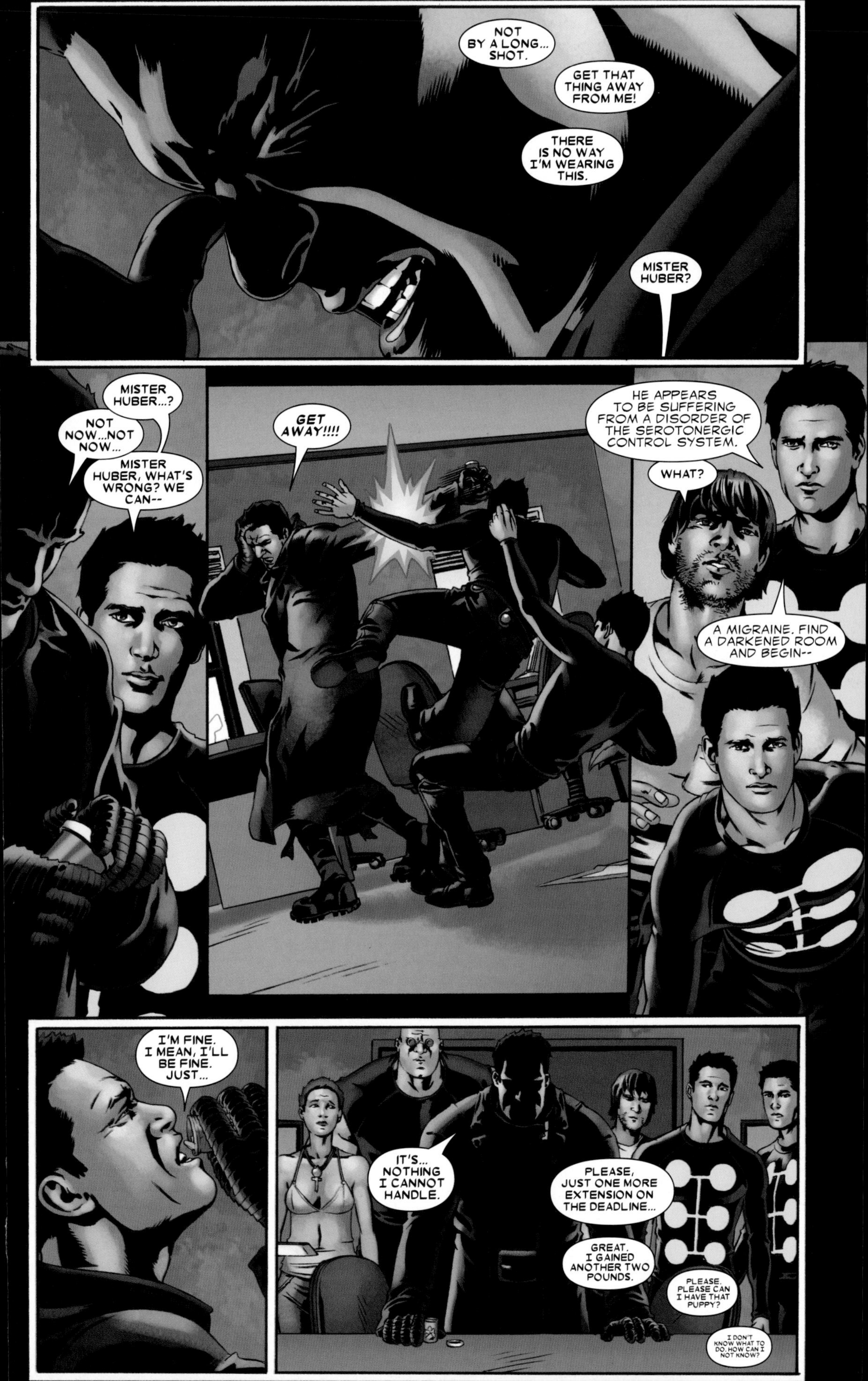
NOT BY A LONG... SHOT.
GET THAT THING AWAY FROM ME!
THERE IS NO WAY I'M WEARING THIS.
MISTER HUBER?
MISTER HUBER...?
NOT NOW...NOT NOW...
MISTER HUBER, WHAT'S WRONG? WE CAN--
GET AWAY!!!!
HE APPEARS TO BE SUFFERING FROM A DISORDER OF THE SEROTONERGIC CONTROL SYSTEM.
WHAT?
A MIGRAINE. FIND A DARKENED ROOM AND BEGIN--
I'M FINE. I MEAN, I'LL BE FINE. JUST...
IT'S... NOTHING I CANNOT HANDLE.
PLEASE, JUST ONE MORE EXTENSION ON THE DEADLINE...
GREAT. I GAINED ANOTHER TWO POUNDS.
PLEASE. PLEASE CAN I HAVE THAT PUPPY?
I DON'T KNOW WHAT TO DO. HOW CAN I NOT KNOW?

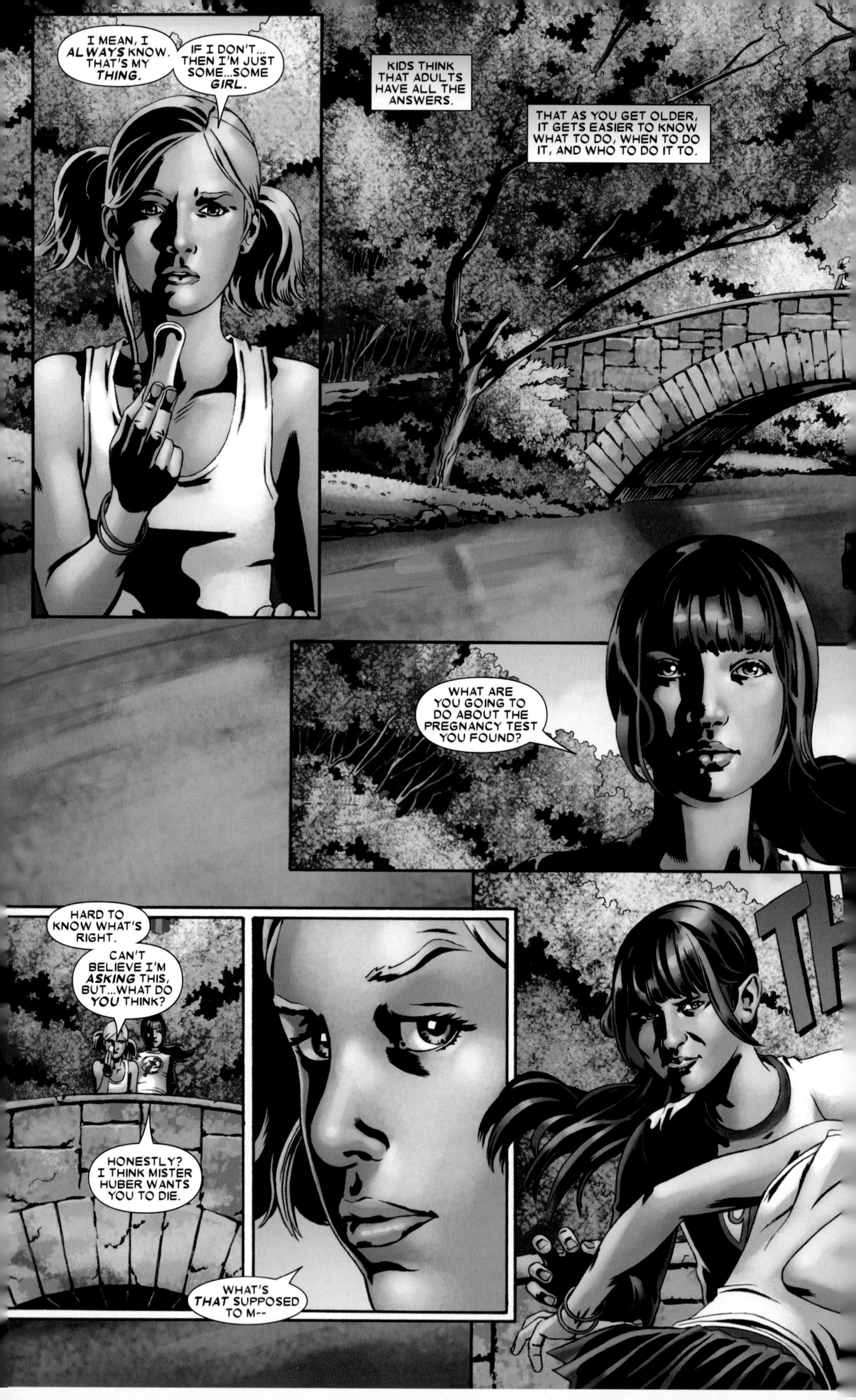

I MEAN, I ALWAYS KNOW. THAT'S MY THING.
IF I DON'T... THEN I'M JUST SOME...SOME GIRL.
KIDS THINK THAT ADULTS HAVE ALL THE ANSWERS.
THAT AS YOU GET OLDER, IT GETS EASIER TO KNOW WHAT TO DO, WHEN TO DO IT, AND WHO TO DO IT TO.
WHAT ARE YOU GOING TO DO ABOUT THE PREGNANCY TEST YOU FOUND?
HARD TO KNOW WHAT'S RIGHT.
CAN'T BELIEVE I'M ASKING THIS, BUT...WHAT DO YOU THINK?
HONESTLY? I THINK MISTER HUBER WANTS YOU TO DIE.
WHAT'S THAT SUPPOSED TO M--
TH

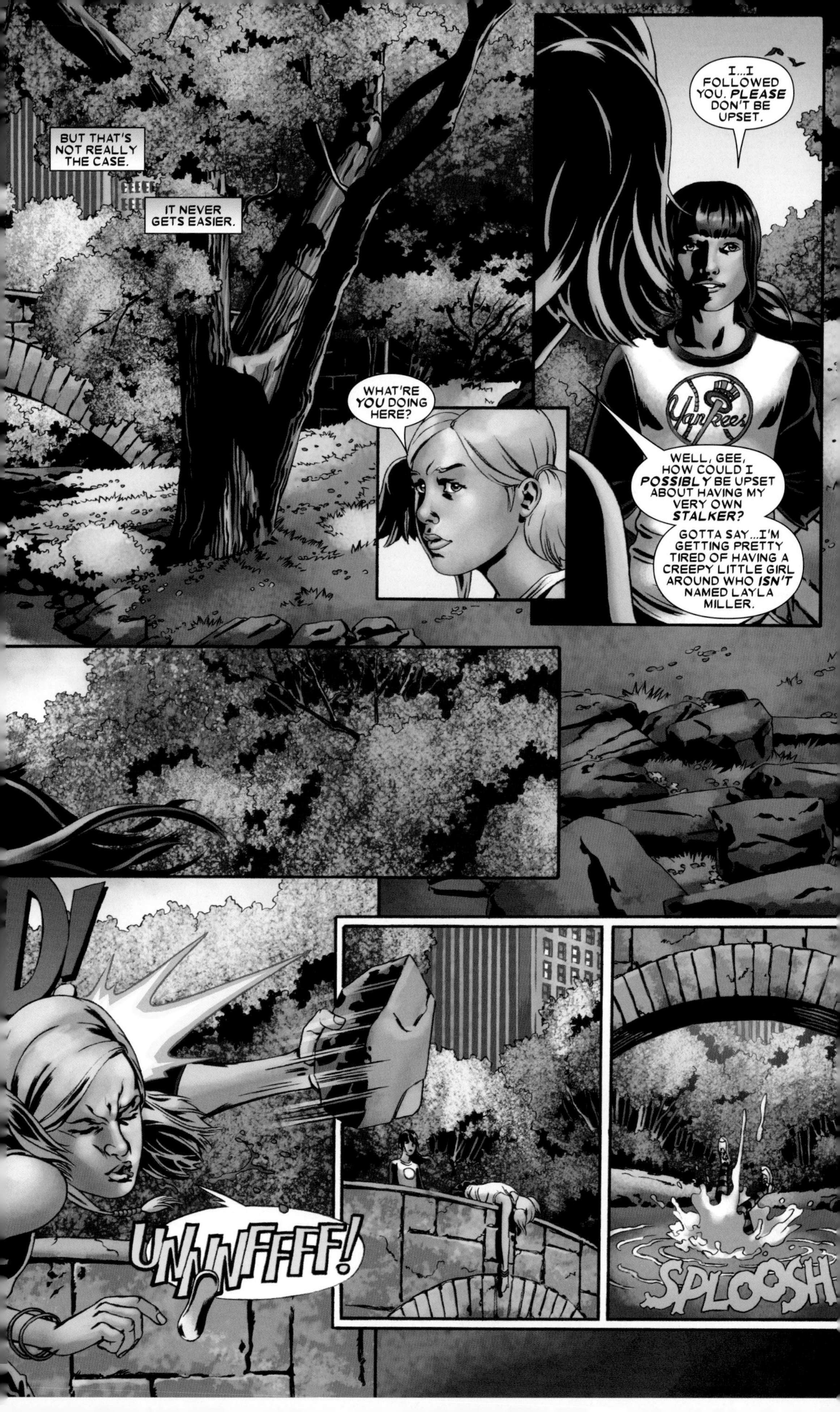

BUT THAT'S NOT REALLY THE CASE.
IT NEVER GETS EASIER.
I...I FOLLOWED YOU. *PLEASE* DON'T BE UPSET.
WHAT'RE *YOU* DOING HERE?
WELL, GEE, HOW COULD I *POSSIBLY* BE UPSET ABOUT HAVING MY VERY OWN *STALKER?*
GOTTA SAY...I'M GETTING PRETTY TIRED OF HAVING A CREEPY LITTLE GIRL AROUND WHO *ISN'T* NAMED LAYLA MILLER.
UNNNFFFF!
SPLOOSH

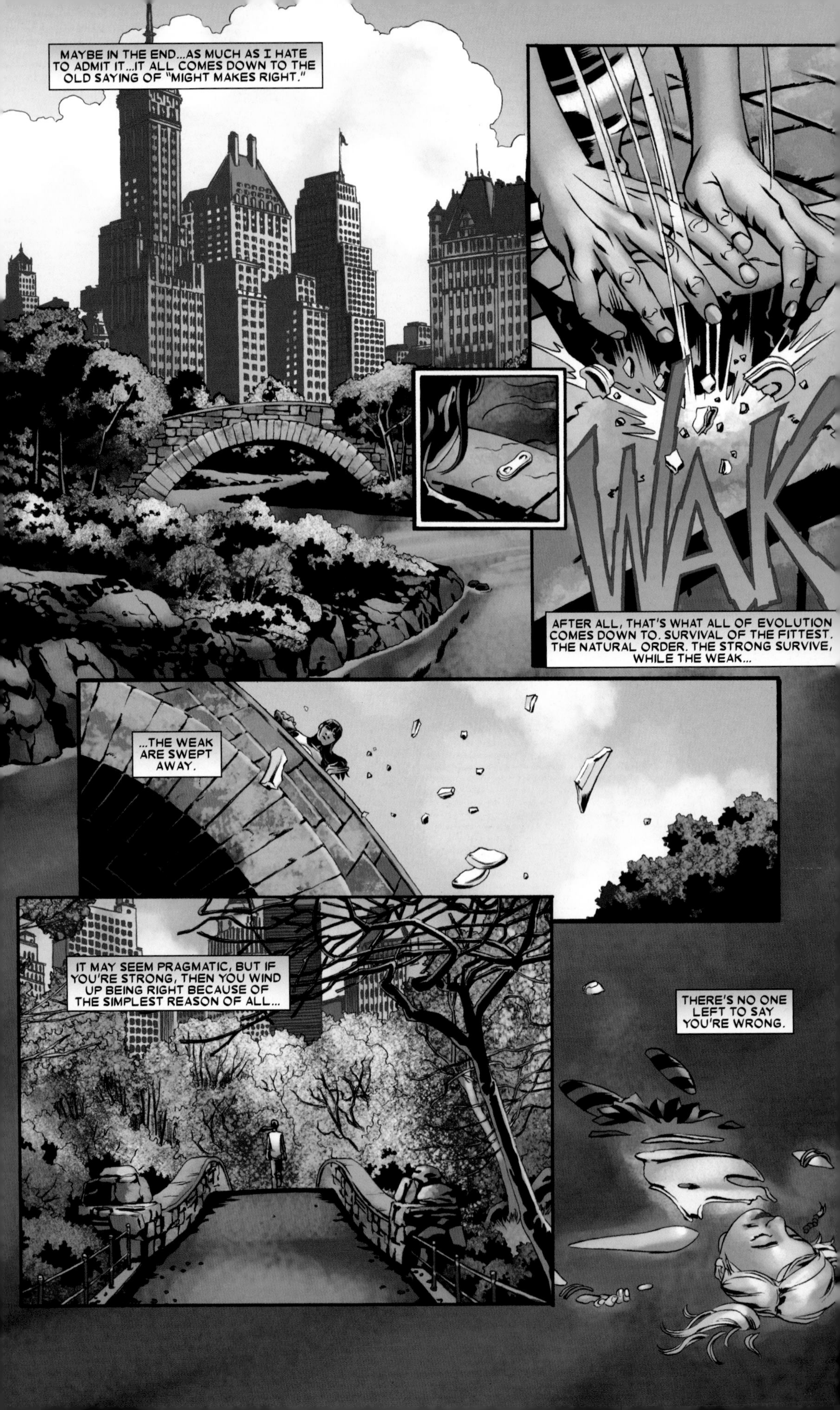

MAYBE IN THE END...AS MUCH AS I HATE TO ADMIT IT...IT ALL COMES DOWN TO THE OLD SAYING OF "MIGHT MAKES RIGHT."
WAK
AFTER ALL, THAT'S WHAT ALL OF EVOLUTION COMES DOWN TO. SURVIVAL OF THE FITTEST. THE NATURAL ORDER. THE STRONG SURVIVE, WHILE THE WEAK...
...THE WEAK ARE SWEPT AWAY.
IT MAY SEEM PRAGMATIC, BUT IF YOU'RE STRONG, THEN YOU WIND UP BEING RIGHT BECAUSE OF THE SIMPLEST REASON OF ALL...
THERE'S NO ONE LEFT TO SAY YOU'RE WRONG.

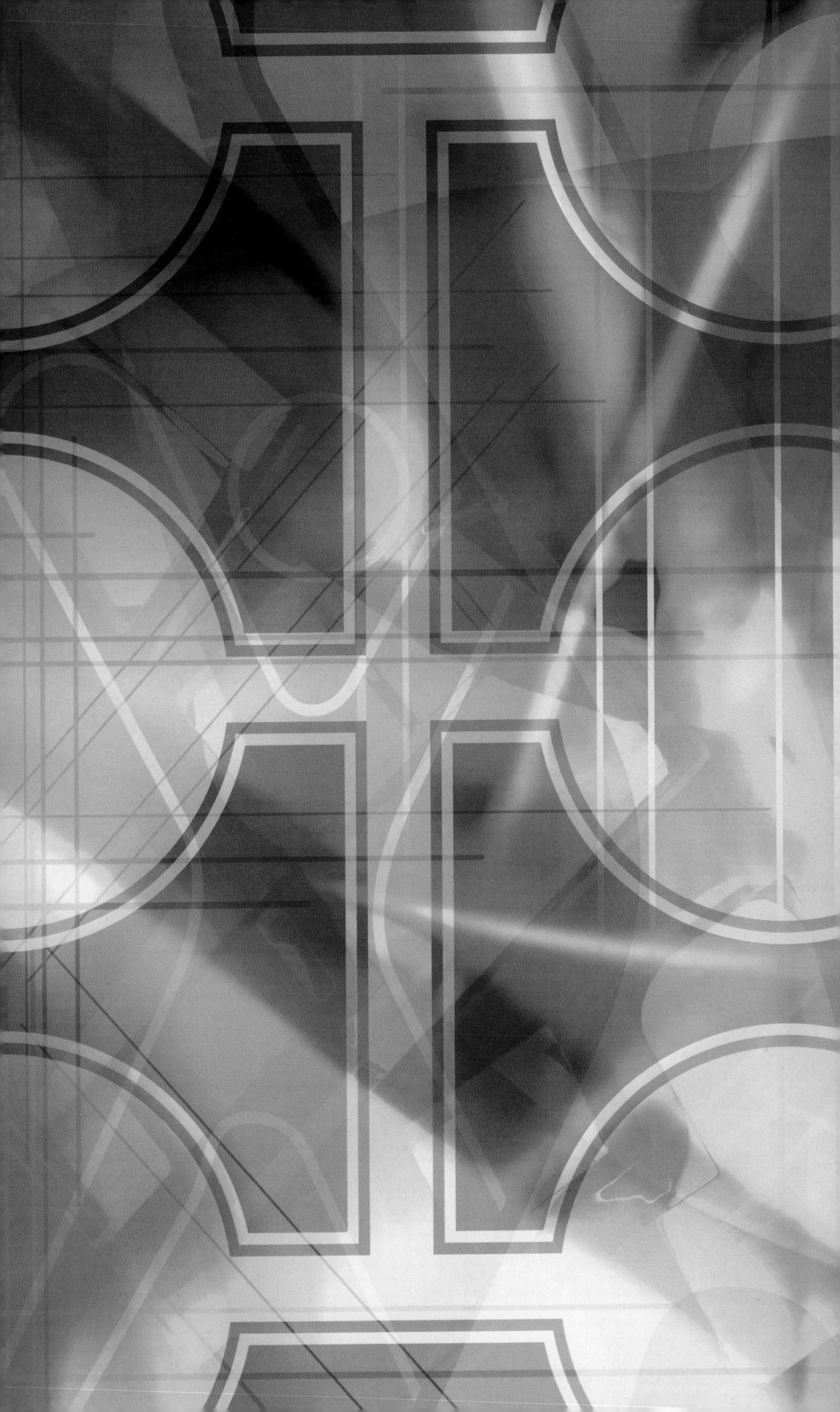

#23

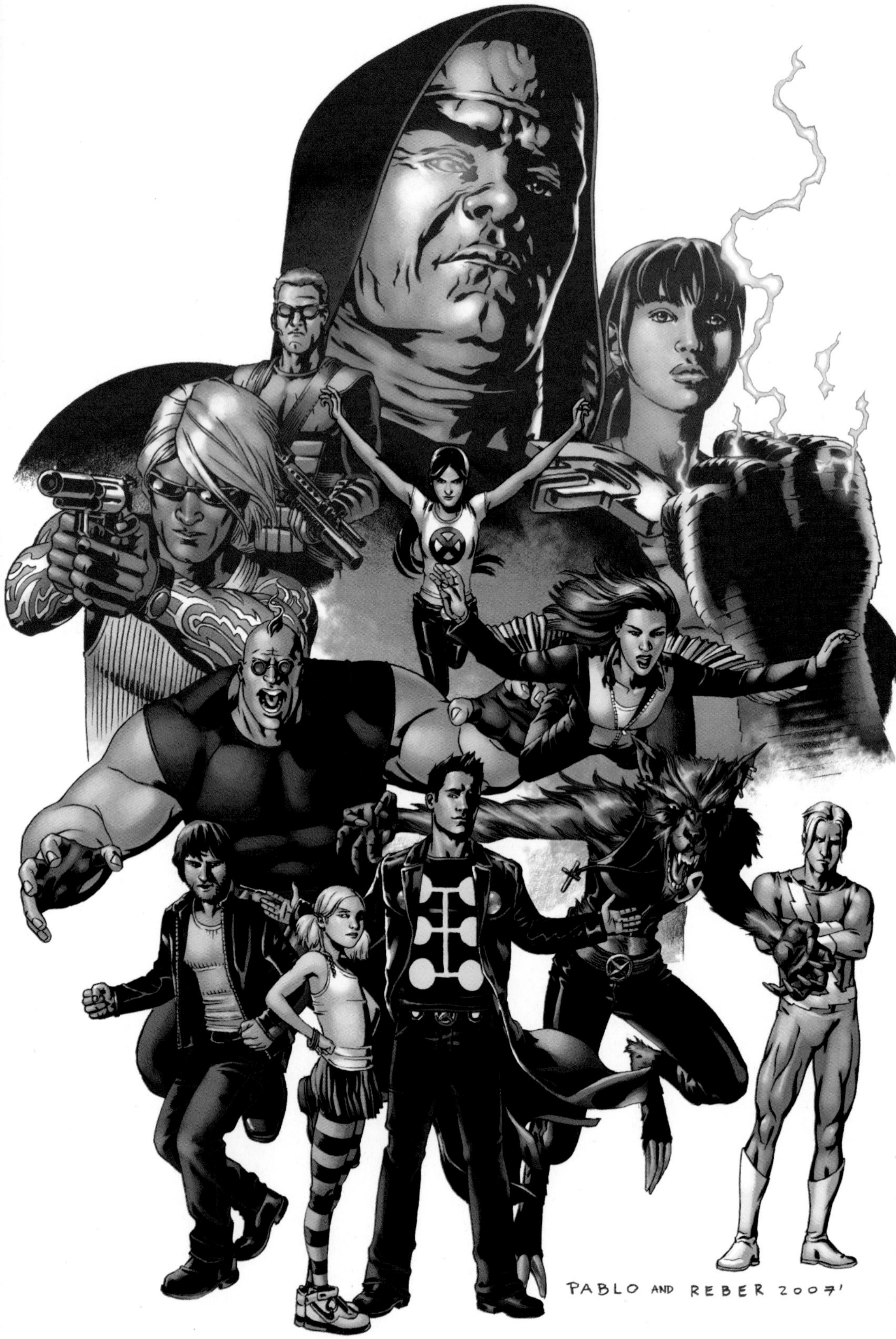
PABLO AND REBER 2007'

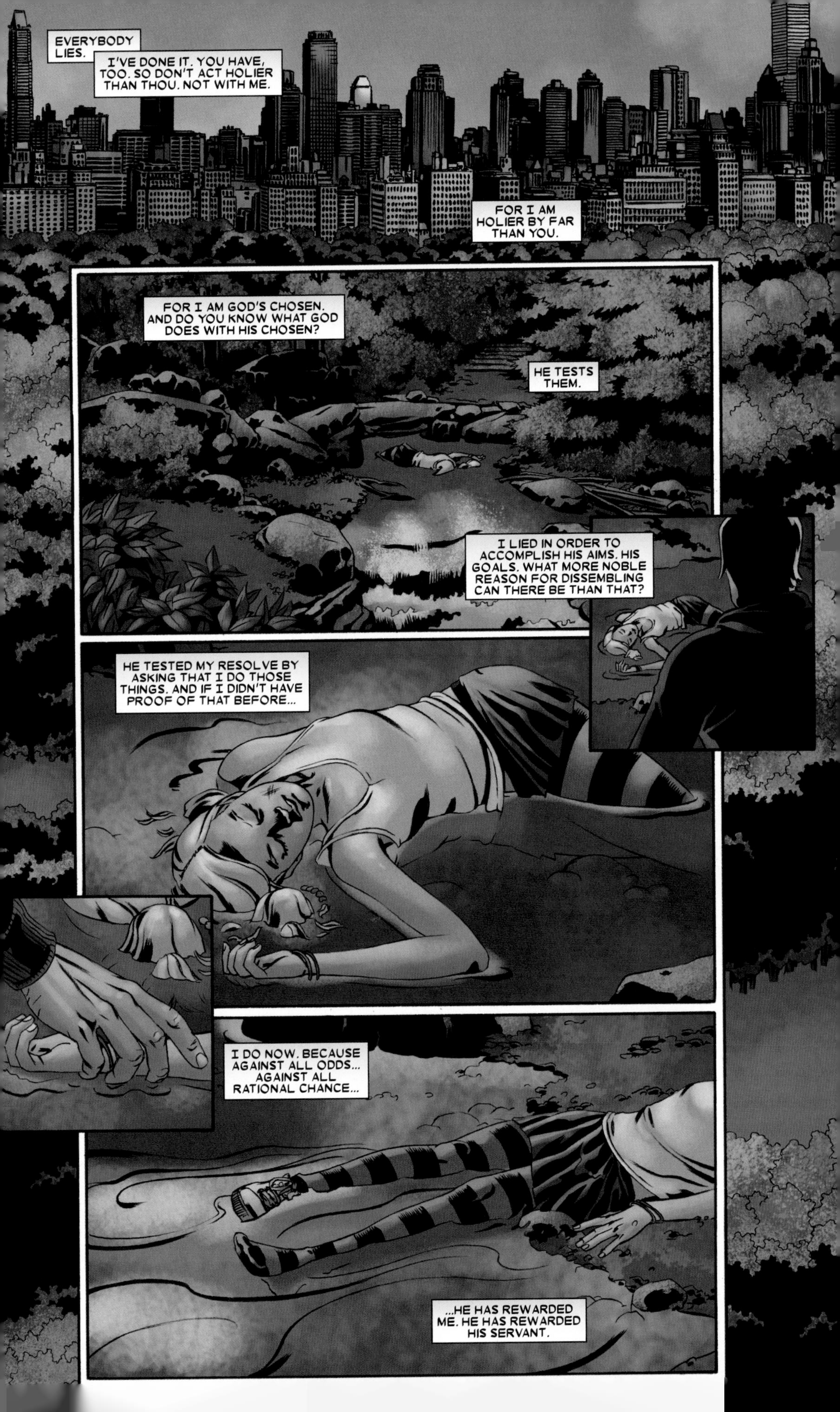
EVERYBODY LIES.
I'VE DONE IT. YOU HAVE, TOO. SO DON'T ACT HOLIER THAN THOU. NOT WITH ME.
FOR I AM HOLIER BY FAR THAN YOU.
FOR I AM GOD'S CHOSEN. AND DO YOU KNOW WHAT GOD DOES WITH HIS CHOSEN?
HE TESTS THEM.
I LIED IN ORDER TO ACCOMPLISH HIS AIMS. HIS GOALS. WHAT MORE NOBLE REASON FOR DISSEMBLING CAN THERE BE THAN THAT?
HE TESTED MY RESOLVE BY ASKING THAT I DO THOSE THINGS. AND IF I DIDN'T HAVE PROOF OF THAT BEFORE...
I DO NOW. BECAUSE AGAINST ALL ODDS... AGAINST ALL RATIONAL CHANCE...
...HE HAS REWARDED ME. HE HAS REWARDED HIS SERVANT.

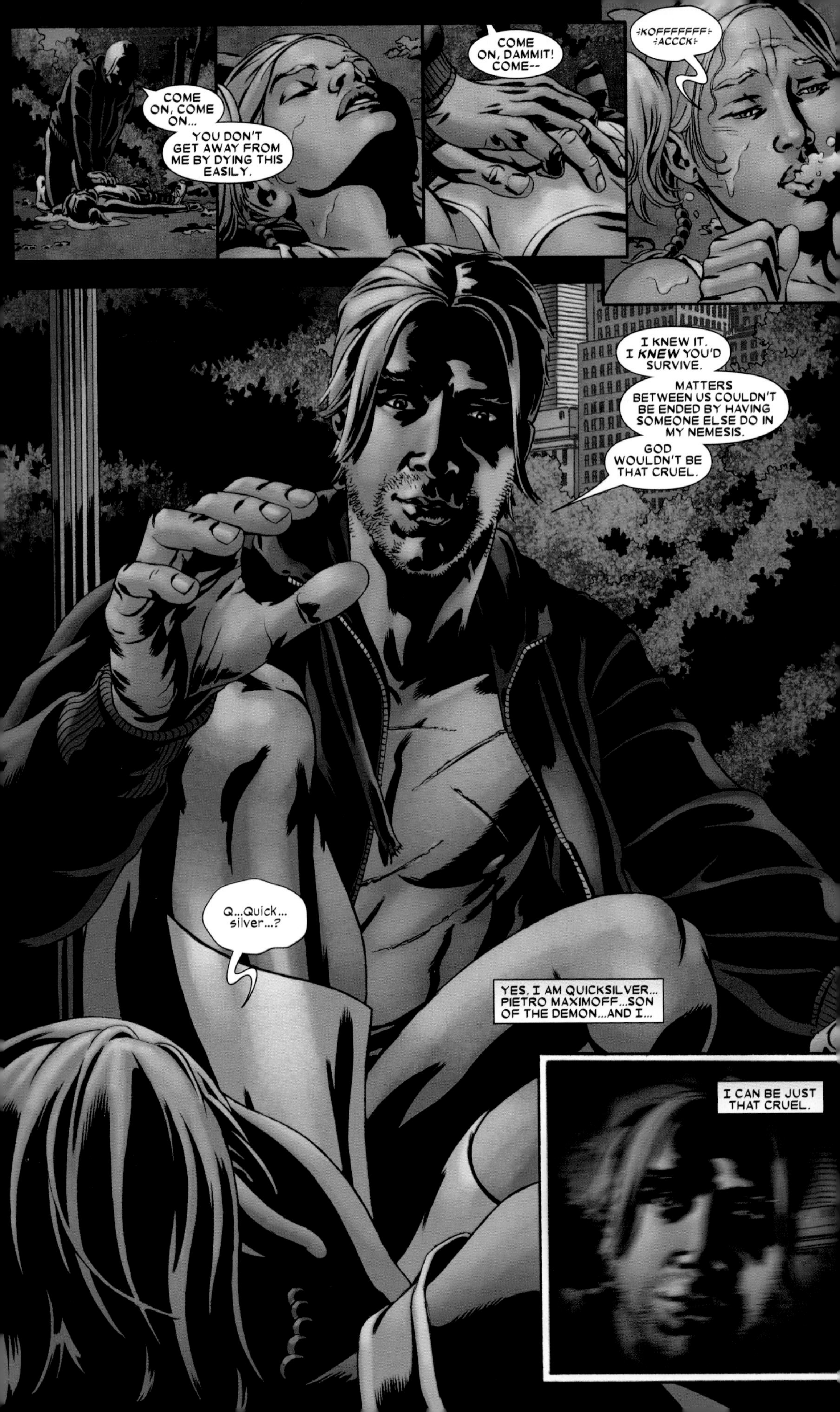
COME ON, COME ON...
YOU DON'T GET AWAY FROM ME BY DYING THIS EASILY.
COME ON, DAMMIT! COME--
KOFFFFFFF ACCCK
I KNEW IT. I KNEW YOU'D SURVIVE.
MATTERS BETWEEN US COULDN'T BE ENDED BY HAVING SOMEONE ELSE DO IN MY NEMESIS.
GOD WOULDN'T BE THAT CRUEL.
Q...Quick... silver...?
YES. I AM QUICKSILVER... PIETRO MAXIMOFF...SON OF THE DEMON...AND I...
I CAN BE JUST THAT CRUEL.

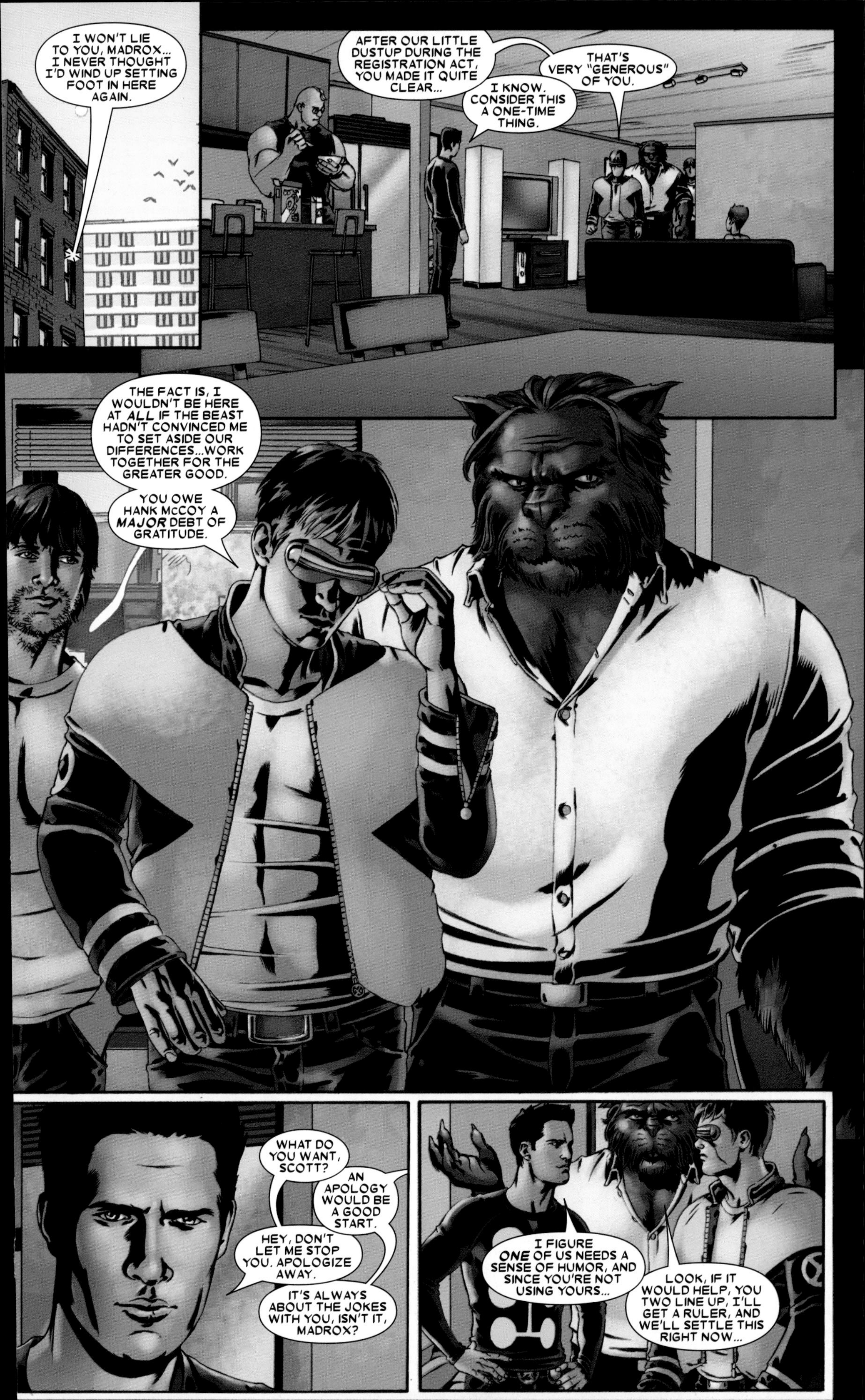
I WON'T LIE TO YOU, MADROX... I NEVER THOUGHT I'D WIND UP SETTING FOOT IN HERE AGAIN.
AFTER OUR LITTLE DUSTUP DURING THE REGISTRATION ACT, YOU MADE IT QUITE CLEAR...
THAT'S VERY "GENEROUS" OF YOU.
I KNOW. CONSIDER THIS A ONE-TIME THING.
THE FACT IS, I WOULDN'T BE HERE AT *ALL* IF THE BEAST HADN'T CONVINCED ME TO SET ASIDE OUR DIFFERENCES...WORK TOGETHER FOR THE GREATER GOOD.
YOU OWE HANK McCOY A *MAJOR* DEBT OF GRATITUDE.
WHAT DO YOU WANT, SCOTT?
AN APOLOGY WOULD BE A GOOD START.
HEY, DON'T LET ME STOP YOU. APOLOGIZE AWAY.
IT'S ALWAYS ABOUT THE JOKES WITH YOU, ISN'T IT, MADROX?
I FIGURE *ONE* OF US NEEDS A SENSE OF HUMOR, AND SINCE YOU'RE NOT USING YOURS...
LOOK, IF IT WOULD HELP, YOU TWO LINE UP, I'LL GET A RULER, AND WE'LL SETTLE THIS RIGHT NOW...

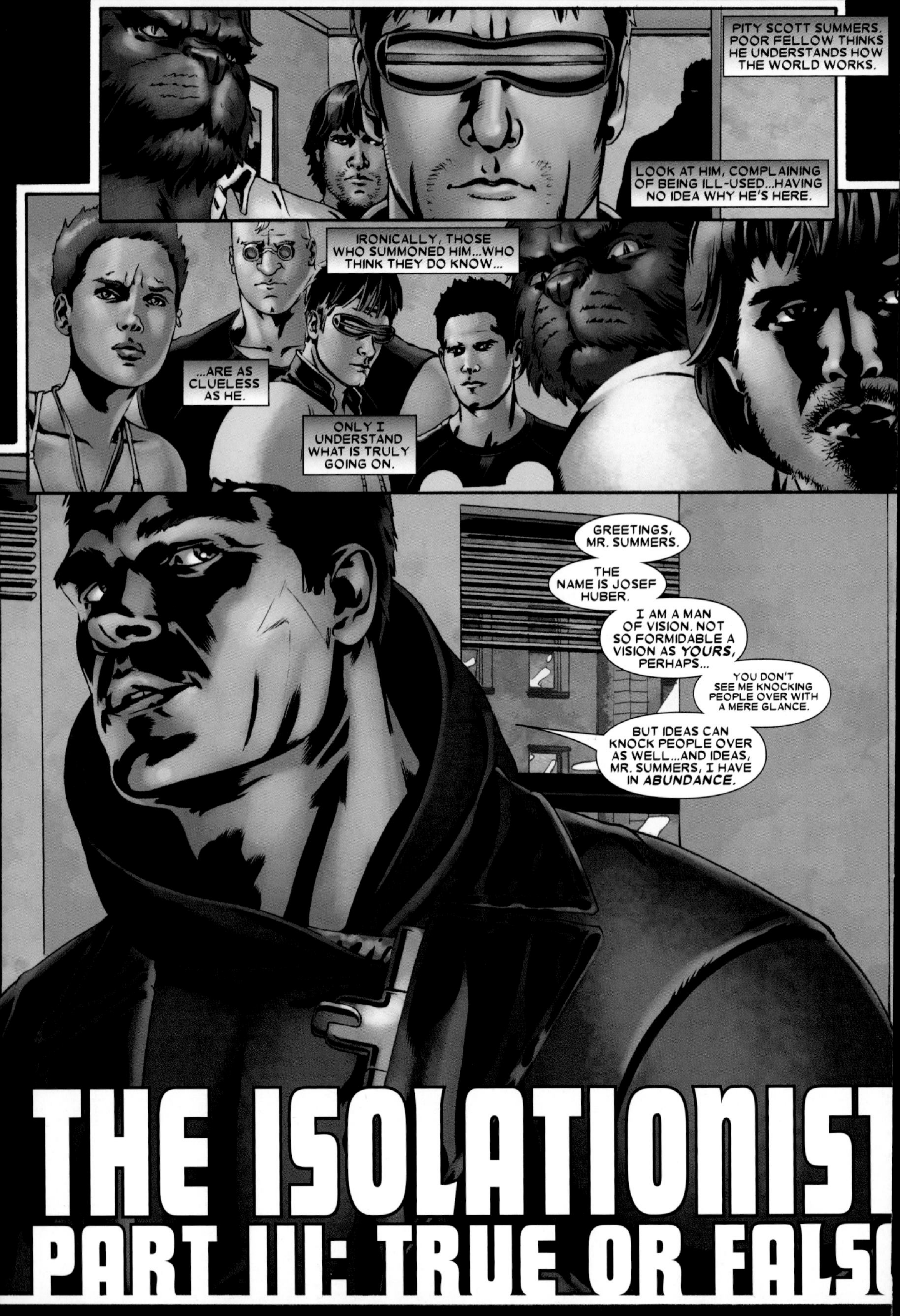
PITY SCOTT SUMMERS. POOR FELLOW THINKS HE UNDERSTANDS HOW THE WORLD WORKS.
LOOK AT HIM, COMPLAINING OF BEING ILL-USED...HAVING NO IDEA WHY HE'S HERE.
IRONICALLY, THOSE WHO SUMMONED HIM...WHO THINK THEY DO KNOW...
...ARE AS CLUELESS AS HE.
ONLY I UNDERSTAND WHAT IS TRULY GOING ON.
GREETINGS, MR. SUMMERS.
THE NAME IS JOSEF HUBER.
I AM A MAN OF VISION. NOT SO FORMIDABLE A VISION AS *YOURS,* PERHAPS...
YOU DON'T SEE ME KNOCKING PEOPLE OVER WITH A MERE GLANCE.
BUT IDEAS CAN KNOCK PEOPLE OVER AS WELL...AND IDEAS, MR. SUMMERS, I HAVE IN *ABUNDANCE.*
THE ISOLATIONIST
PART III: TRUE OR FALS

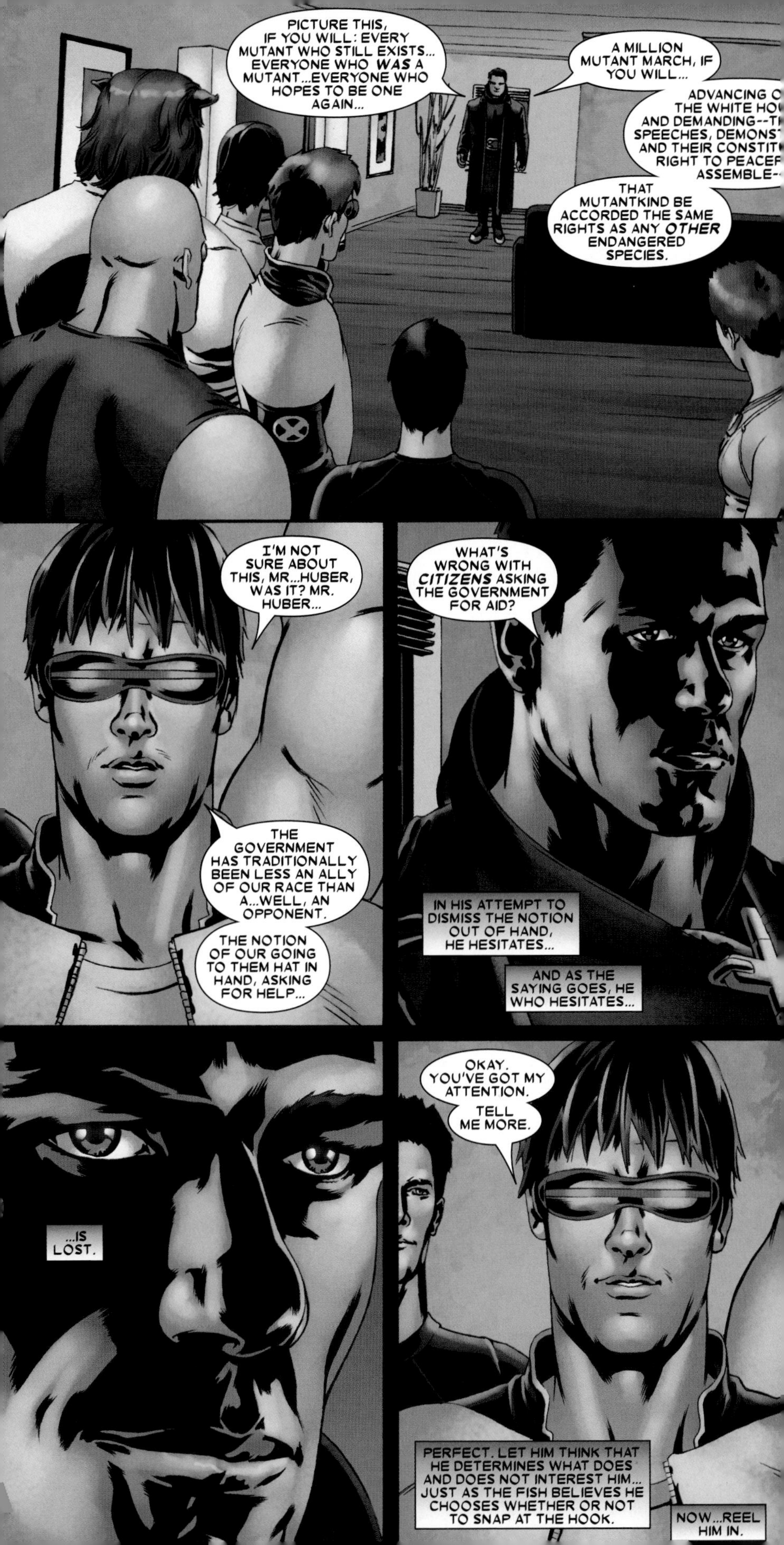
PICTURE THIS, IF YOU WILL: EVERY MUTANT WHO STILL EXISTS... EVERYONE WHO *WAS* A MUTANT...EVERYONE WHO HOPES TO BE ONE AGAIN...
A MILLION MUTANT MARCH, IF YOU WILL...
ADVANCING O THE WHITE HO AND DEMANDING--T SPEECHES, DEMONST AND THEIR CONSTIT RIGHT TO PEACEF ASSEMBLE--
THAT MUTANTKIND BE ACCORDED THE SAME RIGHTS AS ANY *OTHER* ENDANGERED SPECIES.
I'M NOT SURE ABOUT THIS, MR...HUBER, WAS IT? MR. HUBER...
THE GOVERNMENT HAS TRADITIONALLY BEEN LESS AN ALLY OF OUR RACE THAN A...WELL, AN OPPONENT.
THE NOTION OF OUR GOING TO THEM HAT IN HAND, ASKING FOR HELP...
WHAT'S WRONG WITH *CITIZENS* ASKING THE GOVERNMENT FOR AID?
IN HIS ATTEMPT TO DISMISS THE NOTION OUT OF HAND, HE HESITATES...
AND AS THE SAYING GOES, HE WHO HESITATES...
...IS LOST.
OKAY. YOU'VE GOT MY ATTENTION.
TELL ME MORE.
PERFECT. LET HIM THINK THAT HE DETERMINES WHAT DOES AND DOES NOT INTEREST HIM... JUST AS THE FISH BELIEVES HE CHOOSES WHETHER OR NOT TO SNAP AT THE HOOK.
NOW...REEL HIM IN.

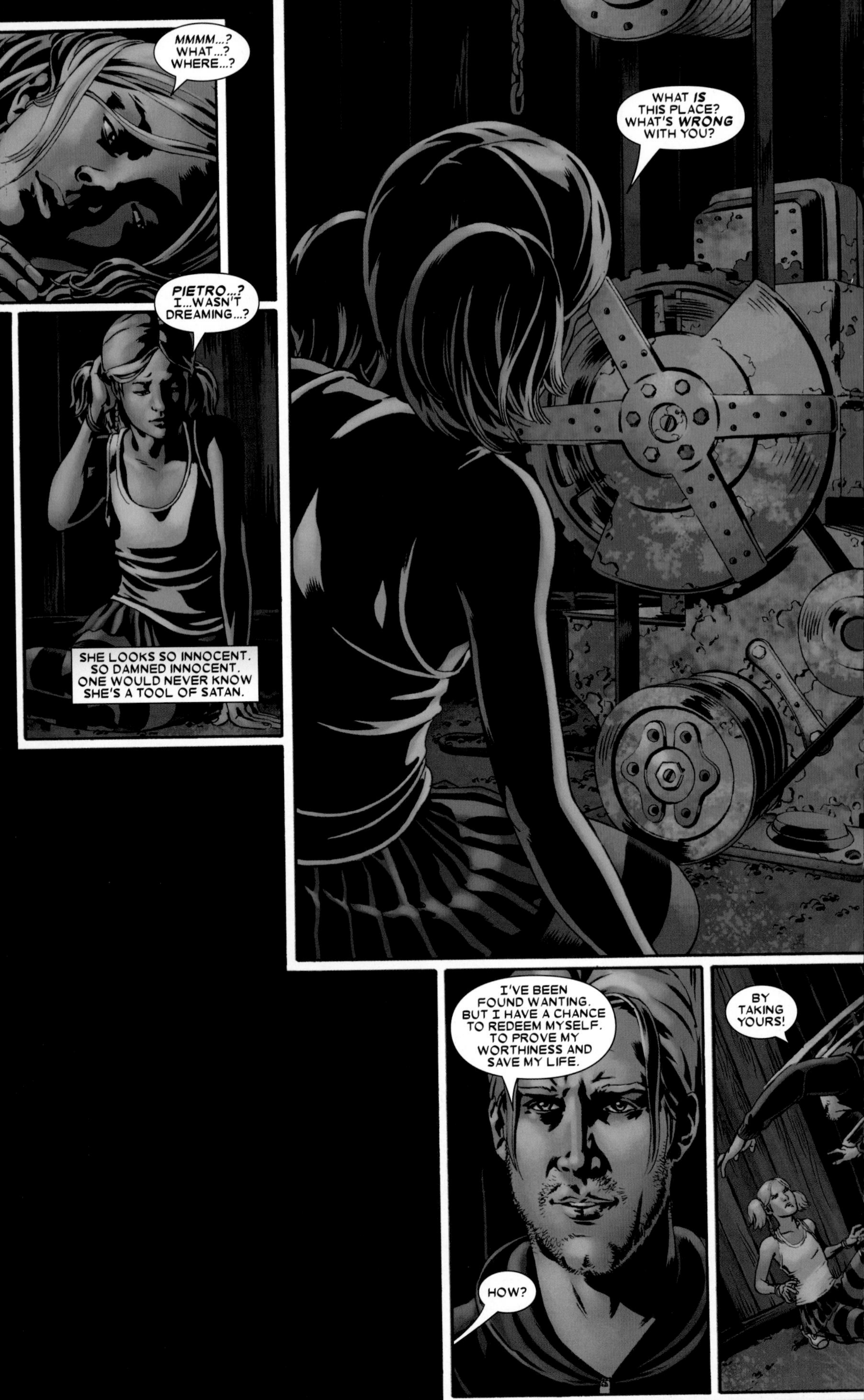
MMMM...? WHAT...? WHERE...?
PIETRO...? I...WASN'T DREAMING...?
SHE LOOKS SO INNOCENT. SO DAMNED INNOCENT. ONE WOULD NEVER KNOW SHE'S A TOOL OF SATAN.
WHAT IS THIS PLACE? WHAT'S WRONG WITH YOU?
I'VE BEEN FOUND WANTING. BUT I HAVE A CHANCE TO REDEEM MYSELF. TO PROVE MY WORTHINESS AND SAVE MY LIFE.
HOW?
BY TAKING YOURS!

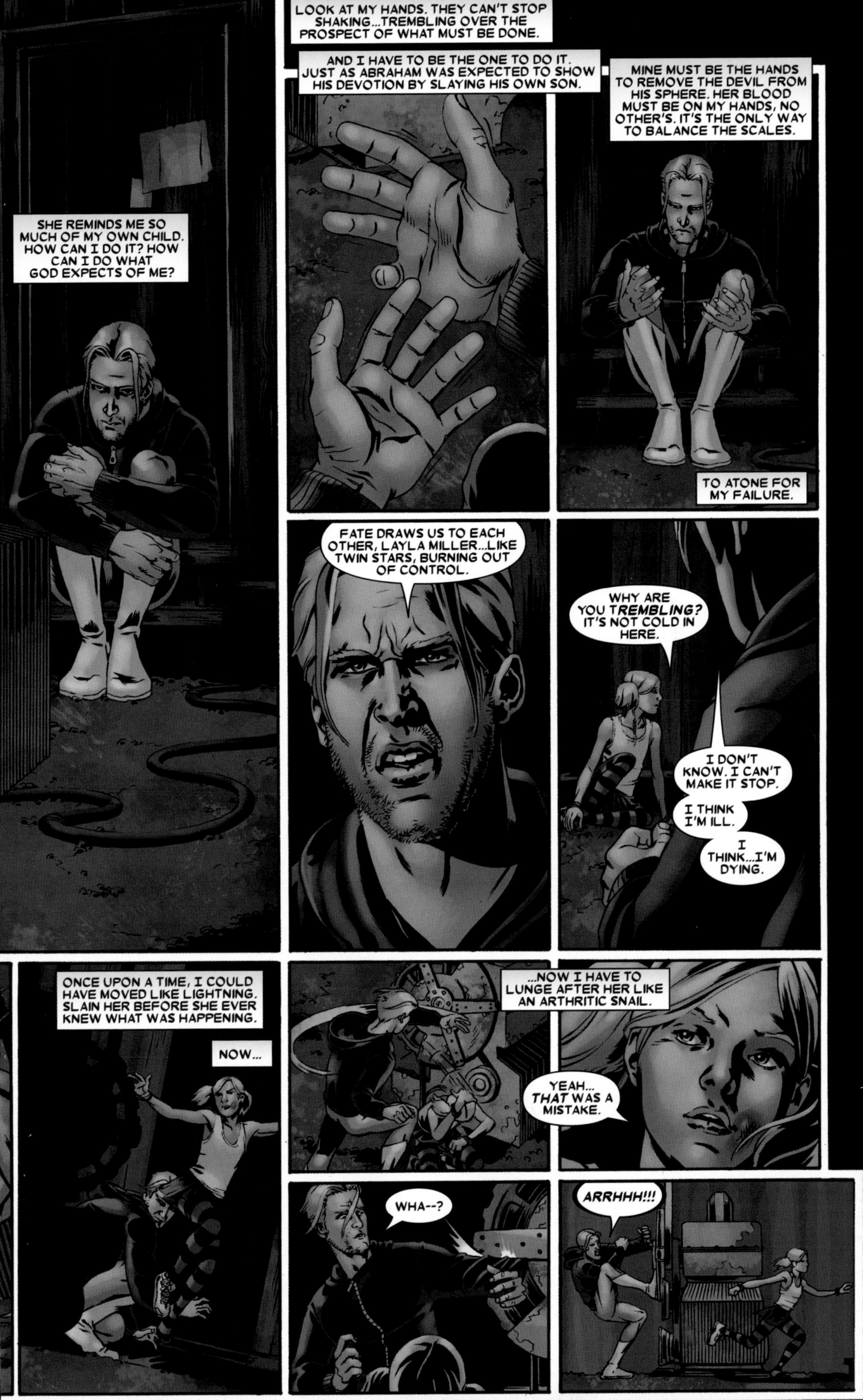
SHE REMINDS ME SO MUCH OF MY OWN CHILD. HOW CAN I DO IT? HOW CAN I DO WHAT GOD EXPECTS OF ME?
LOOK AT MY HANDS. THEY CAN'T STOP SHAKING...TREMBLING OVER THE PROSPECT OF WHAT MUST BE DONE.
AND I HAVE TO BE THE ONE TO DO IT. JUST AS ABRAHAM WAS EXPECTED TO SHOW HIS DEVOTION BY SLAYING HIS OWN SON.
MINE MUST BE THE HANDS TO REMOVE THE DEVIL FROM HIS SPHERE. HER BLOOD MUST BE ON MY HANDS, NO OTHER'S. IT'S THE ONLY WAY TO BALANCE THE SCALES.
TO ATONE FOR MY FAILURE.
FATE DRAWS US TO EACH OTHER, LAYLA MILLER...LIKE TWIN STARS, BURNING OUT OF CONTROL.
WHY ARE YOU TREMBLING? IT'S NOT COLD IN HERE.
I DON'T KNOW. I CAN'T MAKE IT STOP.
I THINK I'M ILL.
I THINK...I'M DYING.
ONCE UPON A TIME, I COULD HAVE MOVED LIKE LIGHTNING. SLAIN HER BEFORE SHE EVER KNEW WHAT WAS HAPPENING.
NOW...
...NOW I HAVE TO LUNGE AFTER HER LIKE AN ARTHRITIC SNAIL.
YEAH... THAT WAS A MISTAKE.
WHA--?
ARRHHH!!!

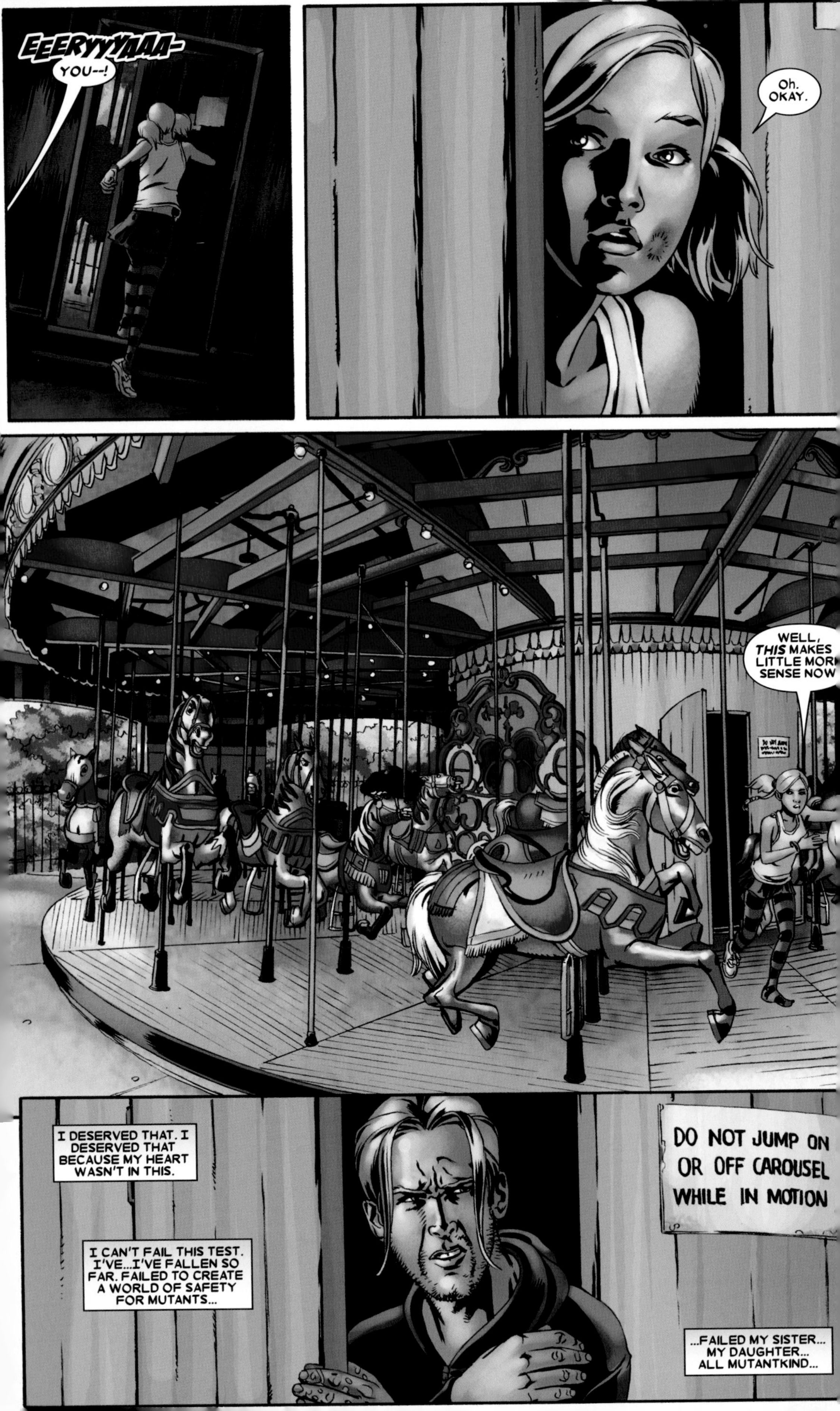
EEERYYYAAA-
YOU--!
Oh. OKAY.
WELL, THIS MAKES LITTLE MOR SENSE NOW
I DESERVED THAT. I DESERVED THAT BECAUSE MY HEART WASN'T IN THIS.
DO NOT JUMP ON OR OFF CAROUSEL WHILE IN MOTION
I CAN'T FAIL THIS TEST. I'VE...I'VE FALLEN SO FAR. FAILED TO CREATE A WORLD OF SAFETY FOR MUTANTS...
...FAILED MY SISTER... MY DAUGHTER... ALL MUTANTKIND...

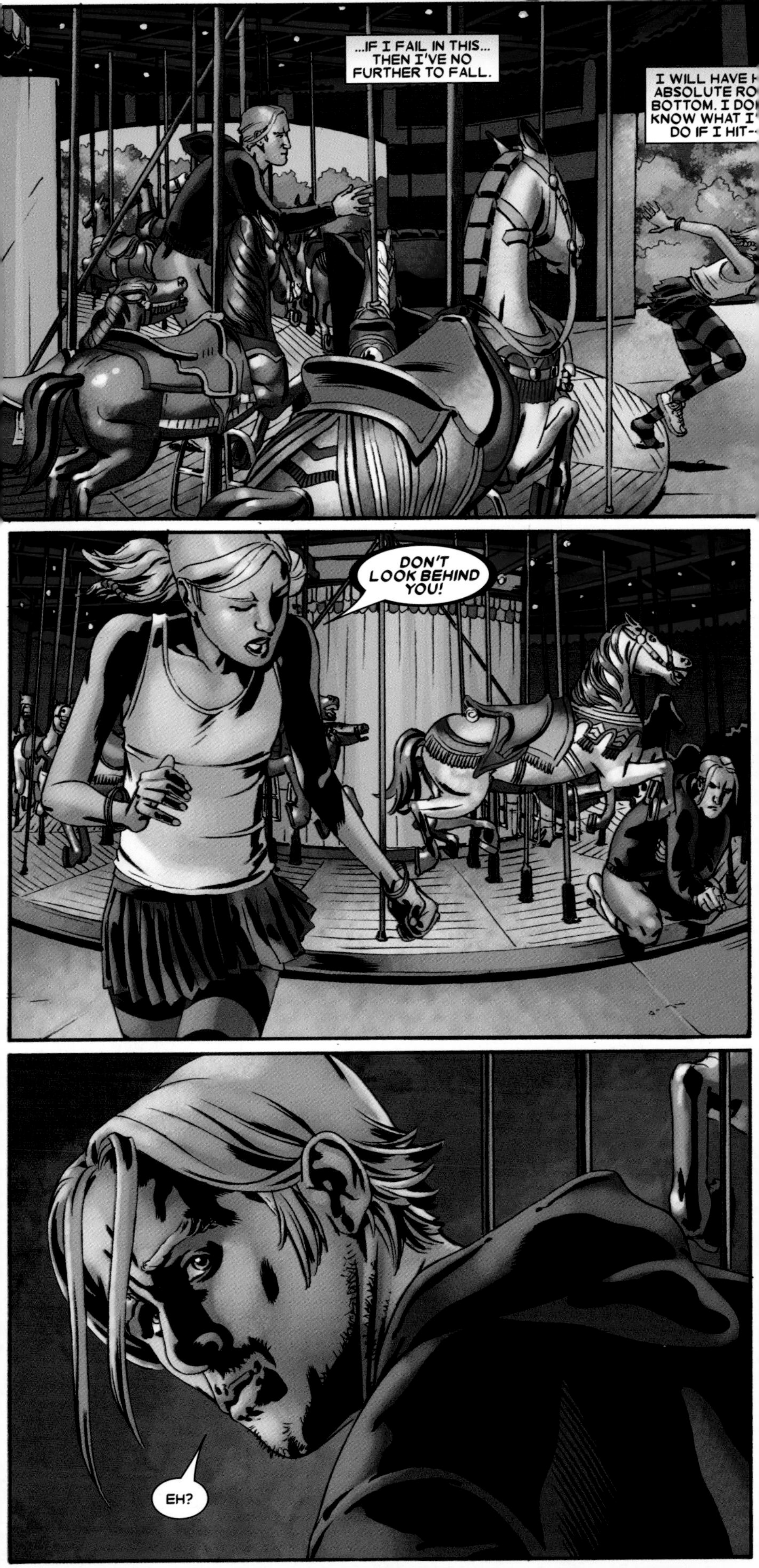
...IF I FAIL IN THIS... THEN I'VE NO FURTHER TO FALL.
DON'T LOOK BEHIND YOU!
EH?

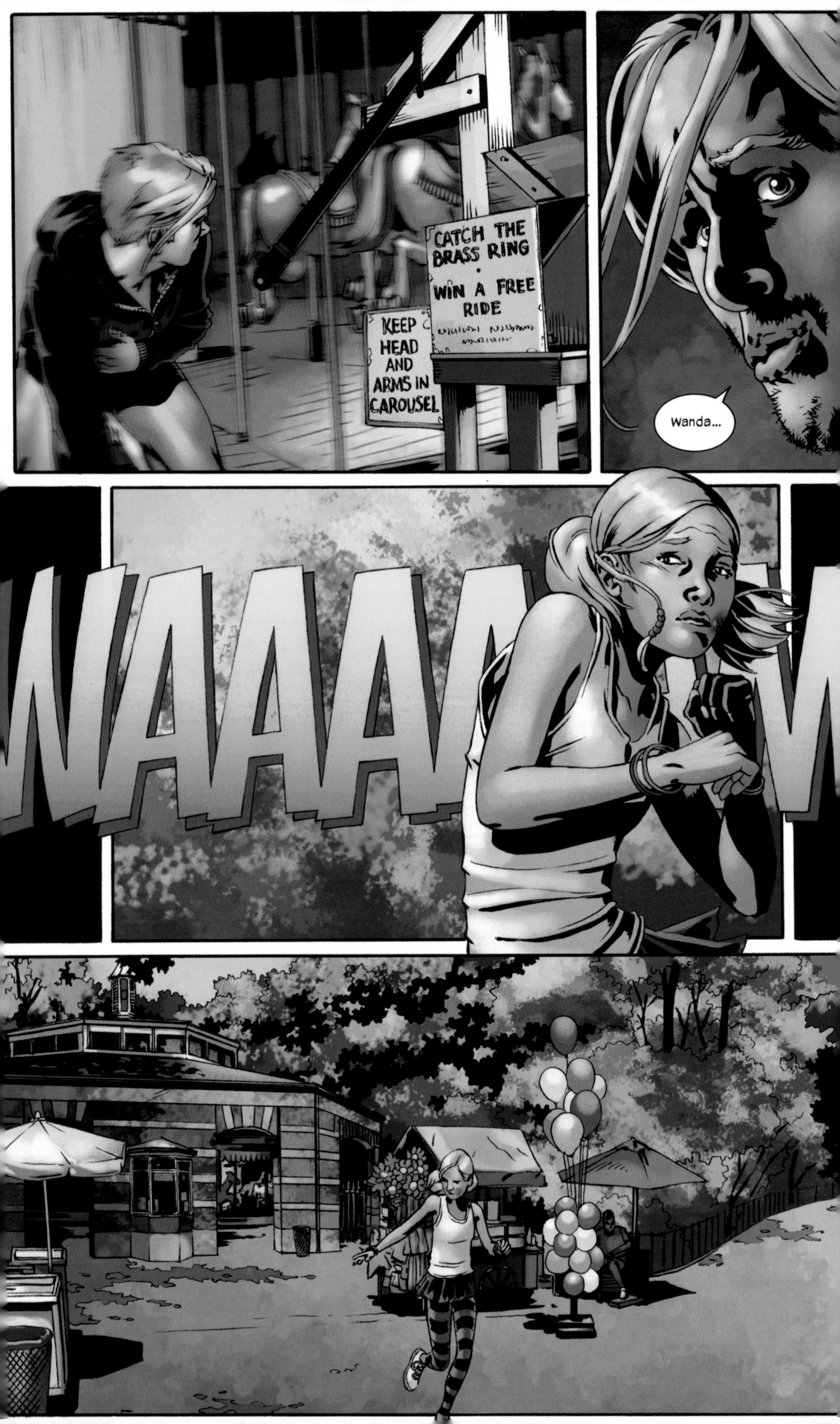
CATCH THE BRASS RING • WIN A FREE RIDE
KEEP HEAD AND ARMS IN CAROUSEL
Wanda...
WAAAAW

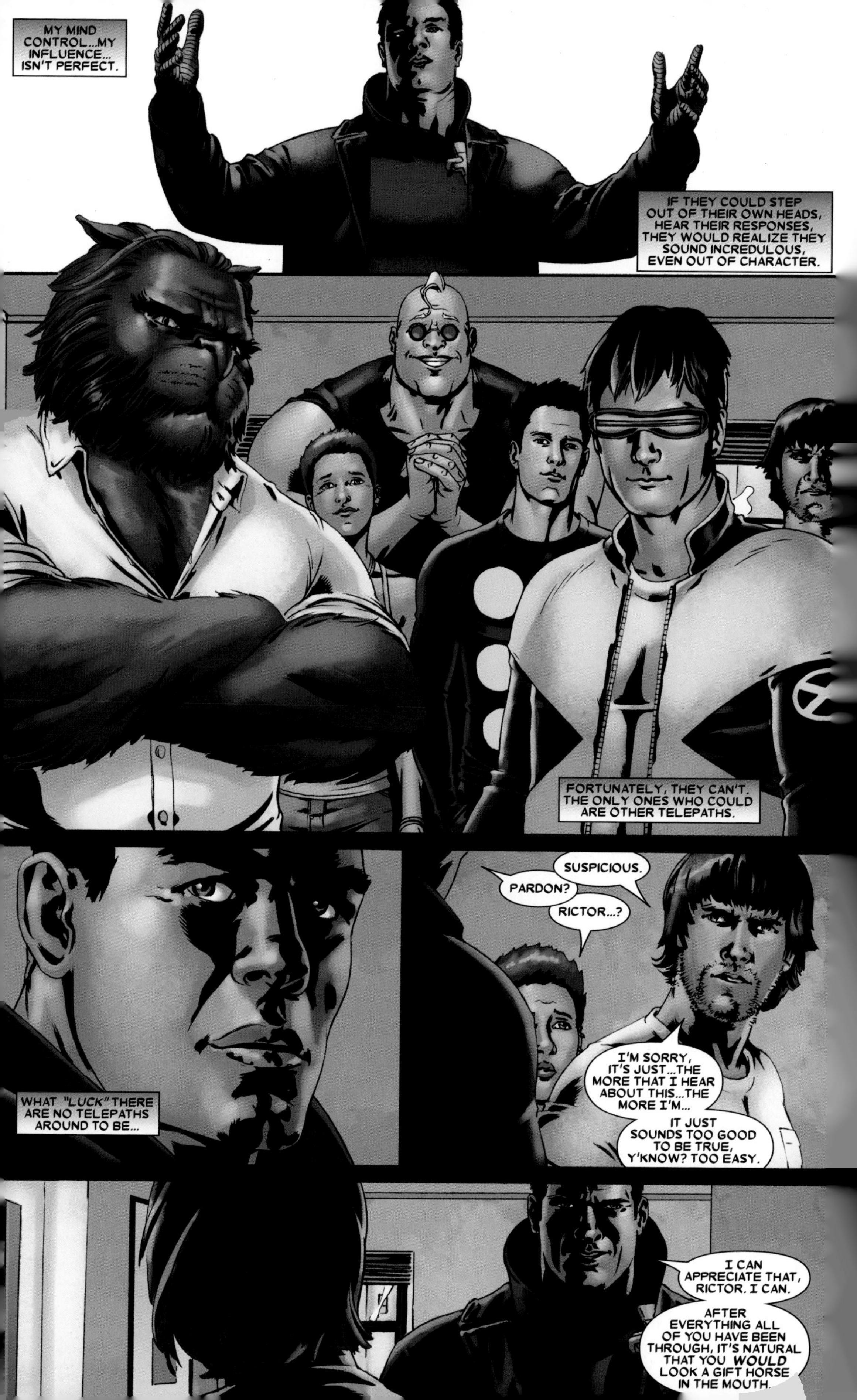
MY MIND CONTROL...MY INFLUENCE... ISN'T PERFECT.
IF THEY COULD STEP OUT OF THEIR OWN HEADS, HEAR THEIR RESPONSES, THEY WOULD REALIZE THEY SOUND INCREDULOUS, EVEN OUT OF CHARACTER.
FORTUNATELY, THEY CAN'T. THE ONLY ONES WHO COULD ARE OTHER TELEPATHS.
WHAT "LUCK" THERE ARE NO TELEPATHS AROUND TO BE...
SUSPICIOUS.
PARDON?
RICTOR...?
I'M SORRY, IT'S JUST...THE MORE THAT I HEAR ABOUT THIS...THE MORE I'M...
IT JUST SOUNDS TOO GOOD TO BE TRUE, Y'KNOW? TOO EASY.
I CAN APPRECIATE THAT, RICTOR. I CAN.
AFTER EVERYTHING ALL OF YOU HAVE BEEN THROUGH, IT'S NATURAL THAT YOU WOULD LOOK A GIFT HORSE IN THE MOUTH.

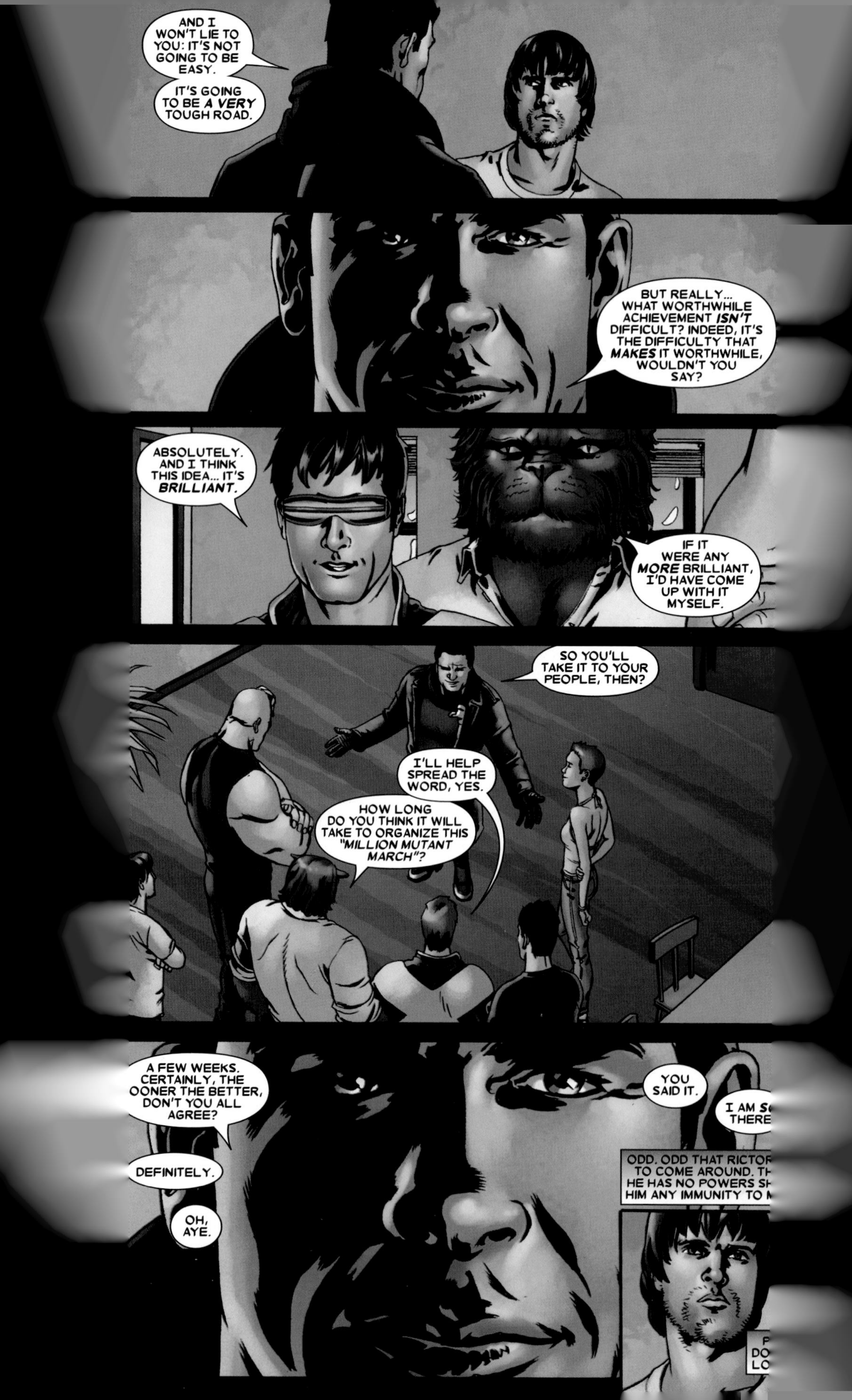
AND I WON'T LIE TO YOU: IT'S NOT GOING TO BE EASY.
IT'S GOING TO BE A VERY TOUGH ROAD.
BUT REALLY... WHAT WORTHWHILE ACHIEVEMENT ISN'T DIFFICULT? INDEED, IT'S THE DIFFICULTY THAT MAKES IT WORTHWHILE, WOULDN'T YOU SAY?
ABSOLUTELY. AND I THINK THIS IDEA... IT'S BRILLIANT.
IF IT WERE ANY MORE BRILLIANT, I'D HAVE COME UP WITH IT MYSELF.
SO YOU'LL TAKE IT TO YOUR PEOPLE, THEN?
I'LL HELP SPREAD THE WORD, YES.
HOW LONG DO YOU THINK IT WILL TAKE TO ORGANIZE THIS "MILLION MUTANT MARCH"?
A FEW WEEKS. CERTAINLY, THE OONER THE BETTER, DON'T YOU ALL AGREE?
DEFINITELY.
OH, AYE.
YOU SAID IT.

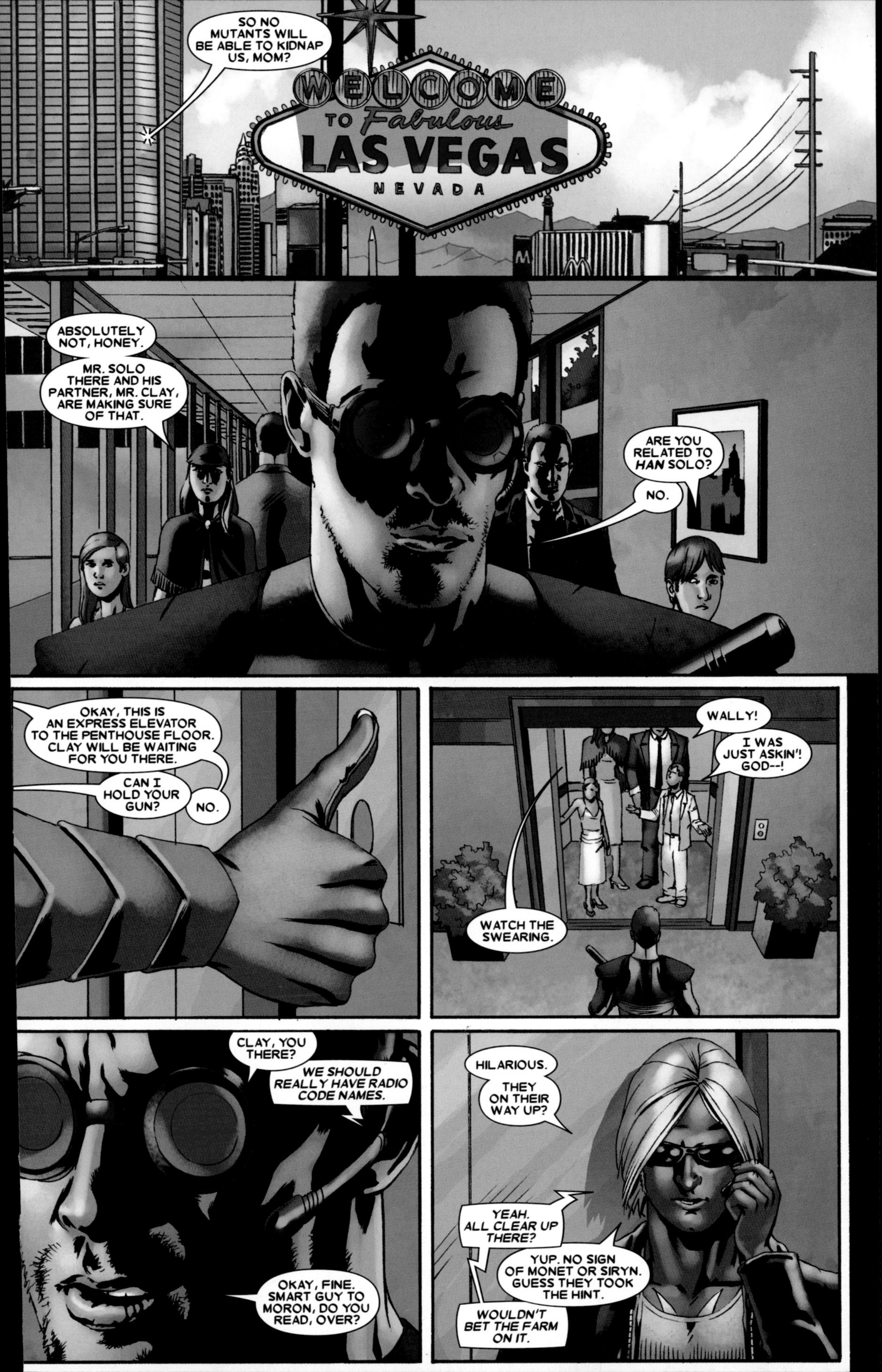
SO NO MUTANTS WILL BE ABLE TO KIDNAP US, MOM?
WELCOME TO Fabulous LAS VEGAS NEVADA
ABSOLUTELY NOT, HONEY.
MR. SOLO THERE AND HIS PARTNER, MR. CLAY, ARE MAKING SURE OF THAT.
ARE YOU RELATED TO *HAN* SOLO?
NO.
OKAY, THIS IS AN EXPRESS ELEVATOR TO THE PENTHOUSE FLOOR. CLAY WILL BE WAITING FOR YOU THERE.
CAN I HOLD YOUR GUN?
NO.
WALLY!
I WAS JUST ASKIN'! GOD--!
WATCH THE SWEARING.
CLAY, YOU THERE?
WE SHOULD REALLY HAVE RADIO CODE NAMES.
OKAY, FINE. SMART GUY TO MORON, DO YOU READ, OVER?
HILARIOUS.
THEY ON THEIR WAY UP?
YEAH. ALL CLEAR UP THERE?
YUP. NO SIGN OF MONET OR SIRYN. GUESS THEY TOOK THE HINT.
WOULDN'T BET THE FARM ON IT.

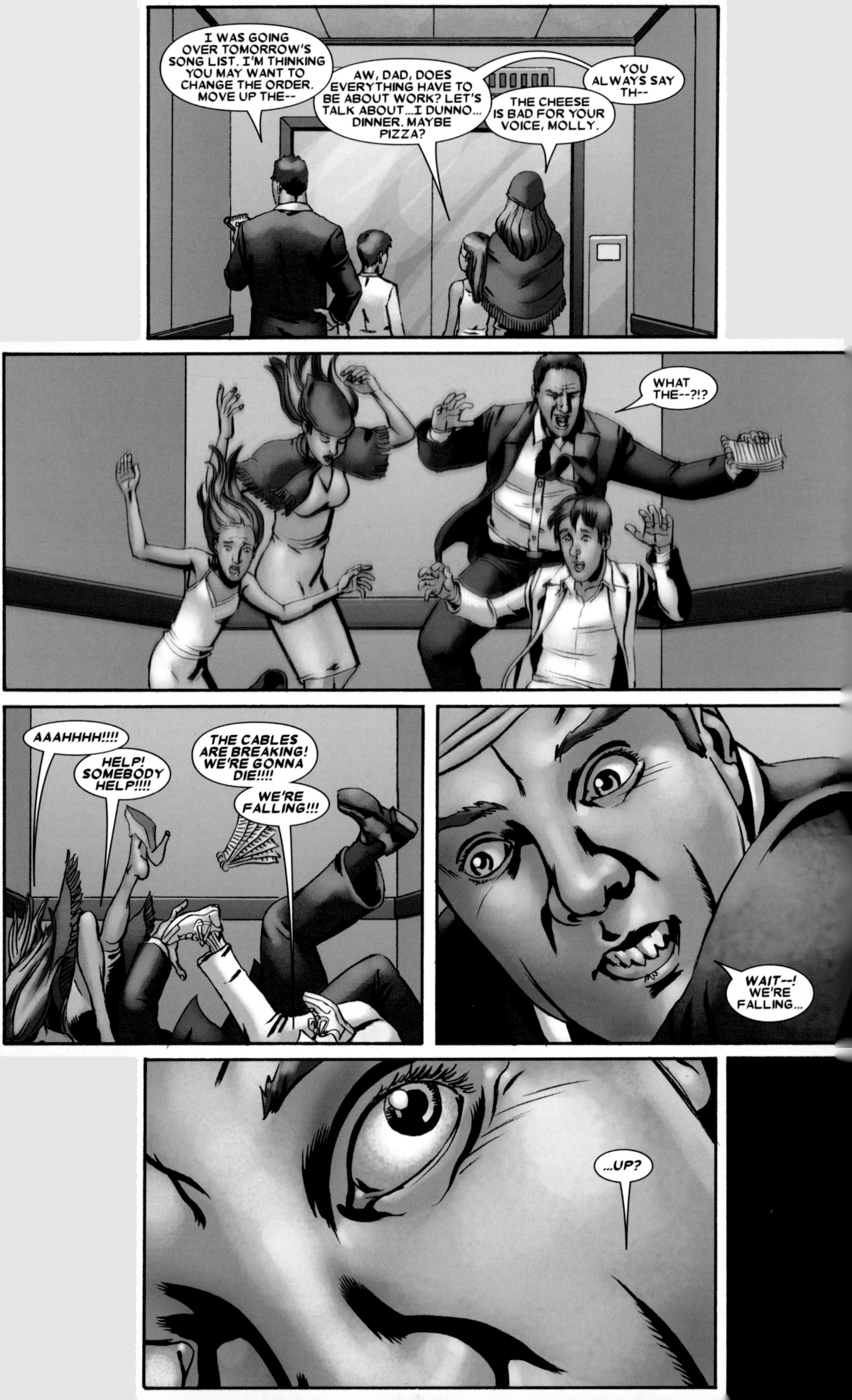
I WAS GOING OVER TOMORROW'S SONG LIST. I'M THINKING YOU MAY WANT TO CHANGE THE ORDER. MOVE UP THE--
AW, DAD, DOES EVERYTHING HAVE TO BE ABOUT WORK? LET'S TALK ABOUT...I DUNNO... DINNER. MAYBE PIZZA?
YOU ALWAYS SAY TH--
THE CHEESE IS BAD FOR YOUR VOICE, MOLLY.
WHAT THE--?!?
AAAHHHH!!!!
HELP! SOMEBODY HELP!!!!
THE CABLES ARE BREAKING! WE'RE GONNA DIE!!!!
WE'RE FALLING!!!
WAIT--! WE'RE FALLING...
...UP?

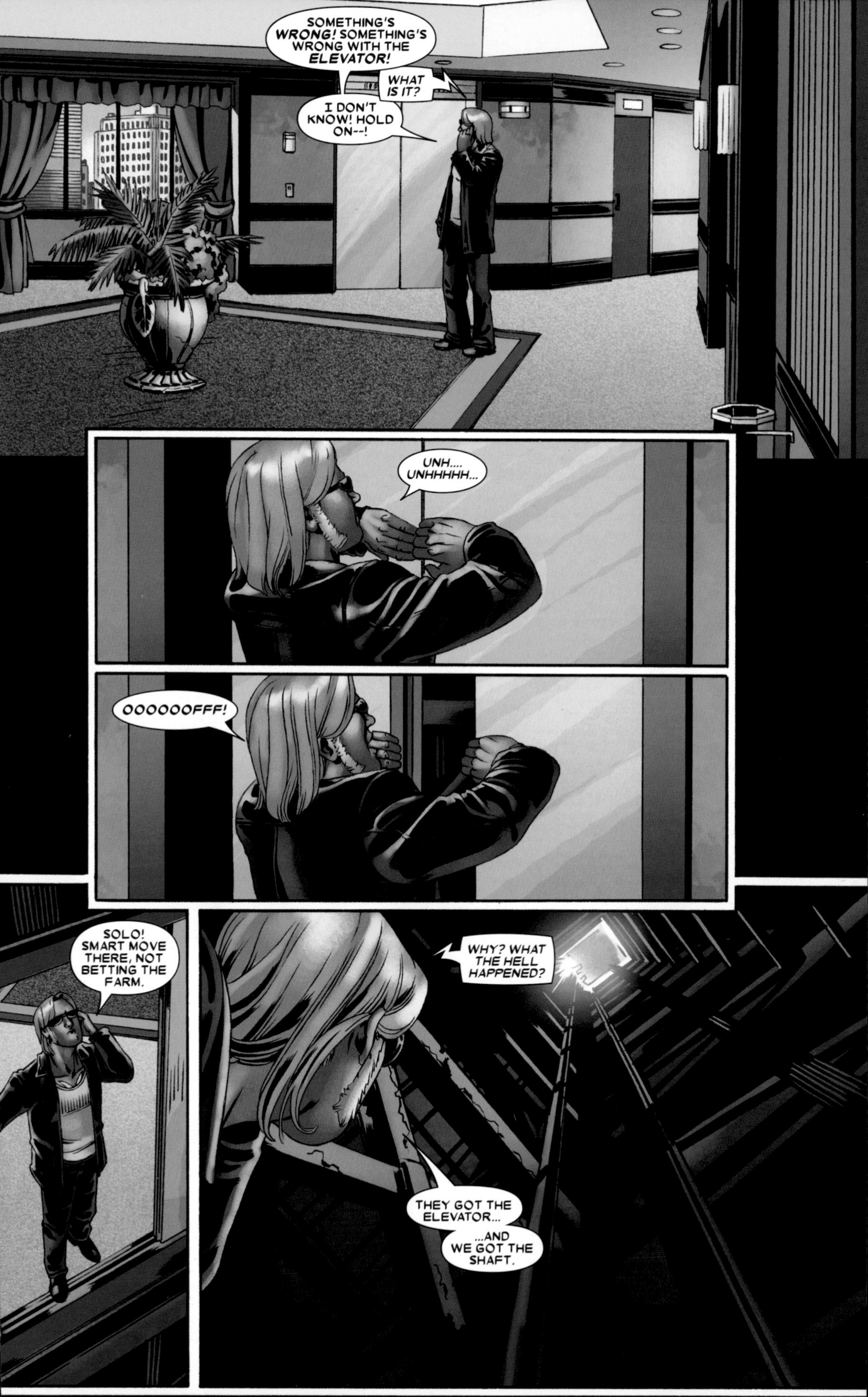
SOMETHING'S WRONG! SOMETHING'S WRONG WITH THE ELEVATOR!
WHAT IS IT?
I DON'T KNOW! HOLD ON--!
UNH.... UNHHHHH...
OOOOOOFFF!
SOLO! SMART MOVE THERE, NOT BETTING THE FARM.
WHY? WHAT THE HELL HAPPENED?
THEY GOT THE ELEVATOR...
...AND WE GOT THE SHAFT.

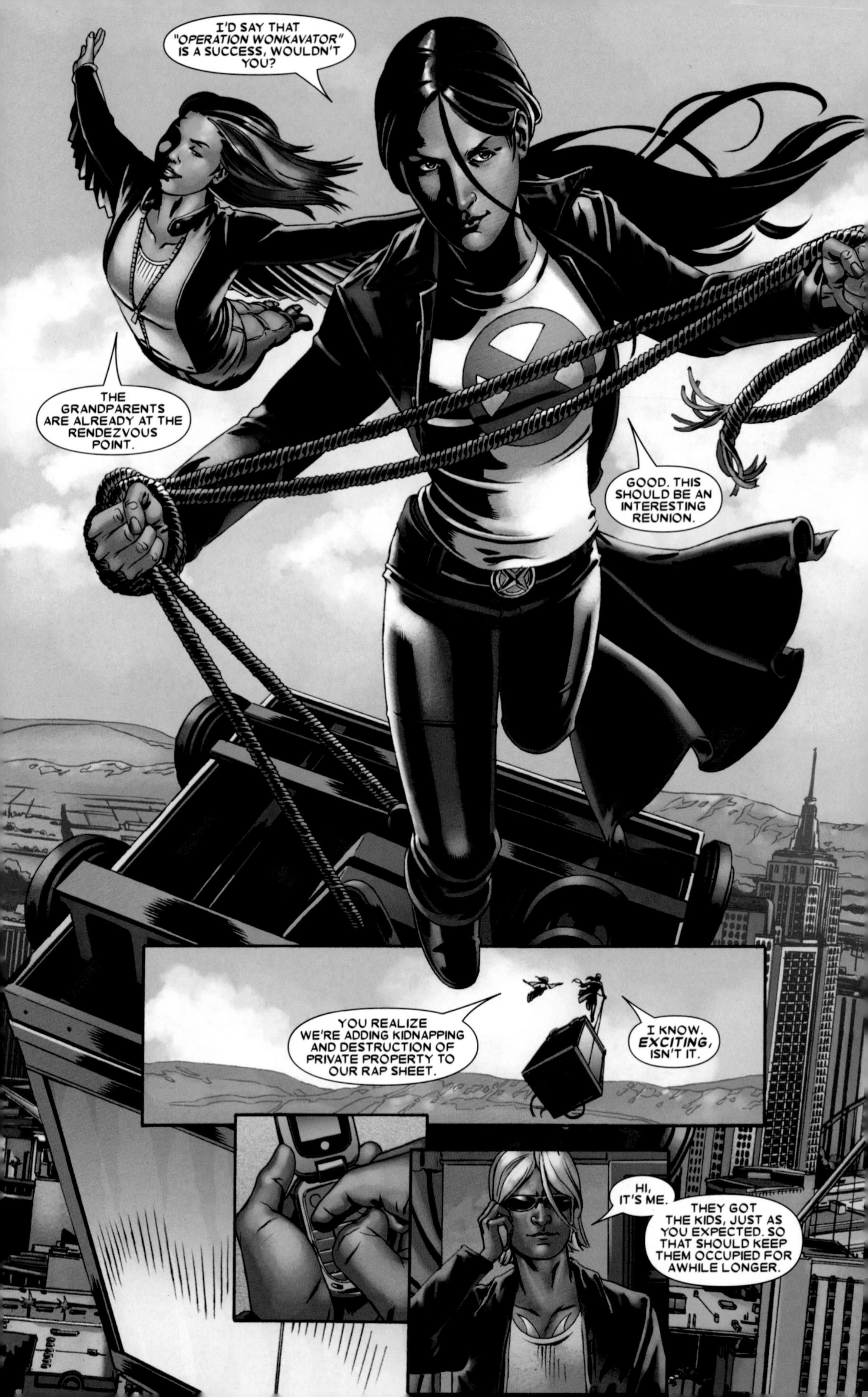
I'D SAY THAT "OPERATION WONKAVATOR" IS A SUCCESS, WOULDN'T YOU?
THE GRANDPARENTS ARE ALREADY AT THE RENDEZVOUS POINT.
GOOD. THIS SHOULD BE AN INTERESTING REUNION.
YOU REALIZE WE'RE ADDING KIDNAPPING AND DESTRUCTION OF PRIVATE PROPERTY TO OUR RAP SHEET.
I KNOW. *EXCITING,* ISN'T IT.
HI, IT'S ME.
THEY GOT THE KIDS, JUST AS YOU EXPECTED. SO THAT SHOULD KEEP THEM OCCUPIED FOR AWHILE LONGER.

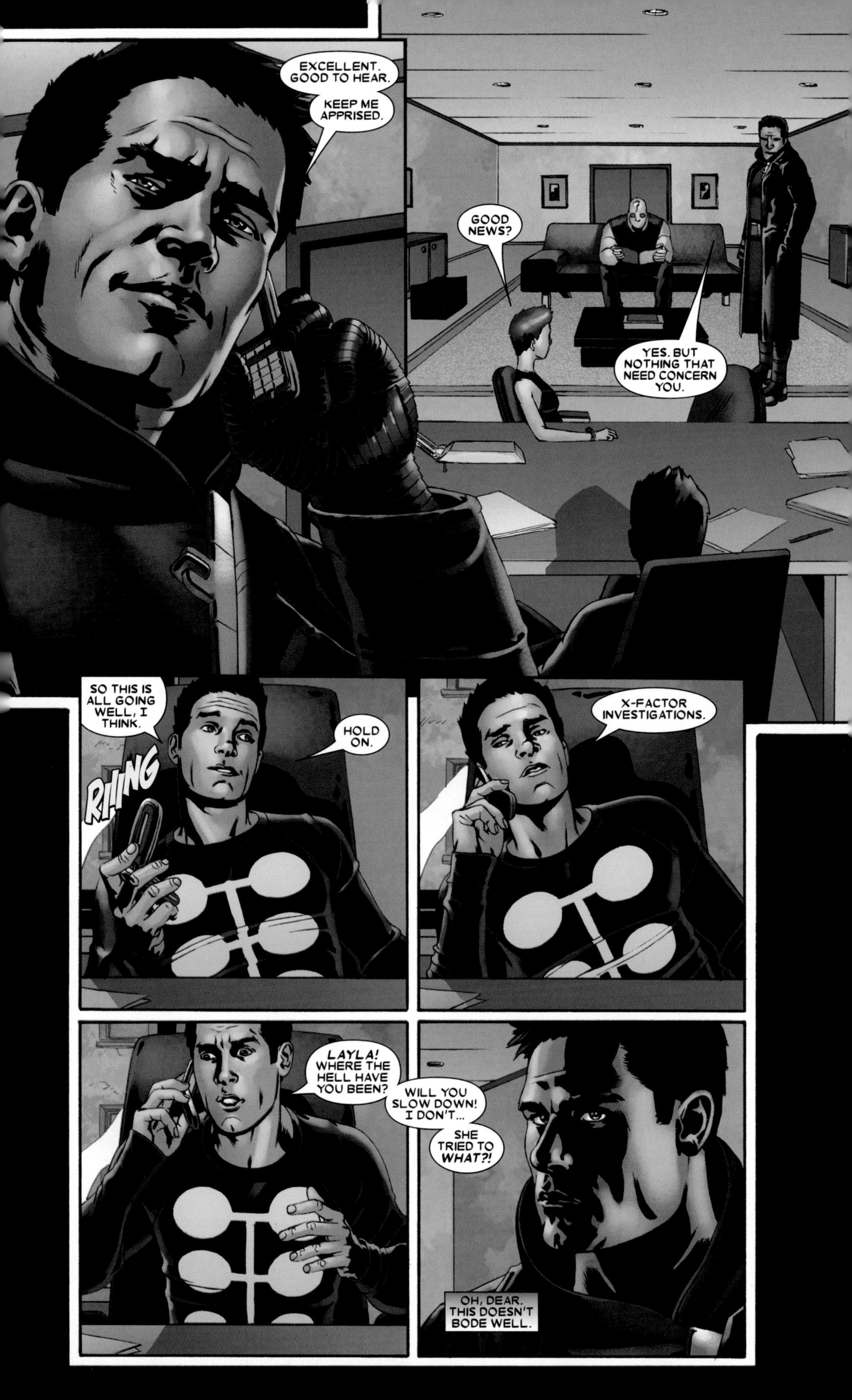
EXCELLENT. GOOD TO HEAR.
KEEP ME APPRISED.
GOOD NEWS?
YES. BUT NOTHING THAT NEED CONCERN YOU.
SO THIS IS ALL GOING WELL, I THINK.
RIIING
HOLD ON.
X-FACTOR INVESTIGATIONS.
LAYLA! WHERE THE HELL HAVE YOU BEEN?
WILL YOU SLOW DOWN! I DON'T...
SHE TRIED TO WHAT?!
OH, DEAR. THIS DOESN'T BODE WELL.

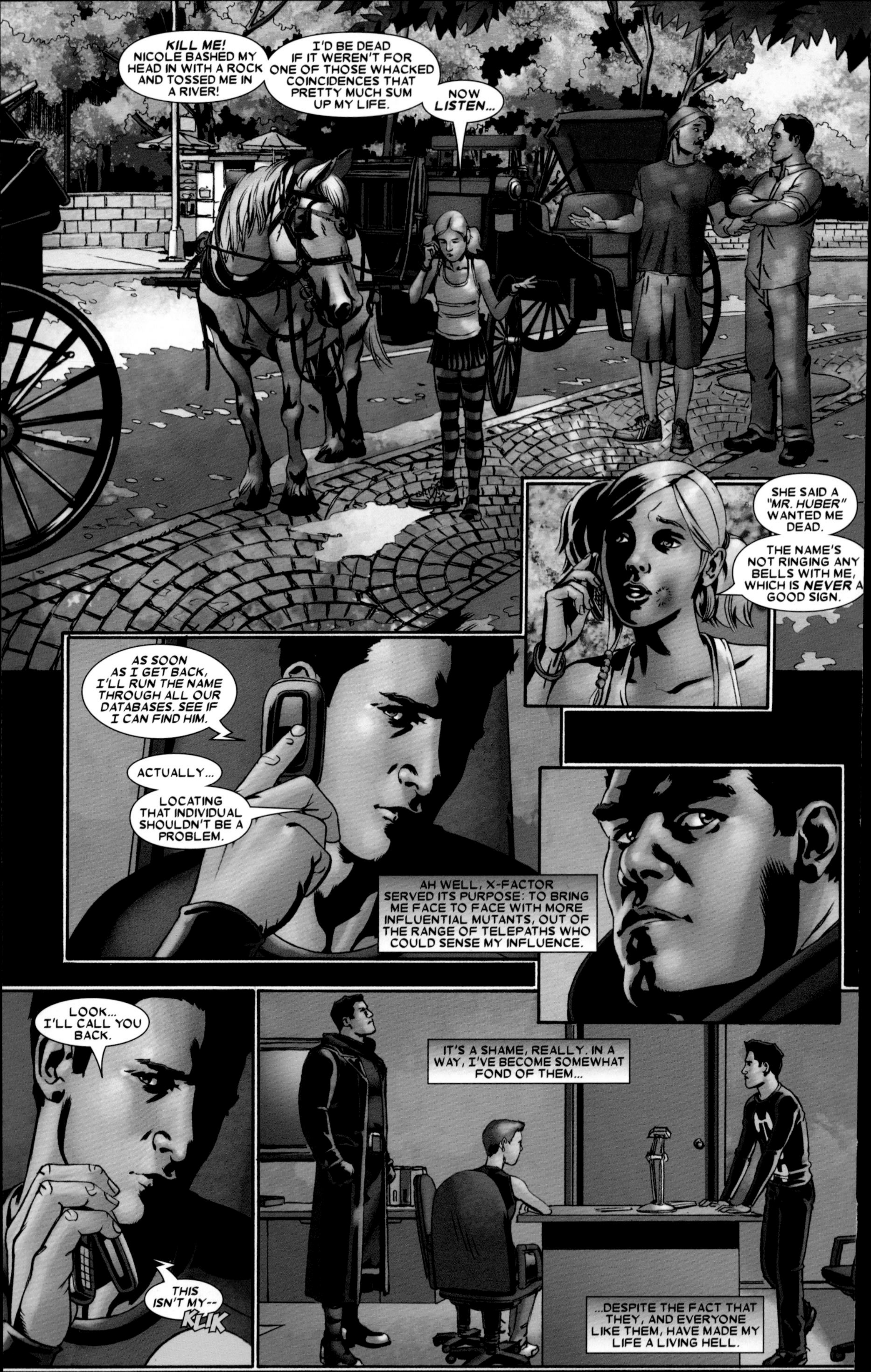
KILL ME! NICOLE BASHED MY HEAD IN WITH A ROCK AND TOSSED ME IN A RIVER!
I'D BE DEAD IF IT WEREN'T FOR ONE OF THOSE WHACKED COINCIDENCES THAT PRETTY MUCH SUM UP MY LIFE.
NOW LISTEN...
SHE SAID A "MR. HUBER" WANTED ME DEAD.
THE NAME'S NOT RINGING ANY BELLS WITH ME, WHICH IS NEVER A GOOD SIGN.
AS SOON AS I GET BACK, I'LL RUN THE NAME THROUGH ALL OUR DATABASES. SEE IF I CAN FIND HIM.
ACTUALLY...
LOCATING THAT INDIVIDUAL SHOULDN'T BE A PROBLEM.
AH WELL, X-FACTOR SERVED ITS PURPOSE: TO BRING ME FACE TO FACE WITH MORE INFLUENTIAL MUTANTS, OUT OF THE RANGE OF TELEPATHS WHO COULD SENSE MY INFLUENCE.
LOOK... I'LL CALL YOU BACK.
THIS ISN'T MY--
KLIK
IT'S A SHAME, REALLY. IN A WAY, I'VE BECOME SOMEWHAT FOND OF THEM...
...DESPITE THE FACT THAT THEY, AND EVERYONE LIKE THEM, HAVE MADE MY LIFE A LIVING HELL.

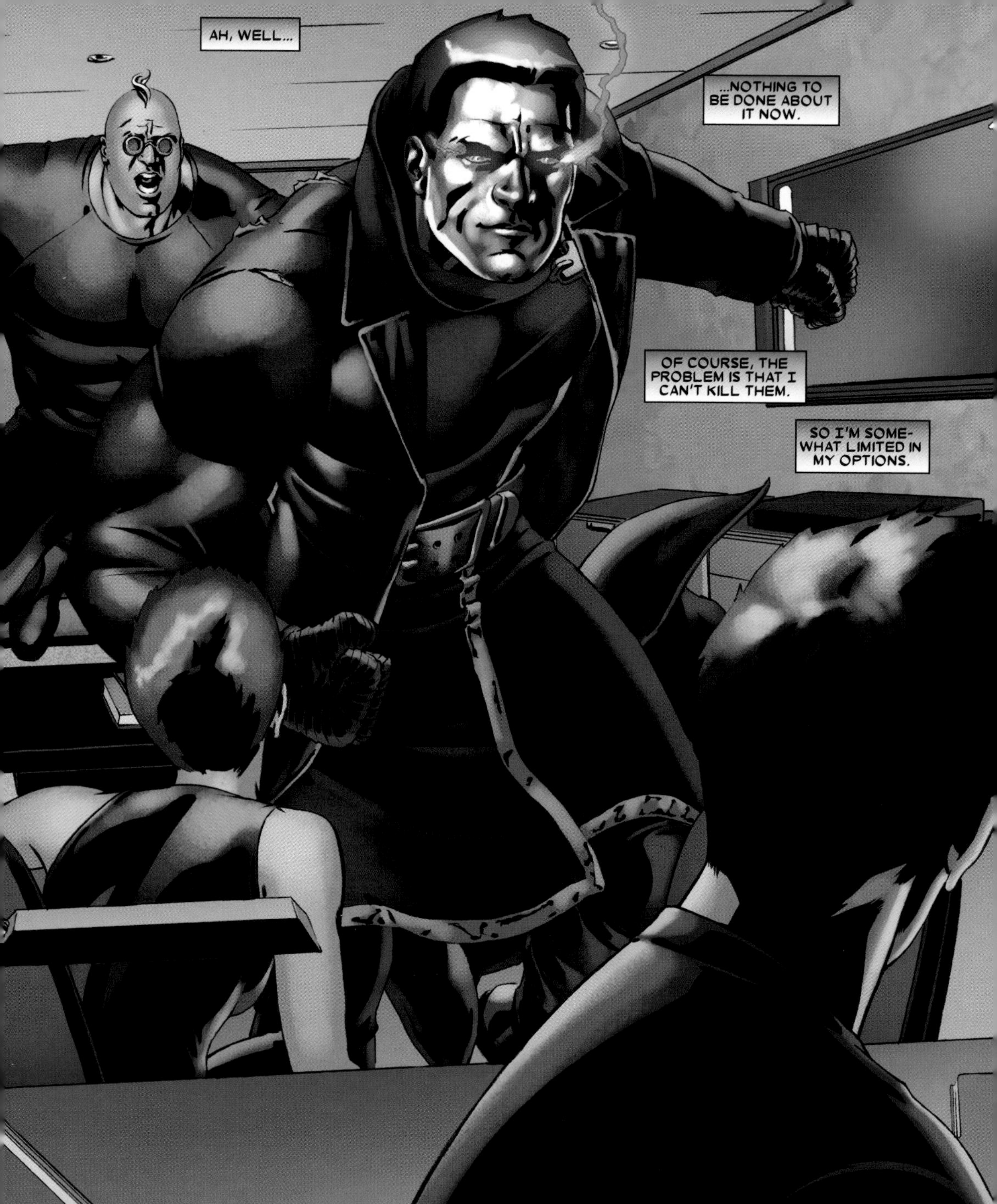
AH, WELL...
...NOTHING TO BE DONE ABOUT IT NOW.
OF COURSE, THE PROBLEM IS THAT I CAN'T KILL THEM.
SO I'M SOME-WHAT LIMITED IN MY OPTIONS.

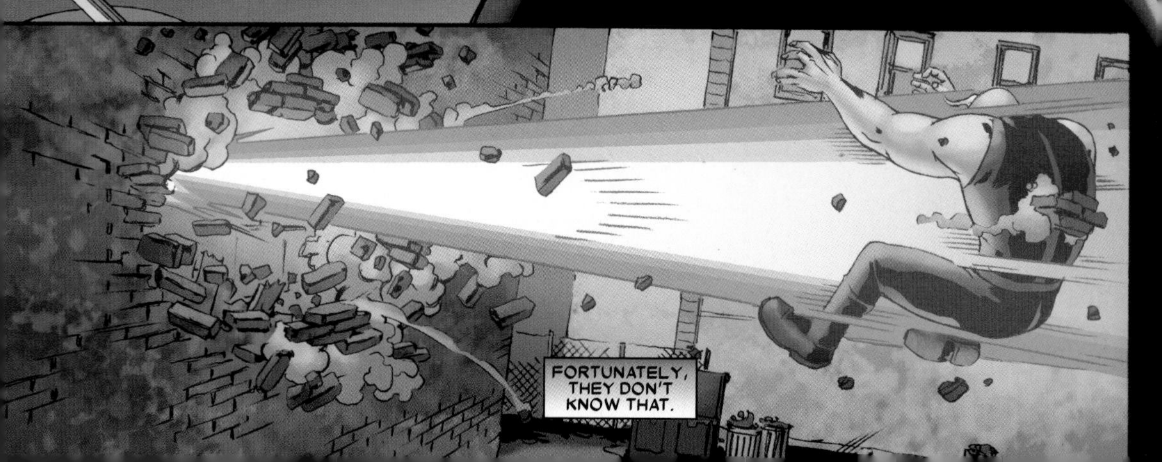
FORTUNATELY, THEY DON'T KNOW THAT.

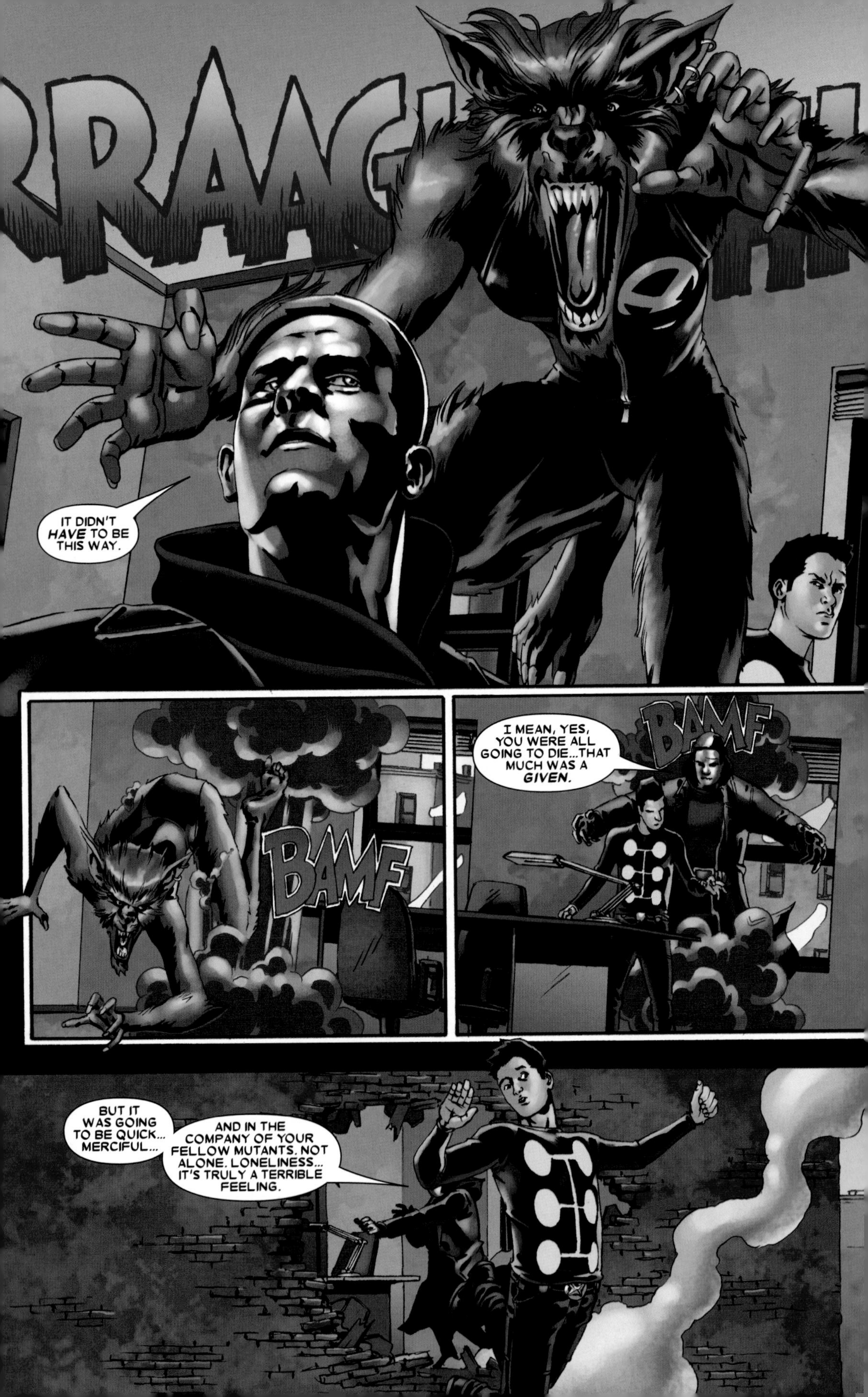
RRAAGH
IT DIDN'T HAVE TO BE THIS WAY.
BAMF
I MEAN, YES, YOU WERE ALL GOING TO DIE...THAT MUCH WAS A GIVEN.
BAMF
BUT IT WAS GOING TO BE QUICK... MERCIFUL...
AND IN THE COMPANY OF YOUR FELLOW MUTANTS. NOT ALONE. LONELINESS... IT'S TRULY A TERRIBLE FEELING.

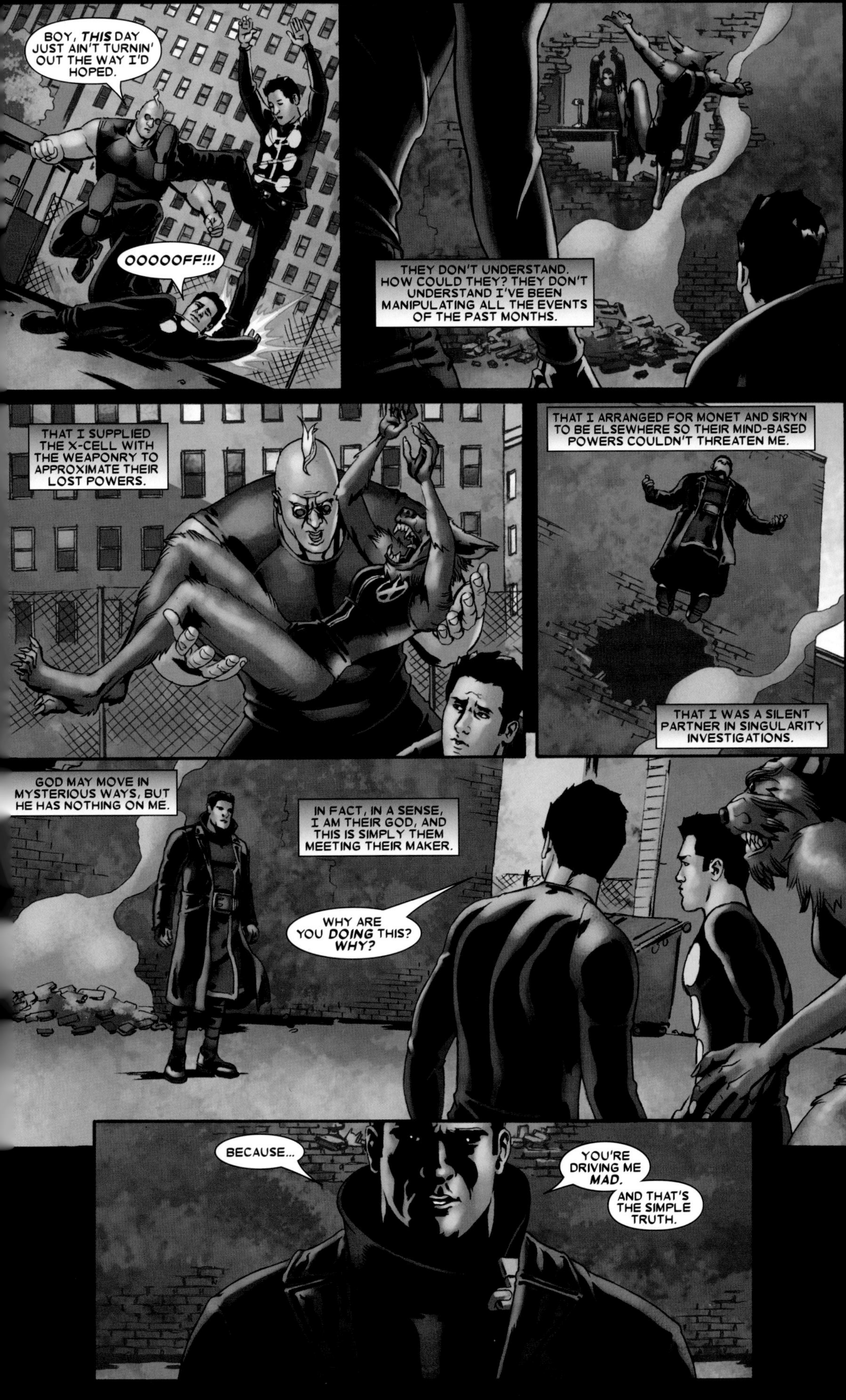
BOY, THIS DAY JUST AIN'T TURNIN' OUT THE WAY I'D HOPED.
OOOOOFF!!!
THEY DON'T UNDERSTAND. HOW COULD THEY? THEY DON'T UNDERSTAND I'VE BEEN MANIPULATING ALL THE EVENTS OF THE PAST MONTHS.
THAT I SUPPLIED THE X-CELL WITH THE WEAPONRY TO APPROXIMATE THEIR LOST POWERS.
THAT I ARRANGED FOR MONET AND SIRYN TO BE ELSEWHERE SO THEIR MIND-BASED POWERS COULDN'T THREATEN ME.
THAT I WAS A SILENT PARTNER IN SINGULARITY INVESTIGATIONS.
GOD MAY MOVE IN MYSTERIOUS WAYS, BUT HE HAS NOTHING ON ME.
IN FACT, IN A SENSE, I AM THEIR GOD, AND THIS IS SIMPLY THEM MEETING THEIR MAKER.
WHY ARE YOU DOING THIS? WHY?
BECAUSE...
YOU'RE DRIVING ME MAD.
AND THAT'S THE SIMPLE TRUTH.

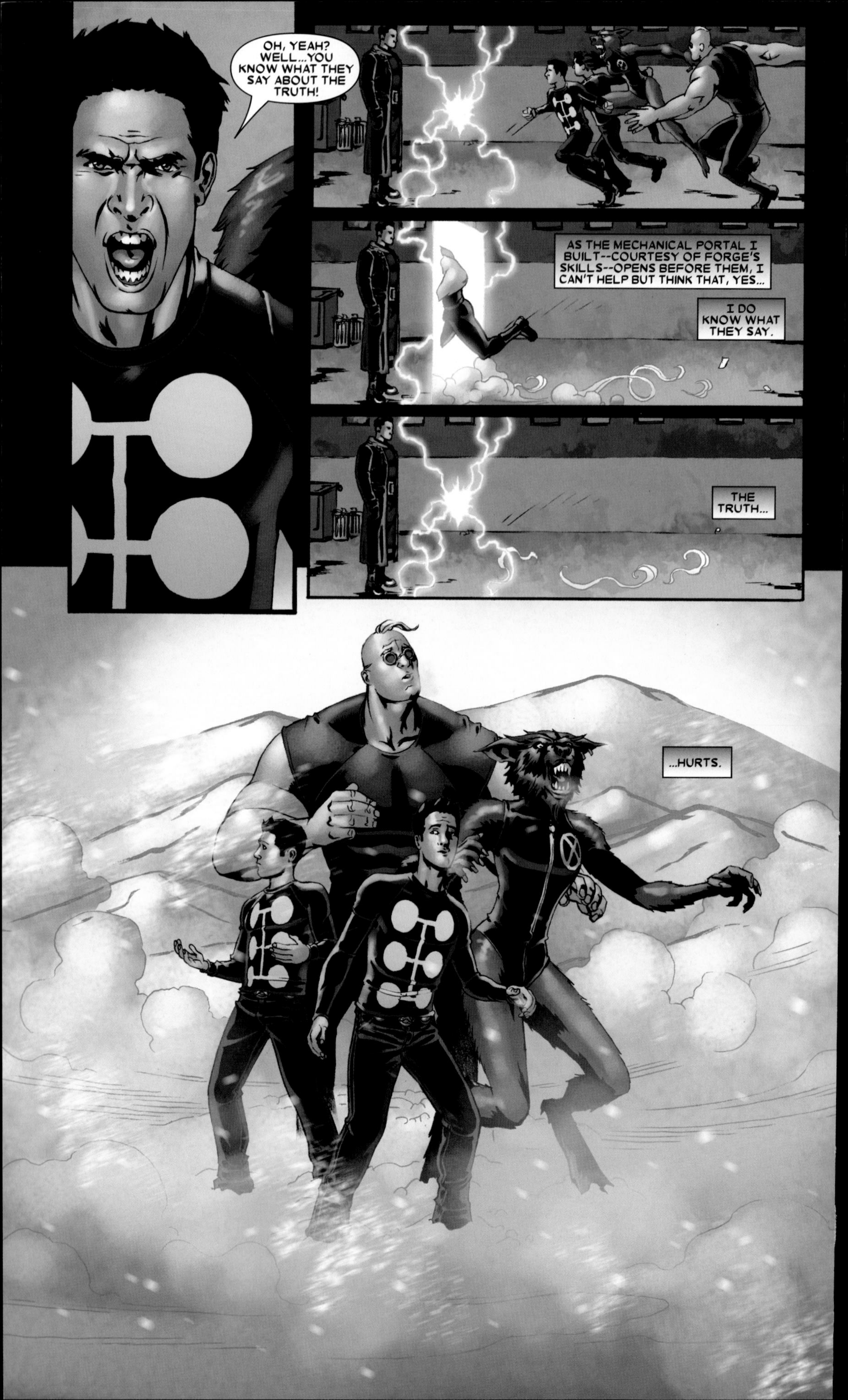

OH, YEAH? WELL...YOU KNOW WHAT THEY SAY ABOUT THE TRUTH!
AS THE MECHANICAL PORTAL I BUILT--COURTESY OF FORGE'S SKILLS--OPENS BEFORE THEM, I CAN'T HELP BUT THINK THAT, YES...
I DO KNOW WHAT THEY SAY.
THE TRUTH...
...HURTS.

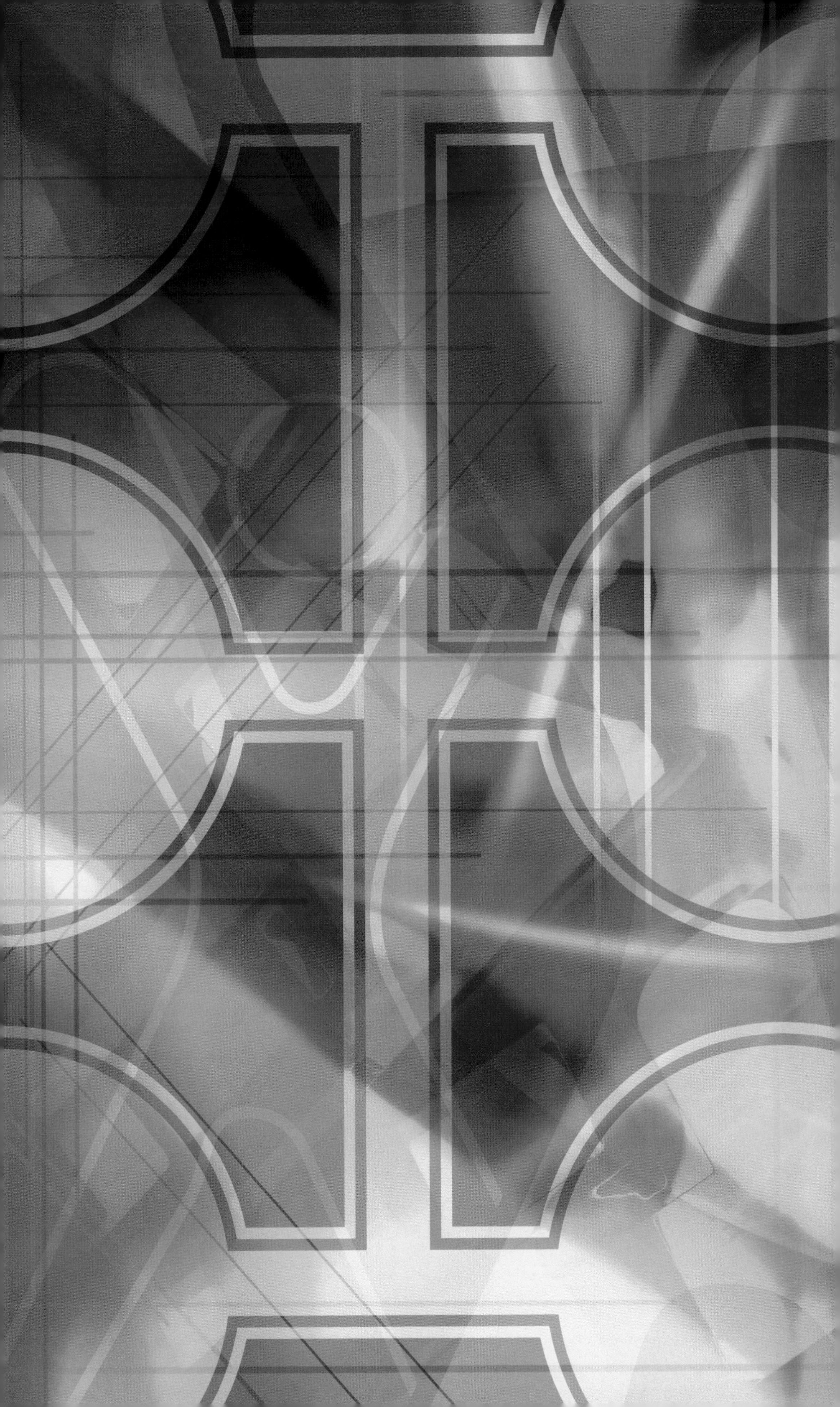

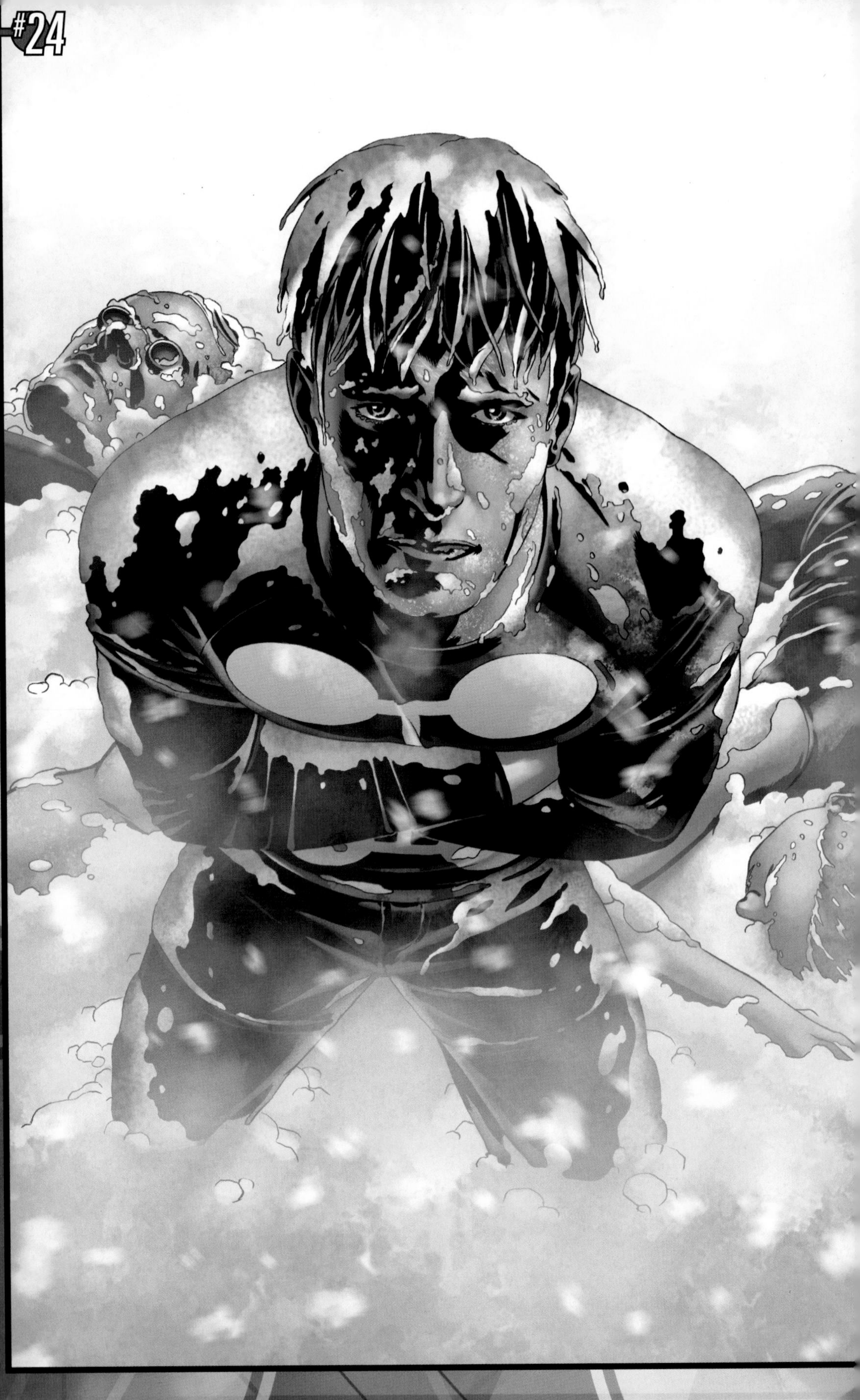
#24

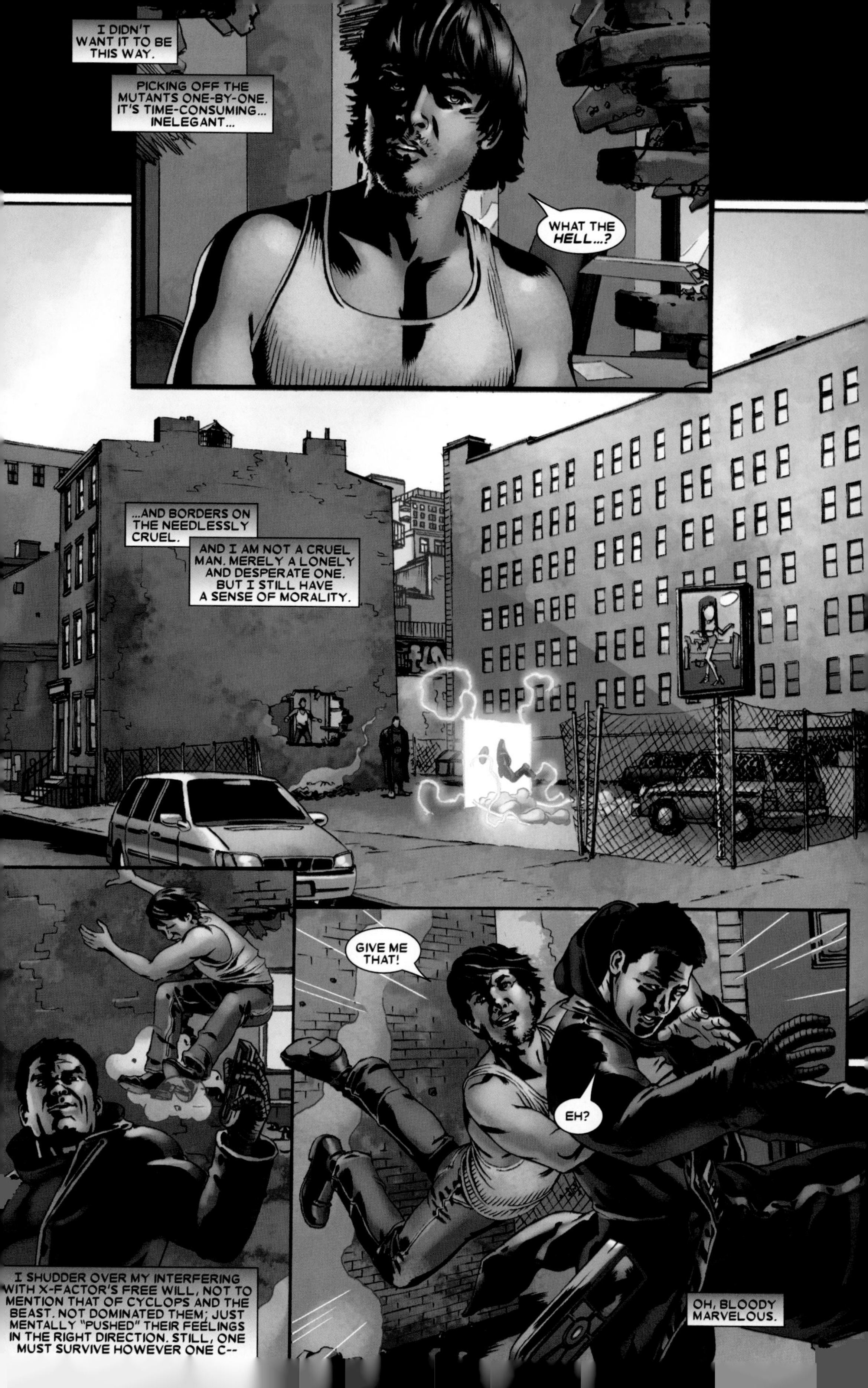

I DIDN'T WANT IT TO BE THIS WAY.
PICKING OFF THE MUTANTS ONE-BY-ONE. IT'S TIME-CONSUMING... INELEGANT...
WHAT THE *HELL*...?
...AND BORDERS ON THE NEEDLESSLY CRUEL.
AND I AM NOT A CRUEL MAN. MERELY A LONELY AND DESPERATE ONE. BUT I STILL HAVE A SENSE OF MORALITY.
I SHUDDER OVER MY INTERFERING WITH X-FACTOR'S FREE WILL, NOT TO MENTION THAT OF CYCLOPS AND THE BEAST. NOT DOMINATED THEM; JUST MENTALLY "PUSHED" THEIR FEELINGS IN THE RIGHT DIRECTION. STILL, ONE MUST SURVIVE HOWEVER ONE C--
GIVE ME THAT!
EH?
OH, BLOODY MARVELOUS.

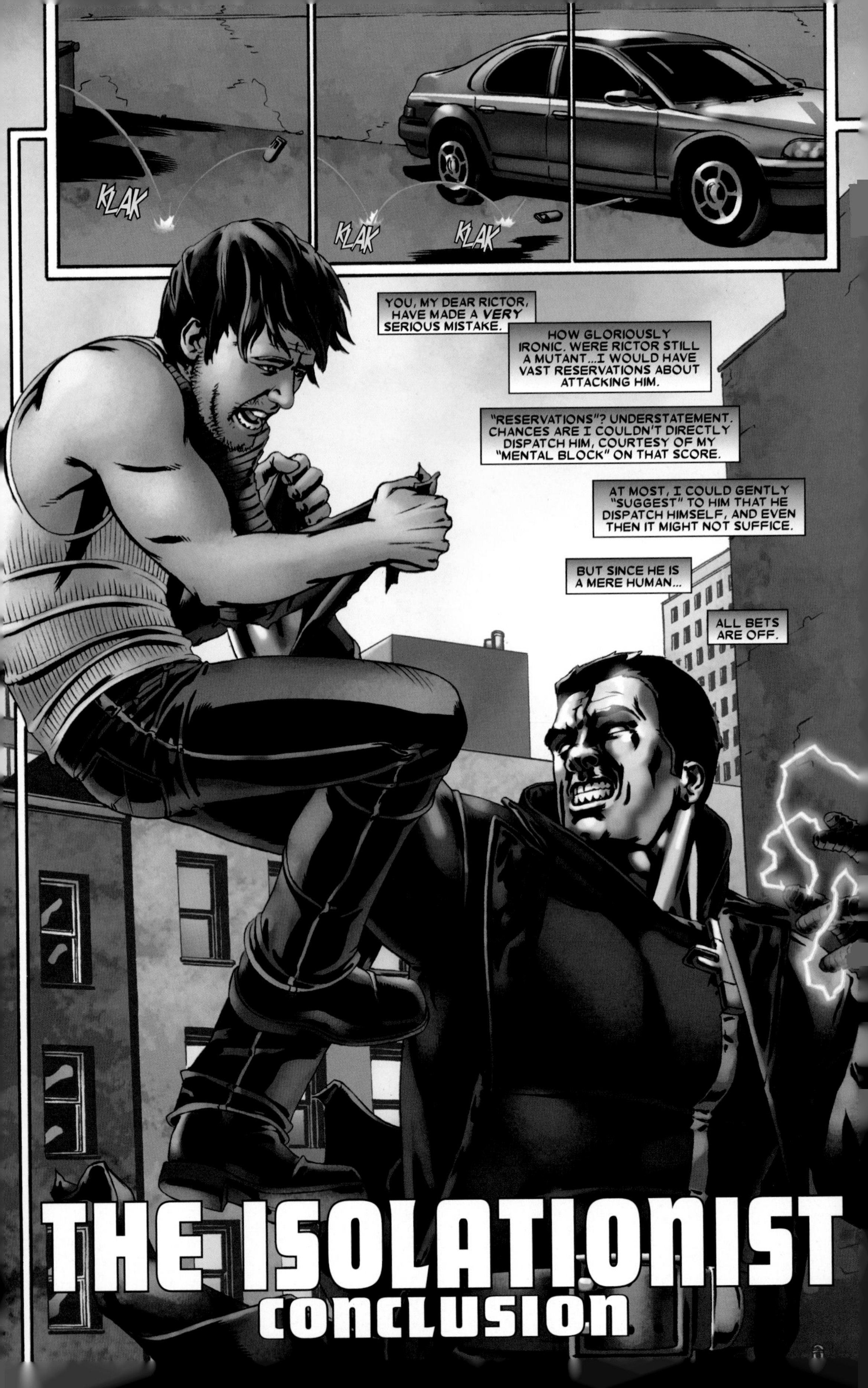
KLAK
KLAK
KLAK
YOU, MY DEAR RICTOR, HAVE MADE A VERY SERIOUS MISTAKE.
HOW GLORIOUSLY IRONIC. WERE RICTOR STILL A MUTANT...I WOULD HAVE VAST RESERVATIONS ABOUT ATTACKING HIM.
"RESERVATIONS"? UNDERSTATEMENT. CHANCES ARE I COULDN'T DIRECTLY DISPATCH HIM, COURTESY OF MY "MENTAL BLOCK" ON THAT SCORE.
AT MOST, I COULD GENTLY "SUGGEST" TO HIM THAT HE DISPATCH HIMSELF, AND EVEN THEN IT MIGHT NOT SUFFICE.
BUT SINCE HE IS A MERE HUMAN...
ALL BETS ARE OFF.
THE ISOLATIONIST
CONCLUSION

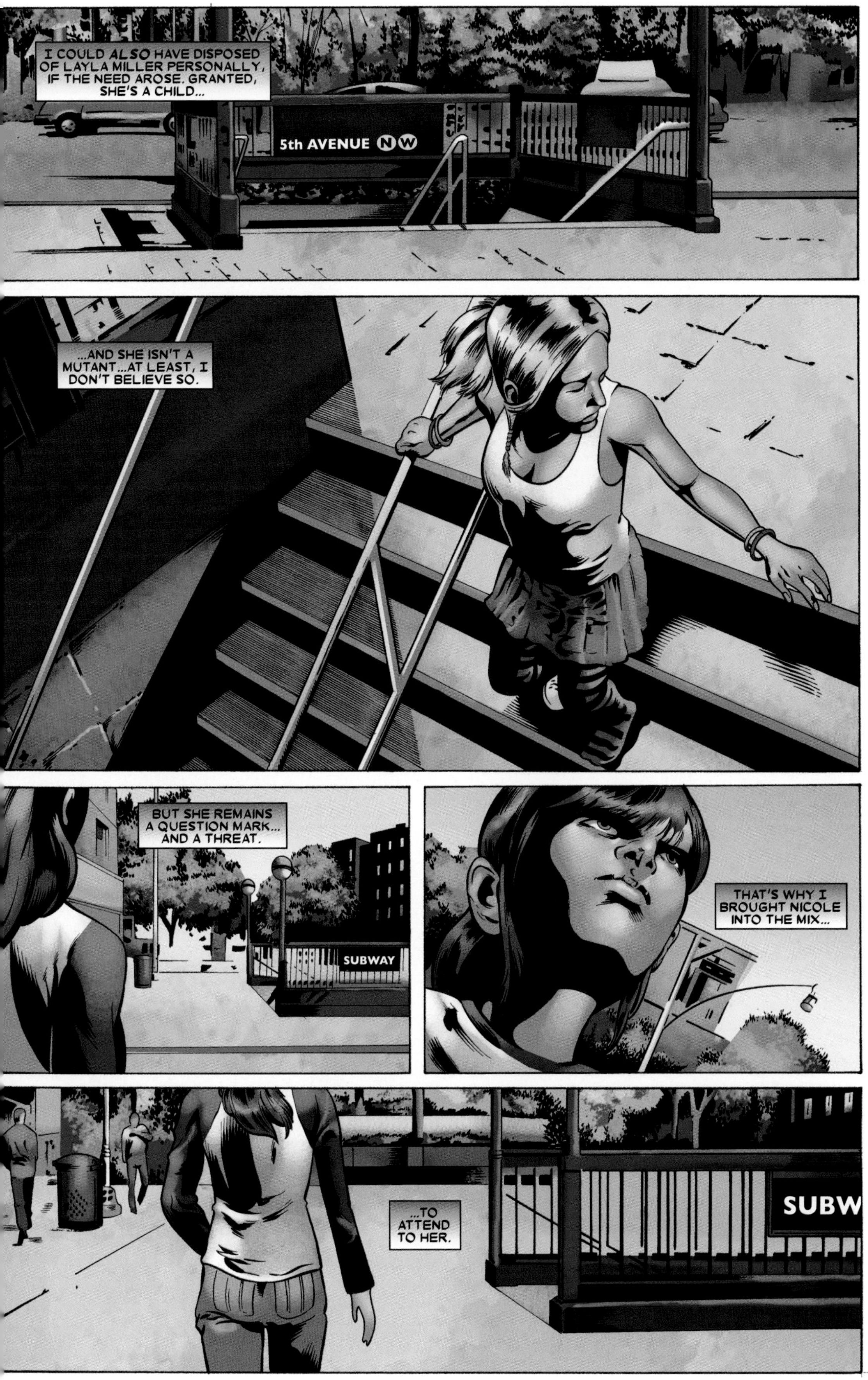

I COULD *ALSO* HAVE DISPOSED OF LAYLA MILLER PERSONALLY, IF THE NEED AROSE. GRANTED, SHE'S A CHILD...
5th AVENUE N W
...AND SHE ISN'T A MUTANT...AT LEAST, I DON'T BELIEVE SO.
BUT SHE REMAINS A QUESTION MARK... AND A THREAT.
SUBWAY
THAT'S WHY I BROUGHT NICOLE INTO THE MIX...
...TO ATTEND TO HER.
SUBW

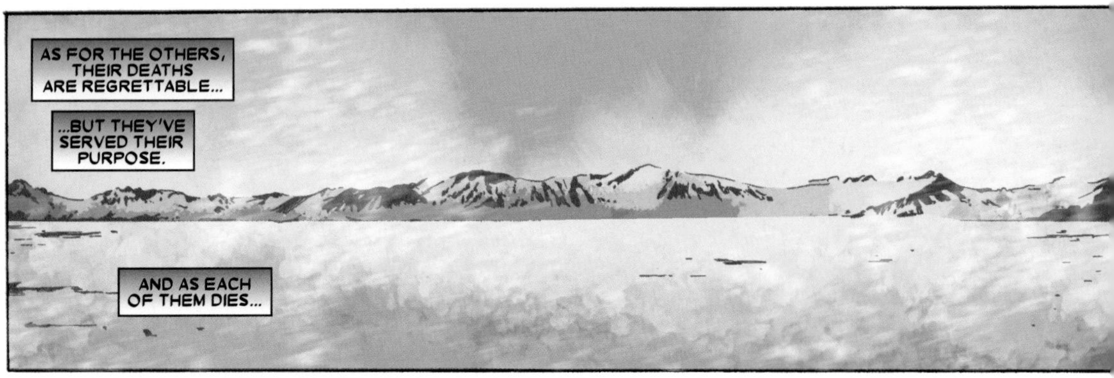
AS FOR THE OTHERS, THEIR DEATHS ARE REGRETTABLE...
...BUT THEY'VE SERVED THEIR PURPOSE.
AND AS EACH OF THEM DIES...
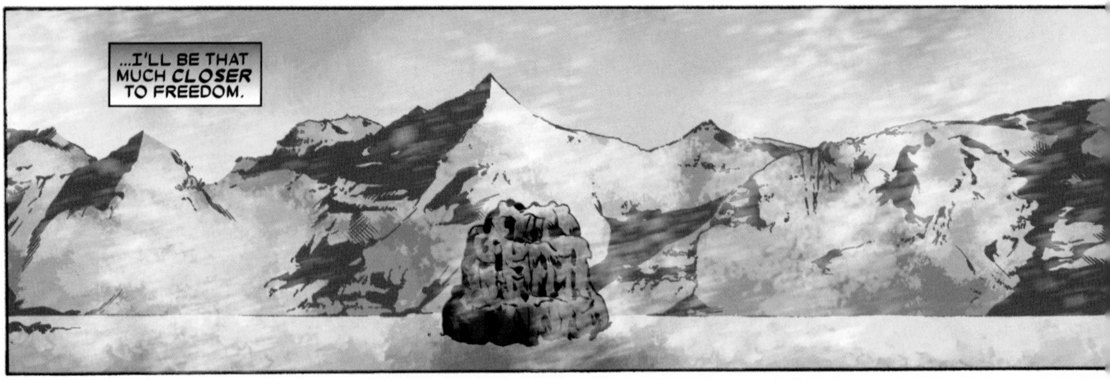
...I'LL BE THAT MUCH CLOSER TO FREEDOM.
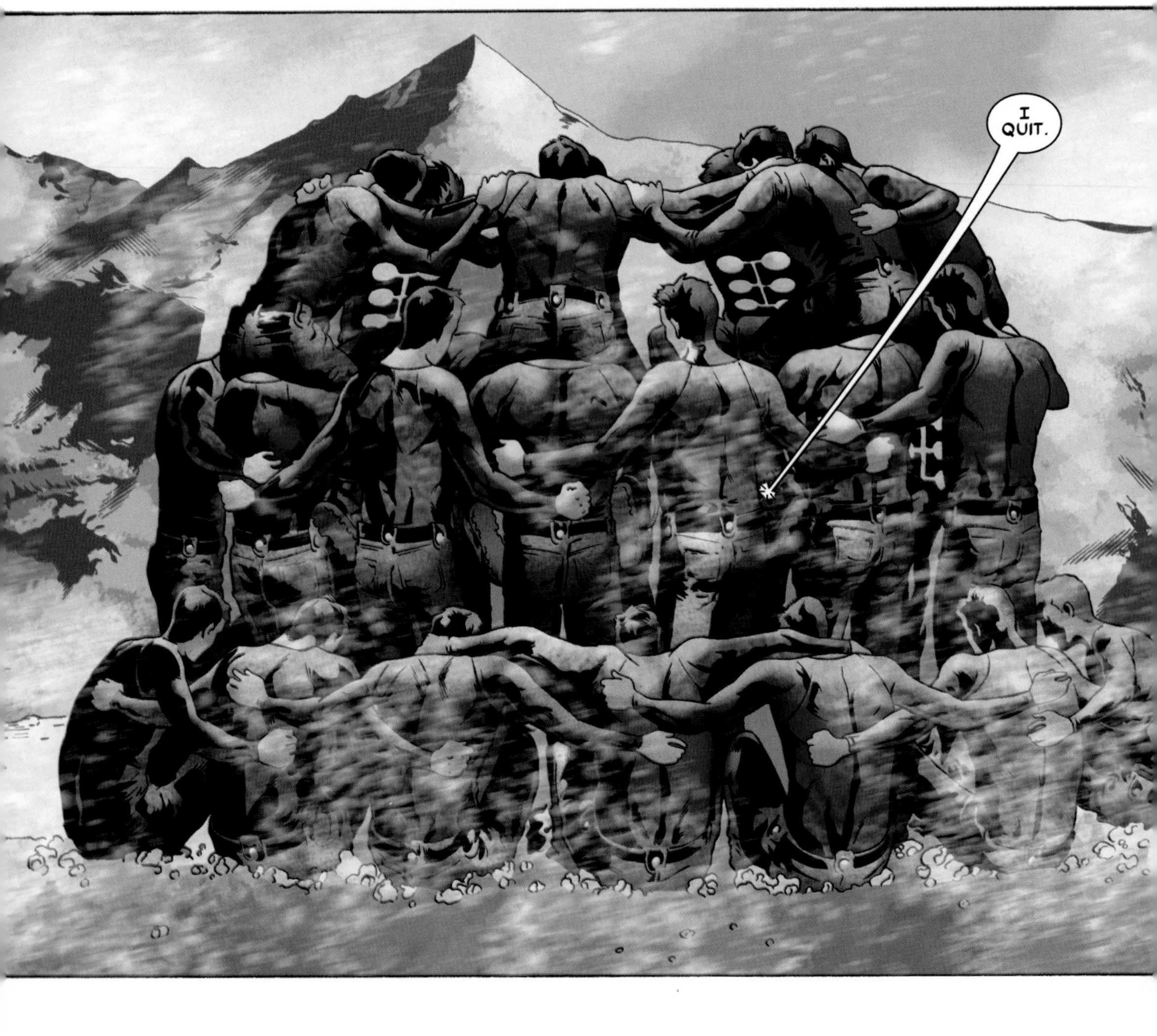
I QUIT.

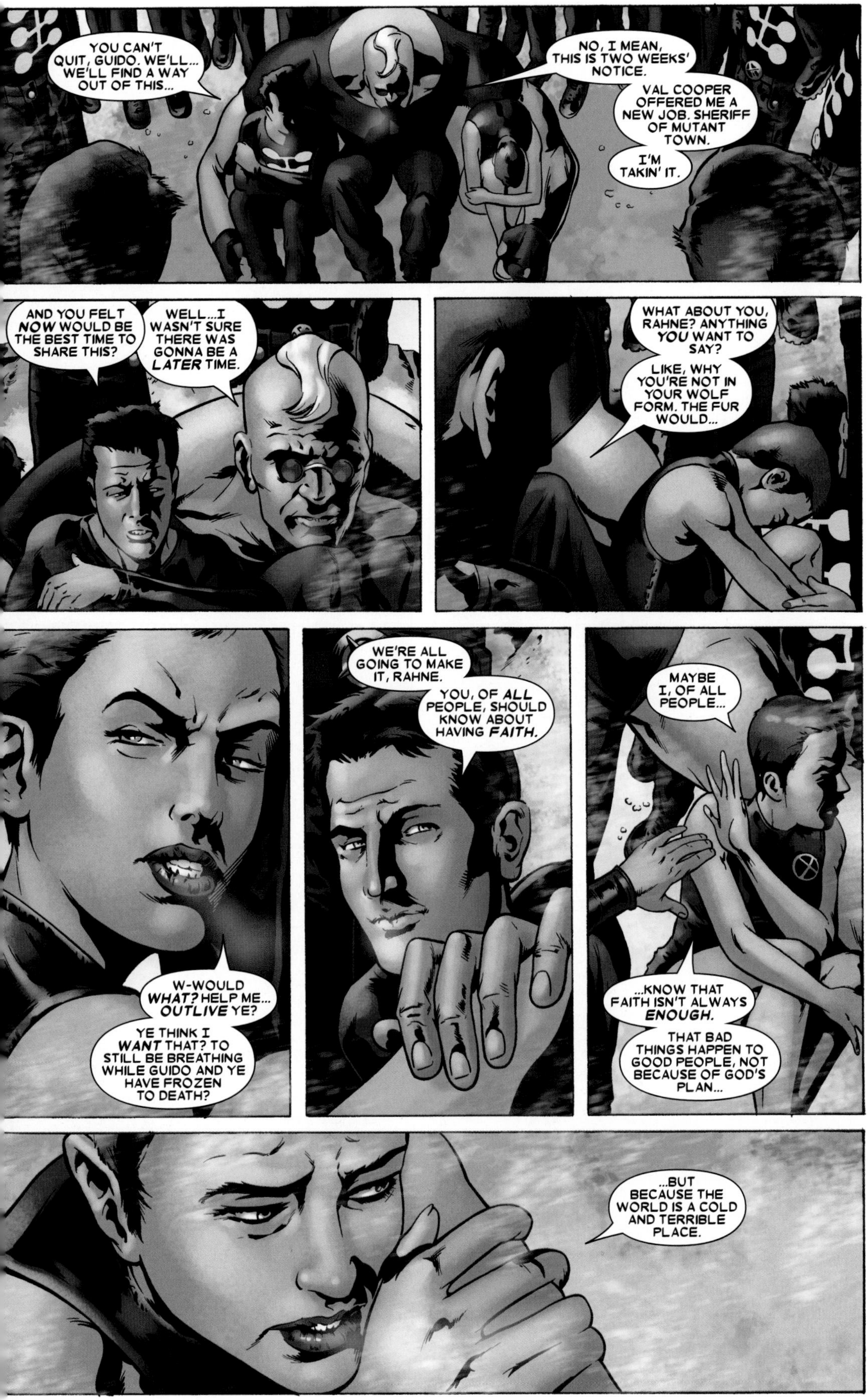
YOU CAN'T QUIT, GUIDO. WE'LL... WE'LL FIND A WAY OUT OF THIS...
NO, I MEAN, THIS IS TWO WEEKS' NOTICE.
VAL COOPER OFFERED ME A NEW JOB. SHERIFF OF MUTANT TOWN.
I'M TAKIN' IT.
AND YOU FELT NOW WOULD BE THE BEST TIME TO SHARE THIS?
WELL...I WASN'T SURE THERE WAS GONNA BE A LATER TIME.
WHAT ABOUT YOU, RAHNE? ANYTHING YOU WANT TO SAY?
LIKE, WHY YOU'RE NOT IN YOUR WOLF FORM. THE FUR WOULD...
W-WOULD WHAT? HELP ME... OUTLIVE YE?
YE THINK I WANT THAT? TO STILL BE BREATHING WHILE GUIDO AND YE HAVE FROZEN TO DEATH?
WE'RE ALL GOING TO MAKE IT, RAHNE.
YOU, OF ALL PEOPLE, SHOULD KNOW ABOUT HAVING FAITH.
MAYBE I, OF ALL PEOPLE...
...KNOW THAT FAITH ISN'T ALWAYS ENOUGH.
THAT BAD THINGS HAPPEN TO GOOD PEOPLE, NOT BECAUSE OF GOD'S PLAN...
...BUT BECAUSE THE WORLD IS A COLD AND TERRIBLE PLACE.

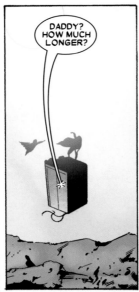

DADDY? HOW MUCH LONGER?

HOW THE HELL SHOULD I KNOW?

RON! LANGUAGE!

SCREW LANGUAGE! WE'VE BEEN TAKEN PRISONERS BY MUTANTS! FOR ALL I KNOW, WE'RE--

WE...WE STOPPED!

WE'RE GOING TO GET OUT!

WE'LL BE ALL RIGHT!

MOLLY! WALLY! JUST... JUST STAY CALM! IT--

ANYBODY LEANING AGAINST THE DOOR?

LET US OUT! LET US OUT!

MAYBE THAT'S WHY SHE WAS ASKING ABOUT LEANING AGAINST THE DOOR, MOM.

THANK GOD SOMEBOD IN THERE HA BRAINS.

WE'RE CLEAR OF THE DOOR.

GOOD.

THIS IS KIDNAPPING! I'M GOING TO HAVE YOU ARRESTED!

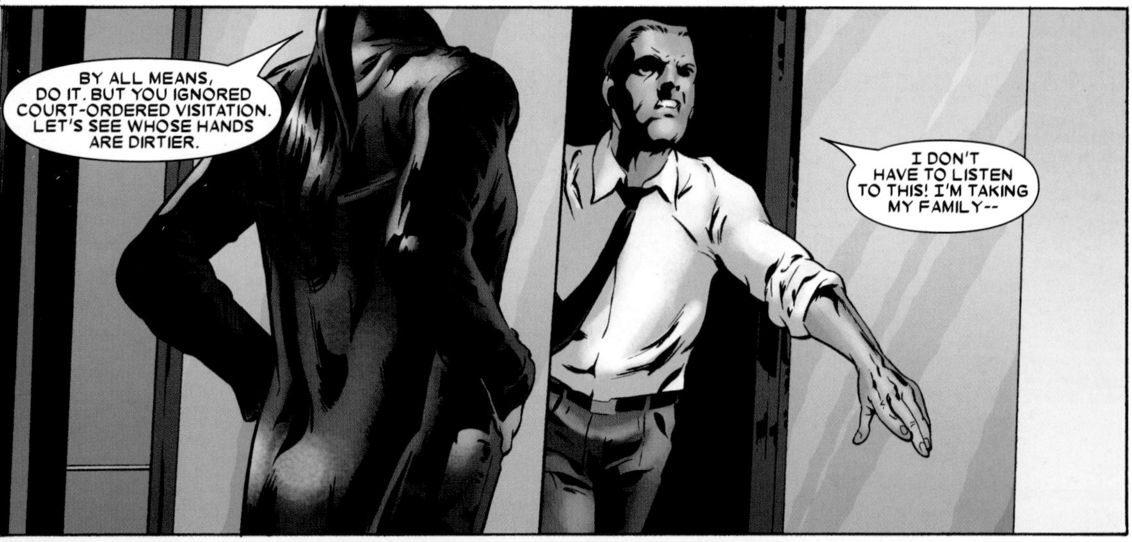
BY ALL MEANS, DO IT. BUT YOU IGNORED COURT-ORDERED VISITATION. LET'S SEE WHOSE HANDS ARE DIRTIER.
I DON'T HAVE TO LISTEN TO THIS! I'M TAKING MY FAMILY--

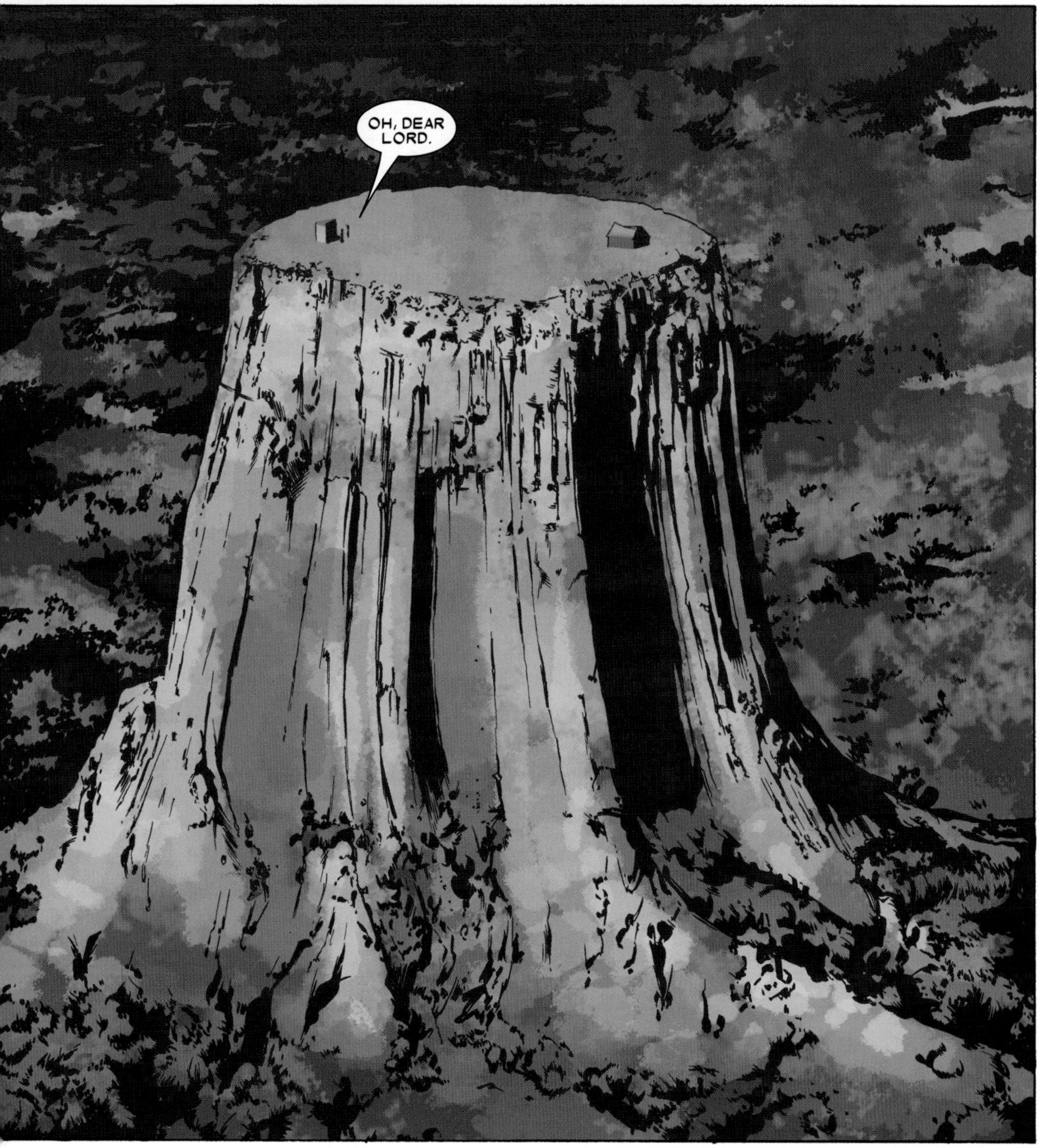
OH, DEAR LORD.

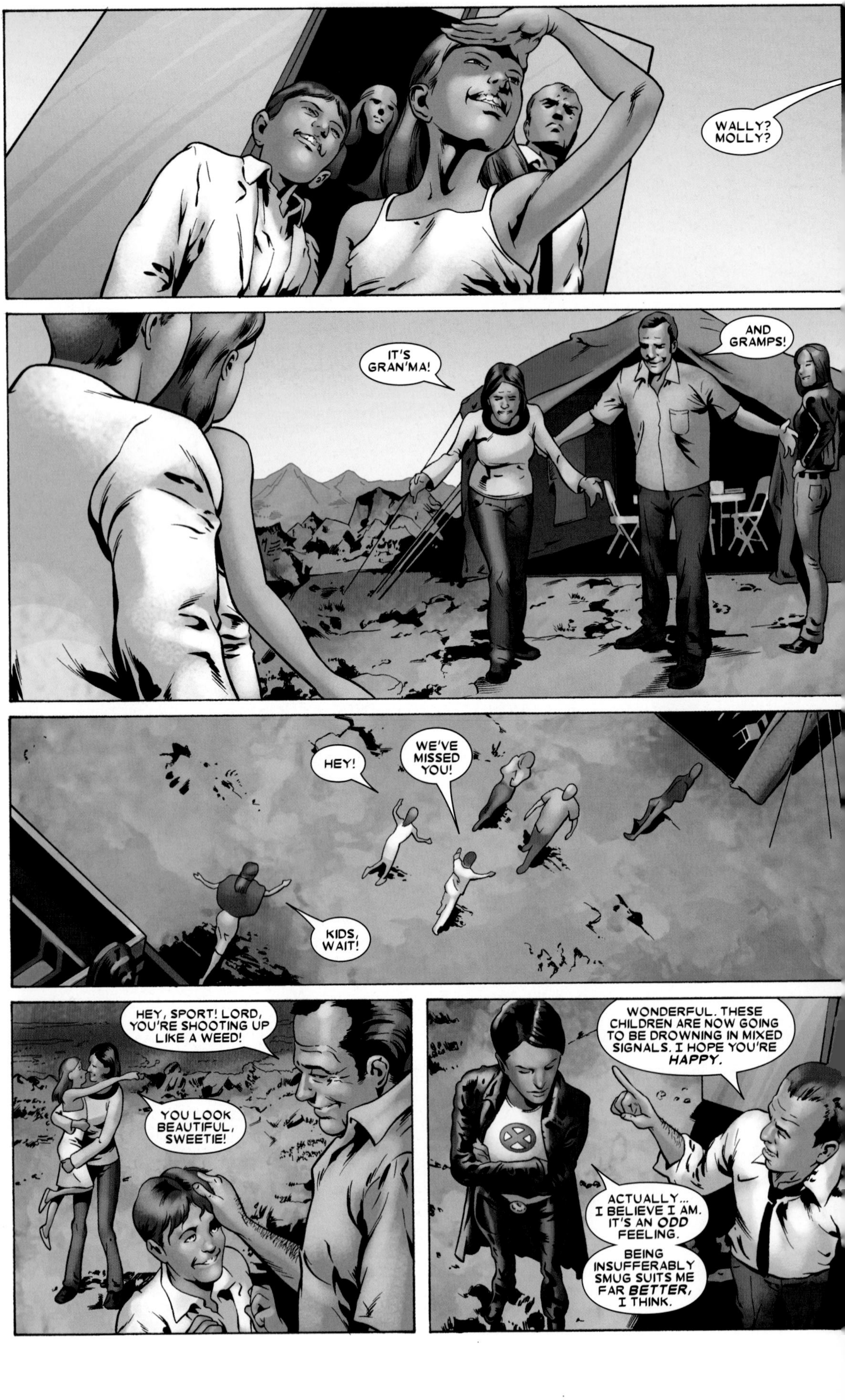

WALLY? MOLLY?
IT'S GRAN'MA!
AND GRAMPS!
HEY!
WE'VE MISSED YOU!
KIDS, WAIT!
HEY, SPORT! LORD, YOU'RE SHOOTING UP LIKE A WEED!
YOU LOOK BEAUTIFUL, SWEETIE!
WONDERFUL. THESE CHILDREN ARE NOW GOING TO BE DROWNING IN MIXED SIGNALS. I HOPE YOU'RE HAPPY.
ACTUALLY... I BELIEVE I AM. IT'S AN ODD FEELING.
BEING INSUFFERABLY SMUG SUITS ME FAR BETTER, I THINK.

WE HAVE EVERYTHING SET UP...CHAIRS, TABLES, SNACKS...

YOU ARE *SO* THOUGHTFUL, MISS CASSIDY.

DON'T MENTION IT. I'D START WITH THE BRIE; NO TELLING HOW LONG IT'LL HOLD UP.

YOU GOT A *HANDLE* ON THINGS HERE?

SURE. WHY? WHAT'S WRONG?

I JUST TRIED TO CHECK IN WITH MADROX, GIVE HIM AN UPDATE. NO LUCK.

NOT GUIDO NOR THE FLEABAG, EITHER. EVEN *RICTOR'S* NOT PICKING UP.

COULD BE *NOTHING*, OR...

HOW FAST CAN YOU GET BACK?

IF I GO *SUPERSONIC?* PRETTY DAMNED. 'COURSE THERE'S NO GUARANTEE THEY'RE AT HQ, BUT...

IT'S A PLACE TO START. DO IT. STAY IN TOUCH.

BOOM

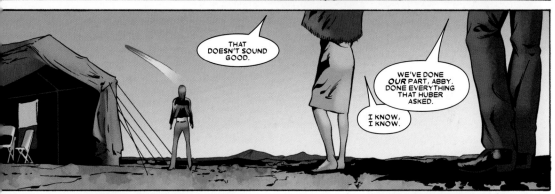
THAT DOESN'T SOUND GOOD.

WE'VE DONE *OUR* PART, ABBY. DONE EVERYTHING THAT HUBER ASKED.

I KNOW, I KNOW.

YOUR PARENTS PLAYED IT *BEAUTIFULLY*, BY THE WAY.

I'LL TELL THEM YOU SAID THAT. THEY'LL BE *SO* PLEASED.

YOU'RE LIKE A SON TO THEM, YOU KNOW. DAD ALWAYS SAYS SO.

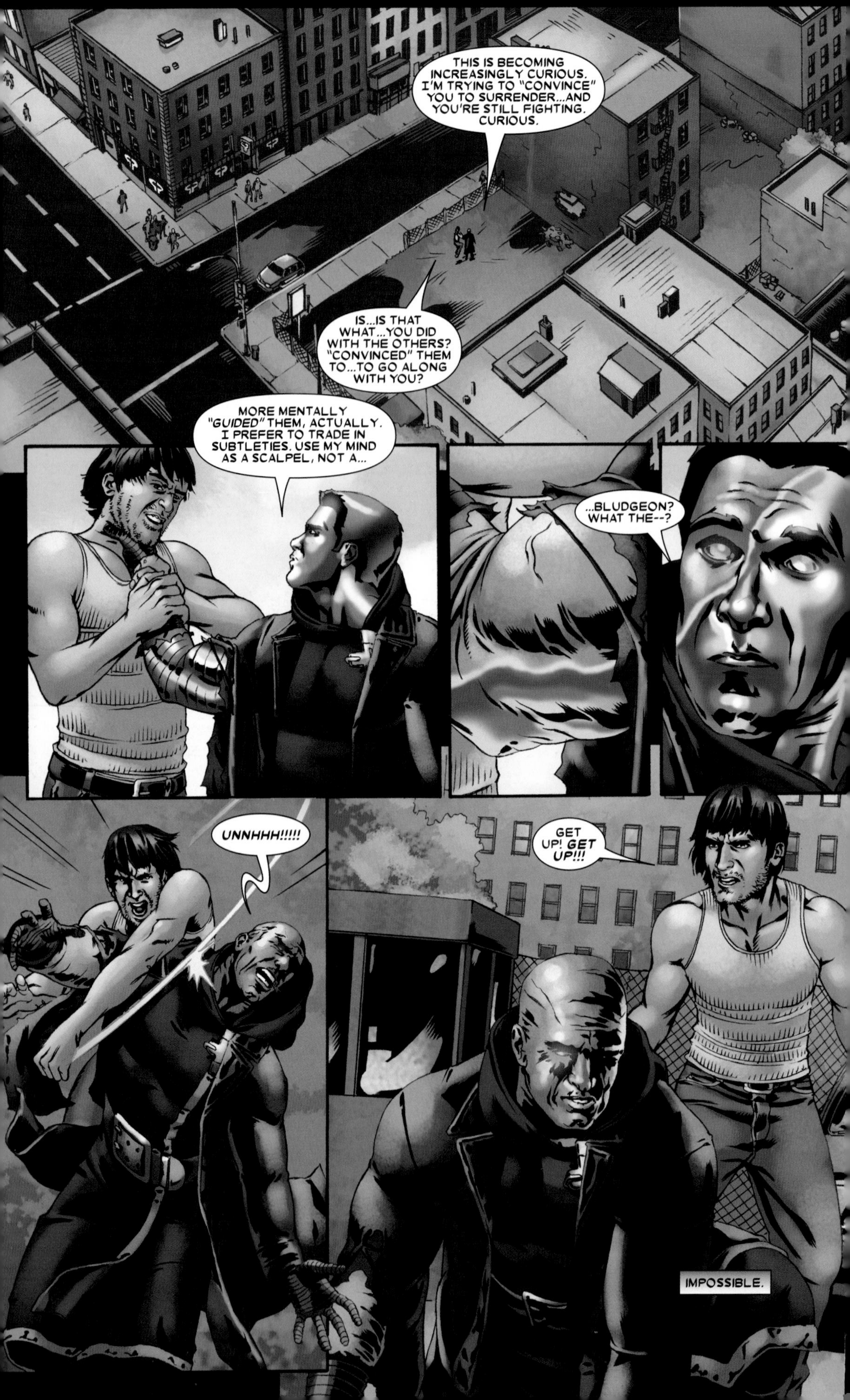
THIS IS BECOMING INCREASINGLY CURIOUS. I'M TRYING TO "CONVINCE" YOU TO SURRENDER...AND YOU'RE STILL FIGHTING. CURIOUS.
IS...IS THAT WHAT...YOU DID WITH THE OTHERS? "CONVINCED" THEM TO...TO GO ALONG WITH YOU?
MORE MENTALLY "*GUIDED*" THEM, ACTUALLY. I PREFER TO TRADE IN SUBTLETIES. USE MY MIND AS A SCALPEL, NOT A...
...BLUDGEON? WHAT THE--?
UNNHHH!!!!!
GET UP! *GET UP!!!*
IMPOSSIBLE.

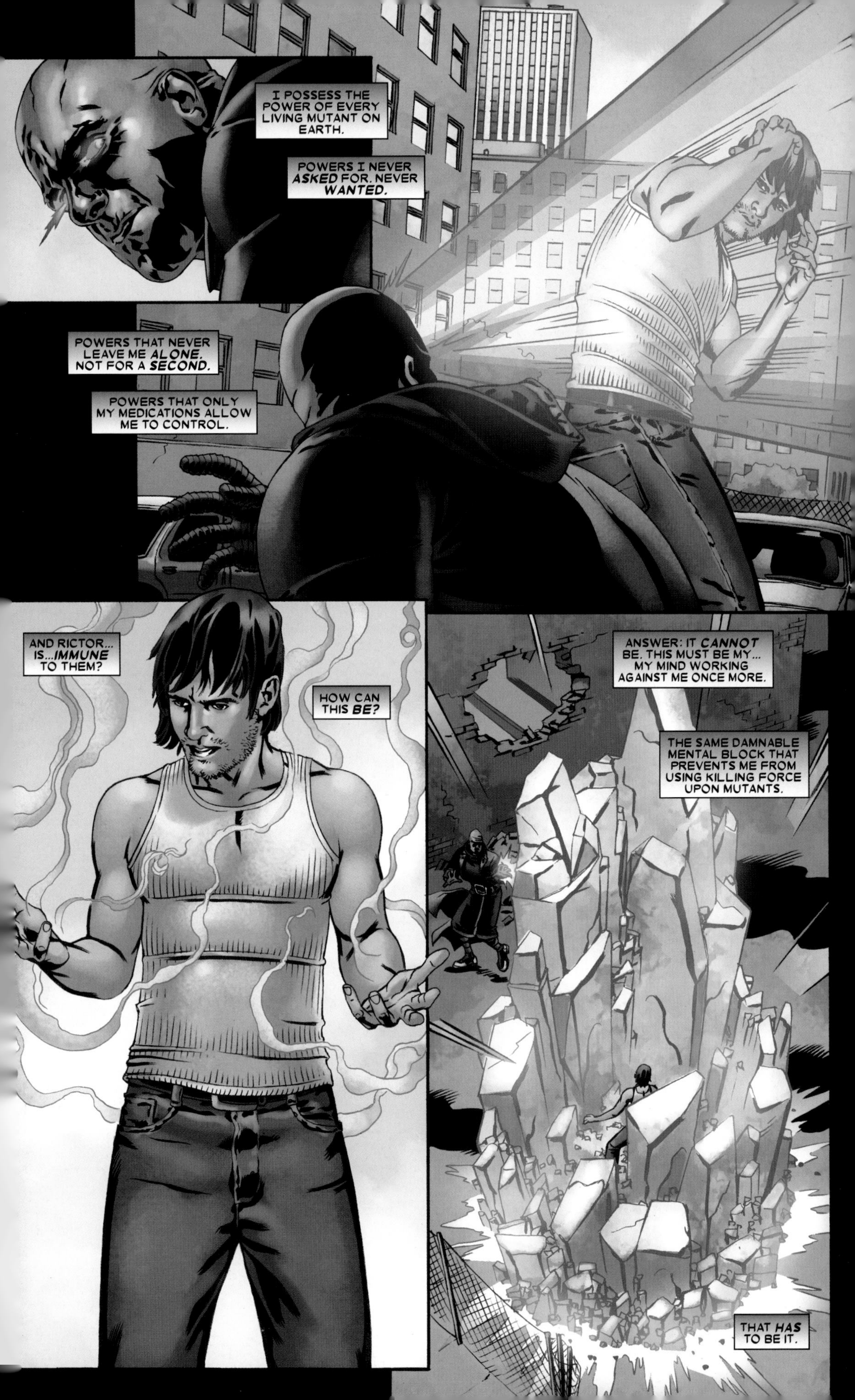

I POSSESS THE POWER OF EVERY LIVING MUTANT ON EARTH.
POWERS I NEVER ASKED FOR. NEVER WANTED.
POWERS THAT NEVER LEAVE ME ALONE. NOT FOR A SECOND.
POWERS THAT ONLY MY MEDICATIONS ALLOW ME TO CONTROL.
AND RICTOR... IS...IMMUNE TO THEM?
HOW CAN THIS BE?
ANSWER: IT CANNOT BE. THIS MUST BE MY... MY MIND WORKING AGAINST ME ONCE MORE.
THE SAME DAMNABLE MENTAL BLOCK THAT PREVENTS ME FROM USING KILLING FORCE UPON MUTANTS.
THAT HAS TO BE IT.

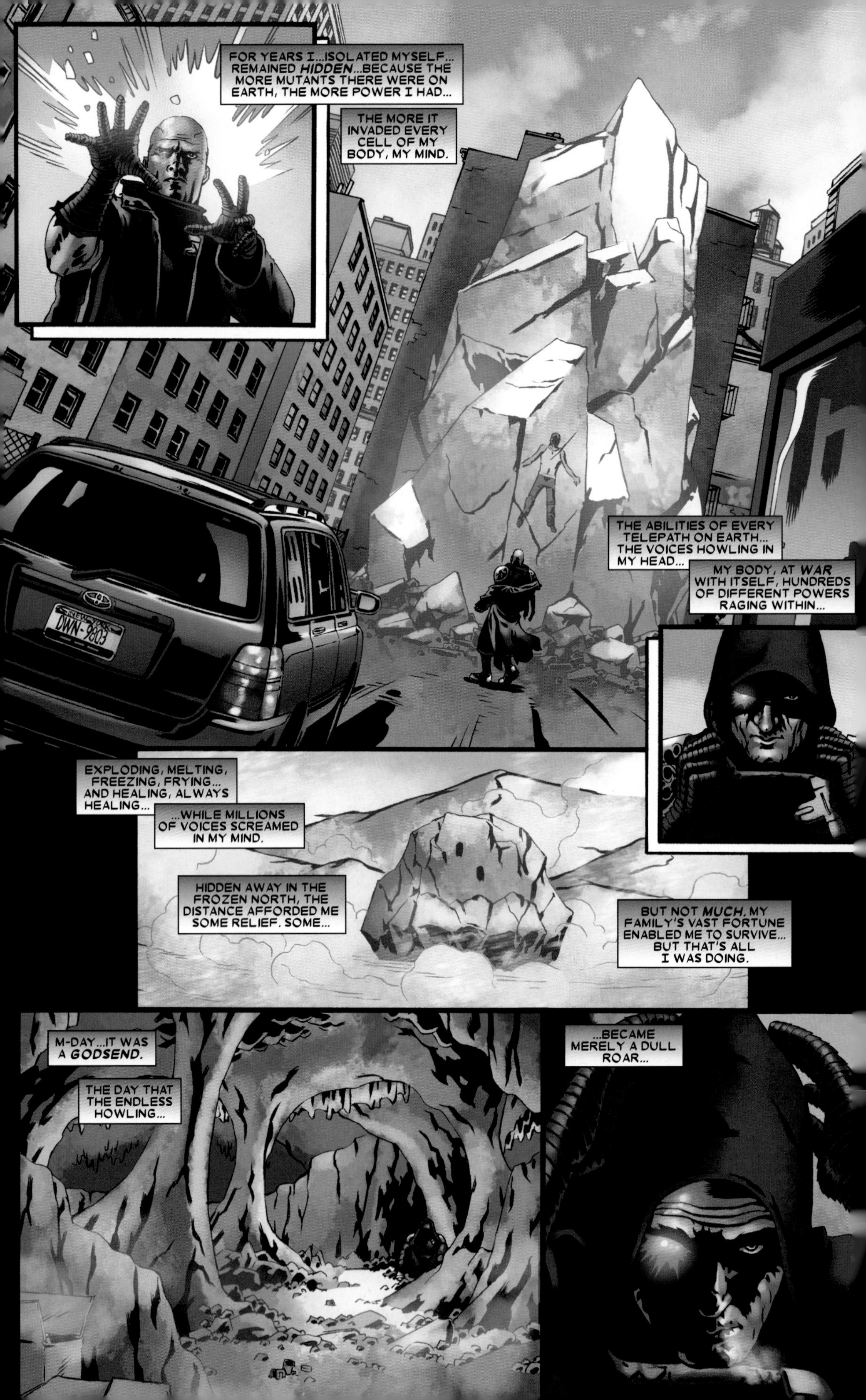

FOR YEARS I...ISOLATED MYSELF... REMAINED HIDDEN...BECAUSE THE MORE MUTANTS THERE WERE ON EARTH, THE MORE POWER I HAD...
THE MORE IT INVADED EVERY CELL OF MY BODY, MY MIND.
THE ABILITIES OF EVERY TELEPATH ON EARTH... THE VOICES HOWLING IN MY HEAD...
MY BODY, AT WAR WITH ITSELF, HUNDREDS OF DIFFERENT POWERS RAGING WITHIN...
DWN-9803
EXPLODING, MELTING, FREEZING, FRYING... AND HEALING, ALWAYS HEALING...
...WHILE MILLIONS OF VOICES SCREAMED IN MY MIND.
HIDDEN AWAY IN THE FROZEN NORTH, THE DISTANCE AFFORDED ME SOME RELIEF. SOME...
BUT NOT MUCH. MY FAMILY'S VAST FORTUNE ENABLED ME TO SURVIVE... BUT THAT'S ALL I WAS DOING.
M-DAY...IT WAS A GODSEND.
THE DAY THAT THE ENDLESS HOWLING...
...BECAME MERELY A DULL ROAR...

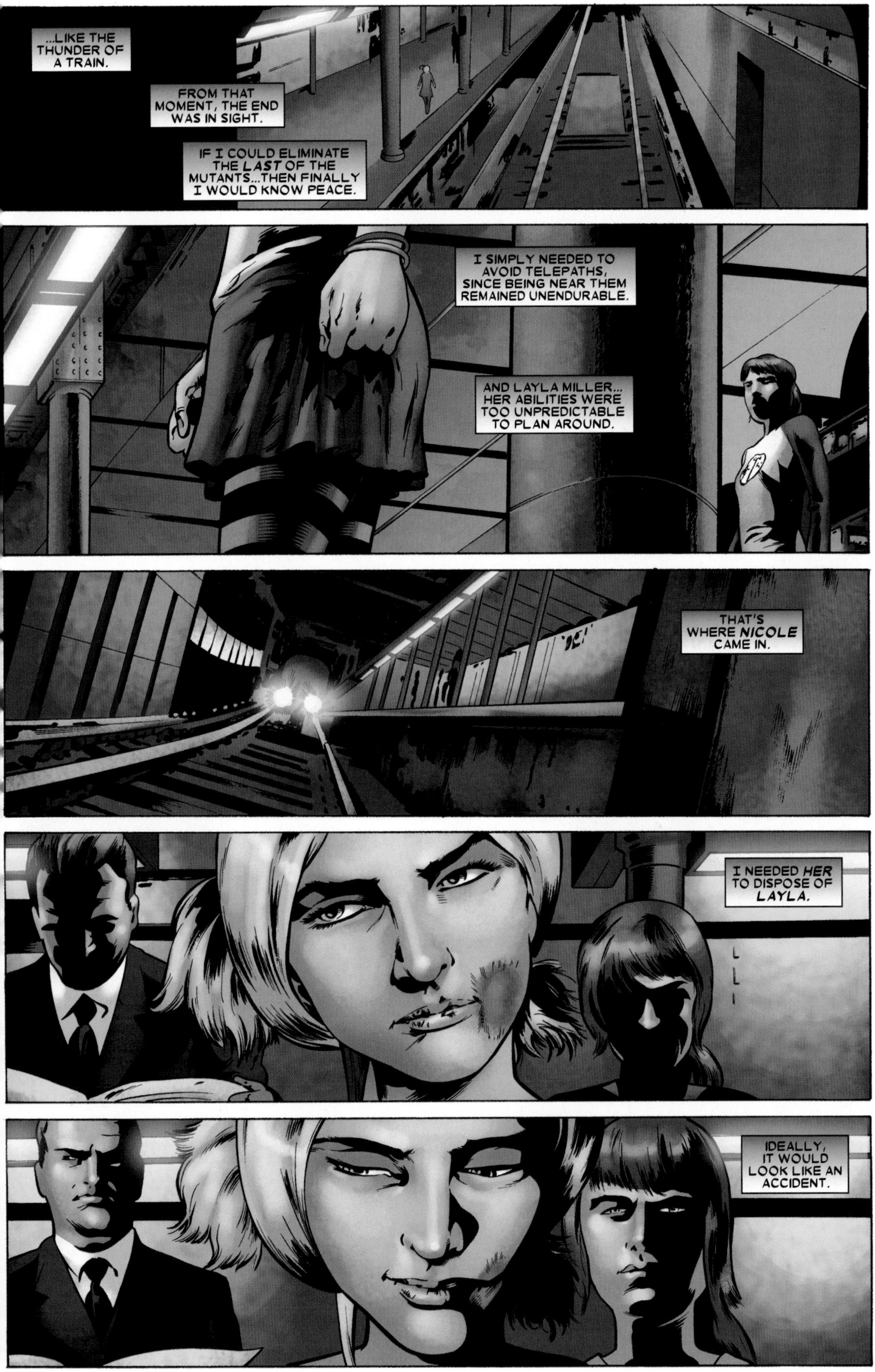
...LIKE THE THUNDER OF A TRAIN.
FROM THAT MOMENT, THE END WAS IN SIGHT.
IF I COULD ELIMINATE THE *LAST* OF THE MUTANTS...THEN FINALLY I WOULD KNOW PEACE.
I SIMPLY NEEDED TO AVOID TELEPATHS, SINCE BEING NEAR THEM REMAINED UNENDURABLE.
AND LAYLA MILLER... HER ABILITIES WERE TOO UNPREDICTABLE TO PLAN AROUND.
THAT'S WHERE *NICOLE* CAME IN.
I NEEDED *HER* TO DISPOSE OF *LAYLA.*
IDEALLY, IT WOULD LOOK LIKE AN ACCIDENT.

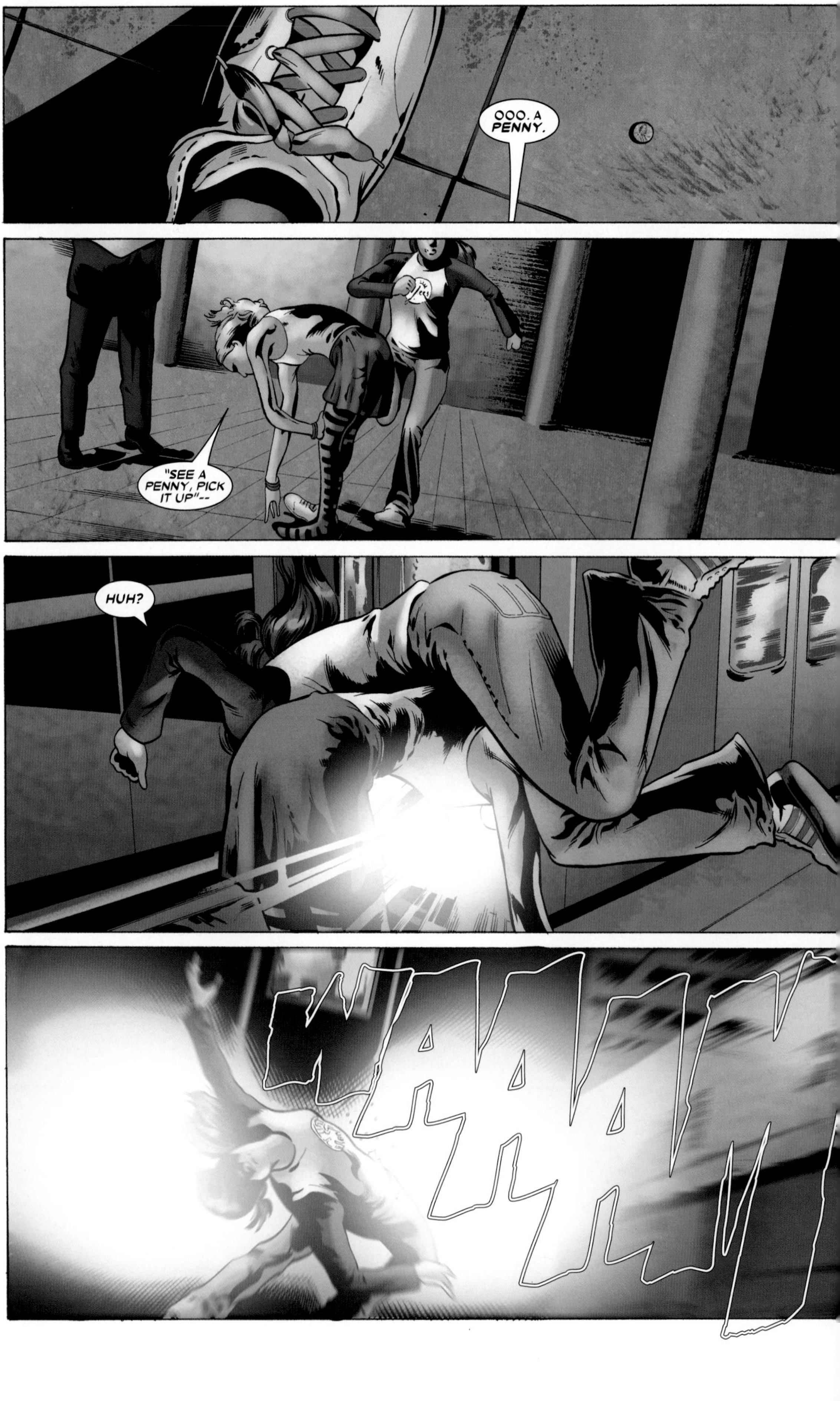

OOO. A PENNY.
"SEE A PENNY, PICK IT UP"--
HUH?
WAAAM

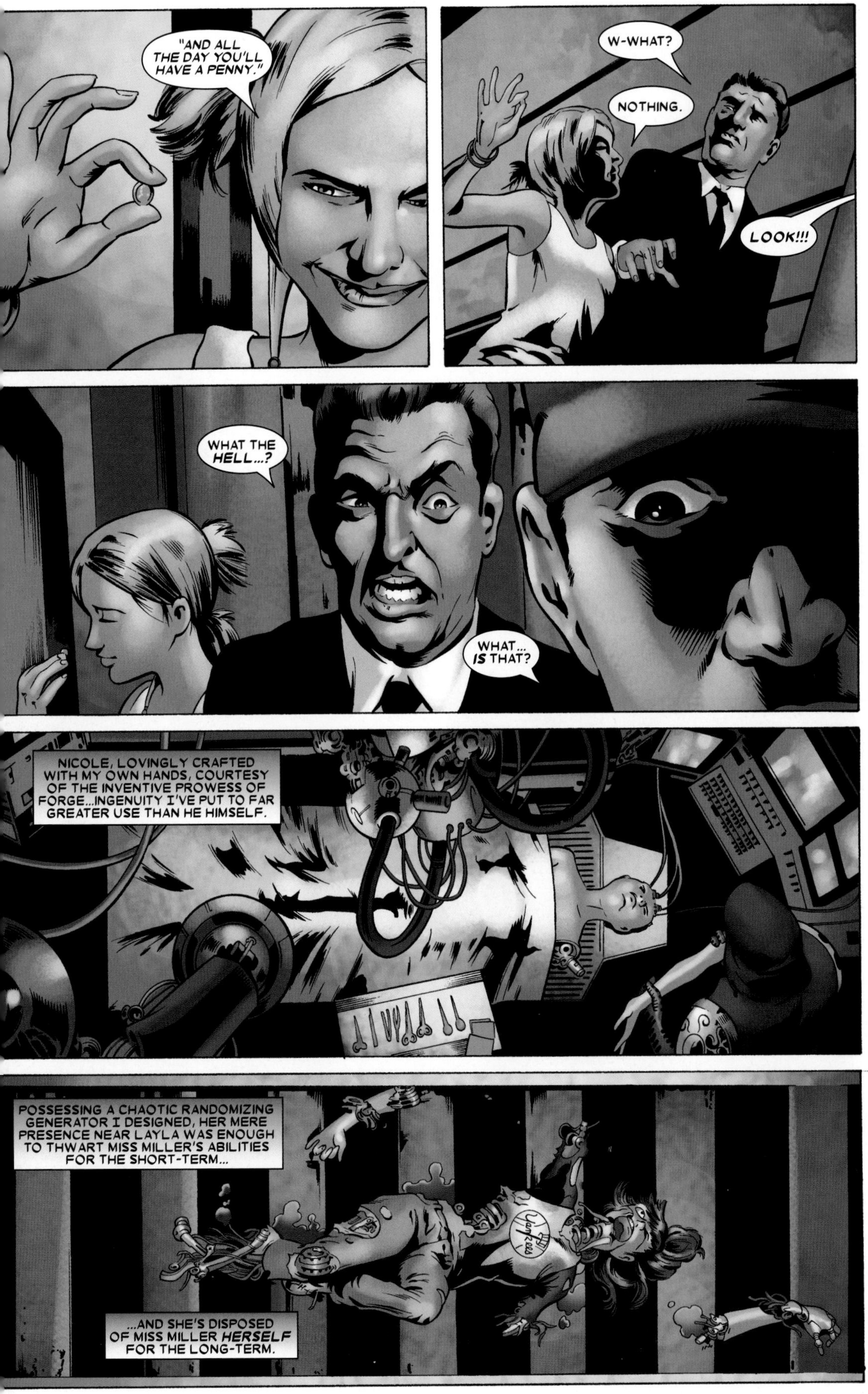
"AND ALL THE DAY YOU'LL HAVE A PENNY."
W-WHAT?
NOTHING.
LOOK!!!
WHAT THE HELL...?
WHAT... IS THAT?
NICOLE, LOVINGLY CRAFTED WITH MY OWN HANDS, COURTESY OF THE INVENTIVE PROWESS OF FORGE...INGENUITY I'VE PUT TO FAR GREATER USE THAN HE HIMSELF.
POSSESSING A CHAOTIC RANDOMIZING GENERATOR I DESIGNED, HER MERE PRESENCE NEAR LAYLA WAS ENOUGH TO THWART MISS MILLER'S ABILITIES FOR THE SHORT-TERM...
...AND SHE'S DISPOSED OF MISS MILLER HERSELF FOR THE LONG-TERM.

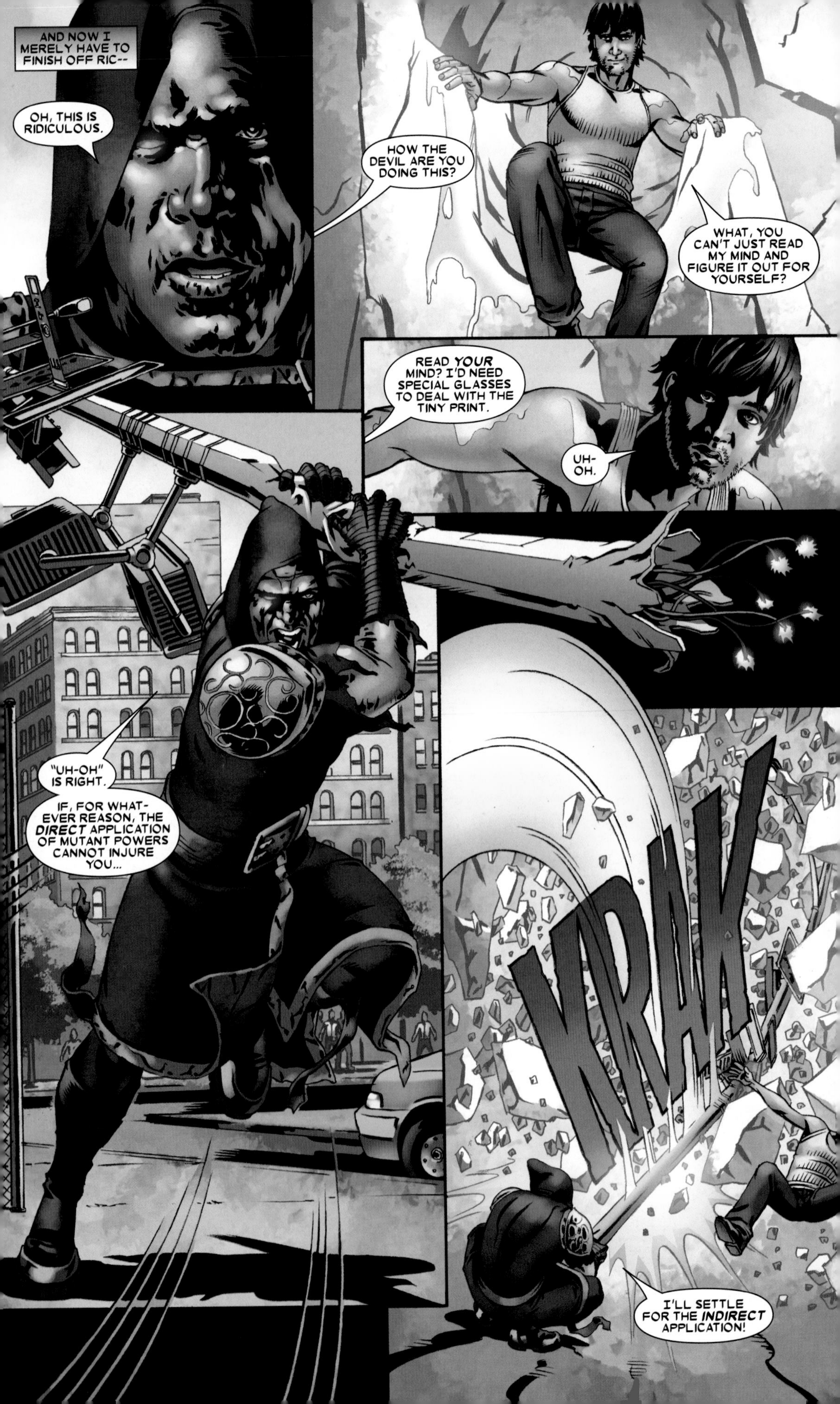
AND NOW I MERELY HAVE TO FINISH OFF RIC--
OH, THIS IS RIDICULOUS.
HOW THE DEVIL ARE YOU DOING THIS?
WHAT, YOU CAN'T JUST READ MY MIND AND FIGURE IT OUT FOR YOURSELF?
READ *YOUR* MIND? I'D NEED SPECIAL GLASSES TO DEAL WITH THE TINY PRINT.
UH-OH.
"UH-OH" IS RIGHT.
IF, FOR WHATEVER REASON, THE *DIRECT* APPLICATION OF MUTANT POWERS CANNOT INJURE YOU...
KRAK
I'LL SETTLE FOR THE *INDIRECT* APPLICATION!

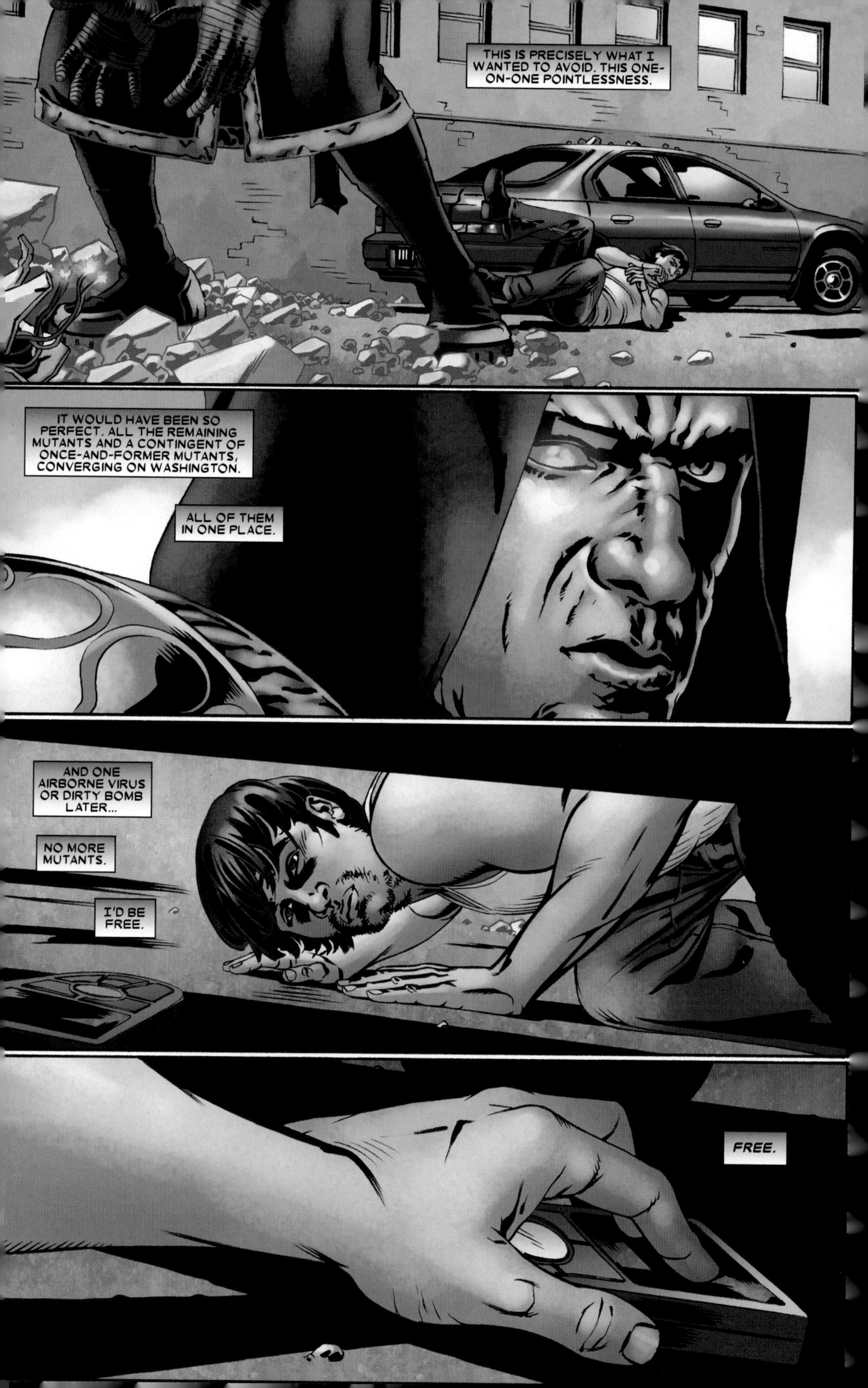
THIS IS PRECISELY WHAT I WANTED TO AVOID. THIS ONE-ON-ONE POINTLESSNESS.
IT WOULD HAVE BEEN SO PERFECT. ALL THE REMAINING MUTANTS AND A CONTINGENT OF ONCE-AND-FORMER MUTANTS, CONVERGING ON WASHINGTON.
ALL OF THEM IN ONE PLACE.
AND ONE AIRBORNE VIRUS OR DIRTY BOMB LATER...
NO MORE MUTANTS.
I'D BE FREE.
FREE.

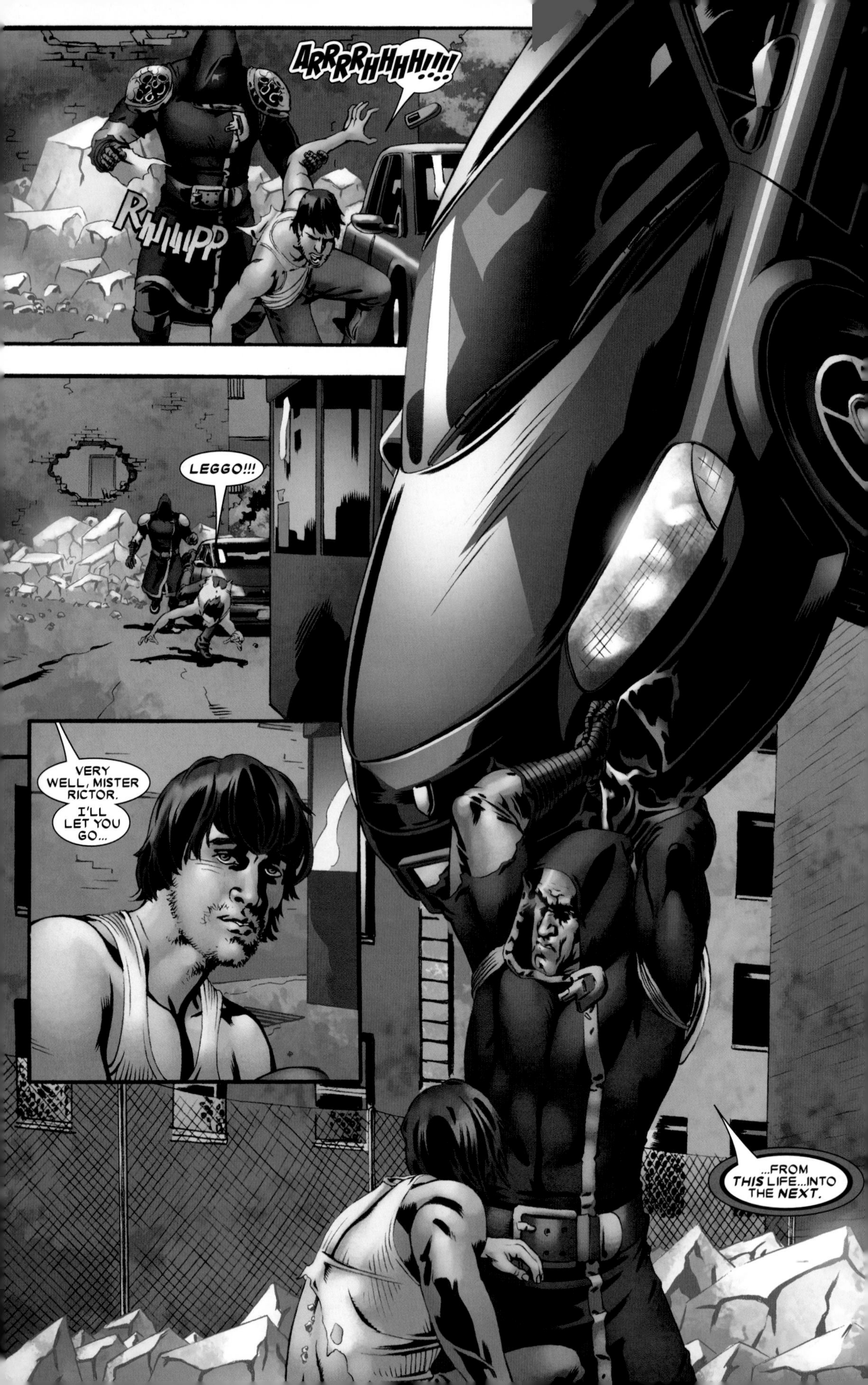
ARRRRHHHHH!!!!...
RHHHIIPP
LEGGO!!!
VERY WELL, MISTER RICTOR. I'LL LET YOU GO...
...FROM THIS LIFE...INTO THE NEXT.

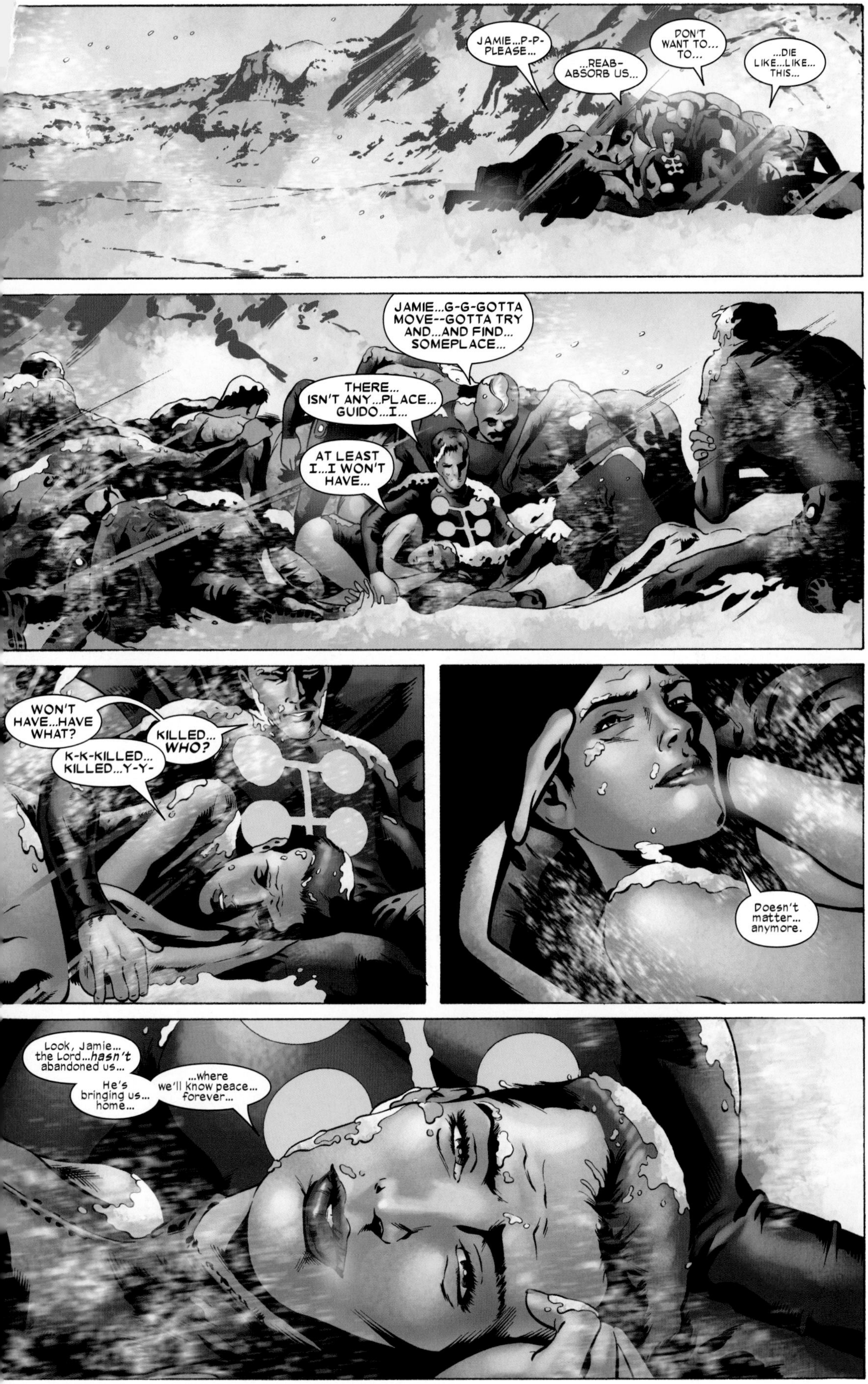
JAMIE...P-P-PLEASE...
...REAB-ABSORB US...
DON'T WANT TO... TO...
...DIE LIKE...LIKE... THIS...
JAMIE...G-G-GOTTA MOVE--GOTTA TRY AND...AND FIND... SOMEPLACE...
THERE... ISN'T ANY...PLACE... GUIDO...I...
AT LEAST I...I WON'T HAVE...
WON'T HAVE...HAVE WHAT?
KILLED... WHO?
K-K-KILLED... KILLED...Y-Y-
Doesn't matter... anymore.
Look, Jamie... the Lord...hasn't abandoned us...
He's bringing us... home...
...where we'll know peace... forever...

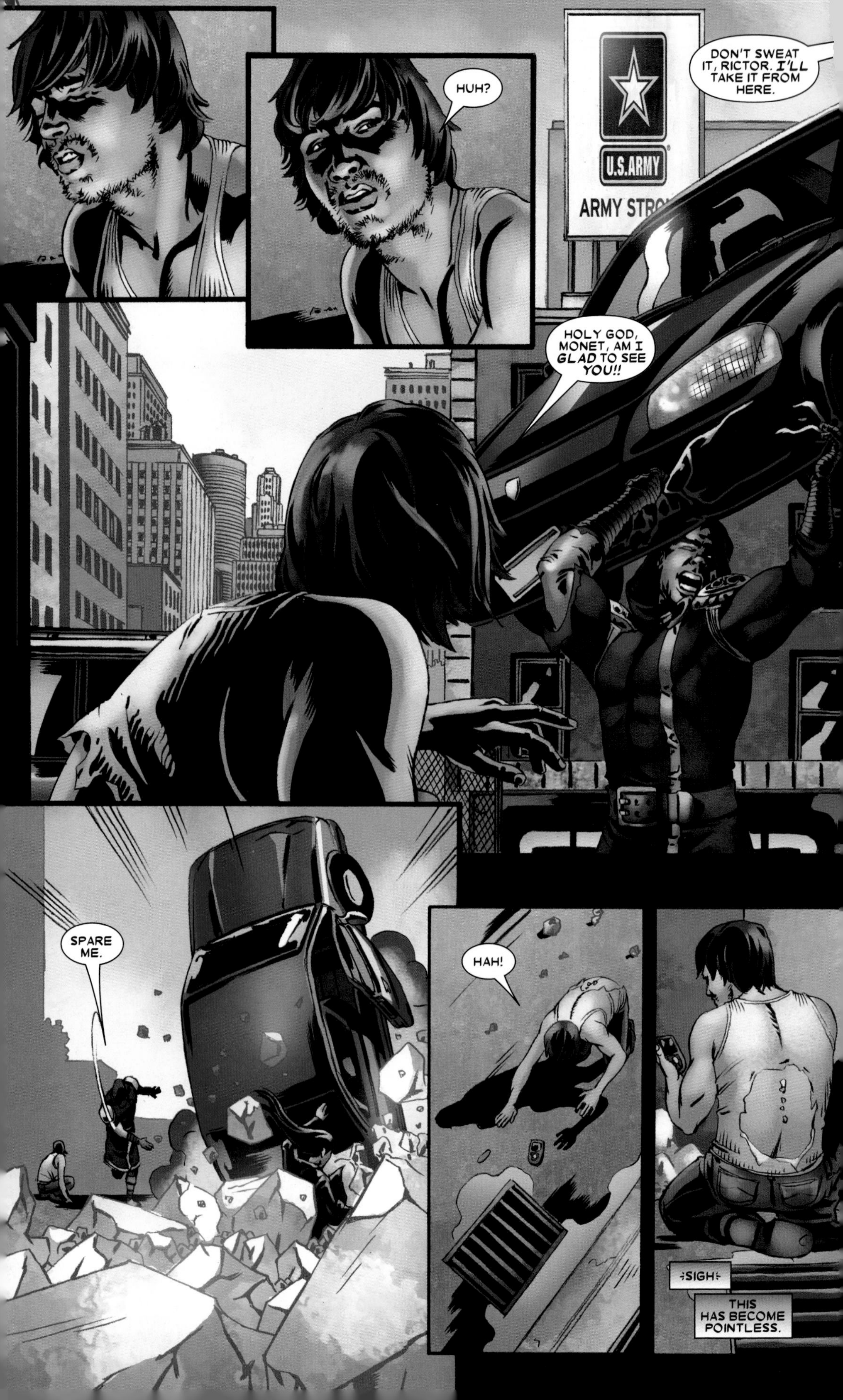
HUH?
U.S. ARMY
ARMY STRO
DON'T SWEAT IT, RICTOR. I'LL TAKE IT FROM HERE.
HOLY GOD, MONET, AM I GLAD TO SEE YOU!!
SPARE ME.
HAH!
SIGH
THIS HAS BECOME POINTLESS.

GOOD. REMEMBER THAT NEXT TIME I WANT YOU TO MAKE ME BREAKFAST.

AS FOR YOU--

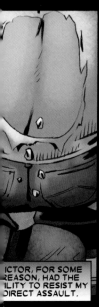

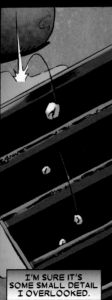

AND NOW THE PRESENCE OF THE TELEPATH, MONET, BRINGS PAIN BACK TO ME IN SWEEPING WAVES. AND MY MEDICATION IS STARTING TO WEAR OFF.

TOO MUCH HAS COME UNDONE. ALL THAT'S LEFT TO ME IS TO LASH OUT IN CALAMITOUS SLAUGHTER...

THAT'S SO... UNCIVILIZED. BESIDES...

WHEN ONE IS ATTEMPTING GENOCIDE...

...WHAT POINT IS THERE IN HOMICIDE?

...CTOR, FOR SOME ...EASON, HAD THE ...ILITY TO RESIST MY ...IRECT ASSAULT.

I'M SURE IT'S SOME SMALL DETAIL I OVERLOOKED.

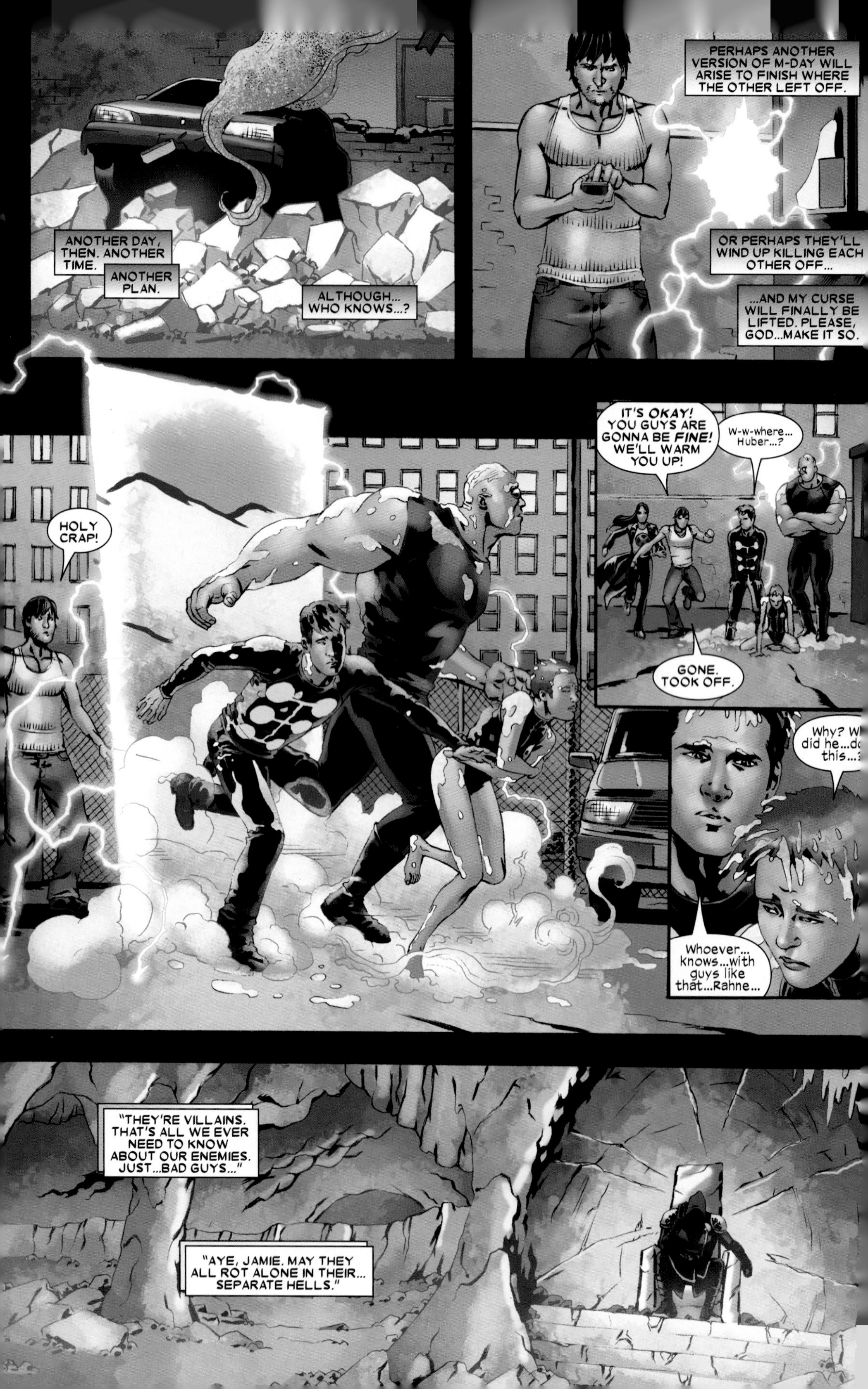
ANOTHER DAY, THEN. ANOTHER TIME.
ANOTHER PLAN.
ALTHOUGH... WHO KNOWS...?
PERHAPS ANOTHER VERSION OF M-DAY WILL ARISE TO FINISH WHERE THE OTHER LEFT OFF.
OR PERHAPS THEY'LL WIND UP KILLING EACH OTHER OFF...
...AND MY CURSE WILL FINALLY BE LIFTED. PLEASE, GOD...MAKE IT SO.
HOLY CRAP!
IT'S OKAY! YOU GUYS ARE GONNA BE FINE! WE'LL WARM YOU UP!
W-w-where... Huber...?
GONE. TOOK OFF.
Whoever... knows...with guys like that...Rahne...
"THEY'RE VILLAINS. THAT'S ALL WE EVER NEED TO KNOW ABOUT OUR ENEMIES. JUST...BAD GUYS..."
"AYE, JAMIE. MAY THEY ALL ROT ALONE IN THEIR... SEPARATE HELLS."